THE IRONIES OF COLONIAL GOVERNANCE

The Indian village council, or *panchayat*, has long held an iconic place in India. *Ironies of Colonial Governance* traces the history of that ideal and the attempts to adapt it to colonial governance. Beginning with an in-depth analysis of British attempts to introduce a system of panchayat governance during the early nineteenth century, it analyses the legacies of these actions within the structures of later colonial administrations as well as that of the early nationalist movement. Particular attention is paid to the ways in which the ideologies of panchayat governance evolved during this period and to the transnational exchange and circulation of panchayat ideologies.

JAMES JAFFE is Professor of History at the University of Wisconsin-Whitewater and a Fellow at the Institute for Legal Studies, University of Wisconsin-Madison. His current work on transnational legal history has received support from the National Science Foundation, the US–UK Fulbright Commission and the Ford Foundation.

CAMBRIDGE STUDIES IN LAW AND SOCIETY

Cambridge Studies in Law and Society aims to publish the best scholarly work on legal discourse and practice in its social and institutional contexts, combining theoretical insights and empirical research.

The fields that it covers are: studies of law in action; the sociology of law; the anthropology of law; cultural studies of law, including the role of legal discourses in social formations; law and economics; law and politics; and studies of governance. The books consider all forms of legal discourse across societies, rather than being limited to lawyers' discourses alone.

The series editors come from a range of disciplines: academic law; socio-legal studies; sociology; and anthropology. All have been actively involved in teaching and writing about law in context.

A list of books in the series can be found at the back of this book.

THE IRONIES OF COLONIAL GOVERNANCE

Law, Custom, and Justice in Colonial India

James Jaffe
University of Wisconsin

CAMBRIDGE
UNIVERSITY PRESS

CAMBRIDGE
UNIVERSITY PRESS

University Printing House, Cambridge CB2 8BS, United Kingdom

Cambridge University Press is part of the University of Cambridge.

It furthers the University's mission by disseminating knowledge in the pursuit of education, learning and research at the highest international levels of excellence.

www.cambridge.org
Information on this title: www.cambridge.org/9781107087927

First published 2015

A catalog record for this publication is available from the British Library

Library of Congress Cataloging in Publication Data
Jaffe, James Alan, 1954– author.
Ironies of colonial governance : law, custom and justice in colonial India / James Jaffe.
pages cm. – (Cambridge studies in law and society)
Includes bibliographical references and index.
ISBN 978-1-107-08792-7 (hardback)
1. Justice, Administration of – India – History – 19th century.
2. Panchayat – India – History – 19th century. I. Title.
KNS132.J344 2015
347.54'0209034–dc23

2015007837

ISBN 978-1-107-08792-7 Hardback

In memory of my parents

Laura Bernice Jaffe (1927–2011) and Stanley R. Jaffe (1923–2011)

CONTENTS

TABLES AND FIGURES

FIGURES

TABLES

ACKNOWLEDGMENTS

It is a commonplace in Acknowledgments to assert the collective nature of the undertaking and in my case this is especially appropriate. Before work began on this project, my career had been spent entirely in the field of British history and particularly in the field of the histories of British industrial relations and trade unionism. In fact, this book began as a legal and social history of English arbitration practices during the nineteenth century. However, as that research proceeded, I continually found references, and very numerous ones at that, to the Indian panchayat, which I found both odd and intriguing. As the work evolved, it became apparent not only that the archival and secondary sources on the panchayat were plentiful, historically significant, and underutilized, but also that I would have to learn the vagaries, disputes, and critical issues confronting historians of British imperialism as well as historians of South Asia.

I was incredibly fortunate to find that the community of South Asianists was invariably generous with their time, advice, expertise, and friendship. I will thank them more fully in a moment, but I would first like to express my profound gratitude to those institutions and agencies that provided the funding necessary to undertake and complete this project. Particularly at this time, when support for the humanities is disappearing and the requirements for gaining such support are most often premised upon "measurable outcomes," I was indeed fortunate to receive support from the US National Science Foundation, the US–UK Fulbright Commission and the University of Leeds, and the Ford Foundation at Jawaharlal Nehru University. The grant from the US National Science Foundation, SES-0849571, provided support for my first lengthy research trip to Mumbai and thus laid the foundation for this work. The US–UK Fulbright Commission and the University of Leeds, and the Ford Foundation at Jawaharlal Nehru University provided the time, space, and financial support necessary to complete the manuscript. Without the support of all of these agencies and institutions, this work could never have been begun, much less completed.

The Fulbright–Leeds University Distinguished Chair Award brought me back into contact with several old "fellow-travelers" in British working-class and trade union history, all of whom brought their critical perspectives to my new endeavor. Foremost among these, I wish to thank Malcolm Chase, whose help in securing the Chair at Leeds was invaluable. Martin Hewitt, now Dean at the University of Huddersfield, helped to ease me into life in West Yorkshire, and, most of all, Quentin Outram, with whom I spent many an evening at the local. At JNU, the faculty at the Centre for the Study of Law and Governance were wonderful hosts who graciously made time for me despite their hectic schedules. I sincerely appreciate the help of Pratiksha Baxi and Niraja Gopal Jayal, who welcomed me to the Centre, and I could not have done without the friendship of Amit Prakash, who helped me in so many ways both large and small.

The staffs at the British Library's Asian and African Reading Room and the Maharashtra State Archive provided expert assistance while carrying the burden of the enormous tomes compiled by the East India Company. At my home institution, the University of Wisconsin-Whitewater, the interlibrary loan staff secured dozens of articles and books from around the country that were absolutely crucial for the completion of this project. I would also like to thank the editors of the *Historical Journal* for permission to reprint Chapter 5, which first appeared there.

However, it is the new friends and new colleagues that I have made during the course of this research that made this project exciting, enjoyable, gratifying, and fun. Even though I was one of their worst students, my Hindi teachers, Virendra Singh and Brajesh Samarth, deserve much credit for their persistence and patience. In Mumbai, Jehangir and Veera Patel were the kindest and most generous hosts imaginable. The Parsi club life and the marriage ceremonies that they introduced me to were experiences I shall never forget. Similarly, Erin Broach welcomed me into her busy life, providing wonderful meals, trips to the theatre, and several adventures in her "classic" automobile. In Delhi, Anita Khemka and Imran Kokiloo were wonderful hosts: Imran's meals were to die for and Anita's willingness to help me settle into life in Delhi was unstinting.

At SOAS, University of London, the group of outstanding South Asianists was especially helpful and welcoming. Among them, Peter Robb was most generous with his time and advice, Roy Fischel helped to arrange and organize my visits there, and my close friends there,

Martin Lau, Eleanor Newbigin, and Amrita Shodhan, helped me in more ways than I can count. Amrita has shared both her expertise and friendship as we both worked on the history of panchayats, an endeavor that we once thought would be a lonely one but have since been pleasantly surprised to find that this is not the case. I owe my sincere thanks as well to the international group of scholars who work on law and/or colonialism, especially Adam Hofri-Winogradow, Binyamin Blum, Pooja Parmar, Peter Andersen, Gopika Solanki, Jothie Rajah, Shalini Randeria, and Nurfadzilah Yahaya.

This book would never have been completed without the friendship, advice, and support of Mitra Sharafi and Marc Galanter. If I were to list all of the ways in which they have helped me, then that would merit a book in and of itself. Instead, let me simply emphasize the fact that I will always be indebted to them for their wise counsel, constant support, and, most of all, their camaraderie and friendship.

I know that others may think that they have the greatest children in the world, but I really do. So thank you, Olwen and Max, for being my greatest joy. Finally, this book is dedicated to the memory of my parents.

ABBREVIATIONS

CWMG	*Collected Works of Mahatma Gandhi*
Hansard	*Hansard's Parliamentary Debates*
IOR	British Library, India Office Records
LHR	*Law & History Review*
MAS	*Modern Asian Studies*
MSA, EIC	Maharashtra State Archives, East India Company Papers
NA, CAB	National Archives, Cabinet Papers
ODNB	*Oxford Dictionary of National Biography*
PP	Parliamentary Papers

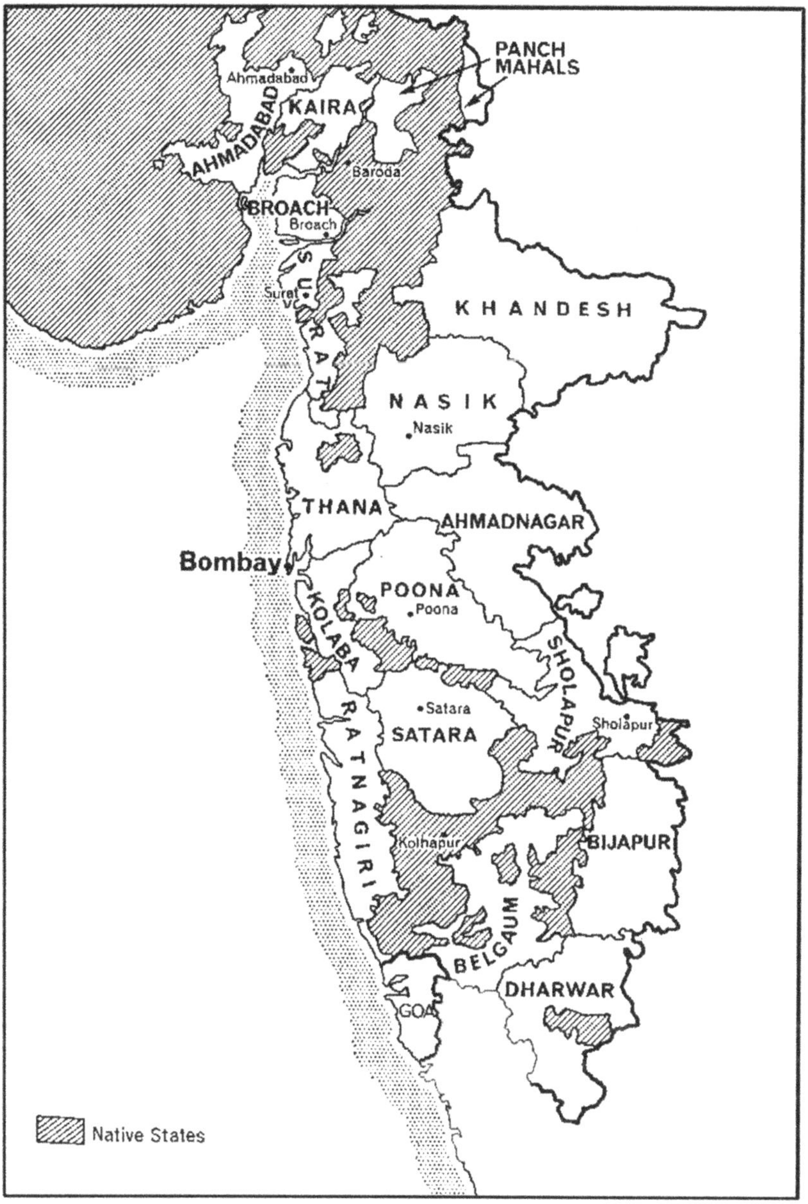

Map 1 Map of Bombay Presidency, c. 1840[1]

[1] "The Bombay Presidency (excluding Sind), c. 1843." Reproduced from Anil Seal, *The Emergence of Indian Nationalism: Competition and Collaboration in the Later Nineteenth Century* (Cambridge University Press, 1965).

INTRODUCTION

This book concerns several discussions, discussions that took place first among British officers and officials serving in India or residing in London and then among Indian nationalists. The discussions concerned the nature and function of the Indian village council – the *panchayat* – its place in Indian society, and its role in the British governance of India. Much like Peter Robb's work on the Bengal Tenancy Act, I have tried to "treat the evolution of events and concepts as the outcome of a dialogue between various, changing, mutually-influenced voices."[1] More specifically, the book is about the colonial imagination of indigenous legal customs and government and the attempts to adapt those imagined customs to the practices of colonial governance. It thus adopts a transnational perspective that emphasizes the ideological sources of Western perceptions of indigenous governing practices, the variety of efforts to "revive" and implement these "authentic" institutions, and the unintended consequences that resulted. Therefore, it recounts the complicated and contested history of the construction of colonial knowledge and the political and intellectual influences that shaped it. In the words of Rosane Rocher, my intent is to examine "the intricate dialectics between the pursuit of knowledge and governmental pursuits."[2] I would not say that this is a cautionary tale, but it is a study of the ways in which customs are

[1] P. G. Robb, *Ancient Rights and Future Comfort: Bihar, the Bengal Tenancy Act of 1885, and British Rule in India* (Richmond, Surrey: Curzon Press, 1997), p. xxi.

[2] Rosane Rocher, "British Orientalism in the Eighteenth Century: The Dialectics of Knowledge and Government," in Carol A. Breckenridge and Peter van der Veer, eds., *Orientalism and the*

imagined and re-imagined, the role of ideology in their creation, and how they developed their own political and social inertia.

Thus this book is about the various incarnations of the Indian "panchayat." I would like to tell the reader that there is a simple and accurate definition for the term "panchayat." However, that is impossible. There is no consensus as to the precise etymology of the word, but it is generally accepted that it is derived from the Sanskrit *pañca*, meaning five, and *āyatta*, depending on. Yet the Hindi word *panchayat* is most commonly defined as a village or caste tribunal or council, five being the customary number of elders on this council or court. The panchayat, however, is protean in both form and function. Over the course of the nineteenth and twentieth centuries, the term has been used to identify and define a number of different institutions, including village councils, municipal councils, conciliation boards, arbitration tribunals, judicial benches, panels of judicial assessors, juries, committees, representative assemblies, and democratic governing bodies. The very indeterminacy of the term has been an essential source of its longevity as well as its contestation. The fact that today the term can be applied equally to the constitutional Panchayati Raj Institutions (PRIs) of local governance and, at the same time, to the infamous "kangaroo courts" of the *khap panchayats* is continuing evidence of the panchayat's political and social significance as well as its resistance to precise categorization.

Nevertheless, since at least the beginning of the nineteenth century, the belief that the panchayat was a fundamental source of Indian authenticity has stood as an iconic idea in both Indian and Western thought. In the early nineteenth century, Sir James Mackintosh, the Scottish Orientalist, described it as "the institution which has preserved society from total shipwreck in India."[3] At that time, other Orientalists, many of whom were among the officer-official corps of the East India Company, fully accepted this description. In their minds, it was chiefly a judicial institution that had been corrupted during the reign of the Mughals or Marathas. Later in the nineteenth century, however, the understanding, adaptation, and implementation of panchayat institutions changed along with the development of liberalism and its imperialist applications. By the last quarter of the nineteenth

Postcolonial Predicament: Perspectives on South Asia (Philadelphia: University of Pennsylvania Press, 1993), p. 215.

[3] James Mackintosh, *Memoirs of the Life of the Right Honourable Sir James Mackintosh*, R. J. Mackintosh, ed., 2nd edn., Vol. I (London, 1836), p. 489.

century, the panchayat was less often imagined as a judicial institution, but instead it had come to be viewed largely, although not exclusively, as an ancient Indian council for local administration. This is the view that came to dominate much of the ideology of the early nationalists, many of whom, from Gandhi to the liberal Gokhale to the radical Tilak, invoked the panchayat as the foundation of self-governance. During the interwar period, this imagining of the panchayat also became one of the foundations of Britain's efforts to devolve the administration of local and provincial affairs within the system of diarchy.

How that transformation came about is the subject of this book. It attempts to trace the lineages of the panchayat ideal, particularly to its origins within the structures and practices of British governance during the nineteenth and early twentieth centuries. The vast subject of caste and *jati* panchayats during this period, therefore, is not addressed in any detail and is left to other scholars. This is largely because the colonial state imagined caste and *jati* panchayats as largely autonomous corporate institutions possessing, like other corporate bodies, the authority to regulate their own members.[4] The colonial state's imagining and implementation of a variety of civil panchayat projects nevertheless had a profound impact upon the political and ideological development of modern India. Those ideological underpinnings of the panchayat ideal today, I would argue, owe as much to the British colonial imagination as they do to the Indian historical experience.

The panchayat was certainly not unknown to British colonial administrators in India before 1800, but during the first three decades of the nineteenth century it took on both a new meaning and new significance. In tandem with the idealization of the Indian village community – the so-called "metaphorical heart of orientalism," – the project of resurrecting and restoring the panchayat to what was believed to be its traditional role in local society became of paramount importance to both East India Company officials in London and

[4] Trade, professional, and artisanal panchayats under British control have received little if any attention, unfortunately. Bankers' panchayats, for example, appear to have been especially prominent in the settlement of commercial disputes in Pune, for example. Nevertheless, for earlier cases, see Nandita Prasad Sahai, "Artisans, the State, and the Politics of Wajabi in Eighteenth-century Jodhpur," *Indian Economic and Social History Review*, Vol. 42, No. 1 (2005), pp. 41–68 and *idem*, "Collaboration and Conflict: Artisanal Jati Panchayats and the Eighteenth Century Jodhpur State," *Medieval History Journal*, Vol. 5, No. 1 (2002), pp. 77–101. On caste panchayats during the earlier era, see Amrita Shodhan, "Caste in the Judicial Courts of Gujarat, 1800–1860," in E. Simpson and A. Kapadia, eds., *The Idea of Gujarat: History, Ethnography and Text* (Hyderabad: Orient Blackswan, 2010), pp. 32–49.

military officer-officials in India, especially in the Company's southern and western possessions on the subcontinent.[5] It was there and then that British officials began to imagine the panchayat as a local judicial institution meting out justice according to the "customs of the country" and without recourse to the Hindu law codes. Along with the village headman (*patel*), the panchayat, it was believed, was an institution derived from Indian common law and the basis of India's ancient constitution.[6] As such, India shared a common history with that of early medieval England. As one local Political Agent wrote, according to this perspective, civil justice in India "seems not to differ much – from what we understand – to be our own antient [*sic*] local Courts."[7] In this manner, India's history was reshaped to fit the mold of British political ideologies. This particular type of Enlightenment historicism continued to be reformulated and reinterpreted throughout the nineteenth and early twentieth centuries in ways that would affect not only British attempts to adapt the panchayat to colonial rule but also the emerging nationalist movement.[8]

Thomas Munro, who served as Governor of the Madras Presidency between 1820 and 1827, and Mountstuart Elphinstone, Governor of the Bombay Presidency from 1819 to 1827, were among the leading proponents of the judicial function of the panchayat during the early nineteenth century. Their efforts to resurrect the panchayat as "the great instrument in the administration of Justice," to use Elphinstone's words, entailed adapting it to their own needs as colonial administrators.[9] Foremost among these was the effort to make the panchayat an inexpensive, accessible, and efficient judicial institution. Thus, much of the British interest in the panchayat here, unlike in Bengal, was adjectival, that is, concerned with legal procedure, rather than uncovering the substance of customary law. Implementing their vision, however, required regularizing panchayat procedures, supervising its

[5] David Ludden, "Orientalist Empiricism: Transformations of Colonial Knowledge," in Breckenridge and van der Veer, *Orientalism and the Postcolonial Predicament*, p. 263.

[6] The theme of India's "ancient constitution" was not an uncommon one and can be traced in the writings of such disparate characters as Warren Hastings, Edmund Burke, and Philip Francis. See Thomas Metcalf, *Ideologies of the Raj* (Cambridge: Cambridge University Press, 1995), Chapter 1.

[7] MSA, EIC, Judicial Department, Civil and Criminal Judicature, Vol. 9A/9A, 1823, John Briggs to William Chaplin, 3 May 1822.

[8] On the development of nineteenth-century historicism and its effects on British rule, see Metcalf, *Ideologies of the Raj*, Chapters 1 and 2.

[9] Mountstuart Elphinstone, *Report on the Territories Conquered from the Paishwa* (Calcutta, 1821), p. 78.

operation, limiting its jurisdiction, and, in general, incorporating the panchayat into the structures of British judicial administration. Inevitably, such attempts to "remove its abuses and revive its energy," Elphinstone's words again, created an altogether new institution that still carried the name "panchayat," but had been remade in the image of its creators.[10] However, by the end of Munro and Elphinstone's tenures as Governors, these panchayat experiments had proven to be a failure. In both the Madras and Bombay Presidencies panchayats would survive, but only as an adjunct and alternative to the British courts, and very few litigants ever sought them out. In Bengal, meanwhile, the steadfast resistance of judicial and other Company officials to its introduction there prevented the panchayat from ever becoming incorporated into the formal systems of justice.

Ideologically, there is much in common here with Robert Travers' recent work on Bengal in the late eighteenth century.[11] As in Bengal, British rulers in western and southern India were immersed in the language and ideology of ancient constitutionalism, and the development of colonial governing practices was often the result of the interaction between these ideological predispositions and their observation and interpretation of Indian custom. However, unlike Travers' Bengal, in the Bombay and Madras Presidencies these practices did not end in the last decades of the eighteenth century. One very obvious reason for the continuity in the south and west was the fact that neither Munro in Madras nor Elphinstone in Bombay were anything like Cornwallis in Bengal whose antipathy to the employment of Indian administrators, separation of executive and judicial authority, and advocacy of a permanent settlement of land revenues under the aegis of large-scale landholders (*zamindars*) marked his tenure as Governor-General there. Indeed, the governing ideologies, revenue settlement, and judicial practices in the south and west were proposed and implemented in direct contradistinction to the perceived failures of Cornwallis' Permanent Settlement in Bengal.

Moreover, the displacement of the ideologies of ancient constitutionalism by those of a commercial and modernizing Enlightenment narrative that Travers describes in Bengal did not occur in the same way in the south and west.[12] Instead, the specific idiom of English

[10] Elphinstone, *Report*, p. 99.

[11] Robert Travers, *Ideology and Empire in Eighteenth-Century India: The British in Bengal* (Cambridge: Cambridge University Press, 2007).

[12] Travers notes this distinction in *Ideology and Empire*, pp. 252–3.

ancient constitutionalism continued to be deployed there and increasingly in a fashion that had been molded by its contact with Scottish Enlightenment thought, thereby forming a properly British ideology of colonial governance. Particularly important in this regard was the reimagining of history as a process that occurred in definable stages of social, political, and economic development, the so-called stadial or conjectural interpretation, as well as the valorization of India as a once-great civilization in and of itself. This form of "Scottish Orientalism" shared with some of the earlier British governors of Bengal the notion that India had been corrupted by the rule of arbitrary despots, both Muslim and Maratha, but in the south and west the goal was to restore India to its proper path of historical development. The irony was that such a restoration was very unlikely, if not impossible, to occur under colonial governance, and its demands for revenue were neither understood nor appreciated by the likes of either Munro or Elphinstone.

In one sense, therefore, British attempts to adapt and reform the panchayat epitomized the bureaucratic complexity of establishing indirect colonial governance. From the East India Company's perspective, the panchayat experiments adopted in Madras and Bombay were just that – experiments. Under Munro's influence, the Company agreed to employ the panchayat as the basis for the administration of colonial justice, but then only after the failure of British-staffed courts in Bengal had become too obvious to ignore. Yet the incorporation of the panchayat into the British judicial bureaucracy required constant tinkering and repeated interventions in order to attempt to correct the unforeseen and unintended consequences of such a policy. One such unintended consequence was the constant expansion of the number of Indians employed in judicial roles to monitor and supplement the panchayat. By 1829, there were already almost eighty Indian commissioners and magistrates in the Bombay Presidency, almost the full complement of subordinate judges that would be employed by the end of the nineteenth century.[13]

In another sense, the adoption of the panchayat to colonial governance during this period revealed not only the ideological sources of such an undertaking but also the very limits of that ideology itself. The Orientalist ideal that the panchayat was an essential component of

[13] PP, *Report from the Select Committee on the Affairs of the East India Company* (1831–1832), General Appendix, No. III, p. 125. By 1887, the number of Indian judges in the Bombay Presidency totaled only 104; see, Christophe Jaffrelot, *Dr. Ambedkar and Untouchability* (Delhi: Permanent Black, 2005), p. 12.

India's ancient constitution and was based upon Indian common law restricted the range of possible reforms. Whether or not any reform of the panchayat might have made it a success is not the pertinent question here. Much more important was the perception that any plans of reform had to be limited to those that did not violate the panchayat's supposed origins in Indian common law. Therefore, in the Bombay Presidency, for example, where the panchayat was understood as an analog to British arbitration practices, litigants could bring their suit to a panchayat, but only voluntarily; any individual could serve on a panchayat, but only upon the request of the litigant; and, panchayats could issue a decision, but they could not enforce it. These kinds of self-imposed limitations ultimately restricted the efficient disposal of suits by panchayats. The resulting failure of the British-reformed panchayat to provide cheap and efficient access to justice was the key factor in that institution's eventual rejection by India's colonial governors as a suitable venue for dispute resolution.

After the first third of the nineteenth century, the idea and symbolic significance of the panchayat only temporarily lost its material embodiment under the British administration of India. During the second half of the century, the panchayat was re-imagined and resurrected once again. This time, however, it came not in the guise of a judicial institution but as an instrument of village and town governance. The first incarnations during the 1860s and 1870s were in the form of appointed bodies for local tax assessment purposes, and then for the levying of taxes to provide for local policing. By the 1880s, panchayats could also be appointed to manage roads, schools, sanitation, and other municipal responsibilities. A key impetus to this transformation was the increasing influence of what Thomas Metcalf has called the "eclectic liberalism" of the later nineteenth century.[14] Of particular importance were the elements of liberalism that emphasized the historicism of the Indian village community as well as those elements of liberalism that emphasized the importance of fostering the growth of Indian civil society. Yet both of these elements of liberalism drew heavily upon the older idioms of ancient constitutionalism and Scottish Orientalism, and both exercised an enormous influence upon the panchayat ideal.

Of special note in this regard was the notion that the panchayat could be employed as a means by which Indians could be educated and trained into the arts of modern civilization. Such notions had already

[14] Metcalf, *Ideologies of the Raj*, p. 33.

been mooted under Company rule, but the institutional means through which this tutelary function might be achieved shifted from the panchayat imagined as a judicial forum to the panchayat imagined as an institution of village and municipal governance. Notably, these local governance panchayats of the second half of the nineteenth century were in no way representative and instead were comprised of "respectable" Indians, appointed by local British officials, who would thereby be educated into the arts of Western-style government. Significantly, by the time of the 1908 Royal Commission on Decentralization, both British and Indian witnesses lauded the ideal of the panchayat as an institution that would promote the growth of civil society in India, but they also offered a wide variety of often-contradictory opinions as to its possible form, function, and composition. Therefore, not only is it true, as C. A. Bayly has written, that the panchayat was continually reinvented during the nineteenth century, but it is similarly true that memories of the panchayat had become muddled and confused.[15]

Yet, once again, the British imagining of an appointed municipal and village panchayat was unsuccessful. In part, the "autocratic structure" of these British-appointed panchayats made them unpopular and their function, to levy taxes, made them even more so.[16] However, the ideological limits of liberalism were palpable as well. Despite liberalism's adherence to the goal of expanding representative institutions, it remained hostile to and suspicious of the political participation of the uneducated masses. Moreover, as several authors have emphasized, liberalism's tutelary project in India faltered in the face of popular political agitation, the growth of Indian nationalism, and the spread of "scientific racism."[17]

The resuscitation and adoption of the panchayat by the British after mid-century was a matter not only of colonial administration through indirect control but also of liberal "nation-building" in a specific historical form. Explicit in the discussions surrounding the panchayat as a tutelary instrument was the desire to use it as a means by which to build a civil society in India. The term "civil society," however, should not be

[15] C. A. Bayly, *Recovering Liberties: Indian Thought in the Age of Liberalism and Empire* (Cambridge: Cambridge University Press, 2012), p. 347.

[16] Hugh Tinker, *The Foundations of Local Self-Government in India, Pakistan, and Burma* (New York: Frederick A. Praeger, 1968), p. 70.

[17] Metcalf, *Ideologies of the Raj*, Chapter 2; Uday Singh Mehta, *Liberalism and Empire: A Study in Nineteenth-century Liberal Thought* (Chicago: University of Chicago Press, 1999), pp. 111–14; 151–2; Karuna Mantena, *Alibis of Empire: Henry Maine and the Ends of Liberal Imperialism* (Princeton: Princeton University Press, 2010), pp. 160–71.

taken to mean the collection of autonomous or independent groups and associations outside of the political sphere, the meaning that became attached to it in the late-twentieth and early twenty-first centuries. Nor should it be taken in the sense expressed in Partha Chatterjee's *Nationalist Thought and the Colonial World*, in which the term is used as a synonym for the political, economic, and moral structure of modern industrial society.[18] Instead, the term as used in this book should be understood in its historical context as indicating a specific set of conservative institutions based not only upon an idea of progress but more specifically upon the rule of law, the right to private property, and the importance of elite civic participation in government.[19]

As José Harris has noted, this was a specifically Anglophone tradition, distinct from both the French and German understanding of "civil society," and stretching back through the works of a great many prominent theorists and moralists, including Adam Smith, Adam Ferguson, Bernard Mandeville, John Locke, Thomas Hobbes, and Richard Hooker.[20] Most important for the first generation of advocates of the panchayat was the influence of the so-called Scottish Orientalists, especially William Robertson, who viewed India as a once-great civilization that had been corrupted by the arbitrary rule of Mughal and Maratha despots. The "civilizing mission" of Munro and Elphinstone, therefore, was not to convert the heathens, but to return India to its "natural" path of historical development toward a civil society. In the British imagination, this entailed the restoration of the social and political standing of the village headman, the definition of property rights, and the revival of the panchayat for the dispensation of civil law.

Once again, such an ideology, based as it was upon the Scottish school of history, possessed its own inherent limits. It was by no means democratic, but it was intended instead to restore the traditional authority of an imagined landed gentry and yeomanry. The authority to administer the criminal law remained the prerogative of the British

18 Partha Chatterjee, *Nationalist Thought and the Colonial World: A Derivative Discourse* (1986; Minneapolis: University of Minnesota Press, 2011), Chapter 4.

19 For a similar point, see Peter Robb, "The Colonial State and the Construction of Indian Identity: An Example on the Northeast Frontier in the 1880s," MAS, Vol. 31, No. 2 (May, 1997), pp. 251–2.

20 José Harris, "From Richard Hooker to Harold Laski: Changing Perceptions of Civil Society in British Political Thought, Late Sixteenth to Early Twentieth Centuries," in José Harris, ed., *Civil Society in British History: Ideas, Identities, Institutions* (Oxford: Oxford University Press, 2005), pp. 13–37.

company-state with little or no role for the "natives." And, the restoration of Indian civil society certainly did not entail the ultimate creation of a democratic, sovereign, and independent India.

When the panchayat ideal resurfaced among British administrators in the second half of the nineteenth century as a body suitable to take on the responsibility of decentralized village and municipal governance, it nevertheless continued to be imagined as a school for civil society. This new liberal ideal of the panchayat, heavily influenced by the works of John Stuart Mill and Henry Sumner Maine, necessarily possessed its own ideological limits. Like previous generations, this new imaginary retained a pronounced antipathy to democracy, preferring instead to educate a cadre of respectable and propertied local officials into the values of civic morality and the science of government. High matters of state, such as defense and foreign policy, were excluded from this training, of course, and, once again, very few British officials ever foresaw the likelihood of yielding ultimate sovereignty over India.

The ironies of colonial governance, therefore, included not only the unintended consequences of British efforts at reforming the panchayat but also the attempts to resurrect the "customary" legal institutions of southern and western India within the ideological parameters of Anglophone political theory.[21] Yet the panchayat was not an "invented tradition." In western India, it was a very real institution that had been a functioning part of the judicial administration of the Marathas before the British conquests.[22] Elphinstone believed that the role of the new British occupiers was only to "remove its abuses and revive its energy," cleansing the panchayat of the venality, partiality, and corruption that had encrusted it under the Marathas' arbitrary and despotic rule.[23] By the late nineteenth and early twentieth centuries, many of these fundamental ideas had found new voices in the writings of Mill and Maine. As Christopher Bayly has noted, it would be a mistake to draw too sharp a distinction between the Orientalist and liberal traditions with regard to their imagining of Indian society. "One reason that Maine's thought was well received in the India of the 1870s and 1880s," he has written, "was that it spoke to the older

[21] In a somewhat similar manner, for South India, Arjun Appadurai notes the ironic tension between "the [British] urge to maximize vertical accountability and the fantasy of *pancāyat* models of local self-sufficiency." See Arjun Appadurai, *Worship and Conflict under Colonial Rule: A South Indian Case* (Cambridge: Cambridge University Press, 1981), p. 141, ff. 6; 153–4.

[22] See V. T. Gune, *The Judicial System of the Marathas* (Poona: Deccan College Post-Graduate and Research Institute, 1953).

[23] Elphinstone, *Report*, p. 99.

pre-utilitarian tradition represented most notably by Elphinstone, Munro and Tod between 1780 and 1830."[24] Although the invented form and function of the panchayat changed significantly under the influence of liberalism, the ideological imperative of restoring the imagined panchayat had not.

By the early twentieth century, the panchayat as reframed and re-invented by the liberal imagination had become an essential element of the nationalist movement. Yet even during these critical moments, the form and function of the panchayat and its role in civil society continued to be a matter of significant debate as some imagined it as a uniquely Indian form of democracy, others as a form of socialist commune or cooperative, and still others, most notably B. R. Ambedkar, as an instrument for the violation of individual rights.

The models of these reinventions and re-imaginings of the panchayat thus rarely were specifically Indian ones. Instead, they were fashioned along the lines of Western ideologies, or analogized to them, and then applied to Indian history, Indian custom, and the perceived necessity of the reform of Indian society. Thus Gandhi, for example, certainly the most famous advocate of the revitalization of panchayats, imagined historical India as populated by "village republics," a phrase first coined by Thomas Munro, and panchayats as democratic institutions.[25] Like others of his generation, however, he also admitted that he had never actually seen a panchayat.[26] In this sense, Sudipta Kaviraj was quite right to point out the irony that European writers helped to construct an image of "eternal India" and presented it to Indians looking for a national identity.[27] Therefore, this study is less about the interaction of distinctly plural legal cultures or the forms of indirect rule than about the processes of the absorption, adaptation, reconfiguration, and re-imagining of "traditional" local practices of dispute resolution and village authority in a transnational environment. It is about, to use Simon Roberts' words, "looking for the exploitation of an existing repertoire, or the artificial sustaining of ancient

[24] C. A. Bayly, "Maine and Change in Nineteenth-century India," in Alan Diamond, ed., *The Victorian Achievement of Sir Henry Maine: A centennial reappraisal* (Cambridge: Cambridge University Press, 1991), pp. 389–90.

[25] *Young India*, 28 May 1931, reprinted CWMG, electronic edition, Vol. 52 (New Delhi: Publications Division, Government of India, 1999), p. 191.

[26] "Speech at a Prayer Meeting," 27 December 1947, CWMG, Vol. 98, p. 121.

[27] Sudipta Kaviraj, "The Imaginary Institution of India," reprinted in *idem*, *The Imaginary Institution of India: Politics and Ideas* (New York: Columbia University Press, 2010), p. 181.

forms" and "an account of ideology as working with what is already to hand."[28]

Thus, this book is also a study of the history of an idea and it is an attempt to locate the history of that idea within the practices of colonial governance and the development of Indian nationalism. That is, it is at one and the same time a history of an idea and a history of an ideology. In working out these relationships, I admit to a rather pronounced theoretical eclecticism, albeit an eclecticism largely drawn from the *marxisant* literature. Thus readers will recognize the influence of both Gramscian and Althusserian theory.[29] However, perhaps the most appropriate way to describe the approach adopted here is what Lauren Benton recently described as "applied theory."[30] That is, the attempts by both British occupiers and Indian nationalists to adopt, adapt, and institutionalize preconceived ideas of the nature and history of Indian culture and society to the needs of colonial administration. In this process, not only did the British administrators re-create the institutions – in this case, the panchayat – through which individuals constituted themselves as litigants or local officials within evolving structures of law and governance, but also it was through these and other interactions with local administrators and judicial officials, both British and Indian, that individuals became conscious of themselves as "subjects," as who they were, how they were expected to behave, and their place in the British Empire. The panchayat, obviously, was not the only institution that served these multiple functions. As Niraja Gopal Jayal has written, the legal status of the imperial subject was "complex and stratified" in several different ways.[31] Yet, along with

[28] Simon Roberts, "Afterword to the Second Edition," in *Order and Dispute: An Introduction to Legal Anthropology*, 2nd edn. (New Orleans: Quid Pro Books, 2013), p. 163.

[29] Of particular importance, see Louis Althusser, "Ideology and Ideological State Apparatus (Notes Towards an Investigation)," in *idem*, *Lenin and Philosophy and other essays* (1971; New York: Monthly Review Press, 2001), pp. 85–126 and the critical analysis provided in Stuart Hall, "Signification, Representation, Ideology: Althusser and the Post-Structuralist Debates," *Critical Studies in Mass Communication*, Vol. 2, No. 2 (June 1985), pp. 91–114. For Gramsci, Partha Chatterjee's explication of his theory's bearing on the study of colonialism, particularly as it evolved in India, is of exceptional significance. See his *Nationalist Thought and the Colonial World*. See also the useful discussion in Christine Sypnowich, "Law and Ideology," *Stanford Encyclopedia of Philosophy*, online http://plato.stanford.edu/archives/fall2010/entries/law-ideology/, accessed 11 June 2013. Marx's classic statement on ideology appears in "On the Jewish Question" (1844).

[30] Lauren Benton, "Under the Protection of British Law: Empire and the Early Nineteenth-century Origins of the Responsibility to Protect," Third Biennial Conference of the European Society for Comparative Legal History, Macerata, Italy, 8–9 July 2014.

[31] Niraja Gopal Jayal, *Citizenship and its Discontents: An Indian History* (Cambridge, MA: Harvard University Press, 2013), pp. 31–3.

revenue collection, the panchayat took primacy of place among British efforts to settle their dominion over southern and western India, especially during the first third of the nineteenth century.

The process of creating the Indian subject was not only a complex one but also lengthy. It has a history. It involved failures as well as successes; it created unintended consequences. Perhaps the most significant irony of the British panchayat project was the fact that in their efforts to revivify the panchayat in order to make it serve their needs, the British sustained its iconic standing in Indian governing ideology only to see it adopted and re-imagined by nationalists and those seeking independence as the only properly indigenous form of government.

There is an already-established literature on the construction of colonial identities that, in many ways, parallels and supplements this project. Much of that work has also focused on the role of the colonial government in establishing identities, particularly those identities of caste, religion, and tribe.[32] In the manner of Foucault, much of that literature sprang from the recognition that the government's desire to enumerate and hence to more effectively tax the Indian population (as well as to deal with famine relief) had the effect of classifying and categorizing individuals and groups in ways that reflected colonial anxieties over race, religion, law and order, and ethnicity. This book, however, is less about establishing colonial taxonomies and classifications, although that was sometimes inherent in the process, and much more about attempts to identify, forge, and foster a specific legal and civic culture.

In this effort, of course, the colonial state was the essential actor. It would be misguided, I think, either to anthropomorphize the state or to attribute an unwarranted degree of uniformity to the implementation of its policies. In the case of the panchayat, its meaning and significance was always heavily contested and remains so today. What David Ludden has written about Munro and village India is equally true of Munro's and Elphinstone's approach to the panchayat. Their "victories" in identifying and resuscitating the panchayat were only

[32] See, for example, Nandini Sundar, "Caste as Census Category: Implications for Sociology," *Current Sociology*, Vol. 48, No. 3 (July 2000), pp. 111–26; Sumit Guha, "The Politics of Identity and Enumeration in India, c. 1600–1990," *Comparative Studies in Society and History*, Vol. 45, No. 1 (January 2003), pp. 148–67; Radhika Singha, "Settle, Mobilize, Verify: Identification Practices in Colonial India," *Studies in History*, Vol. 16, No. 2 (August 2000), pp. 151–98; and, Robb, "The Colonial State and the Construction of Indian Identity," pp. 245–83.

partly victories of a particular ideology or philosophy. Equally, they were political victories fought out in London. Unlike the imagined Indian village, however, which became reified as the essential and timeless unit of colonial administration, by the second half of the nineteenth century, the panchayat also had taken on a mythical status that was shared by many colonial administrators and nationalists alike. To be sure, as Ludden also notes in regard to the colonial categories of the village and caste, there were serious debates not only as to its form and functions but also as to its emancipatory or coercive role. Yet this imagined panchayat tradition would ultimately be adopted as an element of the nationalist critique of imperial governance. Thus the nationalist adoption of the panchayat as a symbol of a uniquely Indian mode of self-governance "came from the treasure chest of orientalism." In this way, nationalism "appropriated orientalism in the name of self-representation."[33]

A final word should also be said about the nature and function of arbitration, a concept and practice that will occur repeatedly throughout this book. Readers will become familiar with the fact that British administrators in India as well as many nationalists were often at odds over the precise function of the panchayat. Some thought it analogous to an English jury, while others thought it analogous to arbitration. Still others saw it as an analog to the British town councils or local boards of guardians. Indeed, throughout the nineteenth century, we will see that the perception of the panchayat would oscillate between the poles of jury, board of arbitration, and municipal and village governments, a testimony to the panchayat's iconic albeit amorphous standing in both British and Indian ideology.

However, during the late eighteenth and early nineteenth centuries, arbitration was often extolled, most notably by William Blackstone and Lord Mansfield, as a remedy to the obvious deficiencies of the English court system, an observation that was then applied to the justice system in colonial India. Throughout the book, the term is used in its specific legal sense and should not be confused with other forms of alternative dispute resolution such as mediation or negotiation. As one legal historian has succinctly put it, "arbitration is a procedure in which one or more people are selected and empowered by the principals to render a binding decision the principals agree to accept beforehand."[34]

[33] This paragraph owes a great debt to Ludden's superb article, "Orientalist Empiricism," pp. 250–78.

[34] William Ian Miller, *Bloodtaking and Peacemaking: Feud, Law, and Society in Saga Iceland* (Chicago: University of Chicago Press, 1990), p. 261.

As we shall see, this voluntary mode of dispute settlement was a potentially attractive alternative to the courts, promising, as it still does, speedy access to justice at a very low cost. However, arbitration was also encumbered by many less attractive features, including its lack of any authority to enforce its decisions; its frequent failure to satisfy either litigant; and, the tendency of some litigants to employ arbitration as a way to delay or deny justice rather than to secure it.[35] Nevertheless, arbitration entailed a specific set of procedures that distinguished it from other forms of dispute resolution, and it was this process that many British officer-officials, especially in western India, believed they had found in the form of the panchayat during the early nineteenth century.

This book is divided into two parts. Part I, Discoveries and Adaptations, is very much a detailed historical analysis of the various imaginings and adaptations of the panchayat to the needs of British governance in India during the early nineteenth century. It opens with a discussion of the origins and functioning of the panchayat system in the Bombay Presidency during the first third of the nineteenth century. The focus upon western India at this time emphasizes the production of colonial knowledge of the panchayat and the problems of the implementation of a supposedly revived and purified panchayat system. To a significant degree, the choice of the Bombay Presidency as the focus of this section was motivated by the desire to contrast the adaptation of the panchayat there with the more well-known efforts of Munro in Madras.

Chapter 1 of the first part, therefore, examines the British "discovery" of the panchayat as an institution analogous to the British system of arbitration and rooted in India's common law and ancient constitution. This chapter analyzes the sources of British perceptions of the panchayat and its roots in Anglophone political theory, and it attempts to more critically locate these perceptions within the context of

[35] The structural problems inherent to arbitration as it was practiced in different cultures in widely different circumstances are well illustrated in Miller, *Bloodtaking and Peacemaking*, Chapter 8. Arbitration is frequently included as an aspect of the anthropological study of law. For a now dated although still very helpful introduction to the general study of disputes by anthropologists, see Francis G. Snyder, "Anthropology, Dispute Processes and Law: A Critical Introduction," *British Journal of Law and Society*, Vol. 8, No. 2 (Winter 1981), pp. 141–80. Max Gluckman's "The Peace in the Feud," *Past & Present*, No. 8 (November 1955), pp. 1–14 is also certainly worthy of re-reading.

Scottish Enlightenment readings of historical India. Chapters 2, 3, and 4 constitute an extended analysis of the functioning of the panchayat-arbitration system, its perceived advantages over the Bengal-style system of judicial administration, and how litigants understood and made use of the new system. There are rarely sources that permit the historian to enter into the panchayat for this period, but the appeals from panchayat cases as well as the Company's own investigations into allegations of corruption on the part of their officials have left some detailed records in which the litigants can be made to speak. To be sure, these are not the voices of the urban poor, nor are they the voices of the rural peasant. They are largely the voices of more prosperous rural landholders and village officials. Nevertheless, they do provide access to at least part of the realm of contemporary legal consciousness shaped, as it was, by the structures and demands of the British panchayat system.

Part I of the book also focuses on the other incarnations of the panchayat before the mid-nineteenth century, as well as on the debates among British administrators as to its proper role and function. British officer-officials in southern and western India gained their first experiences with the panchayat where it was adapted to the process of disciplining Indian troops in Company employment. There is substantial evidence that this variation of the panchayat was regularly used well into the second half of the nineteenth century and that many military officers found it both a useful and effective means by which Indian soldiers and camp followers were tried for minor offenses. It is also likely, although it cannot be proven, that the value placed upon the panchayat by the likes of Munro and Elphinstone was based upon their experiences with it in its military form and that these favorable impressions were confirmed by their Orientalist predisposition.

The panchayat-military court, however, was part of a broader stream of Western theory that the panchayat was an indigenous form of the jury system rather than a system of arbitration. The panchayat-jury, therefore, is also examined in its manifestations as both a civil and criminal jury. During the 1830s, this became an especially salient issue as jury reforms were being promoted in England. Several radicals in London seized upon this opportunity to expand the debate in parliament to include the introduction of the jury system to India in particular and the judicial administration of India more generally. Significantly, this transnational legal debate drew in the participation of the most prominent Indian intellectuals of the era, especially

Rammohan Roy, and thus marked one of their earliest efforts to publicly reform British rule.

Part II, Lineages and Legacies, adopts a much more expansive view of the panchayat by tracing its ideological lineages largely through the period up to Indian independence. During this period, the fate of the panchayat became inextricably connected to several prominent themes of British political ideology, especially Scottish Orientalism, republicanism, and, lastly, liberal imperialism. Ultimately, the liberal imagining of village India as an ancient institution, immune from historical change, and in need of protection and tutelage, penetrated both imperial and nationalist thought. This legacy, of course, is attributed largely to the influence of Henry Sumner Maine, but Maine himself had little to say about the panchayat. It thus was left to others to formulate a new view of the panchayat's role in village society within this new paradigm. While some, such as William Wedderburn, drew upon the legacy of Munro and Elphinstone and promoted the panchayat as a judicial or arbitral institution, most liberal reformists envisioned the panchayat as an administrative institution that historically had been responsible for village services, such as the maintenance of roads and wells, the provision of police, or the establishment of schools. These new visions of the panchayat were of a piece with both the political and social reform movements in the municipalities of England and, by the beginning of the twentieth century, had drawn the approbation not only of liberal reformers but socialists as well.

This period also marks the introduction of panchayat ideology into the nationalist movement. The nationalists of the late nineteenth century showed a significant degree of confusion over the forms, functions, and composition of the panchayat, although they obviously had imbibed the belief that the panchayat was an ancient institution responsible for village governance. As such, the panchayat became symbolic of an authentic Indian tradition of self-governance, although evidence for such a standing was drawn largely from British sources and British observations. Certainly, the most critical intervention in this new understanding of the panchayat was that of M. K. Gandhi, who ultimately imagined the panchayat not only as an ancient form of village governance but, more importantly, as the foundation of a uniquely Indian form of democracy.

By the later stages of the independence movement, the democratic panchayat had become embedded within nationalist ideology. To be sure, there were some dissenting voices, most notably that of B. R. Ambedkar.

However, the imagining of a democratic panchayat as the foundation for a free India brought with it a variety of practical political problems, problems as mundane as the participation of political parties in the electoral process and as controversial as the representation of women and castes. In the immediate post-independence period, the central government exhibited relatively little interest in resolving these issues, a fact that reflected Jawaharlal Nehru's own position on the primacy of economic development. Instead, a variety of panchayat institutions were created by individual states and by 1954 about two-thirds of the Indian states had implemented some form of local panchayat governance. In the end, however, it was not until 1992 that the central government amended the Constitution to introduce a uniform system of *panchayati raj*.

Nevertheless, various incarnations of the panchayat continued to exist and continue to play a prominent role in Indian thought and society. These incarnations, as distinct as the *khap panchayats* of northern India, which regulate and discipline members of the same clan or lineage, the trade union among Pune porters and laborers (*hamal panchayat*) that provides low-cost housing, pensions, and other benefits to its more than 3,000 members, or the government-sponsored *mahila* (women's) panchayats, testify both to the ambiguities of the panchayat ideal as well as to its lasting significance.

PART I

DISCOVERIES AND ADAPTATIONS

1

THE RISE AND FALL OF THE PANCHAYAT IN THE BOMBAY PRESIDENCY

Twice during the nineteenth century, British administrators in India "discovered" the panchayat, or village council. Both times it appeared in a form created to meet the demands of British governance and fashioned by current streams of Western political theory. The first discovery dates to approximately the first third of the century, when several prominent East India Company military officers sought to adapt the panchayat to the needs of the British administration of justice, especially in the newly conquered regions of southern and western India. To meet these requirements, the panchayat was put forth as an Indian analog of either the English jury or European tribunals of arbitration. The second discovery dates to the final third of the century. At that time, the necessities of urban and rural development required new forms of local and municipal administration. The consequent widespread support among British administrators in India for political decentralization therefore involved the desire to recreate the panchayat, but this time as a municipal body often in the image of European local administration.

Despite the obvious differences between the two incarnations of the panchayat under British rule, a further notable distinction existed. By the late nineteenth century, the panchayat as an active part of village governance as opposed to being used for caste regulation was, by all accounts, virtually moribund. Observers noted that it survived in a few scattered places, chiefly in the North-Western Provinces and parts of Burma, but, as one attorney who practiced before the Madras High Court noted in 1915, they had rarely been seen in the rest of India for the previous thirty years.[1] However, during the first third of the century, this had not been the case. Most British officer-officials had had active experience with the panchayat, not the least because in the military it was employed to resolve disputes between soldiers and camp-followers and to court-martial sepoy troops. Furthermore, especially in the areas occupied by the British after the Anglo-Maratha Wars in western India, the panchayat had been an active judicial institution under the later Marathas.[2] We will never be able to answer the question of whether these British officer-officials fully comprehended or understood the role of the panchayat in village society. At the time, it suited one of their most pressing needs, which was to settle the territories by securing the administration of justice. However, for the period following the defeat of the Marathas, their records remain one of the few sources available with which to study the panchayat.

While much of the attention of historians has been directed toward the work of Thomas Munro in this respect in the Madras Presidency, considerably less attention has been paid to the efforts of Mountstuart Elphinstone in the western Bombay Presidency.[3] The focus upon Munro's efforts to adapt the panchayat to British governance is not unwarranted. His work in both London and Madras to promote it were of principal importance for the history of the panchayat. Moreover, the institutional panchayats established by Munro in the Madras Presidency survived much longer than they did elsewhere.

However, Elphinstone's efforts in the Bombay Presidency, especially in western Deccan which was acquired after 1818, were equally important and equally strenuous. Not only did Elphinstone and his officers engage in substantive historical and contemporary research on the panchayat's activities under the Maratha Peshwa, but they also took a very active role in supervising and promoting its use under their own administration. By adapting the panchayat to British needs, most officer-officials believed that they were reviving an ancient and customary

[1] John Matthai, *Village Government in British India* (London: T. Fisher Unwin, 1915), p. 181.

[2] V. T. Gune, *The Judicial System of the Marathas* (Poona: Deccan College Post-Graduate and Research Institute, 1953), pp. 83–6.

[3] Burton Stein, *Thomas Munro: The Origins of the Colonial State and his Vision of Empire* (Delhi: Oxford University Press, 1989); Catherine S. Meschievitz, "Civil Litigation and Judicial Policy in the Madras Presidency, 1800–1843" (Ph.D. thesis, University of Wisconsin-Madison, 1986); Kenneth Ballhatchet, *Social Policy and Social Change in Western India, 1817–1830* (Oxford: Oxford University Press, 1957); T. H. Beaglehole, *Thomas Munro and the Development of Administrative Policy in Madras, 1792–1818* (Cambridge: Cambridge University Press, 1966); and Meera Singh, *British Revenue and Judicial Policies in India: A Case study of Deccan (1818–1826)* (New Delhi: Har-Anand Publications, 1994).

institution that would be welcomed by the people of the country. But, at the same time, they also believed that the panchayat had to be reformed and re-structured to meet the British government's present-day needs. The paradox of attempting to achieve both of these goals did not occur to them. Perhaps the ultimate failure of British attempts to revive the panchayat during this era was therefore inevitable.

Elphinstone had first come to India in 1796.[4] For many years, he served at Pune, conducting diplomatic relations with the Maratha Peshwa. However, after the British victory in the Third Anglo-Maratha War of 1817–1818, Elphinstone was given responsibility to occupy and settle the Deccan, which the Peshwa had been forced to cede to the British. In 1819, he was appointed Governor of the Bombay Presidency, a position he held until 1827.

Upon the occupation of the Deccan, the Marquess of Hastings, Governor-General of India, permitted Elphinstone "to establish such temporary measures as he might deem requisite or proper, and to avail himself of the talents and experience of Brigadier-General Munro, by inviting assistance from the latter in introducing the British authority into the southern territory."[5] However, Hastings also ordered that these temporary measures "were limited to the restoration of [civil administration] as nearly as might be practicable, to the character of its original institutions."[6] Elphinstone dutifully followed these orders. In 1818, he ordered his subordinate Collectors to "scrupulously avoid all sorts of innovations" in order "to show the people that they are to expect no change but in the better administration of their former laws."[7] Therefore, British Collectors, who were responsible for the general administration of individual districts, were to employ former Maratha officials and maintain the system whereby "the Patails might settle village disputes by village Punchayets (arbitration). The Mamlutdars would superintend the trial of more important causes by Punchayets of the most respectable people within their divisions, while those of

[4] C. A. Bayly, "Elphinstone, Mountstuart (1779–1859)," *ODNB* (Oxford University Press, 2004), online edn., January 2008, www.oxforddnb.com/view/article/8752, accessed 25 May 2011.

[5] Marquess of Hastings to Secret Committee, 21 August 1820, in *Papers Respecting the Pindarry and Mahratta Wars; [and], Treaties and Engagements with Native Princes and States in India, Concluded for the Most Part in 1817 and 1818* (London, 1824), p. 422.

[6] Similar instructions were issued for the settlement of Nagpur, Pune, and the North-Western Provinces. See Hastings to Secret Committee, 21 August 1820, *Papers Respecting the Pindarry and Mahratta Wars*, pp. 439; 445.

[7] Mountstuart Elphinstone to Marquess of Hastings, 18 June 1818, in G. S. Sardesai, ed., *Poona Residency Correspondence, Volume 13: Poona Affairs (Elphinstone's Embassy), Part II, 1816–1818* (Bombay: Government Central Press, 1958), p. 408.

greater magnitude and all appeals would come before the Collector himself assisted also by Punchayets and Hindoo Lawyers."[8]

Both East India Company officials in London and Elphinstone himself made it clear, however, that this was only to be a temporary measure until the territory was settled when further improvements would then be made. For his part, Elphinstone appeared somewhat confident that relatively few substantive reforms would be needed in the future. "The present system is probably not bad in itself," he wrote, "as the country has prospered under it notwithstanding the feebleness and corruption with which it was administered. At all events it is generally known and understood; it suits the people whom indeed it has helped form, and it is probably capable of being made tolerably perfect by gradual improvements introduced as they appear to be called for."[9] John Adam, Hastings' Chief Secretary, perhaps was not quite as sanguine but nonetheless approved of and supported the plan: "Such a system [of the panchayat]," he noted, "while it not only secures in the most satisfactory manner of which present circumstances admit, the ends of essential equity, will form the best possible basis for such future ameliorations as the superior integrity and intelligence of the British Agents may enable them to introduce."[10]

By the following year, 1819, Elphinstone, then serving as Commissioner of over 50,000 square miles of conquered territory with about 4,000,000 inhabitants, had become convinced that in the administration of civil law "our principal instrument must continue to be the Punchayet" and that it was "the great instrument in the administration of Justice."[11] It is not exactly clear why or when his previously qualified support had given way to such a vigorous endorsement of the panchayat. Munro's influence may very well have been of great importance, but it must be noted that the two did not share the same understanding or interpretation of the function of the panchayat. Whereas Munro believed that the panchayat was analogous to the English jury, Elphinstone thought it much more akin to a board or tribunal of

[8] Elphinstone to Hastings, 18 June 1818, Sardesai, *Poona Residency Correspondence*, p. 410.

[9] Ibid.

[10] John Adam to Elphinstone, 26 September 1818, Sardesai, *Poona Residency Correspondence*, p. 478.

[11] Mountstuart Elphinstone, *Report on the Territories Conquered from the Paishwa* (Calcutta: Government Gazette Press, 1821), pp. 78; 99. An initial version of the Report was completed in October 1819 and circulated to Elphinstone's Collectors. See, IOR/P/398/71, Bombay Judicial Consultations, "Circular of the Honble the Commissioner to the Collectors in the newly acquired Territories from the late Paishwa," 25 October 1819.

arbitration.[12] In English practice and in English law, these were obviously significantly different institutions with significantly different legal authority. Of greatest significance was the fact that, in England, arbitration was a wholly voluntary process in which suits were pursued largely beyond the purview of the courts, decisions were based upon equity and not precedent, the process was free of pleadings, fees, and lawyers, and an arbitration tribunal lacked any means of enforcing its award. These qualities obviously would not apply if the panchayat were deemed a "native jury."

Nevertheless, as Commissioner of the Deccan, Elphinstone quickly began to make significant inquiries into the jurisdiction and procedures of panchayats. His roughly penciled notes indicate what he understood to be some of their principal advantages:

> Old appeals says Gen Munro were always [stated?] to be made because [there?] had been no Punchayet or because the cause was tried before a [illegible] officer [.] The natives have no confidence in any plan but punchayets.
>
> The Ct. attribute the success of the best Collectors to *their leaving the detailed management of affairs to the natives* according to the [existing?] forms & usages of the Country *& to see they do their duty instead of attempting to do it for them.*
>
> Complaints to be made to Assistants or referred to them by the Courts either party may demand a Punchayet
>
> Punchayets on revenue suits particularly recommended by the Fortescue.[13]

As early as December 1817, a circular had been sent to the various judicial officers in the Presidency inquiring whether the panchayat system could be adapted there as it had been in Madras under Munro.[14] The response from the Judges was noticeably mixed, much of the muddle apparently caused by the confusion between their perception of the panchayat as an arbitration tribunal and the panchayat as a jury trial. Thus, Saville Marriott, the Collector of the Northern

[12] See below, Chapter 7.

[13] IOR/Mss Eur F 88/408, Elphinstone Papers, "Notes, Memorandum and relative Letters regarding the powers of Patails and Punchayets, c. 1819," pp. 63–5. Emphasis in original. In all likelihood, Elphinstone's reference to "Fortescue" indicates Thomas Fortescue, a Company Collector with extensive experience in Orissa and Bengal. Fortescue later testified before the Select Committee on the Affairs of the East-India Company that he had sat on panchayats as an arbitrator and had been favorably impressed by them. See PP, *Select Committee of the House of Commons on the Affairs of the East-India Company*, IV: Judicial (1833), p. 144.

[14] IOR/P/398/69, Bombay Judicial Proceedings, 27 December 1817.

Konkan, described the panchayat as a "mode of trial" while S. Babington, the Judge and Magistrate at Tannah, assumed that the panchayat was "the judgment of arbitrators."[15] Elphinstone also circulated to his principal subordinates questionnaires on the Peshwa's administration of law in the territories. These were quite lengthy, comprising well over 100 questions, many of which related in some way or other to the form and function of panchayats.[16] The responses provided to Elphinstone thus provide a contemporary account of how British officer-officials first understood the work of the panchayat as well as the processes involved in securing panchayat justice. Significantly, the responses to this questionnaire do not always coincide with one another and it is difficult to ascertain whether the discrepancies indicate local differences in the functioning of the panchayat or whether the officer-officials themselves were misapprehending the processes involved. Nevertheless, when taken together, they provide a unique view of how the British came to understand the panchayat system in the Deccan when they first sought to adapt it for their purposes. At the very least, their importance lay in the fact that the British administration of justice in the region would be substantially based upon these initial perceptions and misperceptions for the next two decades.

Four of the five principal regional officer-officials under Elphinstone provided written answers to the questionnaire: Captain Henry Pottinger, Collector in Ahmednagar, Captain John Briggs, Political Agent in Khandesh, Captain James Grant, Resident at Sátára, and William Chaplin, the only civilian, Collector at Dharwar and soon to be Commissioner of the Deccan. The fifth, Captain H. D. Robertson, the Collector of Pune, may very well have been in personal contact with Elphinstone. There was universal agreement among the written respondents that the panchayat decided local disputes that could not be resolved through the personal intervention of the village headman (*patel*). Pottinger explained, for example, that a panchayat was convened to settle disputes only after "amicable arbitration" had failed.[17] The respondents also agreed that the authority to convene a panchayat

[15] IOR/P/398/69, Bombay Judicial Proceedings, 27 December 1817, ff. 160–1; 168–9.

[16] Different selections from the questionnaire and the responses are reproduced in H. George Franks, *Panchayets under the Peshwas*, App. No. 1 (Poona: Poona Star Press, 1930), pp. 77–80; and, R. D. Choksey, *Twilight of the Maratha Raj, 1818* (Poona: The Author, 1976), pp. viii–xii. Both books are based on the Poona Residency Daftar in the Pune Archives. Franks, in particular, provides a reliable, albeit dated, guide to the panchayat system as it was being adapted by the British.

[17] Choksey, *Twilight of the Maratha Raj*, p. 61.

lay exclusively with the *patel*. Hence, they argued, the revival of the ancient panchayat to a great extent depended upon maintaining his authority. Together, an active *patel* and an effective panchayat created the essential administrative infrastructure for the success of Elphinstone's *ryotwari* system of revenue collection and peasant proprietorship in the Presidency.[18]

The *patels* were, as Elphinstone put it, "the most important functionaries in the villages, and perhaps the most important class in the country."[19] Not only was a *patel* responsible for the administration of justice through both his personal arbitration of disputes and the convening of panchayats, but he was also head of the village police and watchmen. Moreover, he was also responsible for the collection of the revenue and functioned essentially as the representative of the village's needs and interests. Therefore, as Elphinstone realized, the *patel* played a critical intermediary role as both an agent of government and as a representative of the people. The *patel*, he wrote, "is not less useful in executing the order of the Government, than in asserting the rights, or at least making known the wrongs, of the people."[20]

While the *patel* possessed the authority to convene a panchayat, there were various explanations as to how the panchayat process might be initiated. According to Pottinger, a panchayat could be "demanded" by the litigants, after which the *patel* "gave his permission to one being assembled." Grant, however, simply indicated that the *patel* "had [the] power to call a Punchayet or not as he judged proper."[21] In Briggs' report from Khandesh, a third possibility was described in which the parties themselves took their dispute "to the patails and elders of the village when they sat as is customary under some large tree at the village gate of an evening."[22]

There was, however, fundamental agreement upon the fact that panchayats were a voluntary mode of settlement and that litigants could not be compelled to accept their intervention in disputes. Thus Elphinstone's *Report on the Territories Conquered from the Paishwa* described Maratha practice in the following way: "the Patail assembled a Punchayet of inhabitants of the Village, who enquired into the matter with very little form, and decided as they thought best; but their

18 The various later interpretations of the "sociological" connection between the panchayat and the land revenue system are analyzed in Ronald Inden, *Imagining India* (Bloomington: Indiana University Press, 1990), Chapter 4.

19 Elphinstone, *Report on the Territories Conquered from the Paishwa*, p. 21. 20 Ibid., p. 22.

21 Choksey, *Twilight of the Maratha Raj*, p. 61. 22 Ibid., p. 64.

decision could not take place without the previous consent of the parties."[23] As Captain Briggs later wrote, "It is one of the invariable rules of the Punchayut as it was originally instituted for the object of doing Justice, not to enter upon business without having the consent of both parties to abide by their judgement."[24] In this respect, the panchayat was often compared to the system of English arbitration and members of panchayats were often referred to in Company accounts as arbitrators.

Once a panchayat was called, the process of selecting its members became of paramount importance. Chaplin and Pottinger agreed that the parties themselves were allowed to choose their own representatives to serve on the tribunal. There were no necessary requirements to serve on a panchayat, although some sort of "respectability" was often referred to. Thus Chaplin noted that its members were comprised of "respectable ryots, merchants, persons out of employ living upon their means or others who were supposed capable of the duty," while Grant described them as "the more intelligent villagers, outcastes and any low castes were excluded."[25] Yet Pottinger also reported, "there was no rule or even established custom on this point. In general disputants selected their friends of whatever rank they might be."[26] Thus British officials later thought it necessary to decide whether eligibility requirements should apply to the members of panchayats. In this, they subsequently accepted what they believed was customary practice and determined that service on the panchayat was to be open to all adult males and that the litigants were to be free to select their own representatives.

The number of people who would serve on a panchayat was also open to question. The term "panchayat" is derived from the word "panch," or five. The prevailing notion was that under the Marathas two representatives were selected by each litigant, while a presiding fifth member, the *sarpanch*, directed the proceedings and represented the state. Thus it was reported that in petty matters the village clerk (*karkun*) would often serve as *sarpanch* while in more significant ones the Maratha district revenue officer (*mamledar*) might do so. However, it is quite clear that this number could vary widely.[27] Some panchayats, as Briggs suggested, were comprised of all the male elders of the village. Elsewhere, in an important inheritance case heard under British

[23] Elphinstone, *Report on the Territories Conquered from the Paishwa*, p. 77.
[24] IOR/P/399/23, Bombay Judicial Consultations, Briggs to Chaplin, 31 May 1822.
[25] Choksey, *Twilight of the Maratha Raj*, pp. 63; 65. [26] Ibid., p. 66.
[27] Franks, *Punchayets under the Peshwas*, p. 15.

authority in 1819, there were seven members of the panchayat.[28] William Charmier, an Assistant Judge at Dindori, explained, "there is a notion that a punchaiet always consisted of 5 persons which as far as I can ascertain does not appear to be the case. When first instituted it most probably was so but that such has been the case latterly I mean for many years, I can no where find out."[29] British officials therefore eventually found it necessary to regularize both the size of the panchayat and the position of *sarpanch* if they were to be integrated into their system of judicial administration.

British officials perhaps welcomed the fact that panchayat justice was often encumbered by a significant amount of documentation, something they found recognizable although not necessarily entirely comprehendible. Perhaps inevitably, therefore, panchayat procedural documents soon became equated to their supposed British cognates and thus more easily integrated into the British system of justice. The *razeenamah*, for example, which Elphinstone explained was the "consent of the parties to the arbitration" by panchayat, soon enough became understood as equivalent to an English "bond," legally binding the litigants to accept the award of an arbitrator.[30] Other forms of documentation bore a much closer resemblance to English legal forms and thus were also readily assimilated. The *sarounsh*, for example, an abstract of the panchayat's decision, was easily adopted as an equivalent to an English arbitrator's "award."

Enforcement was perhaps the final area of panchayat justice that the British sought to reform and regularize. Chaplin reported that the enforcement of a panchayat's decision was often the responsibility of various local officials, including the village accountant, district officer, or village watchman.[31] However, Pottinger indicated that enforcement could also be executed by "personal authority."[32] He undoubtedly was referring to the practice of *tukaza*, a term one mid-nineteenth-century dictionary defined as "dunning" or "exacting."[33] It is fair to say that British officials were sometimes appalled by the practice, which came in

[28] MSA, EIC, Judicial Department, Civil Judicature, Munkeshur's Appeal, Vol. 10/10, 1821–1823, "Minute on the proceeding of Captain Robertson and Mr. Lumsden on their award in the disputed claim of Luximon Row Sadasew and Mulhar Row Appa," 7 July 1821.

[29] MSA, EIC, Judicial Department, Annual and Periodical Reports, Vol. 1/127, 1827, William Charmier, Assistant Judge, Dindoree, to Saville Marriot, 24 April 1827.

[30] Elphinstone, *Report on the Territories Conquered from the Paishwa*, p. 100.

[31] Choksey, *Twilight of the Maratha Raj*, p. 65. [32] Ibid., p. 67.

[33] Charles Philip Brown, *The Zillah Dictionary, in the Roman Character: Explaining the Various Words used in Business in India* (Madras, 1852), p. 120. Elphinstone also defined *tukaza* as "dunning" in *Report on the Territories Conquered from the Paishwa*, p. 87.

a variety of forms. Elphinstone explained that *tukaza* included "every thing from simple importunity up to placing a guard over a man, preventing his eating, tying him neck and heels, or making him stand on one leg with a heavy stone on his head under a vertical sun."[34] Chaplin argued that *tukaza* often amounted "to a degree of torture."[35]

However, there was disagreement among British officials as to whether *tukaza* was intended to enforce a panchayat's award or whether it was intended to forcefully encourage potential litigants to submit their dispute to a panchayat. Ultimately, Elphinstone adopted the latter interpretation. In his 1819 circular on the use of panchayats, he wrote, "it is absolutely necessary to prohibit the use of force, but all restraints and inconveniences that depend on the point of honor ought to be allowed to remain" because "if done away entirely, the great principle which drives men to Punchauts, private arbitrations and voluntary compositions, is put an end to, and every creditor is compelled to come to Court."[36] Similarly, W. R. Morris, Captain Grant's Assistant Political Agent, explained how the reformed *tukaza* system operated in Sátára:

> Tukazza or Tukada as it is termed in this Country still continue to exist, although it is never carried to such lengths as it was under the former Government; during that period there were four different descriptions of it constantly practised; that of obliging a person to stand in the sun to perform the same with a heavy weight upon his head, or with one of his feet raised up; to seat a man at the door of his house and prevent him eating during the day, or to keep him confined in his house & oblige him to afford provision for the man who was seated at his door. In order to abolish the two former of these, orders have been issued strictly forbidding any recourse to violence, for the purpose of effecting a settlement of debts, but any one is at liberty to try and enforce such arrangement by either of the two latter expedients which are generally put in practice for one or two days, after which the plaintiff comes and lays his complaint before the Mamletdar or the Nyadeish.[37]

In Pune, on the other hand, *tukaza* was sometimes understood as a form of post-conviction punishment. There, imprisonment for debt had

[34] Elphinstone, *Report on the Territories Conquered from the Paishwa*, p. 87.
[35] Choksey, *Twilight of the Maratha Raj*, p. 65.
[36] IOR/P/398/71, Bombay Judicial Consultations, "Circular of the Honble the Commissioner," pp. 1538–9.
[37] IOR/F/4/839/22429 (4), Board's Collections, "Replies to Supplemental Queries by Mr. Morris (No. 2), n.d. The *nyadeish*, more commonly spelled *nyayadesh*, was the chief justice minister under the Marathas.

been a common practice under the Maratha government and continued to be so under the British. In 1822, Chaplin reported, "no definite rules have been established in regards to the period of imprisonment for debt, if the debtor failed to satisfy the demand upon him, creditors requiring the confinement of debtors pay them subsistence."[38] Yet H. D. Robertson, the Pune Collector, also suggested that imprisonment was considered to be an alternative to *tukaza*. "Tuggaza," he wrote, "is not carried to excess, and many prefer placing their debtors under restraint in the Debtor's Jail to resorting to it. This is especially the case where the Debtor being rather respectable may be afraid of losing his character by being thrown into Prison, the threat of which frequently makes him pay his debt."[39] Regardless of this confusion, there was general agreement that the panchayats themselves possessed no direct power of enforcement. Their decrees were implemented either through an individual's "personal authority," such as a *tukaza*, or the intervention of the state. In cases of debt, this involved the seizure and sale of property to fulfill the terms of the panchayat award. In the Deccan, Chaplin noted, "decrees are executed in the usual manner by distraint of property and personal restraint, if necessary. Houses are sometimes sold, but the implements of trades are usually, spared, unless no other property be forth coming."[40]

Interestingly, as British reforms of the panchayat proceeded, it sometimes became clear that attempts to restrict the use of *tukaza* adversely affected the poor's access to justice. In 1823, for example, the enforcement of panchayat awards was formally delegated to the civil magistrates (*munsifs*) and *mamledars* whose actions had to be authorized by the Collector. However, the delay involved in getting that authorization, it was reported, often proved to be a hardship upon poorer litigants. Without the threat of direct physical action, poor litigants often did not have the means to initiate a *tukaza* since, at the very least, this required the employment of a peon to stay outside the home of the debtor. *Tukaza*, therefore, had become a weapon of the wealthy against the poor. Chaplin subsequently indicated that further regulation might be necessary to correct this unintended consequence.

38 IOR/P/368/34, Bombay Revenue Proceedings, "From the Commissioner in the Deccan," 20 August 1822.

39 IOR/F/4/837/22427, Board's Collections, "Extract from Revenue Consultations Connected with the Commissioners Report of the 10 August 1822 – Not Included in the Judicial Consultations."

40 IOR/P/368/34, Bombay Revenue Proceedings, "From the Commissioner in the Deccan," 20 August 1822.

"It is said," he wrote, "that those who have means of exercising Tugazar have pressed the execution of Decrees in their favor before the expiration of the period allowed for appealing. It will require the Judges' attention to correct these defects and abuses, but no sale of property should ever take place in my opinion without his previous sanction. The appointment of persons specially responsible for the legal seizure and distraint of goods and chattels under Decrees of Court will perhaps be eventually necessary."[41]

While the observations of these Company officers were thus being solicited, Elphinstone also sought the advice of local Hindu law scholars (*shastris*) and undertook the investigation of panchayat practices under Ram Shastri Prabhune, the legendarily incorruptible chief justice (*nyayadesh*) of the Peshwas during the late eighteenth century.[42] From these investigations, it is clear that the eighteenth-century panchayat had also been encumbered by many rules and therefore need not be romanticized as an informal community-based institution of dispute resolution. The responses of three *shastris* survive. Although the evidence provided does not make this precisely clear, it appears that the *shastris* were all from Pune and that one, or perhaps two, of them had served under Ram Shastri. Thus the picture that they present is one of a panchayat as it functioned in a courtly urban environment at the heart of the central administration of the Maratha government and not in the village community.

Nevertheless, British officials, and Elphinstone in particular, valued these "authentic" sources as the foundation upon which to rebuild the panchayat system under their authority. Elphinstone had explained in the *Report on the Territories Conquered from the Paishwa* that such historical research was necessary for a full understanding of the panchayat. "The Punchayet," he wrote, "may therefore be considered as the great instrument in the administration of Justice, and it is of consequence to determine how the assembly was constituted, what were its powers, and what its method of proceeding, and enforcing or procuring the enforcement of its decrees."[43] Certainly, much of this historicist perspective can be attributed to the Orientalist perspective

[41] MSA, EIC, Judicial Department, Annual and Periodical Reports, Vol. 1/102, 1826, William Chaplin to D. Greenhill, 14 December 1825.

[42] Gune indicates that the panchayat "became the accepted principal of law" only during the mid-eighteenth century when the Peshwas came to control the Maratha government; see *Judicial System of the Marathas*, pp. 47–50. Ramashastri Vishvanath Prabhune served as *nyayadesh* between 1754 and 1789.

[43] Elphinstone, *Report on the Territories Conquered from the Paishwa*, p. 76.

that several important Company officer-officials, including Elphinstone, brought to their work in India. This perspective necessitated an understanding of the ancient constitution of the country in order to revive it.[44] Thus, while the observations of Elphinstone's subordinate officials on the panchayat were important, the remarks of the *shastris* were equally vital.

The most extensive responses to the British investigation were those provided by Ragopunt Tuthe, who had served under Ram Shastri and had also provided information to Arthur Steele for his influential book *The Law and Custom of Hindoo Castes* (1826), but additional replies survive from two other *shastris*, Nukka Ram and Rumeshur, the latter of whom may also have served under Ram Shastri.[45] Two of the three *shastris* agreed that there were two types of panchayats: those that were convened by the government and those that were organized within each caste or profession and independent of government interference. A third *shastri*, Nukka Ram, whose remarks were very brief and quite sketchy, only indicated that a local judicial official (*amin*) was present at all panchayats.

Both Ragopunt and Rumeshur remarked that convening a panchayat without government oversight often required the authority or influence of someone of substance. Thus Rumeshur noted, "Every man who [had] power enough to enforce the decision of a Punchaet could assemble one."[46] However, personal influence was not absolutely necessary. Without it, a government *karkun* might be assigned to assist the panchayat, especially to ensure the attendance of all those concerned in the suit. Ragopunt explained that among bankers,

> if there was no Banker of sufficient weight to assemble the Punchayet [illegible] & to make the Members & Witnesses attend them they met above the Sircar Houses & a Govt. Carcoon was appointed to do this for them. This Carcoon though he sat with them had no voice in the Punchayet but was merely a link between it & the Govt. He was the executive officer of the Punchayet in doing all that could not be done without the influence of a Govt. Officer in assembling Witnesses &

44 See Chapter 9.

45 The investigation into the practices during Ram Shastri's time appears to have been undertaken by two of Elphinstone's subordinates at Pune, Lieutenant Macleod and William Lumsden, and much of their findings was later incorporated into Elphinstone's *Report on the Territories Conquered from the Paishwa*. Macleod notes that two of the people he employed in his court (*kachari*) had also served under Ram Shastri. See IOR/Mss Eur F 88/408, Elphinstone Papers, "Notes, Memorandum and relative Letters," Lieutenant Macleod to Elphinstone, n.d.

46 IOR/Mss Eur F 88/408, Elphinstone Papers, "Notes, Memorandum and relative Letters," Rumeshurs Account of Punchait.

> Parties &c. He might offer his advice but it was not incumbent on the Punchayet to receive it.[47]

The *shastris* appeared to have had almost exclusive experience with government-sponsored panchayats, or at least provided the most details about them. In those cases, the government itself convened the panchayat and a *karkun* appointed a guard to ensure the attendance of the members, the litigants, and the witnesses. Both Ragopunt and Rumeshur indicated that the government had the authority to imprison both the defendant and the witnesses if they did not respond to the panchayat's order. Ragopunt added that the government also had the authority to "place a Mahussul over the contumacious person," which, like the *tukaza*, involved placing one or more peons who had to be fed at the delinquent's door.[48]

The government also had extraordinary powers to convene panchayats. Ram Shastri, it was reported, authorized regional administrators (*sirkars*) and *mamledars* to hear cases and then put the evidence before a panchayat. The *mamledar* was not required to accept the panchayat's verdict although he did have the authority to inquire further into the matter. The government could also refer cases to *karkuns*; however, in these instances, the clerk acted more as an interested observer. Rumeshur explained, "a Karkoon of Govt. often sat with a Punchait (for the purpose of influence) but he was never considered so much a member that he could not be excluded [from?] their sittings whenever the Punch wished to deliberate apart."

In all government cases, the panchayat was composed of members selected separately by each of the litigants to represent them. The litigants also retained the right to object to the government's appointees, which they apparently often did. Nukka Ram noted, "the Govt. added such members [to the panchayat] as it thought proper and always had a Govt Officer present who kept every thing in motion, and superintended & conducted generally the proceedings shaping and preparing the whole for the consideration of the members. The parties would object to every Member proposed by the Officers of Government, and on the other hand the Sirkar often rejected unworthy members proposed by either party."

47 IOR/Mss Eur F 88/408, Elphinstone Papers, "Notes, Memorandum and relative Letters," Queries on Punchaits and answers by Raggopunt Tuttee.

48 IOR/Mss Eur F 88/408, Elphinstone Papers, "Notes, Memorandum and relative Letters," Queries on Punchaits and answers by Raggopunt Tuttee; Rumeshurs Account of Punchait.

The enforcement of panchayat decrees was also the responsibility of government and, once again, there were notable differences between the treatment of the rich and poor. While the poor could be subject to imprisonment for refusing to abide by a panchayat's award, the rich generally could not. Rumeshur indicated that the first step taken to persuade a recalcitrant rich person to perform an award involved government officials "sitting in his house & demeaning him & sometimes keeping him from eating for three or four days." In the cases of both rich and poor, however, the next step was to confiscate property, although there were certain limits. The houses of neither the rich nor poor appear to have been subject to confiscation. For a poor person, his tools or farm implements also were exempt. "His effects . . . were sold," Ragopunt said, "but with great consideration so as not to effect his entire ruin." A rich person, on the other hand, appears to have had no such special exemption, Ragopunt noting that even his horses could be taken.

British officials hoped to ensure that under their administration the panchayat would be resurrected as an efficient, accessible, and inexpensive system of justice. Therefore, many questions sought to uncover existing problems that were believed to be hampering the efficiency of the panchayat system. However, as we shall see, it was in the attempt to rectify these perceived problems that the British most seriously undermined their own admitted goal to rule by "the customs of the country." Among the most common complaints expressed to Elphinstone was the dilatoriness of panchayat proceedings, the difficulty of securing members to serve, and the potential for bribery and other forms of corruption. By 1819, Elphinstone had already distributed a circular to his Collectors cautiously outlining the reforms that he believed were necessary "to purify, and invigorate the native system."[49] According to these orders, the jurisdiction of village panchayats was to be limited to cases valued at Rs. 150 or less; employment of professional pleaders (*vakils*) was prohibited; and suits for debts had to be instituted within twelve years and property suits within sixty years of the origination of the dispute. Elphinstone indicated that several further reforms might be necessary, but withheld any decision for the time being.

After 1819, the inefficiencies of the panchayat system of justice plagued the Collectors and other British judicial officials and,

[49] IOR/P/398/71, Bombay Judicial Consultations, "Circular of the Honble the Commissioner."

ultimately, suits brought before panchayats formed only a fraction of the cases within the British system of justice.[50] Nevertheless, the correspondence from Company officer-officials reveals an immense amount of frustration at being ordered to make the panchayat "the great instrument in the administration of Justice," but, at the same time, to "clear the books" of their accumulating caseloads in the districts under their command. Their chief complaint was the length of time it took for a panchayat to convene, hear a case, and to reach a decision. One example will suffice to illustrate the nature of these complaints, but there were a great many more like it. George Giberne, the Register at Ahmednagar, explained to Henry Pottinger, the Collector, that the panchayat was, in theory, both "expeditious" and "beautiful." In many ways, he suggested, it "may even be considered Superior to our far famed British Courts where the parties can only object to, not choose, their Jury, and on account of the variety of forms and intricate law questions, few men are capable of pleading their own causes." However, the reality of the panchayat system was much different. "It is now my intention," he wrote, "to shew the difference between that beautiful theory and the present base practice." Giberne went on to explain:

> In the first place a person makes a complaint and shews good cause to have an investigation [made?] into his case, the Defendant argues the Plaintiff's right and in short a Punchaiet is ordered; the parties give the necessary Security to abide by the decision, and write down the names of the members they select; they commence sitting upon [the?] question, but [now?] one day, half of the members will attend, the next day not so many, the day after very likely not one; and for several successive days, sometimes indeed weeks, nothing whatever will be accomplished; in this case what is to be done. The Custom is, to send a Peon to exhort them to attend, and this must be done four or five times a week, and even then the attendance is precarious.[51]

British officers and officials further complained that it was also often difficult to find people who were willing to serve on a panchayat. Many argued that too few people were willing to take the time away from their businesses or other personal pursuits and this compounded the problem of delays and postponements. Thus, Captain Pottinger reported, "the

[50] See Chapter 2.
[51] MSA, EIC, Judicial Department, Civil and Criminal Judicature, Vol. 9A/9A, 1823, George Giberne to Captain Pottinger, 1 August 1822.

Members [of a panchayat] usually consider it a tax on their time, and are careless as to the question before them unless they have an interest at stake either directly or indirectly. In the latter event they are partial, and in the former they are inattentive, and occupy them selves [sic] with any thing else than that which should demand their whole thoughts."[52] As early as January 1819, Captain Briggs in Khandesh requested the authority to pay the members of a panchayat in order to encourage participation.[53] Elphinstone quickly refused the request, noting that the payment of panchayat members "would take away the principal motive they now have to use Dispatch."[54] However, Briggs continued to believe that such payments would improve the panchayat system. Three years later, he was still lamenting, "at a very early period I perceived the great reluctance with which almost all persons attended Punchayuts excepting on occasions where Cast was concerned, and I accordingly recommended that an allowance should be granted to the members while sitting, but it was considered that it might be an encouragement to them to delay decision, and it was not authorized, and has therefore never been again agitated."[55]

Among the most grievous complaints, however, were often those alleging bribery or corruption, and these grievances were very often suffused with racist condemnations of Indian culture and character. Once again, one example here represents many others. Captain Pottinger, who otherwise might be considered a staunch advocate of the panchayat system, wrote in 1818:

> The system of receiving Bribes in adjusting all disputes was universal before the War, and has taken such deep root that nothing but time and the example of an upright and good Government will extirpate it. I have been obliged to turn apparently respectable Brahmuns and Soukars ignominiously out of the Court, when it has been shown that they

[52] IOR/P/121/28, Bengal Political Consultations, No. 20, 12 December 1818, Pottinger to Elphinstone. Letter dated 29 October 1818.

[53] IOR/P/121/40, Bengal Political Consultations, No. 27, 13 February 1819, Briggs to Elphinstone. copy letter dated 20 January 1819.

[54] IOR/P/121/40, Bengal Political Consultations, No. 27, 13 February 1819, Elphinstone to Briggs. copy letter dated 20 January 1819.

[55] MSA, EIC, Judicial Department, Civil and Criminal Judicature, Vol. 9/9, 1822, Briggs to William Chaplin, 3 May 1822. Nevertheless, Briggs, who later became the Resident at Sátára, remained a staunch advocate of the panchayat. *See his Letters Addressed to a Young Person in India; Calculated to Afford Instruction for his Conduct in General, and more especially in his Intercourse with the Natives* (London, 1828) in which he states with regard to the panchayat, "I can with truth assert, that it is a most simple, cheap and efficient mode of administering justice, and is admirably calculated for a people situated as is the present state of Indian society," p. 176.

> took a few Rupees from each of the Parties on whose cause I had requested them to sit. On such occasions they have acted with great effrontery and showed no symptoms of remorse at their disgrace. The better classes of our subjects, I am grieved to say seem to me to be deficient in almost every fine or honorable sentiment, and a total absence of a sense of shame is a marked deformity in their characters; My anxious and fullest endeavours have been, and are directed to reform this degraded state of the Native Society, and I trust my exertions will not be unavailing.[56]

In the summer of 1822, H. D. Robertson, the Collector at Pune, sought further advice from local *shastris* and *amins* as to how best to remedy the perceived ills of the panchayat system. To do this, he employed the services of Harry Borradaile, whose indefatigable labors produced both the *Reports of the Civil Causes adjudged by the Court of Sudur Udalut for the Presidency of Bombay* (1825), the first of its kind in western India, and the massive compilation of *Gujarat Caste Rules*, which would lay unpublished for more than half a century. As was the case when Elphinstone sought the advice of *shastris* in 1819, the Pune experience of the *shastris* and *amins* in 1822 was unlikely to have reflected panchayat practices outside of the city. Yet their testimony is most revealing for the fact that there was a general agreement among them that to be effective the panchayat needed to become more systematized and regularized. In a word, the panchayat needed to be bureaucratized. One should be careful, however, to distinguish between whether the respondents had previously believed that panchayat reforms were essential and whether, when asked, the interrogatories necessitated the articulation of both grievances and suggestions for reform that heretofore had lain dormant. That is, the question remains as to whether the *shastris* and *amins* would have thought it necessary to recommend further reforms to the panchayat system if they had not been prompted to do so by British officials. In this regard, unlike the extensive documentation of the complaints of British officers and judicial officials, there is no surviving evidence to suggest that either the *shastris* or the *amins* had previously proposed or demanded reform.

Nevertheless, many of the panchayat reforms later adopted by Elphinstone reflect the suggestions collected by Borradaile. The

[56] IOR/P/121/22, Bengal Political Consultations, No. 49, 17 October 1818, Pottinger to Elphinstone. Copy letter dated 10 September 1818.

introduction of a variety of fines to ensure that panchayats functioned expeditiously was the most common recommendation. Wishnoo Kushen, a Pune *amin*, suggested fines be imposed upon either litigants or witnesses who delayed the panchayat's proceedings. He explained, "many Plaintiffs, after giving in their petition stay away for many days, and when they do reappear there is considerable delay from the Defendant, who refuses or puts off giving an answer; and there is delay on both sides in collecting all the papers, so that a considerable time elapses before the business is prepared to be laid before the Punchayet. It is recommended above all, however, that when all the papers are collected, and the list of evidence given in, that some penalty should be inforced [sic] both on Plaintiffs and Defendants and witnesses, who do not attend when wanted."[57] Chintanum Leley, a *shastri*, further recommended that both parties be required to promise that their version of events is true "and that if found to be false they will submit to be fined."[58]

The imposition of time limits on panchayat proceedings was also frequently suggested or specifically recommended. The *amin* Anunrow Pandooring submitted a variety of time restrictions depending upon the type of case being adjudicated. However, in no case was a panchayat to take longer than six weeks to come to a decision.[59] Others were much less definite about the time restrictions that might be necessary. Wishnoo indicated, "I recommend strongly that the Punchayet should be bound to a particular time to decide in" while Chintanum advocated that "when a suit is referred to a Punchayet, the Punchayet ought to be bound to settle it within a given time, otherwise the Suit to be rendered liable to be taken from before it, and referred by Government to any one person it may please to appoint."[60]

[57] IOR/F/4/837/22427, Board's Collections, "Extract from Revenue Consultations Connected with the Commissioners Report of the 10 August 1822 – Not Included in the Judicial Consultations," pp. 47–8.

[58] IOR/F/4/837/22427, Board's Collections, "Extract from Revenue Consultations," pp. 44–5. Chintanum used the term *khutbee* to refer to this guarantee of the truth. *Khutbe*, as it is usually transposed, is more commonly translated from the Arabic as "prayer," but I have not been able to find a suitable definition that indicates its use in colonial India as a legal or judicial term. The early nineteenth-century *Missionary Journal of the Rev. Joseph Wolff*, who sought to convert the Jews of Palestine and Syria, however, defines it as a marital engagement "promise." I have therefore adapted this usage of the term. See Joseph Wolff, *Missionary Journal of the Rev. Joseph Wolff, Missionary to the Jews*, Vol. II (London, 1828), p. 197.

[59] IOR/F/4/837/22427, Board's Collections, "Extract from Revenue Consultations," pp. 69–71.

[60] IOR/F/4/837/22427, Board's Collections, "Extract from Revenue Consultations," pp. 44–5; 48–9.

The variety of other recommendations for reform indicates further areas in which delays were experienced. From Anunrow's extensive set of suggestions we can infer that many hurdles had to be overcome even before a panchayat could begin to hear a dispute. Problems might arise if only one of the litigants sought to refer their case to a panchayat while the other preferred a Judge or if the parties could not agree upon the *sarpanch* of the panchayat. In either case, Anunrow urged greater government intervention to resolve the deadlock, leaving much of the ultimate authority in the hands of the regional *sirkar*.[61]

A still further delay might be caused by the failure to secure the attendance of the defendant before the panchayat. Anunrow recommended the employment of sepoys to deliver written summonses to defendants who would then be provided with a receipt noting the time and date of their appearance. In the event that the defendant was able to avoid being served or the sepoy accepted a bribe to report that the defendant could not be found, then "either fining him or letting judgment go against him would be easy and justifiable." Similarly, recommendations were made to remedy the perceived problem of frivolous litigation, that is, the practice whereby litigants applied for a panchayat only in order to prolong judicial proceedings and delay judgment.[62] Wishnoo, an *amin* himself, therefore suggested that *amins* should be authorized to proceed by summary judgment in suits whenever "the justice of litigiousness . . . is clear."[63]

Finally, Anunrow proposed that panchayat meetings be held only at the courthouse (*cutcherry*) "to act as a check against evasion." Otherwise, he noted,

> if the Plaintiff or Defendant are asked any questions by the Punchayet [and] they will not give direct or proper answers; one says he will tomorrow, and in this manner procrastinate; the Plaintiff and defendant occasionally absent themselves altogether and a Punchayet entirely composed of persons not in the employment of Government, has no power over them: Punchayets should therefore sit where the Aumeen is, instead of in the Bazar [sic] or purgunnah where he cannot be to give them

61 IOR/F/4/837/22427, Board's Collections, "Extract from Revenue Consultations," pp. 60–4.

62 See the statement by Kuchoo Appajee, an *amin*, at IOR/F/4/837/22427, Board's Collections, "Extract from Revenue Consultations," pp. 45–6.

63 IOR/F/4/837/22427, Board's Collections, "Extract from Revenue Consultations," pp. 48–9.

instructions; if the Punchayet sits in presence of the Sircar and any hindrance takes place, an order can be readily given and the Punchayet will not be delayed.[64]

Therefore, in almost all instances, the Pune judicial officials and *shastris* recommended greater government scrutiny, greater government supervision, and greater government interference in order to ensure the efficacy of panchayats. Perhaps this should have been expected. These were, after all, government-appointed judicial officers and high-ranking legal scholars, most of whom had previously served the Peshwa. However, their view from the top coincided to an extraordinary degree with the perspective of the leading officer-officials of the British occupation. Thus it should not be surprising to discover that a great many of the recommendations proposed by the *shastris* and *amins* found their way into British judicial policy.

By January 1823, Elphinstone had become convinced that further and much more significant reforms of the panchayat were needed. Writing from the field, he reluctantly admitted that the panchayat had failed to live up to his expectations and instead had exhibited all of the potential weaknesses he had warned of in his *Report on the Territories Conquered from the Paishwa.* "The Judicial arrangements, I am sorry to say, have not been so successful as the Revenue," Elphinstone wrote. "Few causes have been decided, and those with considerable delay and dissatisfaction to all concerned ... The Punchayet on which so much depends under the Native System, has shewn all the inconveniences ascribed to it in my report of 1819, while the remedies applied to them have been less efficacious than was then expected."[65]

He remained convinced, however, that the problems could not be solved by more intensive British supervision or more extensive intervention. Like Munro, Elphinstone believed that authentic Indian customs and practices lay beyond the comprehension of most British officials. "It is indeed one of the great inconveniences of the system of Punchayets," he wrote, "that it is so ill adapted to European Superintendence; the want of regularity in the proceedings of Punchayets make them difficult to revise; their decisions being founded on traditional maxims are not easily understood by a foreigner; no

[64] IOR/F/4/837/22427, Board's Collections, "Extract from Revenue Consultations," pp. 66–7.
[65] IOR/F/4/837/22427, Board's Collections, "Extract of a Minute by the Governor. Camp, Coomailee Ghaut, 14 January 1823," pp. 1A–2A.

European improvements can be grafted on a traditionary [*sic*] body of law, and no hope can be entertained in such circumstances of ever framing a simple Code, alike intelligible to the Judge and to the people."[66]

Elphinstone concluded, therefore, that a greater number of Indian Civil Magistrates (*munsifs*) with summary jurisdiction needed to be employed and that a stricter set of rules was required for panchayats. He summarized the plan that would be adopted later in the year:

> The principal features in the plan are, that the number of Moonsifs is encreased; that the Moonsifs are empowered to try all causes, not specially excepted, without obtaining the previous consent of both parties; that Punchayets are confined to particular classes of causes, unless when both parties desire that mode of trial; that the Members of Punchayets are named from a rotation list, when they cannot otherwise be procured; that it is obligatory to serve on Punchayets; that greater strictness and regularity of proceeding is introduced, and greater facilities given to appeals both from Moonsifs & Punchayets.[67]

The 1823 reforms therefore restricted the original jurisdiction of panchayats to ten specific classes of suits, including those regarding local customs and privileges, marriage, maintenance, partition of property, "old and intricate" accounts, and disputes involving less than Rs. 50.[68] Thus, the panchayat's authority was limited generally to administering family disputes, small debts, and questions of local customs. Even in this much more limited sphere of action, litigants were not required to initiate their cases before a local panchayat. Instead, if they preferred to do so, they could submit a written request to have their case heard by one of the new *munsifs*. The responsibility for hearing suits concerning larger debts and property disputes, except those regarding village boundaries, was also shifted to the *munsifs* and *mamledars*, both of whom were also authorized to convene panchayats, if they deemed it necessary. However, ultimate

[66] Ibid., pp. 3A–4A. [67] Ibid., pp. 12–13A.

[68] MSA, EIC, Judicial Department, Vol. 6/178, 1829, "Rules Respecting Punchayets," pp. 94–8. The ten categories were: religion, marriage, peculiar customs of places, hereditary estates (*watans*) and privileges (*huks*), division of property, maintenance, old and intricate accounts, disputes between two inhabitants of the same village for personal property worth less than Rs. 50, personal injuries or other personal damages, and boundary disputes. A reliable overview of the administrative changes in the panchayat system under British rule in the Deccan is provided by Singh, *British Revenue and Judicial Policies in India*, Ch. V.

authority was reserved for the Collector. No panchayat award could be executed without his authorization.

The new rules did not so much displace the panchayat as the principal locus of justice as restrict its independence, limit its jurisdiction, and regularize its procedures within the administrative structure of the British judiciary. In the courts of the *mamledars* and *munsifs*, for example, panchayats were restricted to no more than five members. The *sarpanch* was to be jointly selected by the litigants, but, if they could not agree, then one was to be appointed for them. Litigants were required to sign both a *razeenamah*, now interpreted as an "arbitration deed," as well as a "penalty bond," the latter of which subjected the plaintiff to a maximum fine of ten percent of the value of the claim, if they failed "to substantiate their allegations." This fine was intended to prevent frivolous litigation. In one sense, such a fine was not altogether new, but it is another example of the extraordinary ways in which customary procedures were constantly being redefined for contemporary ends. Under the Peshwa's government, such fines, called *goonhangari*, had been levied as a penalty upon the party who lost their cause. Here, however, the British shifted the burden entirely onto the plaintiff, who became solely subject to the potential fine in order to inhibit litigation.

Further restrictions were placed upon panchayats intended to routinize their proceedings. Panchayat deliberations were limited to three months, after which both parties had to agree in writing to an extension. If they could not agree, the case was then sent before the Collector or a British magistrate for summary justice. Panchayat members were to be drawn from among "respectable people of the class or degree of the parties." However, if no one was willing to volunteer their services, then rotation lists were to be created of respectable people, such as the hereditary police and revenue officers (*desmukhs*), hereditary revenue accountants (*despandes*), and other hereditary landholders. Those who refused to serve when called upon became subject to a fine of up to Rs. 5. If witnesses or litigants failed to appear upon the summons of a panchayat, they became subject to fines of Rs. 2. Plaintiffs who continued to fail to appear could be non-suited with costs while a defendant's failure to appear could result in the panchayat proceeding *ex parte*.

It should be clear, therefore, that rather than reviving the panchayat according to the customs of the country, what had developed within the space of five years was largely a hybrid of British arbitration practices and British law-court procedures that was called a "panchayat." Perhaps not surprisingly, this does not appear to have been apparent to even its most ardent advocates. Elphinstone himself did not find it paradoxical that in his *Report on the Territories Conquered from the Paishwa* he recommended both that the panchayat "must continue to be exempt from all new forms, interference and regulation on our part" and, at the same time, that action needed to be taken "to remove [the panchayat's] abuses and revive its energy."[69] He appears to have believed that changes in "the mere administration of the law" could only improve, and not radically alter, the panchayat. Similarly, William Chaplin, Elphinstone's successor as Commissioner of the Deccan and also a keen proponent of the panchayat system, noted, "it is obvious that if left to work spontaneously, without a well-regulated authority to stimulate them to action, they can be of very little utility as Engines of Justice."[70] However, it does not appear that either Elphinstone or Chaplin understood that the imposition of a "well-regulated authority" would inevitably reshape the form and function of the panchayat system.

Ironically, one of the few instances in which this inherent contradiction in panchayat policy was recognized came from the East India Company's Judicial Department in London. Their observations are worth quoting at length for they emphasize the logical flaw in attempting to incorporate what was assumed to be a voluntary system of dispute resolution into a formal system of judicature. Unfortunately for the Bombay Presidency, the relevant passage quoted here was later excised from the Department's final version of the dispatch:

> Suits in which the parties can be persuaded to agree may be conveniently determined by arbitration, and if the Punchayet were restricted to this, which no doubt was its original function, it would perfectly answer the purpose, and would still be regarded with affection by the Natives, but the great mass of litigation consists of cases in which the enforcement of a claim is peremptorily insisted on by one party or pertinaciously resisted by another. For the decision of all such Suits, whatever the subject of the claim may be, there should be regular Courts, freely accessible to the people and subject to safeguards for the due observance of the Law. Till these are established there is no general protection. To refuse their

[69] Elphinstone, *Report on the Territories Conquered from the Paishwa*, p. 99.
[70] IOR/P/399/12, Bombay Judicial Consultations, 17 April 1822, William Chaplin. original letter to Elphinstone dated 23 March 1822.

> aid to a Suitor, sending him to arbitration against his will, is to deny him justice.
>
> The objects of arbitration and those of Judicature are so essentially different, and the means best adapted to the one are so ill calculated for the other, that every attempt to assimilate them must be impracticable. The superintending and regulating of Punchayets by Officers of Government, are represented as necessary to their success, but, by the interference of authority, these bodies are rendered unfit for arbitration without being made fit for judicature.[71]

The 1823 reforms did little to improve the efficiency of the panchayat or to reduce the backlog of cases in the British courts of justice. A detailed analysis of the surviving data will be presented in the following chapter, but, by 1827, the panchayat experiment in the Bombay Presidency had been deemed a failure. The Elphinstone Code of that year relegated the panchayat to a marginal and very subsidiary role as an aid to British Judges who might or might not seek their advice. In a rare moment of reflection, Elphinstone appeared to regret the fact that the evolving superstructure of British governance in India was tending not only to destroy village India, but also to segregate the occupied from their occupiers. "The native system," he wrote shortly before he retired as Governor,

> may long be tried with success in a moderate portion of an extensive Government at a distance from the Presidency and out of the neighbourhood of a supreme Court, but in a country situated like ours in the Deckan, it is in vain to attempt to preserve that system unimpaired.
>
> The first effect of the introduction of forms and the divisions of authority, is, I think, very unfavorable to the natives. They have no longer any head to look up to. Each person being charged with a Department, no one looks after the whole, and it is only in the duties connected with Justice, Revenue or Police that our functionaries come in contact with any class of the Natives. The effect of these circumstances is already observable in the Deckan. The intercourse between those of the higher orders and Europeans is already much less than it used to be and will probably diminish with every new arrival.
>
> Our forms and regularity, which even in the mode of administration first adopted, were found to exclude the upper classes of Natives from our service, operate still more powerfully under the subsequent change, and the love of uniformity inseparable from our system gradually leads to the

[71] IOR/E/4/1047, Bombay Dispatches, Judicial Department, "Administration of Justice in the Deccan," 31 January 1827, pp. 486–9.

> abolition of separate authorities and privileges and to encroachment even on those Jageerdars whose lands are secured by express agreement.
>
> The effects have by no means taken place to their full extant in the Deckan and the design of many of our present arrangements is to prevent or at least delay that result. The whole system there is still much more conformable to the Native habits and less repugnant to their feelings than in most other parts of India, but there is nevertheless a tendency to an opposite state of things which it will probably be impossible altogether to withstand.[72]

Whether the local, voluntary, and informal panchayat that the British imagined had been characteristic of India's ancient constitution could ever have been made an effective tool for the dispensation of justice is a moot, albeit highly contentious point. It is clear though that British attempts to "revive" and "purify" the panchayat to serve their judicial administration made it increasingly less flexible and bound by an increasingly more complex set of procedural rules, all of which were based upon the assumption that Indians preferred to settle disputes through some form of a community-based arbitration forum rather than seek a winner-take-all decision in the British courts. This is not to say that access to justice was better or worse under the new British-style panchayat or that substantive justice was better or worse served by these changes. It is to say, however, that the British attempts to resuscitate an imagined ancient panchayat inevitably killed the patient.

Once again, the Company's Court of Directors in London understood this inherent contradiction, although their imagining of the panchayat was based wholly upon their preconception of a despotic Maratha system of justice as well as their own understanding of English legal custom and practices. As the failure of Elphinstone's panchayat experiment increasingly became apparent, they wrote of "the true and correct idea of the Punchayet." Under the Maratha despots, they explained, people preferred to avoid the government's courts:

> Not choosing to go before such imperfect tribunals, they had recourse to a plan of settling their disputes among themselves, the plan general throughout India, that of referring them to private arbitration. The whole of the proceeding was voluntary. The parties resorted to it by

72 MSA, EIC, Deccan New Judicial Arrangement, Vol. 10/136, 1827, "Extract of the Honorable the Governor's Minute dated the 4th January, connected with his late visit to the Deccan."

mutual agreement, and they had recourse to such Arbitrators as they could induce to undertake the arbitration. This was not an institution of the Government, it was an expedient of the people to *supersede* an institution of the Government which they could not trust, or to supply the place of one where it did not exist. It was to mistake the nature of this expedient of Individuals to make it an institution of Govt. and the attempt has accordingly failed.[73]

[73] IOR/E/4/1047, Bombay Dispatches, Judicial Department, "Administration of Justice in the Deccan," 31 January 1827. Perhaps it was the harshness of this evaluation that later led to the excision of this paragraph from the final version of the dispatch.

2

BRINGING JUSTICE TO EVERY MAN'S DOOR

Sir William Blackstone famously wrote of the English judicial system, "the policy of our ancient constitution, as regulated and established by the great Alfred, was to bring justice home to every man's door, by constituting as many courts as there are manors and townships in the country."[1] In their judicial policies for southern and western India, the most important Company officers and officials in both India and London, especially Thomas Munro and Mountstuart Elphinstone, viewed the panchayat in just this way. In part, officers such as Munro and Elphinstone were motivated by the Orientalist desire to restore the greatness of Indian civilization by resuscitating its ancient constitution. This ideological imperative will be discussed in a later chapter. But they also made frequent reference to Blackstone's adage. The "great argument" in favor of the panchayat system, the Company's Court of Directors wrote in 1814, was that "it will bring home the administration of justice to the very doors of the parties; and thus relieve them, and particularly the common ryots, from that expense and vexation, and sometimes ruinous loss of time, to which they are now subject when they seek judicial redress."[2]

As a profit-making venture, of course, Company policy was not solely motivated by either Orientalist ideology or jurisprudential philosophy.

[1] Sir William Blackstone, *Commentaries on the Laws of England*, Vol. III (1765–1769; repr. Chicago: University of Chicago Press, 1979), p. 30.

[2] PP, *East India Affairs: Papers Relating to the Police, and Civil and Criminal Justice under the Respective Governments of Bengal, Fort Saint George, and Bombay from 1810 to the Present Time* (1819), Judicial Letter to Bengal, 9 November 1814, p. 42.

There were intense fiscal and bureaucratic pressures that dictated the necessity of attempting to adapt the panchayat to the British administration of justice as well. Especially important in this regard was the immense backlog of cases that had accumulated in the British courts of the Bengal Presidency since the adoption of Cornwallis' reforms there in 1793. In an undated memorandum to the Company, Munro had reported:

> the forms of process in Civil Suits induce such endless delays that justice is almost at a stand for it cannot be said to go on when it proceeds so slowly as not to keep pace in any degree with the demands of the Country. The great accumulation of Causes in arrear, amounting in one Court only in Bengal to above a hundred thousand, shew the inefficiency of the System clearly enough – and its defects would be still more glaring were the numberless suits added to the list of undecided Causes which are now kept back from the parties despairing of ever seeing them settled.[3]

His solution was "to restore to the heads of Villages their ancient jurisdiction in petty causes – to make all causes of importance be decided by Punchayets or Native Juries – to throw as much as possible of the administration of justice into the hands of intelligent natives, instead of confining it to European Judges who can seldom be qualified to discharge the duty."[4]

In 1814, therefore, after the renewal of the Company's charter and obviously under the influence of Munro, the Company ordered both the Bengal and Madras Presidencies to implement the panchayat system.[5] Citing the obvious failures of the courts, the Company's Court of Directors noted that British procedures with "such a minute and tedious mode of proceeding, in a country where the courts are so few, compared with the vast extent and population of it, must be quite incompatible with promptitude and despatch."[6] In 1818, after the third Anglo-Maratha War, the panchayat system was therefore also adopted in the newly ceded Deccan territories of the Bombay Presidency.

In the case of the panchayat experiment in the Deccan, no attempt has yet been made to thoroughly examine the surviving data on the tribunal's frequency, success rate, caseload, or trends during this era.

[3] IOR/H/686, "Colonel Munro's Observations on the Judicial System," n.d., pp. 753–5.
[4] Ibid., pp. 763–4. [5] See Chapter 7.
[6] PP, *East India Affairs: Papers Relating to the Police, and Civil and Criminal Justice*, p. 293. The dispatch to Madras was dated 29 April 1814 and that to Bengal 9 November 1814.

Although a good deal of data exist, especially in the Annual and Periodical Reports submitted by the Presidency's Collectors, they are by no means perfect. There are significant gaps, taxonomical confusions, and other more or less significant obstacles to its interpretation and analysis. Nevertheless, the surviving information is bountiful enough. Moreover, it is unique and for the first time allows the historian to gain significant insights into the workings of the panchayat system under British rule. In order to avoid confusion with modern territorial boundaries and jurisdictions, I have maintained the early nineteenth-century spelling of place names where and when appropriate. Finally, those who may be averse to numbers, charts, graphs, and other forms of data analysis may wish to skip to the Conclusion of this chapter for a summary of the results.

THE STRUCTURE OF CIVIL JUDICIAL ADMINISTRATION UNDER THE COMPANY

Before entering into an analysis of the relevant data, it is necessary to briefly outline the nature and development of the British administration of local justice in the Deccan and the Bombay Presidency.[7] It is important to emphasize that this was a system in transition and thus it should not be surprising that both judicial offices and their jurisdictions were created, abolished, altered, and amended during this period. These changes were not only the result of policy decisions at both the Company and Presidency levels but were also responses to the significant demands for justice in the newly conquered territories.

The judicial system of the Bombay Presidency was divided into several distinct jurisdictions. In the Presidency town of Bombay itself, justice had been administered through a Mayor's Court since 1726.[8] Comprised of a Mayor and nine aldermen, the jurisdiction of the Mayor's Court was confined to the town and Company factories of Bombay. The Court's authority extended to the passage of by-laws and ordinances as well as to the imposition of fines and punishments. Notably, however, the Mayor's Court was limited by the provision "that all such By-Laws, Rules and Ordinances, and all Pains and

[7] For a fuller account of the many variations in the administration of justice before 1827, see William H. Morley, *The Administration of Justice in British India; Its Past History and Present State* (London: Williams and Norgate, 1858), pp. 95–102.

[8] For earlier judicial administration, see *Materials towards a Statistical Account of the Town and Island of Bombay, Vol. III: Administration* (Bombay: Government Central Press, 1894), pp. 1–10.

Penalties thereby to be imposed, be agreeable to Reason, and not contrary to the Laws and Statutes of *England*."[9]

In 1798, the Mayor's Court was reformed by Letters Patent and renamed the Recorder's Court.[10] While its territorial jurisdiction remained largely unchanged, its judicial purview now specifically encompassed jurisdiction over criminal, equity, ecclesiastical, and admiralty cases. A judge, who was required to be an English barrister of not less than five years' experience, was appointed to oversee the Court. The Mayor continued to serve as a judge although the number of eligible aldermen was reduced from nine to three. More significant perhaps was the fact that the Court was now mandated to try all matters relating to landed inheritance, rents, and contracts according to Islamic or Hindu law, depending upon "the Laws and Usages of the Defendant." However, the forms, processes, and legal representation before the Court remained identical to contemporary English practices; that is, slow, expensive, and largely inaccessible to the majority of the population. In the following year, 1799, the Governor of the Presidency, Jonathan Duncan, sought to regularize the judicial system by establishing district and high courts on both the civil and criminal sides.[11]

Before Duncan's 1799 judicial reforms, outside of the presidency town of Bombay, the surrounding British-held territories were subject to a patchwork of judicial institutions. The "acquisition" or, more properly, conquest of the island of Salsette in 1774–1775 led to a fascinating judicial *interregnum* in which official policy promoted the settlement of disputes by English-style arbitration until a satisfactory system of administration could be established. This *interregnum* lasted for almost twenty-five years until the reforms introduced by Duncan. After that date, local civil justice was administered by Indian Commissioners whose jurisdiction was limited to cases in which claims were for less than Rs. 500. This court was also prohibited from

[9] *Charter Granted to the United Company of Merchants of England, Trading to the East Indies, Bearing Date the Twenty-fourth of September, in the Thirteenth Year of the Reign of George I, Anno Domini, One Thousand Seven Hundred and Twenty-Six*, reprinted in John Shaw, *Charters Relating to the East India Company from 1600 to 1761* (Madras: Government Press, 1887), pp. 245–6. Emphasis in original.

[10] *Letters Patent Establishing New Courts of Judicature at Fort St. George and Bombay in the East-Indies* (1798).

[11] Amrita Shodhan, "Caste in the Judicial Courts of Gujarat, 1800–1860," in E. Simpson and A. Kapadia, eds., *The Idea of Gujarat: History, Ethnography and Text* (Hyderabad: Orient Blackswan, 2010), pp. 33–4.

exercising its jurisdiction over inhabitants of Bombay or over property disputes within the city.[12] Between the years 1817 and 1819, the jurisdiction of Salsette was transferred to the control of a Collector and the newly expanded territory renamed the Northern Konkan.

Further northward along the Gujarat coast in Surat, prior to 1800, judicial administration had been shared by the Company and the Nawab. As in Salsette, local civil jurisdiction in the towns of Broach, Kaira, and Surat was exercised by Indian Commissioners known as *sadr amins*.[13] In the bordering Broach collectorate, which was transferred to the British in 1805, a district court was established as well. As territorial acquisitions continued to proceed in modern-day Gujarat, the Company's judicial administration also soon expanded and the district of Kaira was created under the charge of a Collector. At the same time, in 1805, a new Provincial Court of Appeal was created for civil cases comprehending the collectorates of Surat, Broach, and Kaira, which was later moved to Surat in 1810 and then abolished in 1820.[14]

Despite the directive to try certain cases according to the "laws and usages" of Hindus and Muslims, as in Bombay, these Company courts were nevertheless modeled on English legal procedures, and legal representation before them was restricted to qualified English-trained barristers. Moreover, until 1830, the Bombay and Gujarat courts remained independent of one another, creating what one historian has called "two conflicting systems of judicature" within one Presidency.[15] However, an even more pronounced conflict came about only after the acquisition of the Peshwa's territory in the Deccan, the event that provided Elphinstone with the opportunity to construct, or reconstruct, a system of civil justice based upon "the customs of the country."

In December 1817, Elphinstone was able to secure the consent of the Governor-General in Calcutta to establish a separate provisional Commissioner for the conquered territories of the Deccan. Until the

[12] IOR/H/Misc/692, [James Cumming], *Account of the Progress of Judicial Administration in the Bombay Territories, 1809*, pp. 217–28; Rev. A. K. Nairne, "History of the Konkan," in *Gazetteer of the Bombay Presidency, Vol. I, Pt. II: History of the Konkan, Dakhan, and Southern Maratha Country* (Bombay: Government Central Press, 1896), p. 124.

[13] IOR/H/Misc/692, [Cumming], *Account*, pp. 229–30; see also S. M. Edwardes, "District Administration in Bombay, 1818–1857," in H. H. Dodwell, ed., *The Cambridge History of India, Volume VI: The India Empire, 1858–1918* (Delhi: S. Chand & Co., 1958), pp. 58–60.

[14] IOR/H/Misc/692, [Cumming], *Account*, pp. 232–3; Morley, *Administration of Justice*, p. 101; *Gazetteer of the Bombay Presidency: Gujarat, Vol. II: Surat and Broach* (Bombay, 1887), p. 228. A circuit court for criminal appeals was similarly established in 1805.

[15] Edwardes, "District Administration in Bombay," pp. 63–4.

position of Commissioner of the Deccan was abolished in 1826 and Elphinstone's new law code implemented the following year, the Bombay Judicial Regulations that governed the Company's other possessions were not applicable to the Deccan territories and Elphinstone was left largely free to construct a system of judicial administration as he saw fit.[16] Elphinstone's initial plans for the judicial administration of the occupied territories were contained in and later published as the *Report on the Territories Conquered from the Paishwa*.[17] His goal, as we have seen, was to adapt the Maratha system of justice to the British aim of "affording protection to men's rights" without changing the system's "fundamental principles."[18] In rural areas, this entailed the maintenance of the authority of the Maratha district revenue officers (*mamledars*), local revenue officers (*kamavisadars*), and village headmen (*patels*). The latter were considered to be especially important for their ability to amicably intervene in village disputes or to promote the use of panchayats. Both the *mamledars* and *kamavisadars* were henceforth given new titles: The former were now styled Native Commissioners at the *sadr* station and the latter Native Commissioners in the *parganas*. In the towns, the district officers were also assisted by the creation of urban magistrates, for whom the term *amin* was adopted, and they similarly were encouraged to employ the panchayat system to settle civil disputes.[19]

The adoption and incorporation of Maratha *mamledars* and *kamavisadars* as well as the creation of *amins* in the towns heralded a significant expansion of Britain's judicial bureaucracy in the occupied Deccan. A position once occupied by men of significant landed or commercial interests under the Peshwa, the *mamledars*, now styled Commissioners, became paid employees of the Company and the office was increasingly filled by men of lesser distinction.[20] Soon after 1818, however, it became readily apparent that the Peshwa's system of judicial administration was incapable of dealing with the rapid increase in judicial caseloads throughout these territories. Thus, judicial Registers and Assistant Registers, or Assistant Judges, were appointed to the courts in Poona, Ahmadnagar, and Dharwar in 1822. Then, as the number of

[16] Kenneth Ballhatchet, *Social Policy and Social Change in Western India, 1817–1830* (Oxford: Oxford University Press, 1957), Chapters 2 and 6.
[17] Mountstuart Elphinstone, *Report on the Territories Conquered from the Paishwa* (Calcutta: Government Gazette Press, 1821).
[18] Ibid., p. 76. [19] Ibid., pp. 99–103.
[20] Ballhatchet, *Social Policy and Social Change in Western India*, pp. 96–103.

cases being litigated continued to increase and judicial backlogs swelled, Indian civil magistrates (*munsifs*) were also created in 1823.[21]

The relative autonomy of the Deccan Commissionerate formally ended in November 1819 when Elphinstone succeeded Sir Evan Nepean as Governor of Bombay and the Deccan collectorates were officially annexed to the Presidency. For nearly a decade thereafter very little else changed. The position of Commissioner of the Deccan, now under the direct authority of the Governor-in-Council, was retained and filled by William Chaplin, who had been trained in Madras under Thomas Munro and thus was quite sympathetic to Elphinstone's policies in the region.[22] Moreover, it was agreed at the time that the internal administration of the Deccan collectorates was to remain unchanged until a new set of regulations for the entire Presidency could be prepared and implemented, an event that did not occur until 1827.[23]

Therefore, after 1799, the Presidency was comprised of several distinct juridical units. Separate courts held jurisdiction over the towns of Bombay and Salsette; the six "old Bombay territories," as Kenneth Ballhatchet described them, comprised of the collectorates of Surat, Broach, Kaira, Ahmadabad, Northern Konkan, and Southern Konkan, were each possessed of their own district courts as well as an appeals court;[24] and the four Deccan territories, comprised of Khandesh, Ahmadnagar, Dharwar, and Poona, reported to the Commissioner of the Deccan. The Bombay Supreme Court would not be inaugurated until 1824.

SUMMARY OF DATA

The data used in the following charts and tables were collected largely from the Annual and Periodical Reports in the Company's Civil Judicature files preserved in the Maharashtra State Archives. They were supplemented by reports surviving in the Bombay Judicial Consultations files at the British Library. While the reports in London

21 PP, *Appendix to the Report from the Select Committee of the House of Commons on the Affairs of the East India Company, 16th August 1832*, Appendix H, No. 53, pp. 187–90.

22 One of Chaplin's annual reports from the Deccan was published as *A Report Exhibiting a View of the Fiscal and Judicial System of Administration Introduced in the Territory above the Ghauts* (Bombay, 1824). In the *Report*, he was determined to refute any claims that the panchayats were inefficient so long as local officials were "constantly stimulated to an observance of their Judicial duties," p. 115.

23 Meera Singh, *British Revenue and Judicial Policies in India: A Case Study of Deccan (1818–1826)* (New Delhi: Har-Anand Publications, 1994), pp. 31–2.

24 The districts formally were Surat Zillah, Broach Zillah, Eastern Zillah North of the Myhee, Western Zillah North of the Myhee, Zillah of the Northern Konkan, and Zillah of the Southern Konkan.

tend to provide annual or semi-annual compilations of cases, the Annual and Periodical Reports in Mumbai are largely comprised of bi-monthly reports submitted to the Collectors. Neither set of records has survived fully intact nor, unfortunately, are they fully comprehensive when taken together. The bi-monthly reports from the individual collectorates are rarely complete for the entire period between 1819 and 1827; the annual or semi-annual compilations reported to London are similarly non-continuous for this period. In the following calculations, there have been a few attempts to fill in the gaps by substituting means or averages for the missing data. However, considering the wealth of data that do exist (over 212,000 reported cases), to do this to a considerable extent was thought to be largely unnecessary and perhaps misleading. Thus, the data presented here are comprised largely of cases actually reported and therefore almost invariably represent an undercount of the full extent of the litigation activity that was taking place. Where statistical adjustments to the raw data have been made, this has been clearly noted. Despite these limitations, the surviving data remain extremely robust and present a unique opportunity to study and analyze the workings of the early colonial panchayat system.

Table 2.1 displays the surviving data of the adjusted total caseload from both the "old Bombay territories" and the Deccan collectorates between the fall of the Peshwa and the introduction of the new Bombay Regulations, the so-called Elphinstone Code, in 1827. Certainly, the two most obvious results displayed in this table are the large volume of cases brought before these courts as well as the relatively small number of cases that were finally resolved through contact with the judicial process. Of the 212,087 cases recorded, the mean number of cases before the courts in each collectorate between 1819 and 1827 was 17,583. If the collectorates of Surat and Kaira are omitted from the calculations, for which only two years' caseload survives, the mean rises to 21,035 cases for this period. The average number of cases handled in each collectorate annually during this period was 2,365. However, a more meaningful result may be gained again by omitting the sparse data from Surat and Kaira. Excluding those collectorates from the calculations, the average number of cases per year brought before the courts in the eight remaining collectorates rises to 2,711.

The inability of the courts to keep pace with this volume of cases was a constant concern of the Company. Over the period 1819–1827, only 59.6 percent of the cases were tried, settled, or dismissed. As noted earlier, the resulting backlog of cases led the Company not only to expand its judicial bureaucracy through the appointment of Assistant

TABLE 2.1 Total cases, c. 1819–1827

Collectorate	Adjusted total cases*	Cases dismissed or settled out of court (% of total)+	Cases adjudicated (% of total)
Surat†	10,804	3,025 (28.0)	5,038 (46.6)
Broach	22,775	5,420 (23.8)	6,187 (27.2)
Kaira‡	6,823	1,817 (26.6)	3,841 (56.3)
Ahmadabad	23,861	6,705 (28.1)	7,391 (31.0)
N. Konkan	17,942	2,458 (13.7)	8,122 (46.4)
S. Konkan	29,842	7,699 (25.8)	18,379 (61.6)
Khandesh	5,875	1,716 (29.2)	2,098 (35.7)
Ahmadnagar	40,962	10,159 (24.8)	13,725 (33.7)
Dharwar	13,560	3,431 (25.3)	6,703 (49.4)
Poona	40,363	5,570 (13.8)	7,320 (18.1)
TOTAL	212,087	47,023 (22.4)	78,804 (37.2)

* Most surviving reports recorded "cases on file," but only some distinguished between continuing and new cases. These figures therefore have been adjusted to account for cases continuing on the judicial file from one report to the next.
+ Data for 1825 in this category are missing. Figures for this year have been calculated by multiplying the average percentage of dismissed or settled cases for the period 1819–1827 in each collectorate by the total number of cases reported in 1825.
† Surviving data for 1824 and 1825 only.
‡ Surviving data for 1823 and 1825 only.

Judges, Registers, Assistant Registers, Native Commissioners, and *amins* but also to repeatedly demand greater efficiency from the judicial establishment. The courts were thus encouraged to promote the out-of-court settlements of disputes, a fact that is reflected in the relatively large number of such results. Unfortunately, the data do not allow us to distinguish between cases dismissed (often for non-attendance) and those settled out of court. Nevertheless, this suggests that over 22 percent of all cases did not result in a court's verdict.

Between 1819 and 1827, 78,804 cases, or about 37 percent of the total, were adjudicated either in a Company court or by panchayat. The distribution of these cases among the different judicial fora is presented in Table 2.2. Unfortunately, the relevant data are missing for the year 1825 and are thus omitted from this table. Of the remaining cases, of which there are approximately 57,000, the most striking information to be derived from this data is the overwhelming number of cases that were

TABLE 2.2 Distribution of cases decided, 1819–1827*

Collectorate	Judges & Assistant Judges	Collectors, Sub-collectors & Assistants	Registers & Assistant Registers	*Amins* & *munsifs*	Commissioners at the *sadr* stations & in the *parganas*+	Panchayat
Surat	128	0	476	318	1,611	22
Broach	234	0	915	1,175	2,197	131
Kaira	15	0	254	364	1,057	0
Ahmadabad	152	0	832	479	3,567	23
N. Konkan	77	0	616	2,278	3,398	2
S. Konkan	613	0	2,851	1,795	10,328	5
Khandesh	13	22	49	176	596	254
Ahmadnagar	1,192	913	313	365	8,324	482
Dharwar	85	227	163	1,988	141	917
Poona	54	109	183	210	3,173	889
TOTAL (%)	2,563 (4.4)	1,271 (2.3)	6,652 (11.7)	9,148 (16.1)	34,392 (60.7)	2,725 (4.8)

* Table omits data for 1825 for which this evidence does not survive.

\+ These figures include those recorded for *mamledars*, *amildars*, and *peshkars*, three revenue and judicial positions that briefly survived in Dharwar and Poona. Their positions were eventually incorporated into those of the so-called Native Commissioners.

tried before Indian judicial officers. In all, 81.6 percent of the cases disposed of by the courts during this period were heard by *amins*, *munsifs*, Native Commissioners, or panchayats. "European" judicial officers, therefore, heard only 18.4 percent of the cases.

This distribution of caseloads was expressly the result of British judicial policy decisions taken during the immediate aftermath of the cession of the Peshwa's territories. Munro's criticism of the Bengal system of justice, as we have noted, was focused on the inability of British Judges to comprehend the languages and customs of India. He recommended, therefore, that British Judges be restricted to hearing appeals while the courts in the first instance be staffed by Indians. "It cannot be supposed," he wrote, "that the Company's Service can ever furnish more than a very small proportion of Men properly qualified to fill the numerous judicial appointments which now exist, the number of these employments ought to be diminished, so that those which remain may be more respectably filled, and the business of the European Judge ought rather to be to take care that the Native Arbitrators and Juries do their duty, than to attempt to do it for them."[25]

Elphinstone's *Report on the Territories Conquered from the Paishwa* duly followed these recommendations, laying out the system of Native Commissioners, *amins*, *munsifs*, and panchayats that came to characterize the British judicial administration of the Deccan.[26] In one sense, therefore, British policy was successful for it displaced the administration of justice from British judges and magistrates to Indian judicial officers. However, this reform failed to solve the problem of reducing the backlog of cases that continued to clog the judicial files. As we have seen, less than 60 percent of the cases brought before the courts were resolved during this period.

Company officials in London frequently complained not only about the perceived inefficiency of the judicial establishment but also about the perceived litigiousness of Indians, an issue that has become a standard subject of inquiry into Indian legal history.[27] In order to delve further into the latter issue, Table 2.3 relates litigation rates for selected years in

[25] IOR/H/686, Papers concerning revenue, administrative and judicial matters in India, "Colonel Munro's Observations on the Judicial System," n.d., pp. 756–7.

[26] Elphinstone, *Report on the Territories Conquered from the Paishwa*, pp. 101–4.

[27] See Oliver Mendelsohn, "The Pathology of the Indian Legal System," *Modern Asian Studies*, Vol. 15, No. 4 (1981), pp. 823–63; Robert Moog, "Indian Litigiousness and the Litigation Explosion," *Asian Survey*, Vol. 33, No. 12 (December 1993), pp. 1136–50; Marc Galanter and Jayanth K. Krishnan, "'Bread for the Poor': Access to Justice and the Rights of the Needy in India," *Hastings Law Journal*, Vol. 55, No. 4 (March 2004), pp. 789–834 and the related footnotes therein.

TABLE 2.3 Litigation rates: selected years, 1823–1827

Collectorate (year)	Estimated population, c. 1820*	Adjusted total cases	Litigation rate (per 1,000)
Surat (1824)	360,000	8,321	23.1
Broach (1826)	229,000	3,681	16.1
Kaira (1823)	371,000	3,002	8.1
Ahmadabad (1826)	550,000	4,987	9.1
N. Konkan (1827)	420,000	2,354	5.6
S. Konkan (1826)	632,000	5,181	8.2
Khandesh (1827)	418,000	778	1.9
Ahmadnagar (1826)	453,000	4,586	10.1
Dharwar (1824)	684,000	3,910	5.7
Poona (1824)	500,000	7,223	14.4
TOTAL	4,617,000	44,023	9.5

* Population estimates drawn from Ballhatchet, *Social Policy and Social Change in Western India, 1817–1830.*

the ten collectorates of "old Bombay" and the Deccan.[28] Obviously, it would be unwise to make any overbroad generalizations from this data, which provide only a snapshot of litigation during this period. Nevertheless, several views may be put forward.

First, the overall litigation rate of 9.5 per thousand is quite high compared with the data from contemporary India. In Robert Moog's study of civil filings in the district courts of Uttar Pradesh, the litigation rate ranged from a high of 1.6 per thousand in the 1950s to a low of 0.88 per thousand in the 1970s.[29] Much closer to the region of this study, Christian Wollschläger calculated the Maharashtra litigation rate at 3.5 per thousand in 1992.[30] Thus, the early nineteenth-century litigation rates appear to have been almost three times higher than those of the late twentieth century.

[28] Relevant years for analysis were selected based upon the completeness of the returns in the Annual and Periodical Reports. Not all reports for the same year from all districts possessed the same level of completeness. Therefore, different years were selected based upon the robustness of the surviving data. Since the use of the gross numbers for the entire period may have tended to skew the results toward those districts with more complete returns (and hence more data), this "snapshot" was deemed to be a more reliable indication of litigation rates.

[29] Moog, "Indian Litigiousness and the Litigation Explosion," Table 1, p. 1139.

[30] Christian Wollschläger, "Exploring Global Landscapes of Litigation Rates," in Jürgen Brand and Dieter Strempel, eds., *Soziologie des Rechts: Festschrift für Erhard Blankenburg zum 60. Geburtstag* (Nomos: Baden-Baden, 1998), p. 587 cited in Galanter and Krishnan, "'Bread for the Poor'," fn. 1, pp. 789–90.

However, Table 2.3 also reveals a marked difference among the ten collectorates. Most notably, Surat, Broach, and Poona had significantly higher rates of litigation than the other collectorates. Taken together, these three collectorates had a litigation rate nearly twice that of the overall average at 17.6 cases per thousand. Without further data, one can only conjecture as to why this was so. Two reasons, however, immediately suggest themselves. First, Surat, Broach, and Poona were all locations of established courts providing litigants with easy access to the law. Second, these were all relatively significant towns, thus linking the degree of urbanization to litigation rates.[31] Poona alone was estimated to have had a population of 110,000 people in 1819.[32] In 1828, Walter Hamilton estimated that Surat contained over 157,000 people.[33] The same author reported that the population of the town of Broach was over 32,000 in 1812, while the Broach sub-district (*pargana*) numbered nearly 158,000 people.[34] Such concentrations of population may well have promoted access to the courts and thus raised litigation rates.

Anecdotal evidence derived from surviving case records suggests that a rise in litigation may also have accompanied the transfer of power to the British in this era. At least some claimants took this opportunity to press new claims, especially for land, or to renew old ones that had not been successful under the Marathas.[35] Indeed Figure 2.1 suggests that there was a marked rise in litigation during the first years of the British expansion in the area, followed then by a retreat to a lower norm. Unfortunately, the data for these calculations are quite sparse for the earliest years. The reports of cases between 1819 and 1822 are spotty, but relatively full and reliable reports exist for 1823–1827. Between 1823 and 1827, the number of adjusted bimonthly cases ranged from a high of 11,031 cases reported at the beginning of March 1824 to a low of 2,031 cases reported in November 1825. The mean number of adjusted bimonthly cases reported for 1823–1827 was 6,200. Cases during this period reached an obvious peak between January and September 1824, when they spiraled to over 9,800 for each bimonthly reporting period. The proximate cause of this spike in cases may very well be linked to the introduction of *munsifs*, the judicial office that had been introduced the previous year.

31 I owe this point to Marc Galanter.

32 Ballhatchet, *Social Policy and Social Change in Western India*, p. 7.

33 Walter Hamilton, *The East-Indian Gazetteer; Containing Particular Descriptions of the Empires, Kingdoms, Principalities . . .*, Vol. II, 2nd edn. (London: Parbury, Allen & Co., 1828), pp. 610–11.

34 Walter Hamilton, *A Geographical, Statistical, and Historical Description of Hindoostan, and the Adjacent Countries*, Vol. I (London: John Murray, 1820), p. 706.

35 See Chapter 5.

Figure 2.1 Total adjusted bimonthly cases, 1823–1827

The data also suggest some degree of seasonality in the appearance of suits filed in the courts. Cases tended to increase in the first two bimonthly reports of the year in January and March and then to subside thereafter. This may indicate that disputes over land, rents, or other issues related to the agricultural cycle were being reflected in court caseloads. Unfortunately, the surviving data do not allow for such disaggregation for the entire period. However, there are two surviving accounts that break down the courts' decisions for the six-month period between 1 January and 30 June 1826. While it cannot be assumed that these reports fully represent the caseloads of all the collectorates during this period, they may be indicative of broader trends throughout the region nonetheless.

Tables 2.4 and 2.5 display these results for the collectorates of Ahmadnagar and Khandesh, apparently among the only results of this kind that survive for this period. What is most apparent is that the vast majority of suits filed before the courts were for matters of debt and that they were lodged before the *munsifs*.[36] Of the total of

[36] It is interesting to note the striking parallels between this breakdown of cases and the eighteen titles of law in Hindu jurisprudence. See Donald R. Davis, Jr., *The Spirit of Hindu Law* (Cambridge: Cambridge University Press, 2010), Chapter 3.

TABLE 2.4 "Statement shewing the description of suits on which decisions have been passed within the Adawlut of Ahmednuggur during the six months from 1st January to 30th June 1826"

	By the Judge		By the Assistant Judge		By Register		By panchayat	By *munsifs*		
	Original	On Appeal	Original	On Appeal	Original	On Appeal		Original	As referees	As arbitrators
Customs of caste & particular places	0	0	1	0	0	0	0	4	0	0
Marriage & repudiation	0	0	1	0	0	0	1	7	0	0
Maintenance of children	0	0	0	0	0	0	0	0	0	0
Adoption	0	0	0	0	0	0	0	0	0	0
Inheritance & partition of property	0	0	8	1	0	0	0	21	1	0
Gifts & wills	0	0	0	0	0	0	0	0	0	0
Service & salary	0	0	0	0	0	0	1	3	0	0
Contracts of sales, hire, & deposit	0	0	3	0	0	0	0	4	1	0
Money debts & interest	0	0	43	2	0	0	1	1,385	12	1
Personal injuries	0	0	0	0	0	0	0	1	0	0
TOTAL (%)	0	0	56 (3.7)	3 (0.2)	0	0	3 (0.2)	1,425 (94.9)	14 (0.9)	1 (0.1)

Source: MSA, EIC, Judicial Department, Annual and Periodical Reports, Vol. 1/102, 1826.

TABLE 2.5 "Statement shewing the description of suits on which decisions have been passed within the Court of Adawlut in Candeish during the six months from 1st January to 30th June 1826"

	By the Judge		By Register		By panchayat	By *munsifs*		
	Original	On appeal	Original	On appeal		Original	As referees	As arbitrators
Customs of caste & particular places	0	0	0	0	3	2	0	0
Marriage & repudiation	0	0	0	0	0	2	0	0
Maintenance of children	0	0	0	0	0	0	0	0
Adoption	0	0	0	0	0	0	0	0
Inheritance & partition of property	0	0	1	1	5	9	1	1
Gifts & wills	0	0	0	0	0	0	0	0
Service & salary	0	0	0	0	0	4	1	0
Contracts of sales, hire, & deposit	0	0	0	1	1	26	1	0
Money debts & interest	0	2	0	4	11	223	8	3
Personal injuries	0	0	0	0	1	2	0	0
TOTAL (%)	0	2 (0.6)	1 (0.3)	6 (1.9)	21 (6.7)	268 (85.6)	11 (3.5)	4 (1.3)

Source: MSA, EIC, Judicial Department, Annual and Periodical Reports, Vol. 1/102, 1826.

1,502 cases recorded in Ahmadnagar during the first six months of 1826, fully 1,444, or 96.1 percent, were for "money debts and interest." In Khandesh, the figures at first glance appear to be not quite so startling. There, 251 of a total of 313 cases, or 80.2 percent, were for debts and interest; however, there were also a significant number of cases, twenty-nine or 9.3 percent, categorized by the British as concerning "contracts of sale, hire, and deposit." If these cases are added to those for debts and interest, then the total number of what may be generously termed "exchange cases" rises to 280, or 89.5 percent, in Khandesh.

These vast numbers of "exchange cases" were also overwhelmingly decided in local forums of adjudication, especially before Indian *munsifs* and panchayats. In the Ahmadnagar collectorate, only 59 of the 1,502 total cases, or a mere 3.9 percent, were decided by British judicial officials. In Khandesh, the percentage of cases handled by British judicial officials was even smaller. There, only 2.9 per cent, or 9 of 313 cases, were decided by the British Judges or Registers.

Of the small number of remaining cases, inheritance and property partition disputes were certainly the most numerous. In Ahmadnagar, there were 31 cases, or 2.1 percent of the total, of this type, while in Khandesh there were 18 cases, or 5.8 percent. In both instances, however, litigants exhibited a similarly marked preference to present these types of cases, including marriage, to Indian magistrates and *munsifs*. The general avoidance among litigants of bringing their suits before panchayats will be discussed in further detail later.

Interestingly, even the cases categorized as 'customs of caste & particular places' were frequently resolved by local judicial officials. These cases, British officials often noted, were best resolved within each caste and thus outside of the courts, preferably by caste panchayats. However, this may not have been as common as British officials had hoped. Although it is unclear as to why the litigants chose to resolve caste disputes in the local courts as opposed to the caste panchayats, this tendency does reflect the more general drift among litigants away from the panchayat.

Finally, as noted previously, *munsifs* were enjoined to promote arbitration and mediation rather than to act solely as British-style Judges. These reports indicate that they did do so, but only in a small number of the cases brought before them. In the Ahmadnagar collectorate, the *munsifs* acted as referees or arbitrators in only 15 of 1,440 cases, or only 1 percent of the cases. In Khandesh, the number was slightly higher. There *munsifs* refereed or arbitrated 15 of 283 cases, or 5.3 percent. Thus, although British judicial policy explicitly promoted dispute resolution through arbitration or mediation, litigants appear to have adopted a clear preference for the winner-take-all system of the courts.

PANCHAYAT JUSTICE: TRENDS AND DISTRIBUTION

Despite Elphinstone's injunctions to employ panchayats as the main engine of civil justice, only a very small percentage of cases ever followed this path of dispute resolution. Several reasons for this have already been noted.[37] However, Table 2.6 provides quantitative evidence to support the qualitative evaluations previously presented from the reports and letters of contemporaries.

It is quite apparent from these data that the panchayat as a form of civil dispute resolution played a relatively unimportant role in the Bombay Presidency as a whole, hearing less than 5 percent of all cases that went to adjudication. Indeed, in the collectorates of the "old Bombay territories," panchayat justice was restricted to settling suits within castes and other self-regulating groups. There, substantive evidence for the period 1819–1822 is lacking, although panchayats did occasionally

TABLE 2.6 Panchayat cases, 1819–1827

Collectorate	Adjusted total cases	Cases adjudicated	Panchayat cases (% of cases adjudicated)
Surat	10,804	5,038	48 (1.0)
Broach	22,775	6,187	151 (2.4)
Kaira	6,823	3,841	0 (0)
Ahmadabad	23,861	7,391	43 (0.6)
N. Konkan	17,942	8,122	2 (0.02)
S. Konkan	29,842	18,379	5 (0.03)
Khandesh	5,875	2,098	368 (17.5)
Ahmadnagar	40,962	13,725	493 (3.6)
Dharwar	13,560	6,703	1,223 (18.2)
Poona	40,363	7,320	1,191 (16.3)
TOTAL	212,087	78,804	3,524 (4.5)

[37] See Chapter 1.

appear in cases brought upon appeal, as will be discussed in the following chapter.[38] After 1823, however, the historical record became much fuller, due largely to the administrative change in recording practices. Still, only in the Broach collectorate was more than 1 percent of adjudicated cases ever heard by a panchayat. In three of the collectorates, Kaira, North Konkan, and South Konkan, the number was at or very nearly close to zero.

The newly conquered Deccan territories, however, were the sites of Elphinstone's panchayat experiment. There, Elphinstone wrote, the panchayat was to settle "every man's claim among his own neighbours who are best acquainted with his character and the circumstances of the case and among whom he is least likely either to advance a false claim or to succeed in establishing it."[39] Moreover, he constantly encouraged the Collectors there to work harder to promote dispute resolution through the panchayat and this policy was continued under his successor as the Commissioner of the Deccan, William Chaplin.

Nevertheless, Table 2.7 indicates that the number of panchayat cases throughout the Presidency, after reaching a peak of 2,093 cases in 1825, declined dramatically in the following years of 1826 and 1827. Indeed, by the latter year, there were only sixty-two recorded cases throughout

TABLE 2.7 Annual panchayat cases, 1819–1827

Year	Total panchayat cases	Panchayat cases in the Deccan
1819	337	337
1820	531	531
1821	236	236
1822	inc	175
1823	479	238
1824	956	908
1825	2,159	2,093
1826	112	48
1827	62	14

38 See, for example, *Hurrukchand Mooteechund* v. *Khooshalchund Goolabchund and Ten Others*, the Punchayut of Shravak Beesa Ooswal Bunyans in Harry Borradaile, *Reports of Civil Causes Adjudged by the Court of Sudur Udalut, for the Presidency of Bombay, between the Years A.D. 1800 and A.D. 1824*, pt. II, p. 38 cited in Marc Galanter, ed., "Legal Materials for the Study of Modern India" (1965), pp. I-1–I-8. Manuscript in author's possession.

39 IOR/P/121/28, Bengal Political Consultations, Elphinstone to Pottinger, 9 November 1818.

the ten collectorates of "old Bombay" and the Deccan, the fewest of the entire British period since the acquisition of the Peshwa's territory. Even in the four collectorates of the Deccan where panchayats had been most prevalent and most vigorously promoted the decline was both obvious and precipitous. There seems little doubt that whereas panchayats were hearing hundreds or perhaps thousands of cases per year before 1825, they were hearing fewer than fifty per year, and often many fewer than that, thereafter.

Just why this was so is not absolutely clear. In some collectorates, especially in Dharwar, the introduction of *munsifs* appears to have taken on a significant amount of the caseload, contributing to the decline of panchayats. That collectorate reached a peak of 309 panchayat cases in 1824, but by 1826 there were only fourteen cases recorded. At the same time, the first recorded cases brought before *munsifs* in Dharwar appeared in the December 1823 report, and by October 1824 the *munsifs* reported over 1,700 cases in their files. A judicial dispatch to the Company's Court of Directors in 1826, for example, noted "the institution of Moonsiffs and Ameens is found to answer the most sanguine expectations," but "the total arrear has been some what augmented since our last dispatch."[40]

However, a similarly precipitous decline in panchayat cases may also be found in collectorates where *munsifs* had not yet been appointed or had yet to try any cases. Thus in Ahmadnagar, the number of panchayat cases peaked in 1824 when 165 cases were reported. But by the next year, 1825, the number had dropped to forty. In the following year, 1826, the number had fallen even further to thirteen panchayat cases and then rose very slightly to fourteen in 1827. Yet, during this period, the Ahmadnagar collectorate recorded no cases before *munsifs*. Perhaps in this instance the cases had been absorbed into the files of other Indian commissioners, but the drift away from panchayat justice was noticeable nevertheless.

The shift away from dispute resolution through the panchayats may well have been both a matter of British policy and of popular preference. On the one hand, it is quite clear, as we have noted, that British officials recognized the weaknesses of the panchayat system and sought to compensate for this. While the likes of Elphinstone and Chaplin continued to promote dispute resolution through the panchayats throughout the mid-1820s, they nonetheless also recognized the

[40] IOR/L/PJ/3/917, Judicial Letters from Bombay, 1823–1827, 31 May 1826.

mounting caseloads on the files of the courts throughout the Presidency, a recognition that led to the creation and appointment of *amins*, Registers, Assistant Registers, and *munsifs*.

On the other hand, several British administrators suggested that the populace preferred the commissioners' and magistrates' courts to the panchayat and thus litigants had voted with their feet. The Collector of Dharwar, for example, suggested litigants preferred the enforcement powers exercised by the courts, especially after the customary enforcement of claims by *tukaza* went into decline. "The discontinuance of the violent kinds of tugaza has diminished the power of Creditors, and recorded many of them Suitors," he noted in 1822.[41]

Nevertheless, the preference of litigants for the courts rather than panchayats was noted in many places. In Pune, for example, referring to the introduction of *amins* and *munsifs*, "the great increase of the demand for justice" was attributed to "the improved system of administration."[42] Indeed, in 1825, Chaplin noted for the Deccan generally, "the demand for justice may however be expected to Encrease [*sic*] now that the Judicial officers there are more numerous & efficient," explaining that "the demand for justice increases with the supply."[43]

However, the precepts of political economy do not fully explain this phenomenon. Instead, the great attraction of the British courts may well have been their powers of enforcement. The Company's Court of Directors, as was noted in the last chapter, came to this conclusion in 1827, noting that "the great mass of litigation consists of cases in which the enforcement of a claim is peremptorily insisted on by one party or pertinaciously resisted by another. For the decision of all such Suits, whatever the subject of the claim may be, there should be regular Courts, freely accessible to the people and subject to safeguards for the due observance of the Law."[44] Thus, the enforcement powers of the British courts may well have been seen by litigants as one of that institution's great benefits and the winner-take-all system of the courts a more satisfactory site to determine verdicts and pass judgments.

41 MSA, EIC, Judicial Department, Civil and Criminal Judicature, Vol. 9A/9A, 1823, St John Thackeray to William Chaplin, 12 August 1822.

42 IOR/L/PJ/3/917, Judicial Letters from Bombay, 1823–1827, 31 May 1826.

43 MSA, EIC, Judicial Department, Annual and Periodical Reports, Vol. 3/83, 1825, William Chaplin to David Greenhill, 18 May 1825.

44 IOR/E/1047, Bombay Dispatches, 5 May 1826–13 June 1827, Judicial Department, *Administration of Justice in the Deccan*, 31 January 1827, pp. 486–9.

TYPES OF CASES AND DECISIONS

For the purposes of statistical analysis, certainly the most difficult information to uncover is the types of cases that came before the panchayats and their eventual disposition. Very few records with this detailed information were maintained by the British judicial officers. However, during the early years of the British administration, a few intensive investigations of panchayat administration were undertaken and upon this information some preliminary conclusions may be hazarded. The most fulsome data were collected in response to a set of queries posed by W. R. Morris, the Acting First Assistant Political Agent in Sátára.[45] Sátára was not one of the ten collectorates that have so far been the subject of this chapter, but it was contiguous to them. Sátára had been conquered by the British in 1819 and Pratap Singh installed there as raja. Until 1822, governance of the territory was effectively in the hands of the British Political Resident, Captain James Grant Duff.[46]

Morris collected information on a total of 1,362 disputes in five Sátára districts between late 1820 and late 1821. These data are displayed in Table 2.8. The data presented in the table are remarkably consistent with that collected from the "old Bombay territories" and the Deccan collectorates. The vast number of settled cases, 77.3 percent, was either disposed of by the Indian judicial officer or settled out of court. Only 4.7 percent of cases were being heard by or had been settled by a panchayat. This suggests that even in the territories in which the judicial administration had not been reconstructed by the British authorities there was nonetheless a pronounced bias against the panchayat system among litigants.

Moreover, the data provide a much more comprehensive and detailed view of the types of cases that were litigated, especially when this information is compared to that compiled in the Annual and Periodical Reports. For example, while litigation for debts continued to dominate the judicial files, the Sátára data illuminate the wide variety of property disputes that characterized rural society. The Annual and Periodical Reports apparently grouped all such cases under the single rubric of "inheritance and partition of property."

[45] IOR F/4/839/22429 (4), Board's Collections, 1825–1826, *Administration of Justice in the Deccan*, pp. 18–55.

[46] Grant Duff was the author of *A History of the Mahrattas* (1826) where his story is told. See also *Gazetteer of the Bombay Presidency, Volume XIX: Sátára* (Bombay: Government Central Press, 1885), pp. 306–10.

TABLE 2.8 "General Abstracts of all the complaints made within the Districts of Koreygaon, Waee, Kattoo, Punderpoor & Beejapore" [1821]

	Numbers	Settled by a Punchayet	Settling by a Punchayet	Settled by an order from the Mamlutdar	Amicably adjusted	Have not returned	Remaining to be investigated
Debt	416	2	17	323	37	17	20
Share of Family Property	85	1	4	52	13	5	10
Meiras	72	–	11	29	9	11	12
Wuttun	194	4	14	90	18	24	44
Enam	61	1	2	34	5	9	10
Assault Trespass &ca	237	–	–	162	42	22	11
Land (Koombaira)	183	1	–	150	9	1	14
Furnishing maintenance	11	2	–	4	1	–	3
Site of a House	10	–	–	9	–	–	1
Mango Trees	5	–	–	5	–	–	–
Adoption	5	–	–	1	–	1	3
Marriage &ca	31	–	–	18	7	6	–
Disputes Jungle	1	–	1	–	–	–	–
Precedence Man Paun [?] &ca	3	–	1	1	1	–	–
Mortgage of a Field	1	1	–	–	–	–	–
Contract	1	1	–	–	–	–	–

Cattle	15	–	1	7	4	2	1
Security	3	–	–	1	–	1	1
Agency	1	–	–	–	1	–	–
Cast	3	–	–	1	–	–	2
Articles Pawned, deposits &ca	3	1	–	2	–	–	–
Boundary Disputes	4	–	–	1	–	–	3
Wages	5	–	–	5	–	–	–
Pressing Beggries	7	–	–	7	–	–	–
Paper respecting property	1	–	–	–	1	–	–
Huks upon Custom	4	–	–	2	–	–	2
TOTAL (%)	1,362	14 (1.0)	51 (3.7)	904 (66.4)	148 (10.9)	108 (7.9)	137 (10.1)

Source: IOR F/4/839/22429 (4), Board's Collections, 1825–1826, *Administration of Justice in the Deccan*, p. 60. Originals in MSA, EIC, Judicial Department, Civil and Criminal Judicature, Vol. 9A/9A, 1823.

However, the Sátára data indicate that property disputes ranged from those over jungle lands and mango trees to the specific rights and privileges accorded to various types of property (*watan*, *mira*, and *inam*). Interestingly, the significant presence of *koombaira* (*kumbhara*) land disputes may also indicate the widespread presence of petty conflicts among the *kumbhara*, or potter caste. Village potters often held small parcels of property from which they supplemented their incomes or gathered clay for their work.[47]

More revealing perhaps is the fact that litigants rarely agreed to a panchayat in cases other than those for debts, inheritance, or disputes over hereditary estates and harvest rights. Fully, fifty-six of the total of sixty-five cases pending before or settled by panchayats were cases of this nature. Further, of the remaining nine cases, only three were not related in some way to matters of financial exchanges (pawned articles, contracts, or mortgages) or land. Of these three cases, two were for matters related to maintenance and one for ritual precedence.

Of the evidence collected by Morris, among the most valuable perhaps is that relating to the duration of panchayat cases. As we have seen, the slowness of panchayat proceedings was a complaint often lodged against this type of judicial proceeding. However, neither contemporaries nor historians have heretofore been able to precisely gauge their duration. In the five Sátára districts, very few cases seem to have been settled promptly. For example, a list of twenty-nine panchayat cases from the Koreygaon district reveals that more than half of the cases, sixteen in number, referred to a panchayat between February 1818 and November 1820 had not yet resulted in an award. Of the remaining thirteen cases, the average duration was 758 days, that is, almost two years. The quickest panchayat decision was reached in 424 days, while the longest took 1435 days.[48] In Punderpoor, none of the six cases submitted to panchayats between July 1818 and September 1820 had been decided by January 1821.[49]

[47] According to H. H. Wilson's *A Glossary of Judicial and Revenue Terms*, published by the East India Company, a *khumba* in Gujarat denoted a parcel of land of approximately 4,600 square yards.

[48] IOR F/4/839/22429 (4), Board's Collections, 1825–1826, *Administration of Justice in the Deccan, List of Punchayets which are proceeding and of complaints which remain to be investigated at the time of settling the Jummabundie last year within the districts of Koreygaon, Waee, Kattao, Punderpoor, & Beejapoor*, Enclosure No. 3, p. 70.

[49] IOR F/4/839/22429 (4), Board's Collections, 1825–1826, *Administration of Justice in the Deccan, List of Punchayets*, p. 71.

There is also evidence that panchayats could reach decisions with a great deal more alacrity. A case for debt in the Kuttao district was resolved in only 97 days.[50] In Waee district, although the dates in this manuscript are somewhat unreliable, it appears that of the cases settled by panchayats, the average duration was only 120 days. Yet one must be wary of taking these numbers as at all typical. In Waee, for instance, it represents only six of thirty-six recorded cases. Of the remaining thirty cases that had been instituted between July 1818 and January 1821, none had yet been reported as settled. Indeed, by January 1821, only three of twenty-one cases referred to panchayats since 1818 and 1819 had been decided.

Although Elphinstone intended the decisions of the panchayat to be final in all cases, the rules of judicial administration did allow for appeals in cases of "gross error or corruption." In Chapter 3, the appeals process and the character of petitions for appeal will be discussed in detail. For the moment, however, it should be noted that only the slightest amount of data exist relating to the frequency of appeals from panchayats. One such report survives for the calendar year 1824.[51] In that year, fifty-six of 459 cases were appealed from panchayats in the Poona collectorate and three of 222 panchayat cases were appealed in the Ahmadnagar collectorate. In Khandesh, none of 100 panchayat cases was appealed, while in the Carnatic it was none of 493 cases. Of these appeals, only eleven had been decided by the end of the calendar year, all of them relating to cases in Poona: six appeals had been confirmed and five reversed.

The prominence of appeals in Poona once again may be related to its longstanding position as the judicial center of the Peshwa and to the relative familiarity with and ease of access to the court system. It is perhaps most noteworthy that outside of Poona very few cases were ever appealed. Unfortunately, it is not possible to statistically reconstruct why this was so, but it is likely that a combination of time, distance, and money were the most important determinants of appeals, as they often are today.

CONCLUSIONS: THE JUSTICE SYSTEM IN PRACTICE

The Orientalist vision of resurrecting and sustaining the panchayat as the foundation of civil judicial administration was intended "to bring

[50] Ibid. [51] IOR/L/PJ/3/916, Judicial Letters from Bombay, 1819–1822, pp. 402; 408.

justice to every man's door" according to "the customs of the country." Judging from the existing data from the "old Bombay" and Deccan collectorates, however, the project both then and now must be deemed a failure. Generally, between 1819 and 1827, litigants chose the panchayat to resolve their disputes in less than 5 percent of all recorded cases. The overwhelming number of cases were brought before and disposed of by Indian judicial officials acting as *amins*, *munsifs*, and commissioners. When litigants did choose a panchayat, it was almost inevitably in cases involving disputes over debts, land, or land-related rights, perhaps because these disputes were more amenable to a negotiated settlement or perhaps because specific local knowledge was demanded or expected. Somewhere in the order of 90–95 percent of all panchayat cases may have been of this sort. It appears from the surviving data that disputes concerning family issues, such as marriage, adoption, property shares, and maintenance, rarely went before a panchayat. Similarly, misdemeanors, such as trespass, were unlikely to be heard by panchayats. These may have been types of cases in which litigants were much less likely to seek a negotiated or mediated settlement and preferred a winner-take-all forum of adjudication.

One reason often proffered at the time for the failure of the panchayat system was the delay involved in reaching a decision. The surviving data certainly support this observation. While it was possible for panchayats to conclude their investigation and issue an award within ninety days or so, this was uncommon. Many, if not most, panchayat deliberations dragged on for years. Thus, if a litigant was seeking a quick resolution to their dispute, the panchayat was not a suitable forum of adjudication.

The few "successes" of the panchayat system during these years were relegated almost entirely to three of the four Deccan collectorates: Khandesh, Dharwar, and Poona. In these collectorates, the percentage of cases adjudicated by panchayats could reach as high as 26 percent. Observers at the time almost invariably attributed these successes to the diligence and active supervision of the Collector and other British officials on the spot. As William Chaplin noted in 1822:

> [T]he District Officers require to be constantly stimulated to the due discharge of their duty in superintending the operation of Punchaets and to be severely fined or occasionally dismissed for neglect of it; and an unremitting and perhaps more than common interest on the part of the Collectors is no less essential to the success of this instrument of Justice. It is as necessary as oil to the wheels of a machine, the movement of

> which become clogged if not kept constantly greased and lubricated. Long abuse and disuse have much enfeebled the efficacy of Punchaets and they can only be restored to perfect efficiency by a careful and close attention to their invigoration on the part of the local authorities.[52]

However, litigants, as we have said, largely voted with their feet and showed a decided preference for the winner-take-all system of the commissioners' and *munsifs'* courts. In June 1825, Elphinstone commented on this phenomenon as it was reported to be taking place in the Poona collectorate: "The fact as represented by the Collector & Register of Poona that Punchayets are less resorted to than formerly is the natural consequence whenever there is much business & respectable tribunals of easy access to apply to, & where a native resorts to an European Judge or other officer for justice, it is to be presumed that a Punchayet or other mode of adjustment was not acceptable, or he would have assembled one of his [own] accord."[53] The data certainly confirm this general assessment. Nearly 77 percent of all cases adjudicated in the "old Bombay" and Deccan collectorates between 1819 and 1827 were decided in the British courts.

The judicial records also reveal high rates of litigation, much higher than were prevalent in Maharashtra during the last decade of the twentieth century. Between 1823 and 1827, the litigation rate in the "old Bombay" and Deccan collectorates was an estimated 9.5 per thousand. The last modern reliable calculation for Maharashtra was 3.5 per thousand in 1992. When placed in this historical context, therefore, the so-called litigation explosion of the modern era is certainly much more apparent than real.

The transfer of power from the Maratha Peshwa inevitably caused a great deal of social and economic disruption and it may very well be that this is what contributed to the large number of cases that came before the courts and panchayats during this period. However, the pronounced trend to avoid panchayat justice suggests that the desire for a speedy and summary form of justice among litigants was prized more than what the Orientalists constructed as "native custom." British

[52] MSA, EIC, Judicial Department, Civil and Criminal Judicature, Vol. 9/9, 1822, Extract from a Report from the Commissioners in the Deccan dated the 5th November [1821] (paras 58 to the end) transferred from the Revenue Department with Enclosures. No. 20 @ 36A, 24 January 1822.

[53] MSA, EIC, Governor in Council to William Chaplin, Judicial Department, Annual and Periodical Reports, Vol. 3/83, 1825, 14 June 1825. Interestingly, the phrase "it is to be presumed that a Punchayet or other mode of adjustment was not acceptable, or he would have assembled one of his accord" was edited out of the final letter.

officials were probably correct in their assumption that improved access to justice was in part responsible for the large number of cases on their files. However, the cases adjudicated in the local courts also point to a readiness to adapt to changing institutional structures and a decided preference for a system that emphasized enforcement rather than the retention of "customary" forms of adjudication.

3

APPEALS AND THE LANGUAGE OF PETITIONING

From the beginning of his rule in the Deccan territory of the Bombay Presidency, Mountstuart Elphinstone had sought to severely limit appeals from panchayats. In his *Report on the Territories Conquered from the Paishwa*, he claimed that this was necessary in order to ensure the "purity" of the panchayat. That is, Elphinstone believed that village panchayats had functioned autonomously within India's ancient constitution and had to be restored to that position. Therefore, he permitted appeals only in cases in which a litigant claimed that the panchayat's award had been a gross error or corruption was alleged. The regional Collectors, he wrote, "ought on no account to go into an enquiry in any ordinary case, merely because the Punchayet appear to him to have decided erroneously; the object of this appeal being rather to watch over the purity of the Courts than to amend their decisions."[1]

However, like the other village panchayat rules, these restrictions had unintended consequences. In particular, some British officials after 1820 began to blame them for the apparent failure of the panchayat system in general. While appeals were allowed in all cases in the other British law courts in the Presidency, they argued, the limits placed upon appeals from village panchayats only served to deter litigants from using them. Others argued that, as an institution of judicature, restrictions upon appeals from panchayats were an obvious injustice. Elphinstone and several of his most prominent Collectors, however, continued to

[1] Mountstuart Elphinstone, *Report on the Territories Conquered from the Paishwa* (Calcutta, 1821), p. 101.

defend them, especially with regard to village panchayats. In the towns, on the other hand, the constantly growing backlog of cases in the British courts led Company officials to eventually lift these restrictions in an attempt to lighten the caseload of the urban *amins*, Native Commissioners, and other judicial officials. However, that plan had barely been put into effect when, in 1827, the entire experiment was abandoned and the panchayat relieved of almost all of its adjudicatory functions.

Naturally, appeals required petitioning the Court or the Collector and his subordinates for a review of the case. The act of petitioning inevitably placed the appellant in a subordinate position, necessitating the adoption of standard tropes of supplication and deference. From among the relatively few petitions for review of panchayat awards that survive, however, noticeable differences are apparent in the rhetoric of appeals, differences that reveal how the petition was used in often unsubtle ways to attack opponents, supersede local authority, and, in fact, to justify the appellant's efforts to resist subordination.[2] When read in this manner, petitions for appeals from the panchayat are much less about the adoption of modes of deference and much more about the assertion of rights and privileges.

As noted in the previous chapter, the judicial system of the Bombay Presidency, in effect, was a divided one. While Elphinstone had used the recently conquered territories in the Deccan as a laboratory for the panchayat experiment, in the older territories, justice was administered through the system of Company courts established in the eighteenth century. Consequently, there were two possible avenues of appeal applying to different types of panchayats. In the Deccan, appeals from village and town civil panchayats on the grounds of gross error or corruption went primarily to the *amin*, *munsif*, or Native Commissioner and, very unusually, ultimately to the divisional Collector. In addition, these judicial officials were given authority to convene their own panchayats to hear the appeal, if they so desired.

In the older Bombay territories, where the panchayat system in civil cases had not been re-established, civil panchayats had no legal

[2] For an insightful account of petitioning in the Madras Presidency, see Bhavani Raman, *Document Raj: Writing and Scribes in Early Colonial South India* (Chicago: University of Chicago Press, 2012), Ch. 6.

standing. Nevertheless, appeals could be heard from caste panchayats, whose authority was ultimately subject to the jurisdiction of the Court of Appeals (*sadr diwani adalat*), commonly referred to as the "sudder court."[3] In unusual cases, appeals might be made to the Governor or even taken to the Privy Council in London. However, these caste panchayats were considered to be self-governing corporate entities and largely exempt from government interference. Thus it was usually only upon appeal that they were brought into the formal system of British judicature. Although caste panchayats in the old Bombay territories are beyond the purview of this study, in the analysis of appeals they provide an added dimension to an understanding of the complex relationship between British colonial justice and the panchayat.

Given the fact that there were significant restrictions on the necessary grounds for appeals from panchayats in the Deccan, it is not surprising that they were very uncommon. Some data survive for the years 1824 and 1825. Unfortunately, it was recorded differently in those two years and in formats that are not directly comparable. Moreover, the surviving data from the former year are much more comprehensive than that for 1825. Nevertheless, Tables 3.1 and 3.2 can provide a sense of the small number of appeals that were referred to the Collector and his judicial agents in the Deccan. Table 3.1 includes data of the total cases decided by all courts during 1824 in order to provide a sense of the scale of panchayat justice. The data in Table 3.2, on the other hand, are more restricted and place panchayat appeals within the context of total appeals from all courts.

Certainly, the most notable fact to be derived from Tables 3.1 and 3.2 is that the majority of panchayat appeals cases came out of Pune. In 1824, this amounted to 56 of 59 cases and, in 1825, 156 of 256 appeals. It is not unreasonable to assume that this was because Pune residents had easier access to justice and a more plentiful supply of pleaders (*vakils*) to appeal their cases, but this is not how British officials explained it. Harry Borradaile, the judicial Register at Pune, who was employed by the Collector to investigate and report on the causes of delay in panchayat cases, maintained that the rules against most appeals were practically unknown to litigants and there were no pecuniary hurdles that limited or hindered them. "It being a principle strongly inculcated," he wrote, " that no decree of a Punchayet ought to be reversed, unless evidently corrupt or very erroneous. I need only

[3] On caste and *jati*, see Susan Bayly, *Caste, Society and Politics in India from the Eighteenth Century to the Modern Age* (Cambridge: Cambridge University Press, 1999), p. 215.

TABLE 3.1 Total cases decided and panchayat appeals in the Deccan, 1824

Division	Total cases decided	Decided by panchayat	Appeals	Decided by "superior" Panchayat	Confirmed	Reversed
Ahmednagar	8,184	222	3	0	0	0
Candeish	3,398	100	0	0	0	0
Carnatic	9,445	493	0	0	0	0
Pune	9,533	459	56	11	6	5

Source: IOR/L/PJ/3/917, Judicial Letters from Bombay, 1823–1827, *Statement of Original Suits on the File on the 1st January 1824, the number instituted in the twelve following months to the 31st December 1824, and disposed of within that period with the arrears on the 1st January 1825; Statement of Appeals from the Decrees of Registers and of Native Commissioners in arrears preferred from the 1st January to the 31st December 1824, and disposed of within that period*, pp. 401–2.

TABLE 3.2 Panchayat appeals in the Deccan, 1825

Division	Total number of appeals	Appeals from panchayats	% of total appeals
Ahmednagar	12	0	0.0
Candeish	35	5	14.3
Dharwar	53	19	35.8
Pune	156	30	19.2

Source: MSA, EIC, Judicial Department, Annual and Periodical Reports, Vol. 3/83, 1825.

observe that this rule appears to be quite unknown to the Natives, who seem to think an appeal a matter of course and almost invariably resort to it. This appears to be owing to their natural unwillingness to part with their money, until they are absolutely obliged to do so. It is also assisted by the facility given to Appellants, as no security is required, and the Decree is generally allowed to remain unexecuted until the final decision is given in Appeals."[4]

[4] IOR/F/4/837/22427, Board's Collections, "Extract from Revenue Consultations connected with the Commissioners report of the 10 August 1822 – not included in the Judicial Consultations," pp. 34–7.

Like Borradaile, the Commissioner of the Deccan, William Chaplin, explained that the number of appeals from panchayats was in part due to the fact that appellants either did not know of or understand the new rules. In 1822, he wrote, "no time has been limited after which appeals are not received, because it was conceived that the ignorance of the natives regarding our System rendered a considerable latitude necessary until they should become better acquainted with our modes of proceeding."[5] However, the Collector of Pune, H. D. Robertson, was much less charitable. He argued that the "indolence" of respectable men led panchayats to be comprised of poorer and less qualified members who often sought the patronage of one or the other litigants. This circumstance, he suggested, inevitably created the basis for many improper decisions that merited appeal:

> The unwillingness of respectable men to sit in Punchayets, because it interferes with their indolence and *other* pursuits, is certainly a heavy obstacle, and one that cannot be easily removed. The tardy method of investigation to which they were accustomed in former times, contrasted with the speedy decisions insisted upon now, in a considerable degree explains their present backwardness. While those men who consent to sit are generally of a needy description, claiming the attention of men of consideration without the means of supporting the expense attendant on their pretentions [*sic*]. Hence numerous appeals and many of them well grounded on gross injustice, from the decisions of the Poona Punchayets.[6]

Outside of the Pune collectorate, complaints about appeals from panchayats were much less common. In Dharwar, for example, the panchayat system worked so well that the province was initially exempted from the general abandonment of panchayats under the 1827 Elphinstone Code.[7] In Khandesh, Captain John Briggs complained of the "total inefficiency" of the Native Commissioners who were authorized to convene panchayats if they deemed it necessary, but there were only five appeals from panchayats there in 1824 and 1825.[8] In Ahmednagar, the entire British

[5] IOR/P/368/34, Bombay Revenue Proceedings, "From the Commissioner in the Deccan," 20 August 1822, pp. 1337–8.

[6] MSA, EIC, Judicial Department, Annual and Periodical Reports, Vol. 3/83, 1825, Robertson to William Chaplin, 19 November 1824.

[7] IOR/F/4/1425/56221, Board's Collections, "Dharwar: Report of the Judicial Visiting Commissioner of Circuit on that Zillah in continuation of his Report on the Deccan under 18 March '31," pp. 15–17.

[8] IOR/P/368/34, Bombay Revenue Proceedings, "From the Commissioner in the Deccan," 20 August 1822, pp. 1322–3. Briggs also noted that the entire region had been very slow to recover from the depredations of war and famine during the previous years.

system of justice had got off to a rather shaky start and, as late as 1822, the Commissioner of the Deccan observed that the panchayat system there had not yet been successfully implemented.[9] Only three appeals from panchayat awards were recorded there in 1824 and 1825.

Therefore, as British administrators continued to refine and reform the system of justice in the Deccan, Pune garnered much of their attention.[10] In particular, there was growing concern that the panchayats in Pune were not doing enough to relieve the British administration of its judicial burdens. The panchayats, it was reported in 1825, "are less resorted to in Poona than formerly & that the proportion of them in the Town is less than the half of what it is in the Districts."[11] Robertson, the Collector of Pune, was, in fact, quite remarkable for his use of statistical data to evaluate the panchayat. He calculated that during the second half of 1824 "all the decisions of Punchayets are to the decisions of other functionaries as 1 to 7.28 but that this proportion is divided in regard to the City into 1 to 11.18 and to the Country into 1 to 5.43. That is the demand or necessity for justice by Punchayets in the Pergunnas is more than double of that in the City of Poona."[12]

The Pune Collector maintained a staff of six *amins* to deal specifically with the town's caseload.[13] They possessed the authority to refer suits to a panchayat, but only upon the mutual consent of the litigants. However, the Collector and his Register, a judicial office first created in 1822 and intended to relieve the Collector of his judicial business, were not pleased with their performance.[14] Chaplin reported that "one or two seem to be respectable but on the whole the character of their proceeding does not stand very high in the public estimation." Moreover, he noted having received "many complaints of wrongous [*sic*], or arroneous [*sic*] decisions, which I refer to the local authorities for

9 IOR/P/368/34, Bombay Revenue Proceedings, "From the Commissioner in the Deccan," 20 August 1822, pp. 1331–3.

10 Chaplin was especially concerned about the backlog of cases in Pune. See IOR/Mss Eur F 88/207, Elphinstone Papers, Chaplin to Elphinstone, 3 February 1821.

11 MSA, EIC, Judicial Department, Annual and Periodical Reports, Vol. 3/83, 1825, William Chaplin to David Greenhill, 18 May 1825.

12 MSA, EIC, Judicial Department, Annual and Periodical Reports, Vol. 3/83, 1825, Robertson to Chaplin, 26 February 1825.

13 MSA, EIC, Judicial Department, Annual and Periodical Reports, Vol. 3/83, 1825, Chaplin to Greenhill, 18 May 1825.

14 Registers and later Assistant Registers were first appointed in Pune, Ahmednagar, and Dharwar. See IOR/F/4/836/22425, Board's Collections, "Extract Bombay Judicial Consultations," 17 April 1822.

investigation. Several have in consequence been reversed, and some annulled."[15]

According to British judicial officers, the resolution of cases referred to panchayats by the Pune *amins* was plagued by the more general problems of delay in the selection of members and the sluggishness of the proceedings. However, in Pune, there was one additional complication. British judicial officials reported that their greatest difficulty lay in finding suitable inhabitants of the town to serve on panchayats. As a result, panchayats often fell into the hands of "professional" members who undertook the service as a way to collect bribes and other gratuities. Thus R. K. Arbuthnot, Borradaile's successor as Register of Pune, reported, "respectable people may be induced to try the cause of a particular friend as a personal favor, if he has no other mode of redress, but I do not think that even a pecuniary remuneration, would induce them, to be continually called upon to arbitrate the causes of indifferent persons." The consequence was, he wrote,

> if we insist on giving punchaits, the members of them are generally composed of Idle men without any Character, who are glad of the opportunity of making a subsistence in this way, and who in fact become more the advocates to plead the cause before the Sir Punch than the judges who try it. I have no hesitation in affirming that this will be more the case every day, as the people feel themselves independent and instances are even now constantly occurring where person[s] absolutely refuse to become members of Punchait.[16]

In October 1825, however, a chance remark from Chaplin led to a quite significant change. He noted in a letter to David Greenhill, the Secretary to Government in Bombay, that it had been suggested to him that one way to encourage the use of panchayats in Pune was to lift the ban on appeals in cases other than for gross error or corruption. Lifting the ban might encourage not only more litigants to use panchayats but also more people to serve on them. Corruption and gross error being the only two charges subject to appeal, if there were more avenues of appeal, then members of panchayats might be less afraid of being summoned before the British courts by a disgruntled litigant to explain their findings. As Chaplin put it, "It has been thought that suitors

[15] IOR/P/368/34, Bombay Revenue Proceedings, "From the Commissioner in the Deccan," 20 August 1822, pp. 1346–7.

[16] MSA, EIC, Judicial Department, Annual and Periodical Reports, Vol. 3/83, 1825, R. K. Arbuthnot to Captain H. D. Robertson 14 August 1824.

would more readily resort to Punchayets if not thereby deprived of the power of appeal, and on the other hand that members would be less averse to sit when it ceased to be the interest of either party to accuse them of gross error or corruption."[17]

Chaplin himself thought the idea misguided. He explained that opening panchayat awards to all types of appeal would undermine its customary authority in the countryside. Referring to the adage *panch parmeshwar*, variously translated as "God speaks through the panch" or "God is in the panch," he argued that it was only in the cities that the panchayat had broken down. Allowing all types of appeals, he wrote,

> would in my opinion tend to bring Punchayets *in the Country*, where they are still well conducted & respected, into disrepute for it is usual to call the decision of the Punj the decision of the deity which ought not to be set aside. It is in large Towns only such as Poona where all the difficulties of the Punchayet System are most felt, where the System is much abused, and where in consequence none but professional persons can be found to sit as members.[18]

Nevertheless, the idea was quickly taken up by Elphinstone, who appended a note to Chaplin's letter supporting the idea. By the beginning of the next month, November 1825, the plan was already being implemented. Restrictions on appeals from panchayats were lifted "in large towns such as Poona, or places specified by the Commissioner."[19] Eventually, the order was clarified to extend to all towns with a Resident British Magistrate.[20] Moreover, in order to further facilitate the use of panchayats, *amins* were also permitted to accept the award of the panchayat's majority rather than the customary unanimous judgment, although there seems to be some discrepancy on this point.[21]

However, the effect of these reforms and restructuring is extremely difficult to evaluate. As previously noted, by January 1826 Elphinstone

[17] MSA, EIC, Judicial Department, New Judicial Code Deccan, Vol. 11/95, 1825, Chaplin to Greenhill 7 October 1825.

[18] MSA, EIC, Judicial Department, New Judicial Code Deccan, Vol. 11/95, 1825, Chaplin to Greenhill 7 October 1825. Emphasis in original.

[19] IOR/F/4/865/22813 (3), Board's Collections, D. Greenhill to G. W. Anderson, Esq., 3 November 1825.

[20] MSA, EIC, Judicial Department, Annual and Periodical Reports, Vol. 3/83, 1825, Robertson to Chaplin, 9 November 1825; see also, MSA, EIC, Deccan New Judicial Arrangement, Vol. 10/136, 1827, Secretary to Government to G. W. Anderson, Judge of Poona, 4 January 1827.

[21] I have not been able to locate any government-issued order to this effect, but it certainly was the practice of at least one judge stationed at Dindori. See MSA, EIC, Judicial Department, Annual and Periodical Reports, Vol. 1/127, 1827, William Charmier to Saville Marriot, 24 April 1827.

had already admitted that the British panchayat experiment in the Deccan, except Dharwar, had been a failure and had begun to plan the extension of British courts of justice there. Moreover, the surviving data do not lend themselves to distinguishing panchayat appeals from appeals from the decisions of *amins*, *munsifs*, Native Commissioners, Registers, and Assistant Registers. Some anecdotal evidence seems to suggest that the new urban panchayats functioned more in accordance with British demands for speed and efficiency, especially when a unanimous decision was no longer required.[22] Nevertheless, in 1830, Chaplin, referring to his personal observation of panchayats in Pune, testified before a Select Committee of the House of Lords, "there were considerable delays and difficulties in getting the members [of panchayats] of large towns to assemble. I do not think it so well calculated for large towns as for the country."[23]

Regardless of its successes or failures, the introduction of the so-called Elphinstone Code in September 1827 disestablished the panchayat system almost in its entirety. The jurisdiction of the *sadr diwani adalat* was extended to the entire Presidency and six district (*zilla*) courts were established. Upon the request of a district court Judge, the Governor-in-Council could also appoint both Assistant Judges and Native Commissioners to assist them in their work. The new district courts were given jurisdiction over most of the matters formerly tried by the panchayat, including debts, contracts, rents, marriage, succession, moveable and immoveable property, and damages for personal injuries.[24] In addition, village boundary disputes, which panchayats previously had heard, were now to be resolved instead by a commission of civil servants appointed by the Governor-in-Council.[25] As part of these wholesale judicial reforms, the rules regarding appeals were revised with the obvious intent of limiting their numbers. Appeals from lower-level Assistant Judges and Native Commissioners were permitted to the senior *zilla* Judge. However, appeals from the *zilla* Judge to the *sadr diwani adalat* were allowed only if the initial decision had been modified or reversed, but not if it had been confirmed.[26]

22 MSA, EIC, Judicial Department, Annual and Periodical Reports, Vol. 1/127, 1827, William Charmier to Saville Marriot, 24 April 1827.

23 PP, *Report from the Select Committee of the House of Lords Appointed to Inquire into the Present State of the Affairs of the East India Company* (1830), p. 184.

24 PP, *Papers Relating to East India Affairs: viz. Regulations Passed by the Governments of Bengal, Fort St. George, and Bombay, in the Year 1827* (1829), Regulation II, Chp. II, § XXI, p. 63.

25 PP, *Papers Relating to East India Affairs*, Regulation X, Chp. I, § I, p. 138.

26 PP, *Papers Relating to East India Affairs*, Regulation IV, Chp. XVI, § LXXII, p. 99.

The only remnant of the judicial panchayat that remained in the Bombay Code after 1827 was in the form of an investigatory body to aid in a Judge's decision.[27] British Judges were granted the authority to convene panchayats composed of "respectable natives" and to refer to them either individual issues or an entire lawsuit for their advice. The panchayat so appointed carried on their inquiries separate from the court and reported its results in writing. The judge, however, was in no way bound to accept their advice and the court's ultimate decision was vested solely in the presiding British judge. Moreover, the term "panchayat" also continued to be used to refer to the settlement of disputes through English-style voluntary arbitration.[28] However, the vast array of procedural reforms introduced, including, for example, the execution of formal deeds of reference and awards, made arbitral panchayats less like their imagined informal precursors and much more like the evolving forms of arbitration under court aegis in contemporary England.[29]

It may seem paradoxical, but more substantive information regarding appeals from panchayats survives in the older Bombay provinces, where the British civil courts were of longer standing and panchayats were never incorporated into the formal judicial structure. There, as we have seen, the *sadar diwani adalat* had been established in 1799 to hear appeals from the *zilla* courts. The reports of cases heard before the *sadr diwani adalat* were compiled by Harry Borradaile upon the orders of Elphinstone.[30] Of the 185 case reports, approximately 23 refer either to the employment of panchayats at sometime during the case history or involve a panchayat directly as plaintiff or defendant. Unfortunately, this number must only be an approximate one. The reports not only often obscure the distinction between references to panchayats and references to arbitration but the court also occasionally canvassed an

[27] PP, *Papers Relating to East India Affairs*, Regulation IV, Chp. VI, § XXIV, p. 89.

[28] PP, *Papers Relating to East India Affairs*, Regulation VII, p. 121.

[29] On arbitration in England, see Henry Horwitz and James Oldham, "John Locke, Lord Mansfield, and Arbitration During the Eighteenth Century," *Historical Journal*, Vol. 36, No. 1 (March 1993), pp. 137–59.

[30] It has been suggested that the reports were compiled in preparation for the 1827 Elphinstone Code; see, Hiroyuki Kotani, "The 'Caste Autonomy' Policy in the Nineteenth-century Bombay Presidency," in H. Kotani, ed., *Western India in Historical Transition: Seventeenth to Early Twentieth Centuries* (New Delhi: Manohar Publishers, 2002), pp. 86–111. There is, however, no direct evidence to support this conclusion. In fact, the Company ordered Elphinstone to dismiss Borradaile because they saw no reason to employ him for this purpose; see, IOR/E/4/1048, Bombay Despatches, 8 July–8 December 1827, 3 December 1827. Instead, the 1822 investigations referred to by Kotani resulted in the following year's reforms that limited the jurisdiction of panchayats and introduced the *munsifs*.

TABLE 3.3 Panchayat cases before the *Sadr Diwani Adalat*, 1800–1824

Type of case	Number of cases	Average value (Rs.)
Contract	3	1,182
Debt	2	1,254
Property	10	33,088
Caste (damages)	6	1,819
Marriage	1	1,600
Wages	1	3,391

Source: Harry Borradaile, *Reports of Civil Causes Adjudged by the Court of Sudur Udalut, for the Presidency of Bombay, between the Years A. D. 1800 and A. D. 1824* (Bombay, 1825).

entire caste upon questions relating to customs and practices.[31] In some ways, the court's act of canvassing might be considered a type of reference to a panchayat; however, it may also be understood as a Western "democratic" innovation. Therefore, those cases have not been considered strictly as a reference to a panchayat.

Table 3.3 illustrates the types and average value of cases in which panchayats had played a role in a case's history prior to coming before the *sadr* court. Of course, the average values here sometimes masked significant discrepancies. For example, in property cases, the suits ranged in value from Rs. 32 to a claim for the restitution of an entire village valued at Rs. 100,000. In addition, of the three cases involving contracts, no damages were entered in two of them, the plaintiffs instead requesting performance of the agreement.

Not surprisingly, the cases that tended to make their way to the *sadr diwani adalat* were most often those involving significant amounts of money or property. Several of the property cases involved hereditary claims to land while many of the marriage cases concerned the disposition of jewels and other family treasures. However, for our purposes, the

[31] Significant work has already been done on the high court's policy toward caste issues, which, in general, favored "caste autonomy," to use Hiroyuki Kotani's phrase, except in cases of malice, violence, or ill-will. However, as Amrita Shodhan has also shown, while the court may have preferred to permit castes to follow their own customary laws, when these practices became a matter of dispute the court did not hesitate to seek outside assistance in order to judge what was and was not custom. See Kotani, "The 'Caste Autonomy' Policy" and Amrita Shodhan, "Caste in the Judicial Courts of Gujarat, 1800–60," in E. Simpson and A. Kapadia, eds., *The Idea of Gujarat: History, Ethnography and Text* (Hyderabad: Orient BlackSwan, 2010), pp. 32–49.

most interesting cases were those directly involving a panchayat either as the plaintiff or the defendant. The case for wages noted in Table 3.3, for example, was an appeal by the entire caste panchayat of over 400 *Kunbi* sari weavers against a decision of the lower *zilla* court.[32] The suit had been instituted by Lala Joita to recover ten years' worth of wages from the caste. Prior to the suit being lodged, eleven members of the panchayat had signed an acknowledgment (*sammeedustkhut*) of the "justness of the claim", and the lower court subsequently held that these members were then personally liable for the debt of more than Rs. 3,300. The eleven members then appealed, claiming that the entire caste panchayat should be held responsible for the payment of the back wages. However, the caste submitted a statement asserting, "these persons had no authority to act on the part of the Punchayut." The court affirmed the lower court's ruling, declaring "they, and they alone, must be held liable to make good to him the amount of the debt."

The sari weavers' case illustrates the way not only in which panchayats found themselves before the British civil courts but also in which panchayats themselves could become fractured and contentious institutions. A similar case involving the Broach indigo makers and dyers, however, revealed the limits to which the courts were willing to go to restrict the panchayat's autonomy.[33] In this case, Bhaeechund Bhikaree sued the panchayat for Rs. 150 in damages resulting from his expulsion from the indigo dyers' caste. Bhaeechund, who was also a member of the caste panchayat, had long been at odds with its other members. He had previously lodged both civil and criminal complaints against them in a dispute regarding the imposition of fines for breaking the caste's trading rules (*bandobasts*). Their dispute came to a head when Bhaeechund refused to attend a meeting of the panchayat, telling the members "he would neither join them in mourning nor marriage, nor in any thing else, nor permit them to attend him on those occasions at his own house." In early 1821, therefore, the panchayat refused to invite Bhaeechund to a funeral feast.

At the initial hearing, the local Assistant Register found that the panchayat had expelled Bhaeechund and he ordered the panchayat to readmit him. For their part, the panchayat claimed that Bhaeechund

[32] Harry Borradaile, *Reports of Civil Causes Adjudged by the Court of Sudur Udalut, for the Presidency of Bombay, between the Years A. D. 1800 and A. D. 1824* (Bombay, 1825), App. No. 24, pp. 390–1.

[33] Borradaile's *Reports*, No. 84, pp. 434–40.

had actually renounced his caste because of his "dislike to certain articles of a Bundobust, or Set of Bye Laws drawn up by the Jumaut for the Regulation of their Trade." Other witnesses, however, testified that Bhaeechund had been "turned out of Cast because he would not carry on business with them, and continued to trade by himself." The Assistant Register, who was provided with a copy of the *bandobast*, decreed that the rules did not include a penalty specifying expulsion, and therefore Bhaeechund must be readmitted.

On appeal to the *zilla* court, the Judge once again reviewed the *bandobast* and inquired of the Hindu law officers whether any group had the right to enforce its own *bandobast*. The *shastris* advised him that they did, and the Judge overturned the Register's decision on the grounds that every private group had the common right to regulate its own members. Moreover, the Judge used the broadest language in support of the authority of the panchayat, which is worth quoting at length:

> The Cast must be presumed to be the best Judges of their own interests, and as this combination excluded no individual from participating and sharing in common the mutual benefit, profit, or loss, experienced by the collective body, the Court was of opinion that the act of the Majority, grounded upon equality of right and privilege, and contested solely by one dissenting Member of the Punchayut, ought not to be interfered with, unless some specific proof of the existence of oppression or other exercise of arbitrary power were distinctly set forth. In the present instance, the Cast had merely exerted a right common to all classes, that of adopting a system of procedure in their opinion most likely to benefit the general Body, and to which they invited the whole of its members, without any reservation or exception. It would from hence follow that no blame could attach to the Cast relative to the execution of the Bundobust – The only question remaining to be disposed of, was whether their line of conduct in enforcing expulsion in the present instance, was justifiable by Law; in other Terms, whether any offence cognizable by the Punchayut had been committed justifying the severity of the Punishment. The Law Officers had declared the acts of the whole Cast conclusive and binding on Appellant, on the ground of his being the only dissenting member, The only control which could be exercised over Casts by a Court of Justice was the awarding damages to the Party injured or oppressed, but it would be manifestly both impolitic and unjust to interfere on every occasion more especially in a case of mere controversy of opinion. Although a general superintendence is vested in the Courts for the due preservation and protection of the rights and

> privileges of every part of the community, yet still it was far from desirable that every refractory member of a Punchayut should at will make the Udalut the Arbitrary instrument of forcing a large body of men into his own views and interests. For these reasons the present action was dismissed as not tenable on the plea of either Equity, Justice, or Policy, and the Register's Decree was reversed, the Cast and Appellant being left at liberty to carry on the trade in any way they might think most conducive to their several interests.

Upon appeal to the *sadr diwani adalat*, the sitting Judge, E. Ironside, expressed serious reservations about the *zilla* court's ruling. He argued not only that the Judge had allowed a "most cruel and severe" punishment to be imposed upon Bhaeechund but that he had also overreached his authority when interpreting the terms of the *bandobast*. He therefore forwarded the case to the full court for decision. Unfortunately, there is no existing account of the full court's reasoning, but the court ultimately rejected Ironside's argument in its entirety, "seeing no just grounds for interfering with the decision of the Zilla Judge", and affirmed the *zilla* court's decision.

It has been argued that decisions such as this one indicate that the British courts followed a policy of "caste autonomy" during this period.[34] However, it is an odd sort of autonomous body that seeks support from external institutions and, in fact, often relies on those institutions to enforce its decisions and protect its interests. There is perhaps little value in constructing a new paradigm to define the relationship between the panchayat, caste or otherwise, and the British courts in these Regulation Provinces. While the courts may have preferred to relieve themselves of the burden of judging caste panchayat disputes, they nonetheless regularly supervised their decisions. If the panchayats in these regions were not wholly incorporated into the British judicial system, as they were in the Deccan, they were not wholly autonomous either. A policy of panchayat *laissez-faire*, as it were, was still a policy of governance and the courts reserved for themselves the authority to intervene when and where they saw fit to do so.

The examination of one final case may serve to further illustrate the courts' willingness to intervene in disputes involving the authority of panchayats. In September 1822, Henry Agar, the Collector of Sea Customs, sued three prominent members of the Surat silk-weavers and spinners' panchayat to recover back taxes owed on the community's

[34] Kotani, "The 'Caste Autonomy' Policy."

silk-wheels.[35] Agar claimed that as the heads of the community (*jamaat*), they "transacted all its affairs with Government, which knew none but them, and would look to them in this, as in all other business of the Jumaut, and not to individual members." The members of the panchayat, including two *patels*, declared that this had not been Company practice in the past. Previously, they had agreed only to point out tax-defaulters, who then were individually prosecuted by the Company in the courts.

The testimony in the case often obscured rather than illuminated the panchayat's role in the collection of taxes. One witness testified that the panchayat had always farmed out tax collection, another that the panchayat had previously been held responsible only for holding securities from the weavers and spinners, and yet another that the panchayat was responsible for making good the taxes owed only by those who had left the villages. Consequently, the *zilla* Judge decided that there was insufficient evidence to prove that the members of the panchayat were collectively responsible for the back taxes and "that it had been customary for the Patels of the Punchayut to point out the person with whom the Government balance rested, on being called on so to do." Agar then appealed to the *sadr diwani adalat* claiming that the panchayat had entered into the annual revenue agreement (*putta*) with the Collector and thus should be held collectively responsible for the uncollected taxes. The high court, however, brusquely dismissed the appeal, asserting that Agar's claim could "avail him nothing, as it merely shewed that a fixed annual tax was levied and the Patels determined how it was to be paid by each individual. This point therefore was declared not tenable."

As in this and the other cases involving panchayats in the Regulation Provinces, it is perhaps more appropriate to suggest that the courts were willing to carve out certain legal immunities rather than to grant them autonomy. Certainly, the courts consistently relied upon the advice of their *shastris* and frequently sought to uncover local customs and practices when making their decisions. However, the courts showed no obvious reluctance to entertain cases either directly involving panchayats or to hear appeals from their decisions. Like societies, clubs, and, later, trade unions in England, panchayats were possessed of no positive rights under the British judicial administration. Instead, they

[35] Borradaile's *Reports*, No. 105, pp. 548–53. The use of the term *jamaat* suggests that this case pertained to a community of Muslim spinners and weavers. However, the court records clearly indicate that the British understood members of the *jamaat* to be equivalent to *patels* and their form of organization equivalent to a *jati* panchayat.

were granted legal immunities to conduct their affairs as long as there was no "specific proof of the existence of oppression or other exercise of arbitrary power," as the Judge in the Broach indigo makers and dyers' case expressed it. The ultimate determination of what did or did not constitute "oppression," however, was retained by the British courts and thus made the panchayat ultimately subject to their authority.

Appeals cases necessarily involved the process of petitioning. Much historical work has been done in the West on the subject of petitioning; however, it has generally been focused on the petitions of groups or collectives of people to the government.[36] With few exceptions, personal petitions from individuals have received much less attention.[37] In one sense, personal petitions adopted many of the same rhetorical strategies as those delivered by a group. They testified to the magnificence, generosity, and benevolence of their superiors.[38] They often, but not always, sought mercy rather than demanding justice.[39] They almost invariably were "collaborative efforts" involving the intercession of lawyers, pleaders, translators, or other professionals.[40] In another sense, however, private petitions are unique. They relate tales of personal disputes, of fractured relationships with others, and of disappointments with the justice system. That they may be "fictionalized," in the sense in which the term is used by Natalie Zemon Davis, is undoubtedly true, but they also tell us much about the appellant's personal expectations regarding others as well as regarding their governors. As such, petitions can aid in the refinement of our understanding of the place of the panchayat in the social world of early nineteenth-century India, especially by illuminating the discourse of justice that petitioners brought to the presentation of their cases.

36 See, for example, Lex Heerma van Voss, ed., *Petitions in Social History*, International Review of Social History Supplements (Cambridge: Cambridge University Press, 2002); for the Indian case, see, Majid Siddiqi, *The British Historical Context and Petitioning in Colonial India* (Delhi: Aakar Books, 2005).

37 Notable exceptions include Natalie Zemon Davis, *Fiction in the Archives: Pardon Tales and their Tellers in Sixteenth-century France* (Stanford: Stanford University Press, 1987); Laura Bear, *Lines of the Nation: Indian Railway Workers, Bureaucracy, and the Intimate Historical Self* (New York: Columbia University Press, 2007), Ch. 5; and V. A. C. Gatrell, *The Hanging Tree: Execution and the English People, 1770–1868* (Oxford: Oxford University Press, 1994), Ch. 6.

38 Gatrell, *Hanging Tree*, p. 203; Lex Heerma van Voss, "Introduction," Heerma van Voss, ed., *Petitions in Social History*, pp. 2–3.

39 Davis, *Fiction in the Archives*, p. 11.

40 Davis, *Fiction in the Archives*, p. 5; Heerma van Voss, "Introduction," pp. 8–9.

Several of the surviving petitions adopt the grandiloquent but submissive language of that of Ponnjeabhaee Doshawbhoy in a dispute over the legitimate heir to an estate. A panchayat had initially awarded the estate to Ponnjeabhaee, but the award was overturned upon appeal to the *zilla* court. The *sadr diwani adalat* restored the original decision, but left Ponnjeabhaee to pay costs of nearly Rs. 3,800. Ponnjeabhaee subsequently appealed to Mountstuart Elphinstone, hoping to have the costs rescinded. He therefore applied to Elphinstone "with the utmost deference" and "most humbly beg your Majesty in Council will graciously be blessed to take the whole case into your Majesty's candid consideration and mercifully order the sum of three thousand seven hundred and ninety six Rupees for the cost and charges putted [*sic*] on your Petitioner may be freed."[41] Similarly, Moroo Ragoonath Dumdarah, whose father had died of cholera, appealed to Elphinstone after a panchayat decreed that he was liable for certain debts contracted by his father. "I humbly pray to grant me a Compassion," the petition states, "in consideration of my being a minor and supportless child of Dumdarah's family to recommend me to the Commissioner in the Deccan to grant me a rehearing where if I prove wrong after examining my papers and evidence – I shall plead no discord to pay any fine that will be inflicted on me."[42]

The rhetoric of submission and subordination, however, could be deployed in a number of ways, especially when it involved members of the traditional elite. Dadjee Appajee, the son of a principal minister in the government of the Gwaekar of Baroda who had been an ally of the British in the struggles there, for example, applied the language of subordination in his appeal to the Council in Bombay, but at the same time reminded the British of their obligations to him and his family. "I hope and trust," Dadjee wrote, "the liberty I have taken in soliciting your Honble Board's kind intercession will be pardoned. I have been urged to it by a sense of the liberality of your Honble Board to your humble subjects, and by the promise which the Honble the Governor made to my father, during the treaty for the delivery of the Fort, and to me, after my father's death, that my character should not be prejudiced or calumniated."[43]

41 MSA, EIC, Judicial Department, Appeals, Vol. 4/84, "The humble Petition of Ponnjeabhaee Doshawbhoy," 19 August 1825.

42 MSA, EIC, Civil Judicature, Diary 18D, Volume 23, 1823, pp. 137–9, Moroo Ragoonath Dumdarah to M. Elphinstone.

43 MSA, EIC, Judicial Department, Petitions, Vol. 12/96, "Petition of Dadjee Appajee, Severa Nisbut Chowdrey," 25 January 1825.

Other petitions eschewed the language of supplication almost entirely and presented a mere statement of facts. In a disputed inheritance case between two brothers brought before the Collector of Pune, for example, a panchayat was demanded to establish the rightful heir. The panchayat decided to divide the estate equally, upon which an appeal was lodged before Elphinstone. The petition catalogued each step of the judicial process, concluding with the statement that "Under these circumstances I beg to represent that my adversary Damother was not adopted nor was he acknowledged by the Paishwas Government or by the (deceased) owner to be the proprietor of the Estate &c. neither has any separation taken place between us yet notwithstanding this, he was declared to be the proprietor of the Estate &c. I now therefore prefer this Petition to you Honble. Sir in order that having examined the matter in your presence you may be pleased to order the half of the Estate to be given to me."[44]

There was one petition, however, in which supplicatory rhetoric was replaced almost entirely by pleas for justice. The case concerned a dispute over the restoration of hereditary estates (*watans*) to the accountants (*kulkarni*) of two villages that had been seized by the British in Ahmednagar. William B. Hockley, the Assistant Collector, initially restored the estates to them, but subsequently forced the *kulkarni* to re-submit their claim to a panchayat in an effort to extort money from them. Hockley, as shall be discussed in the next chapter, was eventually tried and convicted on charges of bribery and extortion and dismissed from the Company's service. Nevertheless, during the affair, the *kulkarni* petitioned Elphinstone for redress. Expressing their reluctance to appeal to Hockley's superior, Henry Pottinger, they wrote:

> As we should not obtain justice were we to apply to Captain Pottinger, we have come and presented this petition praying that you will have the goodness to take the evidence of Jameedars and Pandurees, and examine the papers and documents, and then order us to be allowed the possession of our wutun. Ever since the wutun was bestowed, our family have lived at Wagerey, whereas the opposite party has not resided there or had any thing to do with the place. Not withstanding this we have suffered the injustice complained of, and can only obtain redress from you.[45]

[44] IOR/P/399/58, Bombay Judicial Consultations, "Translation of a Petition from Narayen Damother Gupchoop Josee . . . Dated 2nd April 1826."

[45] MSA, EIC, Judicial Department, Civil Judicature, Vol. 10/11, "Translation of a petition from Panderong Krishnu and Lumkray Bullal Narsawey Koolkurnees of the Villages of Wajooray Boojoorg Khoord to the Honorable the Governor, Dahot the 7th Magsur Vud 1742 Lalbahan on

Regardless of the matter at issue, the petitions almost always bear evidence of the assistance of a legal intermediary and the attempt to adopt the legal language deemed suitable for such a document. These efforts, however, were extremely uneven and reveal not only the difficulties of translation into English but also the varied understandings of what constituted the proper legal language of their rulers. Some petitions indicate the work of someone who was experienced with British legal language and procedures. The petition of Dadjee Appajee, the son of the Gwaekar's minister, for example, complained, "if I fail to repair to Poonah, the Collector will decide exparte [*sic*] on my case."[46] In a separate case involving a forged note of security on a bill of exchange, the petitioner explained why he should not be held liable for monies disbursed on the strength of the forged note:

> The Question at issue he, in the mean while, referred for arbitration to one Atya Gooroojee, who having consulted with four merchants, came to the following decision – namely That as from a comparison of hand writing the note was an evident forgery, as moreover your Pet^r had warned Keshowraw of its being so, *before* the money was paid, and lastly, as there never had been any one named Gopall Pratunter, in the service of y^r Pet^r; he therefore was not at all bound to refund a sum, which Keshowraw had lost through his own imprudence.[47]

Other petitions, however, reveal a less secure grasp of English legal language but a determined attempt to mimic its abstruse content and style nonetheless. In one long sentence, the appellants tried to explain the basis of their appeal as follows:

> That in the year Hindoo anno 1874/75 the said respondent has been preferred a Complaint in the Court of Adawlut at Surat against your Majesty's appellants for an [*sic*] note dated Hindoo anno 1849 for Rupees 3,477.1.50 Principal named of Rupchund Khemchund Deceased, and Interest thereon 3,477.1.50 are the whole claims being Rupees 6,954.3 – which Justice has been Faithfully quotted [*sic*] by the Judge in the Court of Adawlut, wherein found on examination that the said respondents allegation not proved by proper Proofs on your Majesty's appellants, and the said Complaint dismissed with Costs & charges, because questioned to the said respondent by the Judges, that any such proper witnesses he

26th December 1820." A "jameedar" was a village officer who guarded the crops. "Pandurees," however, is much more obscure. It may refer to the residents of a neighboring village.

46 MSA, EIC, Judicial Department, Petitions, Vol. 12/96, "Petition of Dadjee Appajee."

47 MSA, EIC, Judicial Department, Civil Judicature, Vol. 6/63, Bappoo Dhondew to Mountstuart Elphinstone, 15 November 1824.

> had in this matter to prove on the Contrary, who then sayeth none any sufficient witnesses at all but In Case any one perhaps may be living at Poona because which transactions were made at that place therefore that said Respondent beg leave to request to the Judge that this disputed matter may refer on the arbitrators for their award, but your gracious Majesty's appellant was not consented to it, therefore the said Court of Adawlut dismissed aforesaid suit.[48]

Petitions from poorer appellants are necessarily extremely rare considering the fact that appeals had to be submitted on stamped paper and probably required the employment of a pleader (*vakil*) conversant in written English. One such appeal from Saobriah Bravund Bramny, an assistant to the registrar (*karkun*) of the bullock "contractory" of the Pune Division of the Army, does survive in the Company papers at the Maharashtra State Archives.[49] Saobriah earned Rs. 15 per month and after six years' employment wanted to return to his village. However, when he asked for his entire back pay, the master registrar claimed he was only owed half of the amount. Saobriah, who appears to have known enough English to either dictate this account or to write it himself, explained that when he asked his master for an explanation, "he replied, that is my please, I will give what I think proper, your humble petitioner answered, I will lodge a complaint against your honor. He replied your humble petitioner in abrupt manner you may lodge a complaint where you may think proper."

Saobriah duly lodged a complaint in Pune and was granted a panchayat in Seror, near Aurangabad. Before the panchayat had met, however, the Collector left Pune and Saobriah's master took the opportunity to lodge a separate complaint in Solapur. There, a separate panchayat was convened, which Saobriah attended bringing along with him all of his papers and accounts. When he appeared before this panchayat, he sought to submit his papers as evidence, but "the Punchayut said, they will not take no trouble about the papers, but they will settle it by word of mouth." Obviously angered, Saobriah's response revealed the often-hidden world of a justice system, including panchayat justice, that was inimical to the interests of the poor. In Saobriah's words, "your humble petitioner replied the Punchayut as the

[48] MSA, EIC, Judicial Department, Appeals, Vol. 2/58, *Bhouchund and Khooshalchund, Heirs to the estate of Reepchund Khemchund Deceased, appellants, v. Puntapchund Manuckchund, Respondent*, 7 January 1824.

[49] MSA, EIC, Judicial Department, Civil Judicature, Vol. 6/63, Saobriah Bravund Bramny to Mountstuart Elphinstone, 22 March 1823.

Punch don't take no notice of a poor man's cause and papers; I rejected the Punchayut, and said as they don't take no notice of my papers, I will not undercome [*sic*] their settlements or any arrangement that may be proposed by them."

In his address to Elphinstone, Saobriah reiterated the claim that the panchayat dispensed a rich man's justice while, at the same time, he incorporated his protest into the debasing language of supplication and submission. "Your humble petitioner," he wrote, "Master being a great and well situated person in all respect, therefore may have regard upon him, and your humble petitioner being a poor and miserable soul, they have paid no attention towards a poor man, and, illy [*sic*] treated in every part of the settlement." He concluded the petition by stating that he has been "in a distressed state for these last sixteen months, [on] this affair; therefore your humble petitioner humbly kneel and beg of your honor's favor to bring these few line [*sic*] into your kind consideration."

Although Saobriah's protest is unique, complaints and grievances against panchayats were necessarily common in appeals petitions. As has been argued, British administrators often focused upon their endemic delays, lack of attendance, or partiality and corruption, while British judges often considered caste panchayats to be the governing body of a private club or society, thereby granting them certain legal immunities from prosecution. Litigants, however, had their own separate grievances, the most common of which ultimately concerned the panchayat's inability to enforce its own awards and, as a result, the panchayat's reliance upon litigants' voluntary compliance to its decisions.

The panchayat's inability to proceed to enforcement led some litigants to seek an alternative outcome from a different panchayat. As we have already seen, this occurred in Saobriah's case when his master sought a panchayat in Solapur after a panchayat had been ordered to hear the case in Seror. A similar instance occurred in the case of Bappoo Dhondew, who was the appellant in the case regarding the allegedly forged security note on a bill of exchange.[50] In this case, the initial proceedings were somewhat irregular and combined aspects of both arbitration and panchayat justice. There, the Collector appointed a referee, Atya Gooroojee, to review the pertinent documents. Atya, however, then conferred with four other merchants before issuing an award creating what was, in effect, a type of panchayat.

[50] MSA, EIC, Judicial Department, Civil Judicature, Vol. 6/63, Dhondew to Elphinstone, 15 November 1824.

Six or seven months later, when Atya died, the award had still not been enforced and the respondent took the opportunity of Atya's death to appeal to the courts for a new panchayat. This time, the panchayat functioned in a more customary manner, being comprised of two members selected by the appellant, two by the respondent, and two "neutral" members appointed by the court. Unfortunately for Bappoo, the members of the panchayat appointed by the litigants failed to resolve the dispute and the panchayat became deadlocked. At this point, the Collector intervened, removed the case from the panchayat, and referred it to a *shastri* who ruled against Bappoo. Ultimately, Bappoo found himself in jail, dispossessed of his property, and fined Rs. 1,500.

Bappoo's case reveals a second common grievance. Appellants often noted that panchayats were unable to reach a decision, which, as the British understood earlier custom, was supposed to be unanimous. Instead, the members of deadlocked panchayats often resorted to issuing their own separate awards. In the inheritance case of Narayen Damother, for example, Narayen's petition noted, "the Collector required a written instrument from both parties to conform to the decision of the Punchayet an[d] a Surpunch (umpire) was nominated by that Gentleman after which the arbitrators of Sadasew Damother, and the Surpunch being of the same opinion made out an award declaring Sadasew Damother to be the proprietor of the Estate &c and to this award was affixed the signature of the Surpunch; on the other hand in the award which was drawn out by my arbitrators – I was declared to [be] the proprietor of the half Estate &c."[51] In a similar case regarding the inheritance of a debt, the petitioner explained, "The arbitrators ought to examine the cases of both parties before they come to determine a final decision which the arbitrators of Pandoorang Dumdarah did not and prepared an award exparty [*sic*] wherein they determined that I and Pandoorang was unitedly residing together. This award they given into the Adawlut without obtaining signatures of my arbitrators who however prepared another award by order of the Commissioner determining therein that I and Pandoorang had been divided by separation before the death of my father."[52] One litigant even offered to make provisions for such an outcome by suggesting that if the panchayat "will not be of one opinion and to

[51] IOR/P/399/58, Bombay Judicial Consultations, "Translation of a Petition from Narayen Damother Gupchoop Josee."

[52] MSA, EIC, Civil Judicature, Diary 18D, Vol. 23, Moroo Ragoonath Dumdarah to Elphinstone.

make two separate awards then they will with the consent of both party will chuse the umpire and by their hands get the award made."[53]

In several instances, there were complaints of undue or inappropriate interference on the part of British administrators or judges. This was most apparent in the cases brought before William Hockley, the Assistant Collector convicted of bribery and corruption. Hockley's interference in the proceedings of panchayats was blatantly corrupt by any standards, including extortion, packing of panchayats, and intimidation, but petitions for appeal that complained of British interference were not limited to his activities. Dadjee Appajee, for example, wrote of being "persecuted" by the Collector of Pune and thus suspected that he could not get an "impartial and unbiased" panchayat there. "Captain Robertson," he claimed, "has subjected me to a great many hardships, and will no doubt do all in his power to injure my character both in public and private, which, as it will lead to the entire ruin of my property and family, is tantamount to the destruction of my existence."[54]

In another petition submitted on behalf of an eleven-year-old heir, an appeal was made on the grounds that the Assistant Collector at Pune, Mr. Lumsden, had signed a panchayat award submitted by only one of the parties. "Having got both the parties to select their respective Punchs, (Arbitrators)," the petition stated, "written obligations were obtained to abide by such decisions as might be equitably passed on due enquiry, by 10 Arbitrators, and the Punchayet was set on foot accordingly; after which, the Arbitrators on the part of my adversary having prepared an exparte [*sic*] award, explained it to Mr. Lumsden, and obtained his signature to it, which award bears no signatures of my Arbitrators."[55]

Finally, in the Narayen Damother inheritance case, in which two awards were produced by the panchayat, the appellant argued that both the Collector and the Commissioner of the Deccan had ignored the award submitted by the members nominated by him. Instead, they had both approved the award of the respondent because it also carried the signature of the head of the panchayat, the *sarpanch*. "The Collector,"

[53] MSA, EIC, Judicial Department, Petitions, Vol. 12/96, "Translation of a Mahratta Letter to Captain Robertson dated 18th December 1824."

[54] MSA, EIC, Judicial Department, Petitions, Vol. 12/96, "Petition of Dadjee Appajee."

[55] MSA, EIC, Judicial Department, Appeals, Vol. 5/106, "Memorandum of Moro Ragoonath Dumdherey aged 11 Years Soor-sun-Sit-Ushur-Myantyn-ouluf (A. D. 1825/26)," 1 November 1825.

the petition claimed, "however without examining both awards, put his attestation to that one signed by the Surpunch, and delivered it to my adversary, and furnished me with a Copy – on which a Petition of appeal was delivered by me to the Commissioner and that Gentleman without examining both awards and without instituting an enquiry with regard to my petition of appeal rejected it at once declaring that there appeared no ground in my petition for granting an appeal against the decisions passed by the Collector."[56]

These are among the relatively few surviving petitions that refer to panchayats and it would be hazardous to make any over-broad generalizations based upon them. However, there are several recurring themes that characterize the appellants' grievances about panchayat justice under the British. Foremost among these perhaps was the often-implicit complaint that panchayat awards were not definitive. Because the panchayat lacked any independent authority to enforce its judgments, litigants were often confronted by multiple awards issued by different panchayats. Thus, the fact that during the colonial period litigants often engaged in "forum shopping" is not surprising.[57] Yet multiple panchayats involving a single dispute was an altogether different phenomenon that developed only because panchayats depended upon the litigants' voluntary compliance to their awards. This often entailed long delays or more often a refusal to perform the award, a situation that also provided the opportunity to request new panchayats at a later date or at a different venue.

For their part, the experiences of British judges and officials with appeals from panchayats varied widely. In the Deccan, which was not subject to the Company's official Regulations, Elphinstone's experiment severely limited appeals to only those complaints alleging gross error or corruption. As noted previously, Elphinstone and his supporters hoped that this limitation would restore the authority and preeminence of the panchayat in village society. One unintended consequence of this policy, however, was that litigants understandably preferred to take their case to a British court where appeals were not subject to those restrictions. Thus within five years of the experiment's implementation, reforms were already being introduced to allow appeals from panchayats in all cases in the larger towns and cities of the Deccan.

[56] IOR/P/399/58, Bombay Judicial Consultations, "Translation of a Petition from Narayen Damother."

[57] See, for example, Mitra Sharafi's "The Marital Patchwork of Colonial South Asia: Forum Shopping from Britain to Baroda," *LHR*, Vol. 28, No. 4 (November 2010), pp. 979–1009.

In the old Bombay territories subject to the Company's formal Regulations, the so-called Regulation Provinces, the legal system emulated English criminal and civil procedures. Nevertheless, because the Company courts allowed corporate bodies to exercise a significant degree of self-regulation, caste panchayats continued to survive there. However, the hand of the courts was not invisible. They reserved to themselves the authority to hear appeals on the decisions of these panchayats in cases alleging malicious or oppressive behavior, a standard that could be both broadly and narrowly interpreted. In this sense, it is appropriate to consider the panchayat as operating within a sphere of legal immunities, much as other corporate bodies in England did during the eighteenth and nineteenth centuries.

In all of the cases presented here, the emphasis has been placed on the norms and expectations of procedural, or adjectival, justice, expectations that often went unarticulated but were extremely important nonetheless. Panchayats, however, were expected to dispense substantive justice as well, a perception that is much more difficult to define and assess. It is to this subject that we now turn.

4

THE CONSTRUCTION OF PANCHAYAT LEGALITY

Did the panchayat deliver substantive justice? This is not an unfair question, although it cannot be answered without resolving several more profound issues. How is justice to be defined? Is it procedural or distributive? Is it social or individual? Is it rational or sentimental? It would be very unwise for this author to attempt to answer those questions in their broadest philosophical meanings. However, in the smaller but no less perfect world of the historian, some sense of the multiple meanings of substantive justice in the panchayat can be elicited from the participants themselves. The previous chapter has already given some indication of this. However, the voices described there were necessarily distorted by the customary forms and structures of the act of petitioning. In this chapter, we seek a different perspective, a perspective derived largely from the testimony of witnesses and litigants given before and about panchayats. Of course, these voices were not unmediated either. Like the petition, this testimony was structured, but the structures were of a different nature. Testimonies were guided and directed by members of the panchayat or British judges; questions were often specific and focused. Litigants and witnesses presumably had their own biases and actively participated in the process of "making a case." They also certainly brought to the fore their own perspectives on events, issues, and people. Such biases and perspectives, however, may very well aid rather than hinder us, for their testimonies can be read in a manner that reveals what they thought was just and unjust, what was fair and unfair, and what was right and wrong.

The standards of justice and fairness that litigants and witnesses brought with them before the panchayat were most clearly illuminated when those standards were violated. Then, people complained that that the ruling was "wrong," that the decision was "unfair," and that the award was "unjust." Obviously, this is not a matter of seeking the truth, but it is a matter of trying to uncover normative standards of justice within a particular institutional setting. Despite the enormous ideological burden that the panchayat was made to carry during the late nineteenth and into the twentieth centuries, especially as a privileged source of Indian democracy, the panchayat, when and where it was active, was nevertheless an institution of village and state governance. Thus, in the process of resolving disputes, the panchayat was expected to enforce norms of justice by chastising transgressors and punishing malefactors. When it obviously failed to do so, the foundations of those standards were most clearly revealed.

Panchayats, therefore, were an institution of governance, and in western India, under both the Marathas and the British they were, as we have seen, an especially legalistic one.[1] They required documentary evidence to establish the legitimacy of claims, including deeds, account books, wills, and the like. In turn, the panchayat itself was expected to produce several documents announcing their award and explaining their decision. The composition of panchayats was also significantly regularized. Most commonly, panchayats were supposed to be composed of an equal number of representatives selected by each party to negotiate a settlement. Often a "neutral" head of the panchayat was appointed by Maratha and, afterwards, British officials. Justice, therefore, was arrived at primarily through the interplay of interested parties rather than a disinterested Judge or arbitrator. Perhaps most importantly, the panchayat in civil matters was expected to be a voluntary institution. Although there were a variety of customary forms of "persuasion," such as the *tukaza*, litigants could not be legally compelled to attend or be physically dragged before a panchayat by the increasing numbers of village or town police.

[1] The two leading scholars on the panchayat in the post-Independence era have noted the variety of forms the panchayat has historically taken. See Upendra Baxi and Marc Galanter, "Panchayat Justice: An Indian Experiment in Legal Access," in M. Cappelletti and B. Garth eds., *Access to Justice: Vol. III: Emerging Issues and Perspectives* (Milan: Guiffre; Alphen aan den Rijn: Sijthoff and Noordhoff, 1979), pp. 341–6. On the Maratha panchayat procedures, see V. T. Gune, *The Judicial System of the Marathas* (Deccan College Post-Graduate and Research Institute, 1953), pp. 83–6.

Together, these aspects of the panchayat system helped to create a certain set of expectations that were essential to normative conceptions of justice among Indian litigants during this era. It is noteworthy, however, that litigants rarely appealed to substantive law to support their case. Instead, almost all existing complaints relate to matters of procedural, or adjectival, law. In a sense, this accords well with Elphinstone's imagining of the panchayat as an institution through which the "customs of the country" were adjudicated without recourse to the Hindu law codes. Admittedly, however, we will be left far short of answering the much broader question of what was considered abstract justice to those inhabiting a world comprised of British occupiers, Indian princes, merchant capitalists, village headmen, peasant families, religious diversity, and caste distinctions. Still, within the institutional setting of the panchayat, some preliminary answers can be suggested.

Although panchayats relied upon the production of a number of written documents, they were not courts of record in the English sense and there was no tradition of court reporting in western India. Thus there are extremely few instances in which court interrogatories, witness testimony, or other forms of oral evidence common to the western trial exist. However, in the early 1820s, the activities of an Assistant Collector in Ahmednagar, William Brown Hockley, came under the intense scrutiny of his superiors. Allegations had surfaced that Hockley had extorted bribes from panchayat litigants, packed panchayats, intimidated panchayat members, and engaged in other forms of corruption. The Company's investigation of these charges produced a substantial amount of documentary evidence, almost all of which related to his attempts to manipulate the panchayat system for personal gain.

The remainder of this chapter, therefore, will take the form of three case studies of Brown's interference in disputes heard before panchayats. All three cases concern property disputes evolving out of the transfer of power from the Maratha Peshwa to the British. The analysis of Brown's actions in these cases as well as the responses of both litigants and witnesses provides unique evidence of the normative standards by which the participants evaluated justice in the panchayat.

VEERAMKUR AND SINDEY DESMOOKH V. THE DESHMUKH OF WARRE

Hockley was an Assistant Collector stationed at Ahmednagar, approximately 150 miles east of Bombay. The province had been ceded to the

British by the Maratha Peshwa at the end of the third Anglo-Maratha War of 1817–1818. While Hockley's actions may have come under the scrutiny of Company officials at any other time, his malfeasance in office was considered to be especially serious, not only because it arose within the very first years of the British occupation of the Deccan, but also because it appeared to undermine Elphinstone's panchayat experiment. Over the course of his brief tenure there in 1820 and 1821, Hockley proceeded to cajole, threaten, and intimidate members of panchayats as well as litigants in an effort to extort money from them. Eventually, he was tried, convicted, and dismissed from the service of the East India Company in 1823. Upon his return to England, he later gained a small measure of fame as a novelist of Indian life and manners, but even in fiction he never relinquished his antipathy to the panchayat.[2]

According to Elphinstone's plan for the judicial administration of the Deccan, as we have seen, one of the primary judicial responsibilities of the Collector and his assistant was to promote the settlement of disputes through the convening of panchayats. As happened elsewhere during this period, the cession of sovereignty in this region from the Maratha Peshwa to the British revived long-standing disputes over claims to property rights. More specifically, the case under consideration here involved disputed titles to land and their subsequent income rights between two *deshmukhs*, possessors of hereditary land grants from the Peshwa. The plaintiffs in the case, Veeramkur and Sindey Desmookh claimed that the defendant's family, the current *deshmukh* of Wari, had usurped their family's rights to the income from four villages in the district.[3] Upon receiving the plaintiffs' petition, Warrekur, as the current

[2] His most well-known work was probably *Pandurang Hàrì: or, Memoirs of a Hindoo*. First published in 1826, the novel gained much greater attention when it was republished in the 1870s. Hockley discussed the panchayat in the novel and, not surprisingly, characterized it as a corrupt and unjust institution. The *sarpanch*, or umpire, he claimed, was useless and the members of the panchayat often conspired to force the defendants to accept their judgment. Moreover, since panchayats were called upon too often to settle disputes, respectable people would not sit upon them. Thus, panchayats, he wrote, were filled only by the "depraved and unprincipled." See *Pandurang Hàrì: or, Memoirs of a Hindoo*, Vol. III (London, 1826), pp. 154–60. Even the anonymous reviewer for the *Oriental Herald* was moved to remark "that the punchayet is a favourite theme of abuse with this novelist, whose aversion to it is in proportion to his ignorance of the real nature of the institution." See, "*Pandurang Hàrì; or, Memoirs of a Hindoo*," *Oriental Herald*, Vol. VIII (January–March 1826), p. 78.

[3] MSA, EIC, Judicial Department, Civil Judicature, Vol. 10/11, "'Statement of the Deshmooks of Warrey (the defendants)." Warrey (Wari) was part of a much larger Koorundwar estate, which itself had been a legacy of the powerful Putwurdhun family. The Peshwa had attempted to control and weaken them and the Putwurdhuns themselves had repeatedly threatened to rebel against this, but in 1812 the family invited Elphinstone to mediate the dispute. When the

title-holder was referred to, was summoned before Hockley, who ordered that he submit the dispute to a panchayat.[4] Warrekur refused the order, showing Hockley the written award (*sarounsh*) produced by a previous panchayat that sometime during the 1770s had already decided the dispute in his favor. Hockley, however, refused to look at the award. Instead, he arrested Warrekur's steward, threw him in jail, and placed a *tukaza* upon Warrekur.[5] Three days later, Warrekur relented, agreed to a new panchayat, and appointed two friends to represent him in the case.

When the panchayat met, it initially found in favor of Warrekur, the defendant in the case. But upon the protests of Veeramkur and Sindey, Hockley personally examined the members of the panchayat and at first accepted their decision. Shortly thereafter, however, he became incensed when one of the members of the panchayat appointed by Warrekur was not available to sign the award and thereby finalize the case. He summoned Warrekur to his office and ordered him to name another member immediately. When Warrekur protested that he would need some time to do so, Hockley became enraged, picked up a sandbox from his desk, and threatened to hit him with it. Hockley then dismissed the missing member of the panchayat, took it upon himself to appoint a replacement, and ordered them to re-convene the panchayat and issue the award. The panchayat eventually divided the income from the villages equally between the plaintiffs and the defendant.

Still, this did not end the dispute. The remaining member of the panchayat who had been appointed by Warrekur now refused to sign the award. When Hockley heard this, he immediately fined this person Rs. 20. Warrekur then went to Hockley and, according to his statement, begged Hockley "to let him have a fair Punchayet."[6] In addition, Warrekur argued that the litigants had not submitted bonds (*razeenamah*) to abide by the award of this new panchayat, as was customary.

Peshwa was overthrown, Elphinstone signed treaties with the successor chiefs of the territories. However, this obviously did not end the disputes over the disposition of the family property. In fact, the disputes would go on well into the nineteenth century. See Edward W. West, *A Memoir of the States of the Southern Maratha Country*, No. CXIII, n.s., *Selections from the Records of the Bombay Government* (Bombay, 1869), pp. 129–45; C. U. Aitchison, *A Collection of Treaties, Engagements, and Sunnuds Relating to India and Neighbouring Countries*, Vol. VI (London and Calcutta, 1864), pp. 145–7.

4 In many cases, litigants were identified by their place of origin or residence, which was indicated by the suffix "*kur*" or "*kar*." Today, for example, residents of Mumbai are known as "Mumbaikars."

5 On the practice of *tukaza*, see Chapter 1.

6 MSA, EIC, Judicial Department, Civil Judicature, Vol. 10/11, 1821–1823, "Statement of the Deshmooks of Warrey (the defendants)."

Hockley became enraged once again. He again picked up the sandbox and this time threw it at Warrekur, barely missing him, but hitting someone else in the head. Ten days later, Hockley ordered Warrekur back to his office and threatened to throw him in jail if he did not accept the new award. Warrekur responded that Hockley could give the panchayat's memo (*yad*), which accompanied an award and detailed the panchayat's decision, to Warrekur's brother if he wished, but he would not accept the award. Hockley did send for Warrekur's brother, and when the brother also refused to accept the memo, Hockley ordered both the memo and the award to be put on his head. When the papers fell to the ground, Hockley ordered the brother to be forcibly held down, and the documents were tied to his clothes. Sometime thereafter, the panchayat met again and decided to submit both the original and the new awards to Hockley and tell him to choose between them. Not surprisingly, Hockley confirmed the award issued by the panchayat on which his newly appointed member had served and ordered the villages' income to be divided between the litigants.

Admittedly, this is a rather long and complicated story. However, the case does reveal several contemporary notions of justice, legitimacy, and fairness. First, we must disabuse ourselves of the notion that panchayat justice, even in pre-colonial times, was customary and informal. While the panchayat may not have had a written code of civil procedure, there were nonetheless several important aspects of panchayat procedures that appear to have given them popular legitimacy. Among these undoubtedly was the notion that the panchayat did not act as a Western-style jury composed of theoretically disinterested persons. Nor was it precisely similar to English common-law modes of arbitration. Instead, consultation and negotiation between interested representatives appointed by both the plaintiff and defendant were at the core of panchayat legitimacy. Thus, when Hockley unilaterally appointed a member of the panchayat of his own choosing, Warrekur complained that this was not a "fair" panchayat.

Secondly, the panchayat system was littered with several forms of written documentation, all of which were considered to be essential elements of justice and fairness. The most important of these undoubtedly was the *sarounsh*, or award, a document that required the signature of all the members of the panchayat. As we have seen, when Warrekur's only remaining member of the panchayat, Larko Baboo Row, refused to sign the second award, Hockley fined him Rs. 20. Parenthetically, nothing in Elphinstone's panchayat rules authorized Collectors or their Assistants to impose such a fine. Regardless of this, it appears from the severity of Hockley's response as well as from its inclusion in the complaint that the signatures of all the members of the panchayat were essential to establishing the legitimacy and justice of the award in the eyes of the parties as well as perhaps the state. A partial set of signatures was a manifest sign of illegitimacy and unfairness.

In this regard, several other forms of documentation were similarly required as tangible signs of the panchayat's legitimacy and dispensation of justice. The panchayat's *yad*, which was tied to the clothes of Warrekur's brother, was a synopsis of the panchayat's deliberations. This, too, signaled the legitimacy of the panchayat's final award. The manner in which it was forcibly imposed upon Warrekur's brother indicates just how important it really was. Similarly, the presence or absence of a *razeenamah* to abide by the award was considered an important element of legitimacy. When Hockley constituted his second panchayat, Warrekur complained that no new *razeenamahs* had been signed. When taken together, all three of these documents – the *sarounsh*, the *yad*, and the *razeenamah* – performed a nearly identical function: They provided physical signs of the justice and fairness of the panchayat's decision. Of course, without them the litigant would also have great difficulty defending his claim in any later dispute. Yet given Hockley's manipulation of these "signifiers," Warrekur obviously felt justified in returning to Hockley "to beg to let him have a fair Punchayet."

However, the documents themselves were considered valid representations of a panchayat's fairness only if the procedures that produced them were fair and just. The crux of Warrekur's complaint lay in the manner in which Hockley had violated the norms of procedural justice when he demanded a new panchayat and then selected some of its members. As noted earlier, unlike the Western-style judge and jury system, the panchayat was not considered an impartial body seeking the truth, nor was it precisely a Western-style board of arbitration, although a panchayat's mandate encompassed both of these goals. The panchayats in this region were more akin to a select negotiating body in which parties to a complaint were represented by their kin, friends, or allies and whose brief was to resolve the dispute. Therefore, an essential element of the constitution of a "fair" panchayat was the voluntary selection of each party's members of the panchayat (*panchayatdars*). The number of *panchayatdars* need not necessarily have been five as the word "panch" indicates. In the Deccan, it appears to have been most common for each party to select one, two, or three *panchaytdars*. Thereafter, one additional member, the *sarpanch*, was then either selected by the members themselves or appointed by the local judicial official, either Maratha before 1818 or British thereafter, to head the panchayat.

The important point here though is that a "fair" panchayat was composed of representatives of each party's interests and that these representatives had been selected by the parties themselves without interference, intimidation, or compulsion. Moreover, a fair panchayat was constituted only upon both the voluntary and mutual agreement of both parties. Thus, panchayats could not be ordered to resolve a dispute by either British or Maratha officials, nor could individuals be required to submit their dispute to a panchayat. As we have seen, various forms of persuasion, such as the *tukaza*, could be used to influence parties to do so, but any form of compulsion was considered unjust and unfair and undermined the legitimacy of the panchayat's award.

In Warrekur's words, he first came into conflict with Hockley when the latter "persisted in spite of their solicitations, to order a Punchayet, that they declined the Punchayet, and refused to submit their case to one." Along with instituting a *tukaza* against Warrekur, Hockley also took the extraordinary step of placing Warrekur's secretary in jail. This type of unjust compulsion was then compounded by Hockley's dismissal of one of Warrekur's own appointed members of the panchayat and his replacement with one of Hockley's own choosing. Warrekur subsequently explained that his representative, Abba Deshmookh,

> had some quarrel at home, which prevented him from coming to the Punchayet for several days; that the Punchayet sent for him, but he refused to come, unless Mr. Hockley should send for him, upon which Mr. Hockley ordered him to be struck off the Punchayet; that the defendants represented that if Mr. Hockley would send for Abba Deshmook, he would attend, but that Mr. Hockley would not, and persisted in striking him off, and ordered the defendants to name another, that they declined appointing another, as they had no acquaintance in Nuggur [Ahmednagar], whom they could name, but said that if Mr. Hockley would give them leave for a few days, they would go home and find another person, and protested against any change, that Mr. Hockley rose up in a rage, and seized a sand box or weight, and threatened to throw it at them, and ordered them to be turned out of the Adawlut. That they still persisted in refusing to name another person, upon which Mr. Hockley himself appointed Sudasheo Deo Row, the

> person with whom Abba Deshmook had been quarrelling, to supply his place in the Punchayet, and that this man's name was accordingly entered in the first Sarounsh in lieu of Abba Deshmook.

The weight of this portion of the complaint rests not upon the evidence of Hockley's rage, which was detestable enough, but instead upon the palpable sense of unfairness created by Hockey's refusal to allow Warrekur to appoint his own replacement on the panchayat and his insistence upon appointing someone of his own choosing. The fact that Hockley's appointee was in the midst of a quarrel with Warrekur's appointee only compounded the grievance. It was at this point in the proceedings that Warrekur decided to leave Ahmednagar and travel seventy miles to Pune to lodge a complaint with the Collector, which was then forwarded to William Chaplin, the Commissioner of the Deccan. In 1820, Chaplin reviewed the case and reversed Hockley's decree.

Warrekur's case illustrates that, at least in this instance, the normative prescriptions of justice and fairness were structured in large part around the legal procedures or "games" of the panchayat. Certain documents in this field of force, such as the written award and the bond, were important indicators that the "rules of the game" had been followed and, therefore, became tangible signs of legitimacy. More significantly, however, panchayat procedures evidenced a concept of justice that was based upon the valid representation of interests rather than the impartial decisions of a judge, jury or arbitrator. Finally, the sense of panchayat justice was founded upon its voluntary nature. While forms of customary persuasion were common, excessive methods of compulsion or intimidation threatened the legitimacy of the panchayat and undermined its claim to justice.

Up to this point, the nature of panchayat justice and fairness has been examined based upon the evidence provided by a disgruntled litigant. Certainly, the survival of documents detailing these attitudes and aspirations is quite rare for this period. Yet even more rare perhaps is the existence of full copies of a panchayat's *yad* and *sarounsh*, both of which still survive in translation as a result of the Company's investigation into Hockley's actions. These documents provide a further entry point into an understanding of contemporary notions of justice by describing in detail both the documentary evidence required to establish valid proof and the limits of what may rightly be termed in this context "justice as fairness."[7]

[7] The phrase, of course, is drawn from Rawls, but this account has no connection to his theory of justice.

The panchayat's *yad* from this case is a remarkably detailed and formal document.[8] Its principal function was to adumbrate the history of the dispute, especially through the analysis of documentary evidence provided by the parties themselves. It was distinct from the *sarounsh*, in that the *yad* laid out the facts of the case, as understood by the panchayat, while the *sarounsh* announced the panchayat's decision. According to the *yad*, Warrekur's family once served as the stewards or agents (*gumashta*) of the plaintiffs, Veeramkur and Sindey Desmookh. About 250 years ago, the plaintiffs alleged, Warrekur's predecessors "usurped the whole of the Plaintiff's Wuttun & rights for his own benefit."[9] Since then, the plaintiff's family had tried several times unsuccessfully to recover their patrimony, but each time it was blocked by the actions of Warrekur's family.

To reconstruct the case, the panchayat had access to a number of pertinent documents and certainly avoided relying upon memory or oral histories. Their proceedings, in this sense, were anything but informal. Indeed, their memo attests to the importance of precedence and the primacy of written evidence in the Mughal and Maratha justice systems, a factor that early British administrators found quite amenable to their own predispositions. From these documents, the panchayat was able to determine that the Warrekurs have "unquestionably had possession of it [the estates] for the last 116 years." It was able to trace a deed (*sunnud*) back 138 years to a local Mughal revenue officer (*diwan*) named Assad Khan. Further, the panchayat had access to the Peshwa's grant of a settlement (*niwarput-tur*) from 1775–1776, which not only confirmed Warrekur's rights to the land but also imprisoned Veeramkur and Sindey's ancestors. Even this imprisonment was circumscribed by official documentation. In order to secure their release, Veeramkur and Sindey were supposed to supply Warrekur with a written acknowledgment of their wrongdoing (*ajeet khut*). When Warrekur was unable to produce this document, the panchayat considered it to be a significant weakness in his defense. Only a few years later, in 1783–1784, the situation was confused even further. In that year, both the defendant and the

[8] MSA, EIC, Judicial Department, Civil Judicature, Vol. 10/11, 1821–1823, "Abstract of the case of the Desmookhs Warrey in which the Veeramkur & Sindey Desmookhs are Plaintiffs and the Warreykur Desmookh the Defendant made out from an examination of all the parties themselves, together with the documents and proofs and the proceedings of the Punchayet which sat at Ahmednuggur."

[9] A *wuttun* (or *wutun*) is a hereditary estate or office.

plaintiffs secured revenue contracts (*cowles*) from a local Maratha official. Perhaps because both litigants were able to produce these contracts as evidence, the panchayat ultimately decided to divide the estate.

The reliance upon such disparate forms of written documentation was matched by the extent to which the members of the panchayat attempted to construct a coherent narrative based upon them. For example, the *yad* records several previous times in which the dispute was brought to the attention of both Mughal and Maratha officials. Other documents submitted to the panchayat make specific references to investigations conducted in 1704, 1740, and 1754.[10] However, the most detailed accounts undoubtedly come from the several investigations launched in the decade after 1774.

A period of relative political instability had been ushered in by the death of Peshwa Madhav Rao in 1772.[11] As was the case when the British were ceded control of the territory after the third Anglo-Maratha War, Veeramkur and Sindey appear to have taken advantage of the situation to renew their claims to the villages. Relying on the political confusion in the region, the plaintiffs first appealed to the new Peshwa's regent, Nana Fadnis. Upon rejecting their claim, Nana Fadnis had them imprisoned, at which time the plaintiffs then appealed to one of the local Maratha chiefs, Holkar. Holkar apparently used his influence to get the plaintiffs released in 1777–1778. By 1783, however, the plaintiffs were again to be found appealing to the *mamledar* for the possession of the villages. Despite a brief victory, Warrekur ultimately prevailed yet again and had retained possession of the estates until the latest controversy erupted under the new British occupation in 1819–1820.

At each stage of their investigation, the panchayat relied upon the written legal record to reconstruct the history of the dispute. For the events of 1774–1776, the panchayat relied upon the evidence contained in the settlement grant issued by the Peshwa; for those of 1777–1778, they had the plaintiffs' order of release from prison; and for the claims lodged in 1783–1784, the panchayat relied upon the existence of revenue contracts issued at the time. The panchayat's only concession to the acceptance of unwritten evidence appears to have been in response to the plaintiffs' claim that they had acted as *deshmukhs* of some of the villages in dispute. Even this claim, however, was met with

[10] MSA, EIC, Judicial Department, Civil Judicature, Vol. 10/11, 1821–1823, "Abstract of the case of the Desmookhs Warrey."

[11] André Wink, *Land and Sovereignty in India: Agrarian Society and Politics in Eighteenth-century Maratha Svarajya* (Cambridge: Cambridge University Press, 1986), pp. 78–9.

a good deal of skepticism: "They [the plaintiffs] appear also to have acted in matters of Caste, and such like occasions, without any dependence on the defendants, and to have been sometimes stiled [*sic*] Desmookh by the Mamlutdars and other inferior officers, but without any authority from Government."[12]

Given the preponderance of evidence in favor of Warrekur's claim, it would seem reasonable to assume that the Hockley's corrupted panchayat would have ruled in his favor. Instead, the panchayat equally divided the property between the plaintiffs and the defendant. "In fine," the *sarounsh* finally announced, "it appears to us by the documents of the three parties viz The Warreekur, the Veeramkur and Sindey, and also by the manner in which the Wuttun has been held, that the three ought to enjoy equally the Wuttun of Desmookh – and this is our decision."[13]

The panchayat's decision does appear to have been at odds with the evidence, and this requires some explanation. In an idealized view of the panchayat, it could be argued that panchayat justice was based less upon establishing absolute right from wrong than upon negotiation and compromise. However, one need not resort to explanations based upon such romantic notions of restoring village harmony to explain this phenomenon. In a more practical sense, the members of the panchayat may simply have acknowledged that this was the simplest, most direct, and least contentious way to conclude the panchayat, especially since they may very well have perceived that Hockley was powerful, volatile, and dangerous. Equally possible is the fact that the award reveals the difficult position in which the panchayat was placed between two powerful parties. Contemporary studies of panchayats, such as those by the anthropologist Erin Moore, suggest that the village panchayat can quite easily become a forum in which the wealthy exercise their power over the poor.[14] In this case, it seems clear that panchayats could equally have been sites where local power relationships between elites were played out. Thus the award may indicate a reluctance to antagonize two contending groups of local notables. Admittedly, without further evidence, it is impossible to explain precisely why this panchayat decided as it did. However, the

12 Wink, *Land and Sovereignty in India*, pp. 78–9.

13 MSA, EIC, Judicial Department, Civil Judicature, Vol. 10/11, 1821–1823, "Translation of the Punchayets Summary of their arguments against the defendant as laid down in the Sarounsh."

14 See, for example, Erin P. Moore, "Gender, Power, and Legal Pluralism: Rajasthan, India," *American Ethnologist*, Vol. 20, No. 3 (August 1993), pp. 522–42.

social factors impinging upon the execution of panchayat justice appears to have been an important aspect of reaching a judgment, and both the panchayat members' and the litigants' positions in local society very likely had a significant effect upon their decisions.

PANDERONG KRISHNU AND LUMKRAY BULLAL NARSAWEY V. HUNGEYKUR AND KHATGAONKUR

The case of Panderong Krishnu and Lumkray Bullal Narsawey not only reveals the more grievous intervention of William Hockley but also lends significant credence to the argument that normative prescriptions of panchayat justice were built upon notions of voluntariness, due process, and the valid representation of interests. The sole surviving document from this case is a petition to the Governor-in-Council, Mountstuart Elphinstone, dated 26 December 1820.[15] Once again, the dispute concerned the disposition of property after the transfer of power from the Peshwa to the British. However, in this case, the defendants were village accountants (*kulkarni*) whose office entailed lands and other perquisites for their support. The disposition of three villages near Ahmednagar became the subject of this dispute after they had been seized by the British, and two sets of claimants, Panderong and Lumkray, on the one hand, and Khatgaonkur, on the other, came forward to claim the lands. Subsequently, Hockley examined the papers presented by both claimants and granted the property to Panderong and Lumkray.

The situation remained stable for almost eighteen months thereafter until a third claimant, Hungeykur, appeared. He prevailed upon Hockley to call for Panderong and Lumkray to the *kachari* in Ahmednagar. "We accordingly went," Panderong and Lumkray wrote in their petition, "and explained the nature of the case, when we were directed to refer it to a punchaet. We represented that we had nothing to do with the Hungeykur, but without attending to this, the case was referred to a punchaet."

Once again, there is a palpable sense of injustice expressed by the petitioners when compelled to submit the dispute to a panchayat. In this case, however, the Company's investigation into Hockley's actions left a remarkable record of interrogations of both Panderong and several

[15] MSA, EIC, Judicial Department, Civil Judicature, Vol. 10/11, 1821–1823, "Translation of a petition from Panderong Krishnu and Lumkray Bullal Narsawey Koolhurnees of the Villages of Wajooray [,] Boojoorg [and] Khoord to the Honorable the Governor, Dahot the 7th Magsur Vud 1742 Lalbahan on 26th December 1820."

members of the panchayat. Panderong, for example, testified that upon being ordered to submit the dispute with Hungeykur to a panchayat,

> I said, that I had nothing to do with the Hungaykur, that my Dispute was with the Khatgaonkur, and that I was ready to have a Punchayet with him.
>
> I had originally complained against the Khatgaonkur, who had placed my Papers in pledge with the Hungaykur, had led to my Wuttun being "Zubted" [attached], and he also wanted to establish it, that I was his Gaomashta or agent.
>
> Question – When you expressed your aversion to a Punchayet with the Hungaykur what reply did Mr. Hockley make?
> Answer – He said I must submit to one; and I at length was forced to agree.[16]

The petitioner's sense of injustice arose not only from this element of compulsion but also from the instability surrounding the transition from Maratha to British systems of judicial procedures. Panderong and Lumkray explained that as the discussion with Hockley had proceeded, "we then mentioned that as the matter related to a wutun it should be referred to the Jameedars and Gataururs[17] (Village Officers) and that the Saheb [Hockley] on seeing their decision should issue such orders as were conformable to justice; this being the practice of our former Government and our country."[18] Hockley, however, ordered a panchayat "without listening to this."[19]

The examination of Panderong also provides an interesting insight into precisely how members of a panchayat were selected by the parties. The process was often an exceedingly informal one as litigants endeavored to secure friends, relatives, or allies to serve. Panderong explained that after meeting with Hockley,

> I went to search for members to sit in the Punchayet. I met Mahadjee Punt Joshee Poonakur in the Road and told him that I was seeking for Punchayetdars. He advised me to apply to Moro Madhoo Row Daishmookh of Wankooree. I then went to the Daishmookh's house,

[16] MSA, EIC, Judicial Department, Civil Judicature, Vol. 10/11, 1821–1823, "Examination of Pandoorung Krishen as to allegations against Mr. Hockley," 16 April 1821.

[17] *Jamindars* were local village judicial officials under the Peshwa. The term "gataururs" may refer to members of a *gota*, or village assembly, a judicial body that had fallen out of use under the Marathas in favor of the panchayat. See Gune, *Judicial System of the Marathas*, pp. 54–9.

[18] MSA, EIC, Judicial Department, Civil Judicature, Vol. 10/11, 1821–1823, "Translation of a petition."

[19] Ibid.

> told him I had been ordered to have a Punchayet, and could get no members, showed him my Papers and asked him to be one of my Punchayetdars to which he agreed, and also desired me to try and get Krishnajee Mahayun as the other. I accordingly proceeded to the house of the latter, and told him what I had before said to the Daishmookh and he in like manner consented to sit for me: the following day, I again attended at the Adawlut and gave in the names of my two Punchayetdars.[20]

It appears to have been not uncommon for litigants from the countryside to rely upon the advice of others to secure members of their panchayat, as Panderong was forced to do. Since he was not a resident of Ahmednagar, he had but little choice. As he noted, he "could get no members." Unfortunately, unbeknownst to Panderong, the man who had been recommended to him, Moro Madhoo Row, was one of Hockley's accomplices.[21] At their first meeting, Panderong later testified, "I was told by Moro Madhoo Row Daishmookh to bring 500 Rupees for Mr. Hockley. I replied that I knew nothing of Mr. Hockley, and the Daishmookh then said 'Bring it to me, and I will place it in Hindoo Mull Sowkoers hands and get your Punchayet decided as you wish.'"[22]

Although the judicial systems under both the Marathas and the British were replete with payments, charges, and costs of all kinds – to draw up papers, to feed the members of a panchayat, to pay for travel to and housing near the court, to feed a *tukaza* peon, to make a gift to an official, to name but a few – there is a palpable sense of injustice expressed in Panderong's testimony. Perhaps payments and *douceurs*, as the British liked to call them, were common, but this demand for Rs. 500 had crossed the line between *douceur* and extortion. When Panderong was first approached for the payment, he hesitated, but reluctantly agreed. "As we had no resource," he stated, "and the cause would not be tried without the payment of money, and as we were afraid of losing our wutun, we went round to different places, and having got our relations and a Waree to stand forword [*sic*], we paid four hundred rupees in cash thro' the hand of the mediator (Moro Madhoo Row

[20] MSA, EIC, Judicial Department, Civil Judicature, Vol. 10/11, 1821–1823, "Examination of Pandoorung Krishen."

[21] Moro Madhoo Row was eventually apprehended for his role in the case and agreed to testify against Hockley. See the letter of 4 May 1821, Henry Pottinger to William Chaplin, MSA, EIC, Judicial Department, Civil Judicature, Vol. 10/11, 1821–1823.

[22] MSA, EIC, Judicial Department: Civil Judicature, Vol. 10/11, Pottinger to Chaplin, 4 May 1821.

Deshmookh)."[23] Thus, while panchayats might very well have been costly, the plaintiffs certainly were unprepared to entertain this extraordinary charge.

Shortly thereafter, even further demands for money were made upon them. This time, the plaintiffs balked at the payment. "The next morning," Panderong testified, "after we had eaten something we went to the Adawlut where the Punchayetdars were sitting, and they began to examine us and Pungobha Dahorey [a member of the panchayat] told us the Hungaykurs [the defendant] had agreed to give 1000 Rups., and unless we made up as much we should lose our suit. We said we could not command so much money, and that the Punchayetdars must act as they chose."[24] At this point, Panderong and Lumkray went back to Moro Madhoo Row and demanded their money back, a demand that appears to have been fulfilled but only after several attempts. The extent to which Panderong and Lumkray now acted out of resignation or principle is not altogether clear. The testimony suggests that both sentiments were probably involved. Yet, once again, their actions illustrate the fact that such extortion was contrary to contemporary standards of panchayat justice and not a matter common to the judicial business of the era.

Much of the remaining testimony from the case relates to the procedures adopted by the panchayat itself. It is especially revealing not only of the insight it provides of how the panchayat was expected to function but also of the circumstances in which the standards of panchayat justice were violated. As the discussions of the panchayat dragged on for over two months, Hockley inserted himself into the panchayat process by aborting the panchayat's investigation into the case and ordering it to immediately produce a decision. Although the dispute had evolved into one between Panderong and Lumkray, on the one hand, and Hungeykur, on the other, the panchayat sought to interview the plaintiff's accountant from the original case. According to the testimony of Rungo Moraishwer Dahorey, a panchayat member for Hungeykur, early one morning the members of the panchayat were all called to meet at Hockley's court.

> Mr. Hockley did come to the Adawlut about 11 o Clock. The whole of the Punchayetdars immediately went to him and represented to him "that we require the Khatgaon Takleekur Coolkurnies before we could finish the

23 MSA, EIC, Judicial Department, Civil Judicature, Vol. 10/11, 1821–1823, "Petition."

24 MSA, EIC, Judicial Department, Civil Judicature, Vol. 10/11, 1821–1823, "Examination of Pandoorung Krishen."

> 'Sarounsh,' that the Hooly was at hand and that we therefore begged to be excused till it was over." Mr. Hockley snatched the papers from our hands with some abusive expressions, and told us to get along. We went into the Kucherry where we had been sitting to get our Inkstands &c, and whilst there, a Peon came & called us into the Adawlut. We obeyed the summons, and Mr. Hockley gave back the papers and said "There is no occasion to call the Khatgaon Tankleejurs. Prepare a sarounsh between these two (the Hungaykurs and Wagoondaykur) and let me have it immediately.[']" We five person accordingly went back and prepared a "Sarounsh" to the best of our judgement.[25]

Hockley's interference was also remarked upon in the interviews of other panchayat members and was considered to be a significant contravention of panchayat procedures.[26] Equally notable, however, was the fact that Hockley's accomplice, the panchayat member Moro Madhoo Row, had long ago stopped attending the panchayat's deliberations and had been sending his *gumashta* to attend in his stead. Finally, this irregularity was compounded by the fact that Moro ultimately refused to sign the award and deputed his agent to do so.

Moro's actions may very well have been an attempt to avoid further involvement in the case and insulate himself from possible prosecution for corruption. But the British investigators were clearly troubled by the fact that Moro had not sought Panderong and Lumkray's permission to send a *gumashta* to attend the panchayat's meetings and that he had not personally signed the *sarounsh*. Moro testified as to his role in the case on 16 April 1821. In the following extract, the term "Wagoodaykurs" refers to Panderong and Lumkray, residents of the village of Wagooday.[27]

[25] Ibid.

[26] See the testimony of Mahadew Gondajee Saupkur, MSA, EIC, Judicial Department, Civil Judicature, Vol. 10/11, 1821–1823, "Examination of Mahadew Gondajee Saupkur, Shroff, and member of the Punchayet," 16 April 1821, who noted "The whole of the members immediately went into the Adawlut with the Papers and represented to Mr. Hockley that the 'Sarounsh' was not ready, and that we required the Khatgaon Tankleekur Coolkurries before we could finish it. Mr. Hockley took the Papers, abused us, and told us to be gone, at the same time observing that the dispute had no connection with the Tankleekurs. We returned to the Kucherry where we had been sitting and about a quarter of an hour after a Peon came with the Papers and ordered us to prepare the 'Sarounsh' between the Wagoondaykur and Hungaykurs instantly."

[27] At various times in the petition and examinations, the village is spelled "Wajooray," "Wagooday," "Wagoondy," or "Wagoonday." The spelling that occurs most frequently is "Wagooday," which I have adopted throughout to facilitate identification. This may well refer to the village of Wagunde Budruk in the Ahmednagar District of modern Maharashtra.

> The two Wagoodaykurs (Sumkrajee [Lumkray] Bullalls and Pandooruung Krishen) came to my house to ask me to sit as their member. I refused twice, but the third day when they met me in the street I agreed, and went to the Adawlut with them. I attended there several times, but did not look at the Papers and I appointed a Carkoon to sit on my part whose name is Shakoo Luximon Govindah an inhabitant of Ahmednuggur.
>
> Question – Did the Wagoodaykurs never tell you, that the Punchayet has not acted fairly towards them and that they had suffered injustice?
> Answer – Yes they did; they said that the Punchayet had not been fair.
> Question – What reply did you make to these observations?
> Answer – I told them not to trouble me, but to act as they thought best.
> Question – You were one of their Punchayetdars and why therefore should they not trouble you?
> Answer – I told them that my Goomashtee (who has signed the Sarounsh in my name) had acted like the others.
> Question – By whose authority did you put your Goomashtee into that Punchayet?
> Answer – I informed the other members that I could not attend, and therefore, with there [*sic*] permission, I sent my Goomashtee.
> Question – Did you ask the Wagoodaykurs permission to put in your Goomashtee?
> Answer – No I did not.
> Question – Did you ever tell the Wagoodaykur you had not signed the Sarounsh and give your reason for not doing so?
> Answer – I told him I had not signed the 'Sarounsh' but said nothing of my reason.[28]

Considering the justice expectations of panchayat litigants, the connection drawn here between fairness and justice, on the one hand, and the valid representation of interests, on the other, is not surprising. Panderong and Lumkray had secured Moro's services as their duly deputed member of the panchayat, and his absence did much to de-legitimize the tribunal's claim to those values.

Moro's refusal to sign the *sarounsh* obviously disturbed other members of the panchayat as well. Krishnajee Mahajun, who served as a member of the panchayat for Panderong and Lumkray, testified that when Moro refused to sign the award, he refused as well. According to

[28] MSA, EIC, Judicial Department, Civil Judicature, Vol. 10/11, 1821–1823, "Testimony of Moro Madhoo Row, Deshmookh of Wankoree in the Turuff of Kuwelleenuggur," 16 April 1821.

Krishnajee's testimony, Moro "then said, if you will sign it first, I will do so afterwards. This I did, and he afterwards caused it to be signed by the hand of Shahoo Goomrah, his agent."[29] One of Hungaykur's members of the panchayat similarly testified that he had at first refused to proceed without Moro's signature. Rungo Moraishwer Dahorey explained that Moro "said he had sworn not to do so. On hearing this Krishnajee Mahajun and myself likewise declared we would not put our names to it. At last he agreed to have it signed by one of his Dependants [*sic*] in his name, and then we did so."[30]

The apparent dismay caused by the failure of Moro to sign the award further emphasizes the importance attached to the elements of procedural justice needed to legitimate an award. However, it also illustrates the ambivalence many panchayat members may have brought to their service on these tribunals. Panchayat cases could be long, complicated, and conflictual, as this case certainly was. Service on a panchayat could bring one into conflict with the litigants themselves as well as the judicial authorities. There was thus a certain sense of frustration and resignation in Krishnajee Mahajun's voice when he was interviewed by the British authorities:

> Question – Has the Wagoondaykur Nareesawuz ever complained to you since or not?
>
> Answer – Sunkrajee Bullall did complain to me of the manner in which I decided for him and [I] reminded him that I had asked Mr. Hockley to send for the Khatgaon Tankleekur Coolkurnies, and as he had refused I could do nothing else.[31]

SUKHOO PUNT APTE V. NILKUNT MYRAUL

Unfortunately, very little direct evidence survives from the dispute between Sukhoo Punt Apte and Nilkunt Myraul. Nevertheless, a close reading of the surviving letters from its British investigation further reveals the normative concepts of justice brought to the panchayat system both by Indian litigants and British judicial administrators. Indeed, the extent to which the two shared a common view of justice

[29] MSA, EIC, Judicial Department, Civil Judicature, Vol. 10/11, 1821–1823, "Testimony of Krishnajee Mahajun, Member of the Punchayet on the Part of Nareesawaz," 16 April 1821.

[30] MSA, EIC, Judicial Department, Civil Judicature, Vol. 10/11, 1821–1823, "Testimony of Rungo Moraishwer Dahorey, Member of the Punchayet," 16 April 1821.

[31] MSA, EIC, Judicial Department, Civil Judicature, Vol. 10/11, 1821–1823, "Testimony of Krishnajee Mahajun," 16 April 1821.

may at first appear quite striking. However, this is perhaps less so when one considers both the fact that the British administration of justice was intended to be based upon the restoration of India's ancient constitution and the British perception that the Indian panchayats shared a common adjudicatory role with the English jury and English arbitration. Thus the norms of justice to be expected from these tribunals were in many instances similarly corresponding or complementary ones.

The case apparently came to the attention of William Chaplin, the Commissioner of the Deccan, in April 1820. Initially, Sukhoo Punt had filed a suit seeking to collect his portion of the revenue returns from two districts in the province (*subha*) of Joonur.[32] Sukhoo held these returns in partnership with Nilkunt Myraul.[33] Chaplin, whose initial letter is lost, apparently requested Henry Pottinger, the Collector of Ahmednagar, to inquire into the case, which had resulted in Sukhoo's imprisonment for debt. Relying upon information supplied by Hockley, Pottinger replied that Sukhoo's imprisonment had been the result of two separate panchayat investigations and decisions. Pottinger explained that the first panchayat had found in favor of Sukhoo but had not settled upon the exact amount of award. This led the defendant, Nilkunt Myraul, to deposit approximately Rs. 1,500 with a local goldsmith to settle the debt. A second panchayat was then assembled to establish the exact amount. They awarded Sukhoo Rs. 1,326.3.25. Thus, according to the second panchayat, Sukhoo now had to repay Nilkunt just over Rs. 653. Sukhoo then protested that the money had never been put into his account with the goldsmith, but since he could offer no proof and also refused to pay the amount in question, he was imprisoned for debt.

In December 1820, Sukhoo Punt was released from prison when Nilkunt stopped paying for his daily sustenance. Under the East India Company's regime, imprisonment for debt was supported only so long as the debtor's sustenance was paid for by the creditor. In the 1820s, this rate was fixed at 2 *annas* per diem. Upon his release, Sukhoo immediately went to Pottinger and complained that the final award had not been duly signed by all the members of the panchayat. Pottinger reviewed the award and "was equally vexed and astonished to find

[32] MSA, EIC, Judicial Department, Civil Judicature, Vol. 10/11, 1821–1823, Henry Pottinger to William Chaplin, 25 April 1820; Pottinger to Chaplin, 4 November 1821,

[33] MSA, EIC, Judicial Department, Civil Judicature, Vol. 10/11, 1821–1823, Pottinger to Chaplin, 4 November 1821.

that it was not properly authenticated."[34] He then wrote to his subordinate, Arthur Crawford, asking him to find out why the award had not been signed by all the members of the panchayat. "A Person called Succoo Puntaply," Pottinger wrote to Crawford, "who has been confined in jail at this place for some time for debt having been lately released he appealed against the award of the Punchayet under which he was imprisoned and on examining that document, I find that one of the members (and that too the only one on the part of the appellant) has not signed it."[35] Pottinger, beginning to doubt Hockley's initial report, concluded rather ominously, "I have also other reasons to doubt the fairness of that award."[36]

In fact, Pottinger had only just begun to uncover the web of intrigue and extortion that marked Hockley's tenure in Ahmednagar and that had relied upon the manipulation of panchayats. At this time, Chaplin also had begun to sense the extent of Hockley's malfeasance and within several months requested a Bombay solicitors' firm to conduct a formal investigation. Pottinger's initial investigation revealed that the dispute had begun about two years earlier when the litigants had taken their case to a panchayat, and awarded Sukhoo Rs. 712. Hockley had then reported to Pottinger that Nilkunt had deposited Rs. 1,500 worth of gold as security into the account of the *subah* of Junoor, the site of the dispute. However, Hockley had not informed Pottinger that the panchayat had also examined this account and had found that the gold had never been deposited as a security against Sukhoo Punt's claim. Instead, it had been deposited into another account altogether. "It was proved," Pottinger wrote, "that the deposit of Gold related to quite a different affair, and had only been brought forward in this instance to mislead the members of the Punchayet, whose decision in every respect was final, and apparently very just."[37] In fact, Nilkunt's deposit was made into the account of the Pune province and not Junoor. "The accounts of the two Soobhas," he reported, "were necessarily to be kept distinct from the very agreements made by the Parties with the Paishwa's Government."[38]

[34] MSA, EIC, Judicial Department, Civil Judicature, Vol. 10/11, 1821–1823, Pottinger to Chaplin, 27 January 1821.
[35] MSA, EIC, Judicial Department, Civil Judicature, Vol. 10/11, 1821–1823, Pottinger to Crawford, 23 December 1820.
[36] Ibid.
[37] MSA, EIC, Judicial Department, Civil Judicature, Vol. 10/11, 1821–1823, Pottinger to Chaplin, 27 January 1821.
[38] MSA, EIC, Judicial Department, Civil Judicature, Vol. 10/11, 1821–1823, Pottinger to Chaplin, 4 November 1821.

At this point, Hockley again interfered in the panchayat proceedings and appointed a pair of arbitrators and an umpire to review the original award. The encouragement of English-style arbitration had been a regular feature of the Company's judicial policy since at least the introduction of the Bengal Regulations of 1793.[39] In Pottinger's later account, he noted that the appointment of arbitrators in this situation was appropriate, but only if they were appointed to examine whether the gold was indeed intended as security. Hockley, however, had ordered the arbitrators to review the entire award. In circumstances such as these, Pottinger reflected, while the amount in dispute might be subject to arbitration, the validity of the award was not in question and could not be appealed.

However, this was Pottinger's later assessment of the situation. At the time of the dispute, the arbitrators did meet to review the entire award and found in favor of Nilkunt for an amount of just over Rs. 650. This award had its own complications: not only had it not been signed by all of the arbitrators, but the entire arbitration proceedings appeared to have been conducted without the attendance of one of the arbitrators. Moreover, there were indications that this new award was contrary to the full tribunal's initial recommendations. Pottinger explained that Sukhoo Punt's claim had been fully supported by the first panchayat, but Hockley had seriously mishandled the subsequent inquiry by the arbitrators. After the award of the first panchayat, Pottinger explained,

> The only thing therefore that remained to be done, was to see the award of the Punchayet enforced, but instead of this, it now would appear the [*sic*] Mr. Hockley allowed two persons, who ought to have been simply charged with ascertaining the truth or falsity of the assertion about the Gold, to enter into scrutiny of the sarounsh of the Punchayet, and after setting aside some items, and deducting from others, a second sarounsh was submitted to Mr. Hockley *by one of the members*, in which the charge of 1500 Rupees for Gold was admitted . . . and consequently the Plaintiff instead of having to receive the sum stated . . . was brought in as debtor to the amount of 651.[0].50.
>
> The sarounsh was, as I have said above, presented to Mr. Hockley by one of the two arbitrators and the "Aspree" or Umpire, and that Gentleman I am informed sent for the other member (if such he can be called) and demanded from him why he did not subscribe his name

39 Bengal Regulation XVI, *A Regulation for Referring Suits to Arbitration, and Submitting Certain Cases to the Decision of the Nazim*, 1793.

> to the Paper. The man replied that the award was unjust and that it had been prepared by the arbitrator and the umpire without his concurrence; that a Draft of their real sentiments as settled by all three, was then in his hand, and that he would not sign what he knew to be false and illegal.[40]

Pottinger's further investigations revealed not only that the new award had not been properly signed but also that the arbitrators had relied upon an unsubstantiated memorandum in order to reach their decision. When the province's banker had been called before the arbitrators and asked to produce documents relating to the gold, he replied that he did not have any. The arbitrators then asked the same of Nilkunt, who submitted only a copy of a memorandum purporting to support his claim. Reviewing the arbitrators' decision, Pottinger was clearly aggravated. "It appears," he wrote, "even from the document, that the Gold was admitted on a *copy of a memorandum* given in by Nilkunt Myraul and which should have been utterly rejected on every principle of just arbitration, for had it been proper to receive an alleged *copy of a Paper* on either side, Succo Punt Aptay could have had no difficulty in fabricating one to suit his purpose."[41]

The accumulated evidence of improper procedures in the case eventually led Pottinger to set aside the second award and to restore the original one. Although he was "averse to speak harshly" of Hockley's motives, he indicated to the Commissioner of the Deccan that Hockley had acted improperly by espousing the cause of one of the parties.[42] Moreover, the full extent of Hockley's corruption was becoming too obvious to ignore. Pottinger discovered that several of the same people were repeatedly involved in cases under Hockley's supervision. Nilkunt Myraul, for example, had also been the complainant whose suit had landed Warrekur's agent in jail a year earlier; and another man, Moro Bulwunt, had served as a member of panchayats in both Warrekur's and Sukhoo Punt's case. Eventually, Pottinger would discover that Hockley had extorted over Rs. 30,000 from litigants in return for favorable panchayat decisions.[43]

40 MSA, EIC, Judicial Department, Civil Judicature, Vol. 10/11, 1821–1823, Pottinger to Chaplin, 27 January 1821.

41 MSA, EIC, Judicial Department, Civil Judicature, Vol. 10/11, 1821–1823, Pottinger to Chaplin, 4 November 1821. Emphasis in original.

42 MSA, EIC, Judicial Department, Civil Judicature, Vol. 10/11, 1821–1823, Pottinger to Chaplin, 27 January 1821.

43 MSA, EIC, Judicial Department, Civil Judicature, Vol. 10/11, 1821–1823, "Statement of Kaishao Row Mistry," 18 May 1821.

Pottinger had long held that he had "but one object in view which was to see justice done in the affair."[44] However, the path to justice was obstructed in a number of ways. Most apparent were the numerous violations of procedural justice that were fundamental to panchayat justice. Litigants placed great importance upon the production of valid documents, the valid representation of their interests, and the avoidance of elements of compulsion and coercion as the normative foundations of justice and fairness. Less apparent was the fundamental confusion that existed among British officials about the specific purpose and function of the panchayat. It was not exactly clear to many of them whether the panchayat was analogous to an English jury or English arbitration. British judicial administrators, therefore, often experienced an odd combination of both familiarity and perplexity with the panchayat system. This is nowhere more evident than in Pottinger's attempts to explain Sukhoo Punt's case to his superiors.

The case, as we have seen, was perhaps unique in that it involved first a decision by a panchayat and then a review by arbitrators. Significantly, Pottinger consistently confused terms appropriate to a panchayat with those of English arbitration. In the statement noted above, this linguistic confusion is apparent: "The sarounsh," Pottinger had written, "was, as I have said above, presented to Mr. Hockley by one of the two arbitrators and the 'Aspree' or Umpire."[45] The following November, he then referred to the arbitrators as a "2nd Punchayet" and went on to explain, "the Punchayet was composed of only one arbitrator on each side and an umpire."[46]

Even further confusion existed over the different procedures to be followed by panchayats and arbitrators. Pottinger believed that the umpire of an arbitration should be excluded from the decision. Thus he wrote, "the Punchayet was composed of only one arbitrator on each side and an umpire (who was it may be added, the friend and partizan of Nilkunt Myraul) and I humbly conceive that this last Person should have had no weight in the decision. The undeviating rule, even amongst the natives at Ahmednuggur, is that the decision should be unanimous and this was well known to be one of the standing

[44] MSA, EIC, Judicial Department, Civil Judicature, Vol. 10/11, 1821–1823, Pottinger to Chaplin, 4 November 1821.

[45] MSA, EIC, Judicial Department, Civil Judicature, Vol. 10/11, 1821–1823, Pottinger to Chaplin, 27 January 1821. Emphasis added.

[46] MSA, EIC, Judicial Department, Civil Judicature, Vol. 10/11, 1821–1823, Pottinger to Chaplin, 4 November 1821.

Regulations of the Adawlut."[47] In this sense, the panchayat functioned in a way similar to a jury, with the head of the panchayat as judge. His superior, however, thought the panchayat should follow the rules of English arbitration. William Chaplin wrote in the following terms to Francis Warden, the Chief Secretary to Government of the Bombay Presidency:

> I dissent however entirely from the view taken by Captain Pottinger of the illegality of the second Punchait grounded on the argument that the Punchait ought to have been unanimous and that the umpire ought to have had no Voice in the decision since it does not appear to me that unanimity is at all necessary to constitute the legality of an award of these assemblies and when two arbitrators only are appointed with an umpire to assist them, it is obviously the province of the umpire in case of a difference of opinion, to decide by his casting *Vote*; and this indeed must be the sole object for which he is nominated. The umpire however ought not to have been selected I think by Mr. Hockley except with the joint consent and approval either of the parties or their members.[48]

Perhaps too great a weight ought not to be placed upon the evidence provided by the letters left by Pottinger and Chaplin. Neither man was a legal expert, Chaplin having served in the Madras civil service and Pottinger in the Company army. Nevertheless, as the panchayat was adapted to the needs of British judicial administration, it was simultaneously being refashioned in the light of British legal practices. In this sense, the panchayat experiments in the Bombay and Madras Presidencies did not entail the restoration of the customary institutions of an ancient constitution, as Elphinstone and Munro argued. Instead, a new hybrid institution was created and called a "panchayat."

It was not as easy, however, to refashion normative concepts of justice and fairness. Even before the British occupation, the panchayat in the Deccan was least of all an informal institution. Legitimacy, justice, and fairness were determined by the production of relevant documents, such as wills, grants, bonds, and contracts. Members were selected based upon their ability to represent the interests of the litigants, not to determine guilt or innocence. Various forms of persuasion, but not compulsion, were considered legitimate in order to encourage litigants to settle their cases before a panchayat. The

[47] Ibid.

[48] MSA, EIC, Judicial Department, Civil Judicature, Vol. 10/11, 1821–1823, Chaplin to Francis Warden, 9 November 1821. Emphasis in original.

panchayats themselves issued written and signed documents of which the *sarounsh* and the *yad* were undoubtedly the most important. Within such a formalized institution, procedural justice was of paramount importance.

Unfortunately, there is almost no evidence upon which to decide whether the panchayat delivered distributive justice. In the previous chapter, it was noted that one litigant complained that the panchayat did not deliver justice to the poor. In modern India, the anthropologist Erin Moore has argued that the village panchayat almost inevitably expresses the interests of the rich against the poor. As one panchayat leader told her, "We can't always do justice. We have to be reciprocal."[49] Nor can we generalize about the extent of panchayat justice for different castes. In debates before the Bombay legislature, B. R. Ambedkar famously described Brahmin-dominated panchayats as "an organized conspiracy" against the Dalits.[50] Since the British often insisted that panchayats be staffed by local men of prominence and respectability, it is highly unlikely that Dalits could expect justice from panchayats. Thus British records have left only a partial picture of panchayat justice. For those of wealth and standing, the institutional structure of the panchayat placed great emphasis upon procedural justice, an emphasis that both the Marathas and British valued. For the poor and lower castes of this era, their voices have yet to be heard.

[49] Moore, "Gender, Power, and Legal Pluralism," p. 528.
[50] *Bombay Legislative Council Debates*, Vol. XXXV, 6 October 1932.

5

THE PANCHAYAT AND TRIAL BY JURY, I

The civil trial

During the first half of the nineteenth century, British administrators both in India and in England were unable to define precisely either the form or function of the customary panchayat. Nevertheless, while caste panchayats retained their autonomous roles, Company officials sought to adapt the panchayat to the administration of justice believing, as it were, that they were restoring the ancient customs of the country. Upon close examination, the extent to which attempts were made to adapt and incorporate the panchayat into the British judicial system was quite extraordinary. Panchayat justice was promoted in areas as diverse as civil, criminal, and even military justice. Yet, even as a body to resolve these disputes, there was no clear consensus as to the panchayat's purpose, function, or composition. As we have seen, some British officer-officials, most notably Mountstuart Elphinstone, believed it functioned fundamentally as a board of arbitration and thus provided an inexpensive and speedy forum for alternative dispute resolution. Others, such as Elphinstone's mentor and fellow-officer Sir Thomas Munro, believed that the panchayat's function was more akin to that of the English jury. Certainly, when the panchayat was understood as a form of the common-law jury, it took on a meaning and consequence of immense political and ideological weight. The analogy made between the panchayat and the English jury circulated quite widely among Company officer-officials during the first quarter of the nineteenth century and became an especially salient issue during the 1820s and 1830s, when both radicals and legal reformers in Britain debated the jury's role in the metropole. However, the debate could not be constrained within those geographic limits and the reform of the jury system simultaneously became an imperial as well as an English issue. In India, the question took on a variety of meanings because the role of the panchayat as jury involved not only issues of citizenship but also issues of race, nationality, and religion. In one sense, therefore, the "jury debate" in England was also about the form and practice of colonial governance; in India, moreover, it became part of a more general debate about popular participation in law and civil society.

English custom, ideology, and identity enshrined the trial by jury as one of the fundamental liberties of freeborn Englishmen. As Douglas Hay has noted, during the eighteenth and early nineteenth centuries, the jury was a ubiquitous feature of the English juridical landscape, appearing not only in civil and criminal trials but also in thousands of manor courts, coroner's inquests, and hundred courts.[1] Nevertheless, the role, function, purview, and composition of the jury increasingly became a subject of debate in England, especially as a result of the organized political opposition that grew up during the years immediately after the French Revolution, Pitt's subsequent repression of dissent, and the post-war reform movements that culminated in the Peterloo Massacre and the passage of the infamous Six Acts in 1819.

It is perhaps not surprising, therefore, that, given the growing prominence of the debate over juries in England, British judicial officials and military officers also began to recognize them in the form of the panchayat at about the same time. This appears to have been a new phenomenon. In the quarter century before 1800, Company officials in India already had a variety of experiences with panchayats, but they rarely equated them to an English jury. In nearly every case, panchayats were recognized either as religious institutions that regulated caste discipline or as collective organizations representing specific groups of artisans or traders. In Bombay, for example, the Governor and the Mayor's Court had several issues presented to them regarding the customs and discipline administered by the Parsi Panchayat. In 1778, the Governor of Bombay, William Hornby, was petitioned requesting the authority to shame transgressors before the

[1] Douglas Hay, "The Class Composition of the Palladium of Liberty: Trial Jurors in the Eighteenth Century," in J. S. Cockburn and Thomas A. Green eds., *Twelve Good Men and True: The Criminal Trial Jury in England, 1200–1800* (Princeton: Princeton University Press, 1988), pp. 308–9.

panchayat by hitting them with shoes. Hornby granted the panchayat's request, but he prohibited them from employing any other form of corporal punishment.[2] In 1786, the British government in Bombay again intervened in a dispute involving the Parsi Panchayat, this time not only revoking the panchayat's authority to punish "by the slipper," but, more importantly, reconstituting the panchayat by way of the government appointment of its members.[3]

In western India, the Company's recognition of panchayats was not limited to the judicial oversight of religious discipline. *Jati* panchayats were also well known, especially since they often served as units of revenue assessment and collection. The Company's accounts of the Mughal revenues in Gujarat, for example, list dozens of license fees collected from the *jati* panchayats of opium sellers, tinsmiths, plantain sellers, goldsmiths, well-diggers, turmeric sellers, milk sellers, handkerchief makers, and coral brokers, to name but a few.[4] Not surprisingly, perhaps, some British officials expressed the fear that these artisanal *jati* panchayats were analogous to British trade unions and thus, after 1799, constituted unlawful trade union combinations.[5] John Melville, the Magistrate at Dacca, however, warned against confusing the purpose and function of these two types of organization. "I have heard some persons object to punchauts," he wrote, "because they have known of unlawful combinations under that name, but this, I should observe to them, is speaking of a different matter, and a magistrate would surely not do his duty, who did not prevent such combinations."[6]

Judge Melville, in fact, was among the first Company officials to envision the panchayat as a specifically juridical institution, an idea that later came to dominate British judicial policy in India during the

[2] Dosabhai Framji Karaka, *History of the Parsis Including their Manners, Customs, Religion and Present Position* (1884; Whitefish, MT: Kessinger Publishing, 2004), pp. 186–7.

[3] IOR/P/148/1, Bombay Mayor's Court Proceedings, 26 October 1790, ff. 2629–37; Karaka, *History of the Parsis*, pp. 187–90; Mitra Sharafi, *Law and Identity in Colonial South Asia: Parsi Legal Culture, 1772–1947* (New York: Cambridge University Press, 2014), pp. 78–82. I wish to thank Prof. Sharafi for sharing her work prior to publication.

[4] PP, *Papers Presented to the House of Commons, Relating to East India Affairs, Surat, 1795–1800*, Vol. 27 (1806), pp. 338–9. On *jati* panchayats in eighteenth-century Jodhpur, see Nandita Prasad Sahai, "Collaboration and Conflict: Artisanal Jati Panchayats and the Eighteenth Century Jodhpur State," *Medieval History Journal*, Vol. 5, No. 1 (2002), pp. 77–101.

[5] "Combinations," or trade unions, had been criminalized in England by the Combination Acts of 1799 and 1800 (39 Geo. 3, c. 81 and 39 & 40 Geo. 3, c. 106). For an excellent legal survey, see John V. Orth, *Combination and Conspiracy: A Legal History of Trade Unionism, 1721–1906* (Oxford: Clarendon Press, 1991).

[6] PP, *East India Affairs. No. 3. Copy of the 15th and 35th Interrogatories; Proposed, by the Governor General in Council of Bengal, to the Judges of Circuit, and the Zillah Judges, in 1801: – with, the Answers of the Said Judges to those Interrogatories* (1813), p. 20.

first quarter of the nineteenth century. Indeed, the remarks made in his 1801 letter to the Government of Bengal were often repeated in later communications from London concerning the role of panchayats in the administration of justice.[7] In those remarks, he imagined the panchayat as an alternative to litigation, functioning as an arbitration tribunal and thus serving to mitigate the problems associated with the British courts which were, in his words, "a source of great unhappiness, the parent of multiplied [*sic*] crimes."[8]

The analogy made between the customary functions of the panchayat and those of English tribunals of arbitration was one of the principal ways in which British administrators attempted to understand and adapt the panchayat to colonial governance. But this was only one of several competing perceptions of the panchayat among British officers, administrators, and observers during the early nineteenth century. Equally important was the notion that the panchayat was more closely akin to a British summary court, especially although not exclusively with jurisdiction over petty civil disputes. In addition, there were those who imagined the panchayat as a jury. This construction of the panchayat possessed a special resonance for its adherents, for it complemented a particular imagining not only of India's pre-Mughal past but also England's common-law history and the connections between the two.

Perhaps the earliest expression of this analogy was presented in Mark Wilks' *Report on the Interior Administration, Resources, and Expenditure of the Government of Mysoor*, submitted in 1799 and published in 1805. Wilks had been commissioned into the Company's military service in 1782, served in Cornwallis' army during the third Anglo-Mysore War, and was later the Resident at the court of Mysore between 1803 and 1808.[9] His description of the Mysore panchayats avoids using the term "jury" specifically. However, Wilks does describe the process as a "public trial" before "a Panchaet or Commission of Five, to be assembled in open Cutcherrie; to which all inhabitants of respectability and unconnected with the party, have the right of becoming

[7] See, for example, IOR/E/4/912, Madras Dispatches, 29 April 1814, ff. 589–93 and PP, *East India Affairs: Papers Relating to the Police, and Civil and Criminal Justice under the Respective Governments of Bengal, Fort St. George, and Bombay; from 1810 to the Present Time*, Judicial Letter to Fort St. George, 29 April 1814 (London, 1819), p. 299.

[8] PP, *East India Affairs. No. 3. Copy of the 15th and 35th Interrogatories*, p. 20.

[9] E. I. Carlyle, "Wilks, Mark (c. 1760–1831)," rev. Roger T. Stearn, *ODNB* (Oxford University Press, 2004), online edn., May 2008, www.oxforddnb.com.wam.leeds.ac.uk/view/article/29434, accessed 19 December 2012.

assessors."[10] The term "assessor" is especially significant here. In England, assessors had long been used as expert jurors in admiralty cases, for example, but by the end of the eighteenth century the term had largely become associated with those who were specially chosen and paid to serve on special, or expert, juries.[11] Bentham's attack upon the special jury system, *The Elements of the Art of Packing, as applied to Special Juries*, written in 1808, often refers to these select jurors as assessors.[12] For him, special jurors were nothing less than "a *standing* body of assessors, instruments tenanted in common by the leading members of administration, by the Judges, and by the other crown-lawyers – troops enlisted, trained, and paid by the crown-lawyers, liable to be cashiered, each of them, at any time, without a word of explanation."[13]

Regardless of Bentham's obvious antipathy to the system of special juries, Wilks' own description of the panchayat, perhaps necessarily, drew upon the language of trial by jury in order to comprehend what was, to him, an alien system of justice. Obviously, we will never know what nuances, distinctions, or processes he either missed or misunderstood, because his understanding of the late eighteenth-century panchayat was framed in this manner. However, he clearly was favorably impressed, if only by way of analogy, by the judicial functioning of the panchayat system. Criminal trials in Mysore, he reported, were convened by regional administrators (*subhedars*) and conducted before a panchayat whose decision was then sent for review and sentencing to the *diwan*, Mysore's chief minister. In civil trials, local magistrates (*amins*) exercised summary jurisdiction over petty cases, but cases involving more significant sums were heard by panchayat. Depending on the complexity of the matter, the results of the panchayat's deliberations were then forwarded to the *amin*, *subhedar*, or *diwan* for final judgment.[14]

[10] Mark Wilks, *Report on the Interior Administration, Resources, and Expenditure of the Government of Mysoor, under the System Prescribed by the Orders of the Governor General in Council, Dated 4th September 1799* (Fort William, 1805), pp. 22–3.

[11] On special juries during this period, see James Oldham, "Special Juries in England: Nineteenth Century Usage and Reform," *Journal of Legal History*, Vol. 8, No. 2 (1987), pp. 148–66; on assessors in admiralty law, see J. H. Beuscher, "The Use of Experts by the Courts," *Harvard Law Review*, Vol. 54, No. 7 (May 1941), pp. 1109–10 and Déirdre M. Dwyer, "Expert Evidence in the English Civil Courts, 1550–1800," *Journal of Legal History*, Vol. 28, No. 1 (April 2007), pp. 106–9.

[12] Jeremy Bentham, *The Elements of the Art of Packing, as Applied to Special Juries, Particularly in Cases of Libel Law* (London, 1821). Although not published until 1821, the work was originally written in 1808; see Oldham, "Special Juries in England," pp. 153–4.

[13] Bentham, *Elements of the Art of Packing*, p. 5. Emphasis in original.

[14] Wilks, *Report*, pp. 22–7.

Wilks' *Report* explicitly praised many aspects of the system of trial by panchayat, but only in so far as they reflected English jurisprudence, English trial procedures, and, of equal importance, Enlightenment sympathies. Thus Wilks praised the fact that the members of panchayats were drawn only from "inhabitants of respectability," that the trials were public and not private, and that this "publicity is considered to afford an important security against irregular or partial proceedings."[15] Procedures, he noted, differed significantly from English practices, but he seems to have been impressed by, or at least given tacit approval of, the process whereby both defendants and plaintiffs gave their "narratives" of the affair *viva voce*, after which "this narrative is carefully committed to writing, and twice read over to the party who corrects what has not been properly stated; the document is then authenticated by the signature of the party, of two witnesses, and of a public Officer."[16] Furthermore, he approved of the fact that decisions of the panchayat were subject to appeal and that the penal system was, in his view, proportionate. He appears to have admired the fact that corporal punishment was prohibited, that the death penalty was imposed only upon conviction of charges of murder or "plunder on the frontier," and that "fines are discouraged, as a dangerous instrument in the hands of subordinate authority."[17]

However, where panchayat procedures differed from English jurisprudence, Wilks was much less sympathetic. His most critical comments were reserved for the practice of giving testimony before the panchayat. Unlike in the West, there was neither a presumption of innocence nor a presumption that witnesses were telling the truth. All evidence presented before the panchayat was presumed to be false until or unless it was corroborated by other witnesses. "It is a fixed rule of evidence in Mysoor," Wilks wrote, "to suspect as false the testimony of every Witness, until its truth is otherwise supported."[18] Wilks' further investigations into the matter, including frequent conversations with the *diwan* and "the most intelligent members of these Panchaets," only resulted in the reluctant recognition that these leading members of society did not hesitate "to defend the rule, and to avow, as an abstract proposition founded on experience, that the presumption is infinitely stronger against the veracity, than in favor of

[15] Ibid., pp. 23; 25. [16] Ibid., p. 25. [17] Ibid., p. 23. [18] Ibid., p. 26.

the truth, of a witness."[19] He found great difficulty in "reconciling this rule of evidence to any fixed principles of jurisprudence."[20]

Its significance, to him, was viewed not only in terms of civil and criminal procedure but, more importantly, in terms of "the defective morals of the people."[21] Wilks reasoned that the presumption of false testimony was rooted in the fact that there was nothing equivalent to the Western testimony upon oath. To him, this was the most essential difference between English and Indian jurisprudence. There were many ramifications to this alleged deficiency. Wilks suggested that it might have been the source of Indians' "lamentably deficient" regard for "that ordinary degree of veracity," which so obsessed the colonial imagination. More importantly, however, he drew upon an eclectic combination of common-law tradition and Enlightenment philosophy to condemn Hinduism generally in this regard.

In England, religion and oath taking were inextricably linked together. Indeed, the latter was dependent upon the former.[22] In this regard, oath taking was as much a civil, religious, and moral issue as it was a legal one. The law in Mysore was not based either upon the presumption of innocence or the importance of oath taking because Hinduism failed to bind together "the consciences of men." Drawing upon a relatively brief discussion in Montesquieu's *The Spirit of Laws*, Wilks suggested that the truth or falsity of the theology of Hinduism was not significant here, but its civil function was. Like Montesquieu, he noted "that religion, however erroneous, is the best security we can have for the probity of men; and that its errors may be corrected by civil laws, extending their influence over the morals of the people."[23] Therefore, in the case of rendering testimony and providing for oath taking, considering all of their moral and social implications, Wilks concluded that Hinduism had failed in this essential civic task.[24]

Nevertheless, despite his reservations concerning oath taking and despite avoiding the term "jury" to describe the function of the

[19] Ibid., p. 27. [20] Ibid., p. 27. [21] Ibid., p. 28.

[22] James Oldham, "Truth-Telling in the Eighteenth-Century English Courtroom," *LHR*, Vol. 12, No. 1 (Spring 1994), pp. 102–7.

[23] Wilks, *Report*, p. 28; Baron de Montesquieu, *The Spirit of the Laws*, Vol. II, 1st American edn. (Worcester, 1802), Chapter XIV, p. 134: "As both religion and the civil laws ought to have a peculiar tendency to render men good citizens, it is evident that when one of these deviate from this end, the tendency of the other ought to be strengthened."

[24] Wilks obviously was well-read in Enlightenment philosophy. He also suggested that the moral failure resulting from these errors might be corrected by the hand of a "benevolent legislator," a theme taken up by many in the Scottish Enlightenment tradition. See Wilks, *Report*, pp. 27–8.

panchayat, Wilks' *Report* is the first major analysis that at the very least suggests an identity or analogy between the panchayat and the jury. Yet the circulation of the *Report* was certainly not a wide one nor was it specifically addressed to the public. However, in 1810, Wilks went on to publish the first of the multi-volume *Historical Sketches of the South of India*, a work that was of much greater importance for the British reception and understanding of the panchayat in several regards. The *Historical Sketches* appears to contain the first account in Britain of the panchayat intended for a public audience. Wilks himself noted in a footnote to the first edition that the panchayat was "an institution so entirely neglected or misunderstood, that I believe its existence is now, for the first time, presented to the notice of the English public."[25] In addition, the *Historical Sketches* now specifically invoked an analogy between the panchayat and the English jury, the analogy that had been carefully avoided in Wilks' earlier *Report*. Finally, Wilks posited the logical corollary that if India possessed its own form of the jury, then by extension it must also possess its own form of the common law. Therefore, Wilks contended that if "Anglo-Indian legislators would throw off" their prejudices, "they would find the rules of proceeding prescribed by the Hindoo code (with all its numerous imperfections on its head), combined with local customs, or common law of India, not ill adapted to the state of society to which it is intended to apply; and in the *Panchaiet* or *Indian jury*, which is (or rather was) universally established in the south as the common law of the land, an admirable instrument of practical decision."[26]

Interestingly, Wilks himself realized that his earlier *Report* had contributed to the entrenched British prejudice against Indians and their participation in the legal system. He took the opportunity of the publication of the *Historical Sketches* to accept the fact "that the reproach of English prejudice applies in a certain degree to some of my observations on this subject in 1804: and I regret having made them at all, because they have been misapprehended."[27] In its place, he took up a theme that later would also be taken up by many British Orientalists; that is, to really "know" Indians, it "requires to have lived and been educated among them, as one of themselves." In this

[25] Mark Wilks, *Historical Sketches of the South of India, in an Attempt to Trace the History of Mysoor; from the Origin of the Hindoo Government of that State, to the Extinction of the Mohammedan Dynasty in 1799*, Vol. I (London, 1810), p. 501.

[26] Ibid., p. 501. Emphasis in original. [27] Ibid., p. 501.

regard, he implicitly admits that his previous remarks had been the result of not really "knowing" the Indian. However, after serving as Resident at Mysore for several years, he felt sure enough to declare that "the Hindoo character, like all others, is of a mixed nature."[28]

And yet despite the admissions that Hindus (but not Muslims) were "like all others," that India possessed a common law, and that the panchayat was a trial by jury, Wilks could not concede that Britain's colonial control of India was unwarranted, mistaken, or unethical. He willingly admitted that few, if any, Europeans could acquire the knowledge or experience to "place him on a level with an intelligent Hindoo Panchayet." However, this only meant to him that India could be controlled with a smaller British judicial establishment. "To govern the Hindoos in reality, and not in pretence," he wrote, "by their own laws and customs, civil and criminal, would admit of extensive aid in judges and juries (panchaiets) from among the natives themselves, checked without material danger of corruption by a reduced scale of European controul [*sic*]."[29] In sum, Wilks had reached the limit or barrier of the imperial mentality.

Unfortunately, little is known of Wilks' early personal history, save for the fact that he was born on the Isle of Man and educated there for the clergy.[30] There are no clear indications or suggestions as to how or when he became educated in the works of the Enlightenment.[31] However, his publications place him squarely in the Scottish Orientalist tradition, a

[28] Ibid. [29] Ibid., p. 502.

[30] Carlyle, "Wilks, Mark," *ODNB*; see also, Diocesan Registry, 1776: The Admission of Mark Wilks as an Academic Scholar at Castletown; originally published in *Journal of Manx Museum*, Vol. III (1935–7), Document No. 146, p. 78, available online at www.isle-of-man.com/manxnotebook/jmmuseum/d146.htm, accessed 22 December 2012.

[31] Jane Rendall, "Scottish Orientalism: From Robertson to James Mill," *Historical Journal*, Vol. 25, No. 1 (March 1982), p. 49 notes in passing that Sir James Mackintosh, a prominent Scottish Orientalist, advised Wilks in the writing of his *Historical Sketches*. This was unlikely to have been the case with regard to the first volume published in 1810, from which the material quoted earlier is drawn, although it may have been true for the later volumes. According to his *Memoirs*, Mackintosh first read the initial volume in December 1810 and had a very mixed reaction. He praised it highly for opening a new "era in this branch of literature," but was especially critical of Wilks' view of law and the Indian character. While Mackintosh agreed that there was much to be learned from traditional Indian society and that it was inappropriate to apply the "narrow pedantry" of English law to India, he also noted that "I completely differ from him in that more favorable opinion of the Indian character, to which he now inclines; and I never can disapprove any system of laws for having a tendency, slowly and indirectly, to abolish so detestable a system as that of castes . . . Colonel Wilks, pleased with the manners and understanding of a few Mahometans and Bramins, has borne far too favorable a testimony to the state of society, which elevates these robbers and impostors." Sir James Mackintosh, *Memoirs of the Life of the Right Honourable Sir James Mackintosh*, R. J. Mackintosh, ed., Vol. II, 2nd edn. (London, 1836), pp. 68; 70–1.

tradition that placed great value upon India's historical traditions and sought to revive India's ancient institutions. Perhaps it was his association with Sir John Malcolm, one of the most prominent Company officer-officials of the early nineteenth century, which directed him along this course. Malcolm had been appointed the political Resident at the court of Mysore in 1803. However, illness and service in the Second Anglo-Maratha War had prevented his taking up the position until November 1804. During the interval, Wilks had been appointed as acting Resident there and appears to have been among Malcolm's circle of friends in Mysore, or at the very least one of those who was among his closest associates.[32]

Malcolm was born in Scotland in 1769 and studied briefly at the University of Edinburgh, but from a very young age he had made his career in the service of the army of the East India Company. His rather startling military and diplomatic career in India, including a close friendship with Arthur Wellesley, later the duke of Wellington, was the stuff of which schoolboy stories of the later Victorian era were made.[33] He was also a keen observer and advocate of the panchayat system. However, unlike Wilks, he was less sure that the panchayat was a form of trial by jury and, in fact, never appears to have used the term "jury" to describe the panchayat's form or function.

In his published works, Malcolm first mentioned the panchayat in the *Sketch of the Sikhs*, which appeared in 1812.[34] Here, he described the panchayat only as "a court of arbitration" and the members of panchayats as "arbitrators."[35] Malcolm's later work, *A Memoir of Central India*, published in London in 1823, offered a much more nuanced view of the panchayat than that which had appeared in the *Sketch of the Sikhs*.[36] The material in the *Memoir* was drawn almost entirely from Malcolm's earlier report on the governing of Malwa that

[32] John William Kaye, *The Life and Correspondence of Major-General Sir John Malcolm, G. C. B., Late Envoy to Persia, and Governor of Bombay, from Unpublished Letters and Journals*, Vol. I (London, 1856), p. 296. The friendship is suggested in a letter to Malcolm from Arthur Wellesley reprinted in Kaye's *Life*, p. 376.

[33] See Kaye's, *Life* and, for a more sober discussion, Robert Eric Frykenberg, "Malcolm, Sir John (1769–1833)," *ODNB* (Oxford University Press, 2004), online edn., May 2009, www.oxforddnb.com.wam.leeds.ac.uk/view/article/17864, accessed 22 December 2012.

[34] John Malcolm, *Sketch of the Sikhs: A Singular Nation, Who Inhabit the Provinces of the Penjab* (London, 1812). Malcolm's first published work, *Sketch of the Political History of India* (London, 1811), does not mention panchayats nor does he discuss the administration of justice more generally at any great length or depth.

[35] Malcolm, *Sketch of the Sikhs*, pp. 127–8.

[36] John Malcolm, *A Memoir of Central India, including Malwa, and the Adjoining Provinces*, 2 vols. (London, 1823).

had been submitted to the Marquess of Hastings, the Governor-General, in 1821. Published in Calcutta the following year as the *Report on the Province of Malwa, and Adjoining Districts*, Malcolm not only described the importance of the panchayat in central Indian society but also delineated the variety of its forms and functions.[37] However, in neither the *Report* nor the *Memoir* did he ever draw upon the common-law jury analogy.

Instead, he elaborated on what he believed to be two fundamental forms of the panchayat system of justice serving either as investigatory tribunals, whose results were transmitted to the ruler for disposition, or as tribunals of independent arbitration and mediation. Writing of the variety of panchayats in the territories ruled by the Maratha Peshwas and the Rajput princes of Malwa, Malcolm concluded that

> the forms of Punjayets differ in many places, but the principles by which they are regulated are every where the same. These Courts, as they now exist in Malwa, may be divided into two. The first (composed of government officers and heads of classes) who aid the Prince or his chief officers into enquiring into civil and criminal cases; and the second, Punjayets of arbitration. The former are mere Courts of investigation, and have little, if any, fixed character; and as they depend, both in their formation and proceedings, on the will of the ruler and his delegated officers, they can hardly be deemed an established and recognized part of government: certainly not so much as the second, or Courts of arbitration. These are of two kinds, which may be termed public and private, where the parties (not delinquents) are at issue on any case, and appeal to the ruling authority. A Punjayet sits, in which they have a right to name an equal number, and the Government appoints an officer as umpire to preside. The parties concerned have, however, a right to object to this person if they deem him partial; and, as this Court is one which cannot be constituted but through their assent, the objection, if persevered in, compels the nomination of another. In private arbitration, the Government is not appealed to, but in all cases, where the parties refer by mutual consent to a court of arbitration, they bind themselves . . . to abide by the award.[38]

The inability to precisely classify the functions of the panchayat within the context of contemporary British legal categories was a recurring theme among officials and it was perhaps no more apparent than in the career of Sir Thomas Munro. Without doubt, Munro was

[37] John Malcolm, *Report on the Province of Malwa, and Adjoining Districts* (Calcutta, 1822).
[38] Ibid., pp. 391–2.

the foremost advocate of the restoration of panchayats during the first quarter of the nineteenth century. His early advocacy of the panchayat was based on the perception, as we already have seen in the case of Wilks, that India possessed a common law and that the jury as panchayat was one of its fundamental elements. Although Wilks may very well have been the first to bring this perspective before the British public, Munro's private advocacy of this position predated the publication of Wilks' *Historical Sketches* by three years. First elaborated in a Company report dated 15 August 1807, Munro made the dogmatic and oft-repeated claim that "there can be no doubt that the trial by Punchayet is as much the common law of India in civil matters, as that by Jury is of England."[39]

Munro's 1807 *Report of the Collector of the Ceded Districts* laid less emphasis upon the specific forms and practices of actually functioning panchayats than upon the failures and inadequacies of the operation of the Company's judicial code in the Bengal Presidency. As such, the *Report* reveals much more about the Orientalist desire to revive the ancient institutions of India than about the quotidian realities of implementing a system of judicature based upon panchayats. Decisions in the Bengal Company courts, Munro argued, were slow, costly, liable to corruption, and, most importantly, frequently made by judges ill-informed of the customs, practices, and language of the litigants. "The Native who has a good cause," he wrote, "always applies for a Punchayet while he who has a bad one, seeks the decision of a Collector or a Judge because he knows that it is easier to deceive them." The resurrection of the panchayat would mitigate these problems by encouraging the publicity of judicial decision-making and by providing for judgments to be made by those most familiar with the language, culture, and customs of the litigants. "The natives," Munro concluded, "surely cannot with any foundation be said to be judged by their own laws while the trial by Punchayet to which they have always been accustomed is done away."[40]

Later in 1807, Munro returned to London and for the next several years worked closely with both officials of the East India Company and

[39] IOR/H/686, Thomas Munro, *Report of the Collector of the Ceded Districts of 15th August 1807, on the Advantages and Disadvantages of the Zemindary Permanent Settlements and of the Ryotwar Settlements*, pp. 292–7.

[40] IOR/H/686, Munro, *Report of the Collector of the Ceded Districts*, pp. 292–7. Relevant passages from this report were later extracted and published as "Trial by Panchayat" in Thomas Munro, *Major-General Thomas Munro, Bart., K. C. B., Governor of Madras: Selections from his Minutes and other Official Writings*, Vol. II, Alexander J. Arbuthnot, ed. (London, 1881), pp. 3–6.

members of parliament, promoting reform of the so-called Cornwallis system, which had created a separate British judiciary to govern India, and the restoration of panchayats in the Company's Indian territories.[41] His influence was especially felt among the members of the parliamentary Select Committee on the Affairs of the East India Company, which produced the multi-volume *Fifth Report* in 1812–1813.[42] Although Munro's testimony before the Committee was specifically on matters of trade and settlement, his work with the Company soon bore fruit.[43] After the renewal of its charter in 1813, the Company launched an inquiry into the administration of justice and the system of police in India. Munro appears to have taken a leading role in this investigation. Sometime in 1813, he wrote a memo to the Company on the reorganization of the judicial system in India and, in November of that year, he submitted a further letter on the topic. In both, he argued that the imposition of the British system of justice had created "the most expensive judicial system in the world," which was "attended with vexatious delays, forms, and expense." Moreover, by superseding the traditional village *patel* (headman) and *curnum* (clerk), the Company had undermined their "ancient authority" and thereby weakened their support of the government.[44]

To solve these problems, Munro recommended the restoration of the ancient constitution of "the municipal institution of the village corporations, or little republics, of which India is composed."[45] That entailed the restoration of the traditional authority of local officials and the resuscitation of the panchayat to settle civil disputes. "If we seek to ameliorate the character of the people of India," Munro concluded, "we must maintain their ancient institutions so long as they are respected by themselves: we must support the authority of the

[41] T. H. Beaglehole, *Thomas Munro and the Development of Administrative Policy in Madras, 1792–1818* (Cambridge: Cambridge University Press, 1966), Chapter 4; Burton Stein, *Thomas Munro: The Origins of the Colonial State and his Vision of Empire* (Delhi: Oxford University Press, 1989), pp. 149–67.

[42] PP, *Fifth Report from the Select Committee of the House of Commons on the Affairs of the East India Company*, 3 vols. (1812–1813).

[43] PP, *Minutes of Evidence taken before the Committee of the Whole House, and the Select Committee on the Affairs of the East India Company* (1813), pp. 121–57; 167–75.

[44] Thomas Munro, "Memorandum on the Revision of the Judicial System," reprinted in *Selection of Papers from the Records at the East-India House Relating to the Revenue, Police, and Civil and Criminal Justice, under the Company's Governments in India*, Vol. II (London, 1820), pp. 105–6.

[45] Thomas Munro, "Answers to Court Queries," 22 November 1813, reprinted in *Selection of Papers from the Records at the East-India House*, II, p. 114. This appears to be the first time that the description of the Indian village as an autonomous republic was used. The analogy would later become closely identified with Gandhi and the independence movement.

Potails, as the instruments by which subordination is preserved in the villages, and the trial by punchayet, as that by which litigations are adjusted."[46]

By April 1814, concerned about the enormous backlog of cases that had been accumulating in the Company courts, the Board of Directors in London had ordered the Madras Presidency to reform its judicial system and to incorporate Munro's recommendations.[47] At the same time, Munro was dispatched back to Madras with a special appointment to head a commission to investigate the administration of justice there.[48] The Commission circulated a draft of the new government Regulations in July of 1815, which were then adopted in a series of steps between May and September 1816.[49]

Together, Regulations IV–VII remodeled the Madras judicial system along the lines envisioned by Munro.[50] Judicial and revenue authority was transferred to village headmen, now styled the village *munsif*, and village panchayats were authorized to try and determine cases involving money and personal property. The procedures established by Regulations V and VII for trial by panchayat were an odd mixture of English legal practice and Munro's imaginative recreation of the panchayat's customary rules. In particular, this meant combining the voluntary practices of Munro's imagined ancient panchayat with those elements of compulsion established in English law. Thus, Indian litigants were allowed the option of either submitting their claim to the *munsif* for summary justice or choosing to have their case heard by a panchayat. In all suits, the voluntary approval of both the defendant and the plaintiff was required before proceeding to trial by panchayat.[51] Although "the most intelligent and respectable inhabitants of the village" were bound to serve as jurors only "if he be willing to undertake the duty," fines were nonetheless to be assessed upon those who did not attend and, as in English procedures, a rotation system, or jury list, established. Indeed, the compulsion provided by the implementation of

[46] Munro, "Answers to Court Queries," p. 120.

[47] IOR/E/4/912, Madras Dispatches, 29 April 1814.

[48] *Selection of Papers from the Records at the East-India House*, II, p. 257.

[49] The draft regulation and accompanying letter are reproduced in *Selections from the Records of Fort St. George: Papers regarding the Village Punchayet and other Judicial Systems of Administration, 1812–1816* (Madras, 1916), pp. 43–65.

[50] Catherine Sandin Meschievitz, "Civil Litigation and Judicial Policy in the Madras Presidency, 1800–1843" (Ph. D. thesis, University of Wisconsin-Madison, 1986), pp. 155–67.

[51] In the draft regulations, trial by panchayat could be ordered upon the request of only one of the parties, if the suit was valued at fewer than Rs. 100; see, *Selections from the Records of Fort St. George*, p. 61.

fines occurs repeatedly in the Regulations. Thus fines could be imposed upon witnesses who refused to attend a panchayat, parties or their representatives found guilty of contempt, and panchayat members found guilty of corruption.

The procedures of a trial by panchayat themselves exemplified Munro's complicated or, some might say, confused attempt to merge what he believed to be the practices of the customary panchayat with those of English civil procedure. Parties to the suit could be represented by professional pleaders (*vakils*), but only if the *vakils* were their relatives, servants, or dependents and possessed a *vakalatnamah*, or pleader's license. Plaintiffs were required to submit a written complaint, but defendants only a verbal answer. Both plaintiffs and defendants were required to submit to the panchayat a pre-trial list of their witnesses and exhibits. Witnesses in cases valued at over Rs. 20 were to be deposed by the panchayat and their testimony written down and signed or marked. In suits valued at fewer than Rs. 20, however, oral depositions were permitted. Appeals from the decisions of village panchayats were prohibited, except on the grounds of alleged corruption or gross partiality. Finally, the decisions of panchayats were bound neither by law nor legal precedence. Munro, therefore, seemingly imagined the panchayat as a court of equity whose decisions were to be reached only "according to justice and right."

The failure of Munro's attempt to institute his vision of trial by panchayat was apparent almost immediately. On the one hand, the initial report on the effects of the changes submitted by George Stratton, one of the members of Munro's judicial commission, in April 1818, revealed that the number of suits filed in all of the Company's courts annually had risen by almost 40 percent under the new system. On the other hand, the number of suits decided by village panchayats was infinitesimal. Of the 65,483 cases heard before all of the courts in the Presidency during the year 1817, only 250, or 0.4 percent, had been heard by village panchayats.[52] Moreover, throughout the next several years, the record of the panchayats showed no improvement. Indeed, between 1820 and 1826, village panchayats heard on average only 52 cases each year and, in total, they heard only 0.1 percent of all cases during those years.[53]

52 *Selection of Papers from the Records at the East-India House*, II, "Report of Mr. George Stratton," 13 April 1818, pp. 540–51.

53 Statistics calculated from data in Meschievitz, "Civil Litigation and Judicial Policy," Table 5.3, p. 185.

The fact that Indian litigants had so decisively rejected the British incarnation of trial by panchayat in favor of the summary justice meted out by village *munsifs* and the winner-take-all decisions of the British courts must have been a bitter blow to Munro. Until his death in 1827, he continued to defend the trial by panchayat, but his increasingly strident defense came to rely upon the notions that the failure of the system had been due to the fact that its detractors had forced the introduction of too many rules governing panchayat procedures as well as the idea that a greater degree of compulsion was necessary to make the system work properly. In his *Minute* on the state of India, submitted in December 1824, Munro complained that in order to mollify the opponents of trial by panchayat, the system "was placed under so many restrictions as to deprive it of much of its utility."[54] The revival of the panchayat, he wrote, "was opposed by some very intelligent men, on the ground of its form and proceedings being altogether so irregular as to be quite incompatible with the system of our courts." He insisted that all the evidence collected by Company officials had proven that panchayats had been used extensively in India and that they remained popular "among the natives." Given their popularity and their customary standing, Munro advocated extending the jurisdiction of panchayats to cover criminal cases and making trial by panchayat compulsory. He recommended that both the provincial (*zilla*) and district courts be abolished in favor of a more extensive employment of trial by panchayat and that "neither party should have the option of declining its jurisdiction."[55]

By the time of Munro's *Minute*, however, the discussion of the trial by jury in India had shifted considerably. The changing terms of the debate were influenced by several factors, including the growing recognition that the English-style trial by jury had been successfully introduced in Ceylon, the introduction of a bill in parliament on judges in India, and, most directly perhaps, by the debate surrounding the introduction of reforms to the jury trial in England. Home Secretary Robert Peel had first introduced the subject of jury reform in England before the House of Commons in February 1824.[56] He stated then that the purpose of the bill was to consolidate the statutes relating to the empaneling and composition of juries as well as to

[54] PP, *Copy of a Minute by the Late Sir Thomas Munro, on the State of the Country, and Condition of the People under the Presidency of Fort St. George, Dated 31st December 1824* (1830), p. 21.
[55] Ibid., p. 21. [56] *Hansard*, Commons Debates, Vol. 10, cc. 247–52, 19 February 1824.

introduce new measures designed to compel the attendance of jurors and to transfer the supervision of jury lists to local magistrates, the last of which was later amended to be delegated to churchwardens and overseers. The bill's final version also included important provisions for the significant liberalization of jurors' qualifications and revised rules for the selection of special juries in criminal cases.[57] With the support of parliamentary radicals such as Joseph Hume and John Cam Hobhouse, leave was given to bring in the bill in March 1825 and it quickly became law in June of that year.[58]

At nearly the same time, a now rather obscure Member of Parliament, Charles Watkin Williams Wynn brought in a bill to regulate the salaries of Judges in India.[59] Williams Wynn had been appointed President of the Board of Control of the East India Company in 1822 and the bill, though relatively mundane in this regard, nevertheless drew the attention of the radical MP Joseph Hume. When the bill was brought up for discussion in June 1825, Hume proposed to insert a clause giving Indians the right to serve on juries. He noted that "at the present moment, when an important change is being effected with respect to juries in this country, by calling into action twice the number of individuals who ever were entitled to serve on juries before, it does appear to me that Parliament should not refuse to extend a similar advantage to India."[60]

Like many of his contemporaries, Hume's speech illustrated the ambiguity that surrounded the British understanding of the relationship between the Indian panchayat and the English jury. He first noted that the panchayat was an arbitration tribunal but then immediately proceeded to redefine it as a jury. "Of all the countries in the world," Hume announced,

> India is that which has perhaps the best claim to the trial by jury; for, to a certain extent, it formed part of the old system of Native jurisprudence, under the name of punchayet, on the principle of arbitration. The

[57] Peel pointed out that these last two provisions were among the most important changes provided by the bill. See *Hansard*, Commons Debate, Vol. 13, cc. 799–80, 20 May 1825.

[58] *Hansard*, Commons Debates, Vol. 12, cc. 966–72, 9 March 1825; 6 Geo. IV, c. 50, "An Act for Consolidating and Amending the Laws Relative to Jurors and Juries."

[59] *Journals of the House of Commons*, 15 March 1825, p. 207. On Williams Wynn, see Margaret Escott, "Charles Watkin Williams Wynn (1775–1850), of Llangedwyn, Denb.," in D. R. Fisher, ed., *The History of Parliament: the House of Commons, 1820–1832*, online at www.historyofparliamentonline.org/volume/1820-1832/member/williams-wynn-charles-1775-1850, accessed 27 December 2012.

[60] The proceedings are reprinted in *The Oriental Herald, and Journal of General Literature*, Vol. 6 (July–September 1825), pp. 172–80.

> number of individuals who compose the punchayet is not so large as that of our juries; but that, in my opinion, is of little importance. The trial by punchayet is, in fact, a trial by jury; and it is a benefit which should be extended throughout the Presidencies where the King's courts are established.[61]

Williams Wynn's response was sympathetic, although he ultimately opposed adding the clauses to the bill. He noted that he supported Hume's proposal and indicated that he planned to introduce such a bill the following session. In fact, he said, "I am desirous, whenever a fair opportunity occurs, to secure the jurisdiction of the panchayet to the whole of our Indian empire."[62] However, Williams Wynn could not support Hume's proposal at this time because he believed that such a significant matter required a separate bill. The bill, therefore, limited only to judges' salaries and pensions, became law in July 1825.[63]

The introduction and passage of the East India Judges Act and Peel's Juries Act had encouraged Williams Wynn to inquire into the role and function of juries in India. Even before the parliamentary exchange with Hume, Williams Wynn had written to Alexander Johnston, former Chief Judge and President of the Council in Ceylon, inquiring about the implementation of the jury system there.[64] As one biographer has written, "under Johnston's impulse Ceylon led the vanguard of Indian reform."[65] Among other things, Johnston introduced universal education, promoted the emancipation of slaves, and opened up offices in the British administration of the island to the employment of non-Europeans. Equally important, however, was the fact that in 1810 he had been able to secure from the British government a special charter for Ceylon permitting "natives" and "half-castes" to sit on juries in criminal trials, a plan that had been implemented in November 1811.[66]

[61] *Oriental Herald*, Vol. 6, p. 174. [62] Ibid., p. 176.

[63] 6 Geo. IV c. 85. It actually was a hybrid act, as the title indicates: "An Act for further regulating the Payment of the Salaries and Pensions to his Majesty's Courts in India, and the Bishop of Calcutta; for authorizing the Transportation of Offenders from the Island of Saint Helena; and for more effectually providing for the Administration of Justice in Singapore and Malacca, and certain Colonies on the Coast of Coromandel."

[64] PP, *Report from the Select Committee of the House of Lords Appointed to Inquire into the Present State of the Affairs of the East India Company, and into the Trade between Great Britain, the East Indies and China; with the Minutes of Evidence taken before the Committee* (1830), p. 122.

[65] H. G. Keene, "Johnston, Sir Alexander (1775–1849)", rev. Roger T. Stearn, *Oxford Dictionary of National Biography* (Oxford University Press, 2004); online edn., October 2006, www.oxforddnb.com.wam.leeds.ac.uk/view/article/14927, accessed 27 December 2012.

[66] PP, *Report from the Select Committee of the House of Lords*, pp. 123–4; "Administration of Justice in India: Sir Alexander Johnston's Plan of Reform," *Law Magazine and Review: A Quarterly Journal of Jurisprudence*, Vol. 3, No. 2 (1830), p. 582. Just months before Castlereagh's suicide in

In reply to Williams Wynn's letter of inquiry, Johnston explained in detail how jurors in Ceylon were identified, how juries were empaneled, and the role of the jury in a trial.[67] Subsequently, Williams Wynn duly introduced his Juries in India Bill, which, without any significant debate, received the royal assent in May 1826.[68] The lack of any discussion in either the Lords or the Commons reflected the very weak and anodyne content of the Bill. Unlike the practices introduced in Ceylon by Johnston, in which all freemen over the age of twenty-one were liable for jury service, jurors were selected by lot, and litigants permitted a limited number of peremptory challenges, Williams Wynn's Act was merely an enabling piece of legislation that provided for the eligibility of residents of Calcutta, Madras, and Bombay "to be deemed capable of serving as jurors on grand or petit juries." The rules and regulations regarding qualifications for jury service, the process of selecting jurors, and the role of the jury in a trial all were left unspecified. These procedural issues were to be left to the courts in the respective Presidency towns to decide.

While the Juries in India Act provoked little or no debate in parliament, there was some interest expressed outside of it. In particular, an interesting exchange appeared in the pages of *The Oriental Herald* and *The Asiatic Journal* that revolved specifically around the analogy often made between the English trial by jury and the Indian panchayat. The discussion was initiated by the publication of "System of Punchayet, or Indian Trial by Jury" in the March 1826 issue of the *Oriental Herald*. The anonymous author, most probably James Silk Buckingham, the journal's radical editor, reiterated many of the arguments that had previously been voiced by Munro and others: that the panchayat was the Indian equivalent of the English trial by jury, that it was an institution sanctioned by Indian law and custom, and that its existence

1822, Johnston had also been in contact with him concerning the expansion of trial by jury to India. Johnston's memo on the subject is reprinted in PP, *Report from the Select Committee of the House of Lords*, pp. 136–7.

67 PP, *Report from the Select Committee of the House of Lords*, pp. 123–5. Interestingly, in Johnston's testimony before the House of Lords, he distinguished between the trial by jury and the indigenous panchayat that, he believed, was an arbitration tribunal. In Ceylon, he testified, "they had a system of arbitrations, they did not use the word Punchayet; they called it arbitration, and made use of that word for it in Tamul, which, if translated into English, means arbitration." PP, *Report from the Select Committee of the House of Lords*, p. 133.

68 7 Geo. IV c. 37, "An Act to regulate the Appointment of Juries in the East-Indies." Only two very brief discussions are recorded in *Hansard*; see, Commons Debates, Vol. 15, cc. 1–2, 20 March 1826 and Vol. 15, cc. 107–8, 7 April 1826. In both instances, only Joseph Hume spoke on the matter.

bore witness to the fact that India possessed a common-law tradition, a tradition that needed to be restored, reinvigorated, and reinforced by the British government rather than replaced by British courts and British law.[69] The next month, however, a response appeared in *The Asiatic Journal*, the title of which clearly indicates not only the author's perspective but also the continuing opacity of the panchayat to British observers. The letter to the editor, entitled "The Punchayet, or Hindu Form of Arbitration," denied any British culpability in undermining or superseding the "palladium of Indian liberty," the phrase being an adaptation of the common aphorism used to describe the English trial by jury.[70] Claiming that "the punchayet *has not the least analogy*" to the English jury, the author insisted that "by whatever name the punchayet may be now perversely called, it is, in fact, but a species of arbitration."[71] Moreover, the author continued, under the Madras Code, litigants had always been permitted to voluntarily submit their disputes to the decision of a panchayat, but their manifest failure to do so was clear evidence of the lack of both support and "fond affection" that Indian litigants had for the system.[72]

While the 1826 Act may have been anodyne in content, its application in the different Presidencies was certainly less so. As was typical of the era, property qualifications for potential jurors were adopted in Madras, Bombay, and Bengal. Less typical, however, was the fact that potential jurors in Bombay and Madras were required to understand the English language; in Bengal, they were required to read, write, and understand English. Even more restrictive was the requirement adopted in all three Presidencies that only Christians could serve on grand juries and that only they were allowed to sit on petty juries in cases involving Christian defendants. Regardless of these restrictions, in all of the Presidencies, there still appeared to be a small opening for Indian

[69] Anon., "System of Punchayet, or Indian Trial by Jury," *Oriental Herald*, Vol. 8, No. 27 (March 1826), pp. 457–70.

[70] Anon., "The Punchayet, or Hindu Form of Arbitration," *Asiatic Journal and Monthly Register*, Vol. 21, No. 124 (April 1826), pp. 475–81.

[71] Ibid., pp. 477; 479. Emphasis in original.

[72] Ibid., p. 480. It very well may have been the same anonymous author who submitted a further letter to the *Oriental Herald* entitled "Counter-Evidence Respecting the Punchayet, or Indian Trial by Jury." That short letter repeated several of the same assertions presented in the letter previously published in the *Asiatic Journal*. See A. Y., "Counter-Evidence Respecting the Punchayet, or Indian Trial by Jury," *Oriental Herald*, Vol. 9, No. 28 (April 1826), pp. 129–31. In an appended response, the editor, James Silk Buckingham, catalogued the ways in which the British government had altered the panchayat system, concluding that it is "no wonder [the] punchayet is unpopular."

participation as petty jurors in civil cases. However, this opportunity quickly closed. The separate Regulations issued in Bombay, Bengal, and Madras provided that in cases brought before petty juries, at least one-half of the jurors had to be legally defined British subjects; that is, they could not be "native subjects." This nevertheless implied that one-half of the petty jury could also be comprised of Indian subjects.[73]

However, even this situation was contested. Several years earlier, in 1819, the Board of Control had previously decided that Anglo-Indians or half-castes in Bengal were not eligible to serve on juries. The jury reforms being discussed in 1825 raised the issue once again and, in that year, the Bengal government asked for legal advice concerning the status of Anglo-Indians on juries under the forthcoming Act. The question was therefore referred to J. B. Bosanquet, the Company solicitor, whose opinion was issued in January 1826. In that opinion, Bosanquet narrowly construed the term "British subject" to mean not only that an individual's legal standing was determined solely by the father but also that the male parent had to be British-born to be a "British subject." Thus an Anglo-Indian with a British father could sit on a jury, but male children of a British mother and an Indian father could not. This meant, of course, that "no Native of the British Territories in India though a Subject of the King is qualified to serve on Juries."[74] Indians were thus identified as "subjects," but not "British subjects."

Bosanquet's opinion quite clearly illustrates the way in which race and racial identities were being constructed in this period, although it is also quite clear that unlike some lay opinion on race, which often sought to restrict or prohibit Indian civil participation based upon abstract "scientific" theories of moral, mental, or physical degeneracy, Bosanquet's legal opinion was espoused in terms of what he called "the

[73] PP, *Rules Relating to Juries in the Supreme Court of Judicature at Fort William in Bengal* (1828); PP, *Return to an Order of the Honourable House of Commons, Dated 22 May 1828, and 6 May 1829; – for a Copy of the Regulations That Have Been Adopted by the Supreme Courts at the Several Presidencies in India, as to Natives Sitting on Juries, under 7 Geo. IV c. 37; – So far as Relates to the Supreme Court of Judicature at Bombay* (1829); PP, *Further Return to an Order of the House of Commons, Dated 22 May 1828, and 6 May 1829; – for Copy of the Regulations That Have Been Adopted by the Supreme Courts at the Several Presidencies in India, as to Natives Sitting on Juries, under 7 Geo. IV c. 37; – so far as Relates to Madras* (1829).

[74] IOR/L/L/6/2, Law Cases and Opinions of Council, Case No. 695, "Eligibility of Anglo-Asiatics to Serve on Juries in Bengal," 26 January 1825. Bosanquet's opinion is dated 26 January 1826. He cited to the legal maxim "Lex Angliæ nunquam matris sed semper patria conditionem imiatri partum judicat," or, "The Law of England adjudges that the offspring shall follow the condition of the father, not of the mother."

national character." Of course, this concept in no way precludes racism, as the twentieth century would more than prove. However, it is equally possible, and perhaps even likely, that Bosanquet was expressing himself in the discourse of what Norbert Peabody has described as "Romantic nationalism" rather than scientific racism.[75] Whichever the case, the intended effect was the same: all Indians and a significant portion of Anglo-Indians in Bengal were to be prohibited from serving on juries.

In practice, there appears to have been a very significant degree of variation in the extent to which Bosanquet's opinion was adopted outside of Bengal. In Bombay, for example, Sir Edward West, Chief Justice of the Supreme Court, political economist, and judicial reformer, opened petty juries to Indians shortly before his death in 1828.[76] Robert Rickards, a former member of the council in Bombay and later factory inspector in England, recalled that West "did the honour of permitting the natives into the petit jury; on which occasions the Europeans evinced their utmost displeasure of sitting with them; but the learned judge supported the natives."[77]

Yet, even as the Bombay Chief Judge was acting to open the petty jury to Indian participation, at the same time, the Governor-in-Council of the Bombay Presidency was acting to re-shape, and indeed undermine, the role and function of Indians in the civil judicial process. New judicial regulations eventually passed in 1827 eliminated the jury's role as a finder of fact and refashioned the jury, panchayats, and special juries into mere judicial advisory boards.[78] According to the new Regulations governing civil judicature, European judges were allowed to "derive assistance" from "respectable natives" in three ways: by convening a panchayat, by appointing assessors, or "more nearly as a jury." The remit of the panchayat was to carry out the investigation of any "point or points" at issue in the suit. These assessors, or special jurors, were only to

[75] Norbert Peabody, "Tod's Rajast'han and the Boundaries of Imperial Rule in Nineteenth-Century India," *Modern Asian Studies*, Vol. 30, No. 1 (February 1996), pp. 185–220. Many thanks to Peter Robb for directing me to this article.

[76] See West's obituaries in the *Oriental Herald*, Vol. 20, No. 62 (February 1829), pp. 372–5; *Gentleman's Magazine* (May 1829), pp. 565–6; and, on his contribution to political economy, see Maxine L. Berg, 'West, Sir Edward (bap. 1782, d. 1828)', *ODNB* (Oxford University Press, 2004), online edn., www.oxforddnb.com.wam.leeds.ac.uk/view/article/29079, accessed 9 February 2013.

[77] PP, *Report from the Select Committee of the House of Lords Appointed to Inquire into the Present State of the Affairs of the East India Company* (1830), p. 280.

[78] Bombay Regulation IV, Ch. VI, § XXIV, 1827 reprinted in PP, *Papers Relating to East India Affairs: viz. Regulations Passed by the Governments of Bengal, Fort St. George, and Bombay, in the Year 1827* (1829), p. 89.

submit their opinions or observations to the court. Finally, the newly contrived "near-jury" was to suggest "such points of inquiry as occur to them." No jury comprised of Indians, therefore, was given the authority to determine the facts of a case and, moreover, "it is clearly to be understood," the Regulation stated, "that under all modes of procedure described in the three preceding clauses, the decision is vested exclusively in the [European] authority presiding in the court."

In the Madras Presidency, at the same time, Munro sought to extend the right of Indians to sit on criminal juries, believing that in civil cases litigants already possessed the option of being heard by a panchayat. However, his death from cholera in July 1827 delayed the plan's implementation, yet it was subsequently instituted by the acting Governor, Henry Graeme, as Regulation X of 1827. Entitled "For the gradual introduction of Trial by Jury in the Criminal Judicature of the Territories subject to the Presidency of Fort St. George," the Regulation closely followed the procedures implemented by Alexander Johnston in Ceylon, including the selection of jurors by lot, payment of jurors, the permission of peremptory challenges, and, perhaps most notably, the absence of any property qualification.[79] However, according to the later parliamentary testimony of Thomas Baber, a former senior Judge of the Provincial Court of Appeals in the Presidency, Munro and Graeme's successors "did not think that the natives were morally fit to discharge the duty with integrity and impartiality." Indeed, Stephen Lushington, Munro's successor as Governor of Madras, expressed his dismay at "the precipitancy with which this great change in the administration had been introduced" and immediately suspended the introduction of the Regulation.[80]

Upon Lushington's suspension of the Regulation, Graeme, the former acting Governor, solicited the opinion of Ram Raz, a Telugu Brahmin who was master of the College of Fort St. George and later a Judge at Mysore.[81] Ram Raz's letter, dated 10 May 1828, was a carefully worded account of "whether the Hindu law contemplates any mode of

[79] Madras Regulation X, 1827 reprinted in PP, *Papers Relating to East India Affairs: viz. Regulations Passed by the Governments of Bengal, Fort St. George, and Bombay, in the Year 1827* (1829), pp. 52–6.

[80] PP, *Report from the Select Committee of the House of Lords Appointed to Inquire into the Present State of the Affairs of the East India Company* (1830), p. 202; see also, PP, *Return to an Order of the Honourable House of Commons, Dated 1 August 1833; – for, Copies of the Several Minutes of Council at the Presidency of Madras, by Sir Thomas Munro, Mr. Graeme, and Mr. Lushington and Others, on the Subject of Extending Trial by Jury to the Natives in Criminal Cases* (1833), pp. 34–6; 52.

[81] C. A. Bayly, *Recovering Liberties: Indian Thought in the Age of Liberalism and Empire* (Cambridge: Cambridge University Press, 2012), pp. 67–8.

trial similar to [trial by jury]."[82] He contended that both *sabhas*, which he likened to a king's court or assembly, and panchayats, which he described as "popular tribunals," were similar although not identical institutions to the English jury. Interestingly, he refused to define members of *sabhas* as jurors and instead consistently referred to them as "assessors," thus making the *sabha* more akin to the English special jury rather than the common-law jury. Ram Raz appears to have preferred the term "assessor" to juror because it was commonly accepted that the *sabha* was composed exclusively of Brahmins, a perception that he sought to dispel in the letter.[83]

Ram Raz admitted to knowing much less about the panchayat. "I have not been able to obtain much detailed information on the subject," he wrote, "but, as far as I could collect, there is every reason to conclude, that popular tribunals once prevailed all over India, and still exist in many parts of the country."[84] The scant amount of information that he did collect was drawn exclusively from Ram Raz's personal knowledge of the institution in Mysore and, ironically, from an extract of a report on panchayats in the Deccan that had been written by Mountstuart Elphinstone in 1819, recently republished in the *Asiatic Journal* of 1827.[85] Nevertheless, Ram Raz admired the idea of the panchayat because, unlike the *sabha*, its members were in some cases "composed of all classes of people indiscriminately" and in others "of the same class as that to which the offender belongs."[86]

However, Lushington, the Governor of Madras, remained a determined opponent of the plan and prevented its implementation. A questionnaire he sent on the subject to fifteen district and circuit judges further revealed the almost unanimous opposition to Indian jurors among the British judiciary.[87] With the support of his judicial officers, therefore, Lushington haughtily concluded that "I am sufficiently gratified in the reflection that I arrived in time to prevent the consummation of this pernicious change."[88]

[82] Ram Raz's letter was later reprinted in the *Journal of the Royal Asiatic Society*, Vol. III (1836), pp. 244–57.

[83] Ram Raz, "On the Introduction of Trial by Jury in the Hon. East India Company's Courts of Law," *Journal of the Royal Asiatic Society*, Vol. III (1836), pp. 251–2.

[84] Ibid., p. 252.

[85] Ibid., pp. 252–4. The article referred to appeared as "Judicial System in the Deccan," *Asiatic Journal*, Vol. 23, No. 135 (1827), pp. 329–39.

[86] Ram Raz, "On the Introduction of Trial by Jury," pp. 252; 253.

[87] PP, *Return to an Order of the Honourable House of Commons, Dated 1 August 1833*, pp. 36–51. Two of three sudder judges and ten of twelve circuit judges opposed Indian jurors.

[88] Ibid., p. 52.

For the next several years, the subject lay dormant among parliamentarians and Company officials in both London and India. In 1831, however, the issue was revived in parliament once again by Charles Grant, later Baron Glenelg, who only recently had been appointed President of the Company's Board of Control.[89] In September 1831, in the midst of the English Reform Bill Crisis, Grant indicated to the House of Commons that he intended to bring forward a bill to extend the right of Indians not only to serve on both grand juries and trials of Christians but also to serve as justices of the peace.[90] In the same sitting, Sir Charles Forbes and Joseph Hume submitted two petitions from thousands of residents of Bombay. Recognizing the success of Alexander Johnston's reforms in Ceylon as well as the "mere nominal benefits" of the previous acts of parliament, the petitioners complained of the summary justice meted out by British judges, the lack of the protection of habeas corpus, and the ignorance and deficiencies of British judges. Together, these factors had "stamped upon the natives of India the character of a conquered, distinct, and degraded people."[91]

The petitions requested the institution of trial by jury in all civil cases, extending the right to serve on grand juries to Hindus, Muslims, Parsis, and Jews, and the opening of the office of justice of the peace to all qualified residents.[92] Furthermore, the petitioners expressed the "desire to coalesce with the Crown of the United Kingdoms" and to "reward intellectual and moral merit with honourable and profitable offices." Until this was done, the petitioners argued, "upwards of sixty millions of his Majesty's subjects are at this time disjointed, loose, and floating on the surface of India."[93]

The following year, British and Indian residents of Calcutta rallied to approve their own petition to parliament requesting the implementation of trial by jury.[94] Dwarkanath Tagore addressed the rally and he very well may have been the first prominent Indian intellectual to publicly assert the analogy between the English jury and the Indian panchayat. The reporter, unfortunately, admitted to being "unable to

[89] On Grant, see David R. Fisher, "Grant, Charles (1778–1866), of Waternish, Skye and Glenelg, Inverness," published in *The History of Parliament: the House of Commons 1820–1832*, D. R. Fisher, ed. (Cambridge: Cambridge University Press, 2009), available online at www.historyofparliamentonline.org/volume/1820–1832/member/grant-charles-1778–1866, accessed 11 February 2013.

[90] *Hansard*, Commons Debate, 3rd ser., Vol. 6, cc. 958–60. [91] Ibid., cc. 961–5.

[92] Ibid., c. 956. [93] Ibid., cc. 965–6.

[94] *Calcutta Magazine*, No. 30 (June 1832), pp. 175–188. The petition is printed in the following issue: *Calcutta Magazine*, No. 31 (July 1832), pp. 223–4.

collect the purport of his speech," but surmised that "his remarks were in part directed to showing the similarity between the ancient Punchaut and the system of trial by jury." Tagore's speech was followed by that of Charles Prinsep, a Calcutta barrister, who noted that the residents of Calcutta had previously petitioned for the introduction of trial by jury, but at that time "the institution of trial by jury was then considered peculiarly English, and the Natives of India took no interest in its introduction, but now they were found coming forward to demand it; they had discovered it was an improvement on the ancient system of Punchaut."[95]

These petitions perhaps provided the impetus behind the intervention of Rammohan Roy in the debate on trial by jury. Rammohan, often referred to as the "the father of modern India" for his advocacy of social, political, and religious reforms, was a crucial participant in what C. A. Bayly has called the "liberal constitutionalist moment," when political reform movements in Europe and South America merged with those in India during the 1820s and 1830s.[96] Rammohan's contribution, published in London in 1832, was perhaps more important for the fact that it was published in the metropole by an internationally respected reformer rather than for the fact that it contained any radically new insights or arguments.

Indeed, Rammohan's discussion and prescriptions for the panchayat and trial by jury in India were far less radical than Johnston's policy implemented in Ceylon. His recommendations included the life-time appointment of "native assessors" to serve on the bench with European judges. As we have seen, however, assessors were experts, and thus his plan implied that they would have little or no judicial authority. He imagined instead that such an innovation would lead to a type of cultural exchange in which the assessors would supplement the European judges' knowledge of the language, customs, and habits of the people while the judges would impart "the dignity and firmness of the European" to the assessors.[97] However, to avoid the undue influence of an assessor over a judge, the institution of trial by jury was a necessary bulwark against this type of corruption. Rammohan argued that the principle of trial by jury was "well understood in this country

95 *Calcutta Magazine*, No. 30 (June 1832), p. 183.

96 C. A. Bayly, "Rammohan Roy and the Advent of Constitutional Liberalism in India, 1800–30," *Modern Intellectual History*, Vol. 4, No. 1 (April 2007), p. 28.

97 Rajah Rammohun Roy, *Exposition of the Practical Operation of the Judicial and Revenue Systems of India* (London, 1832), pp. 14–16.

under the name Punchayet."[98] However, as currently practiced, they functioned only as boards of arbitration and were needlessly subject to delay, corruption, and partiality.

In order to revive the panchayat, it had to be reconstructed or re-imagined. In particular, the panchayat had to be "reduced to a regular system, guarded by proper checks, and dignified by judicial forms."[99] Panchayat juries should be limited to three or five members, trials should be in the vernacular, jury lists should be drawn up, limited peremptory challenges accepted, and the selection of jurors should be drawn by lot. However, unlike in Ceylon, Rammohan argued that in India, Europeans should have the responsibility of drawing up the jury lists and that these lists should include only those "respectable and intelligent natives known to be versed in judicial subjects," such as retired *vakils* or retired judicial officers.[100] In effect, the panchayat system imagined by Rammohan was one based on English practices, directed by colonial officials, and staffed only by local élites.

Professor Bayly has recently traced the course of the debate on trial by jury in the context of the development of Indian political liberalism. He has noted the critical intervention in these debates of members of the first generation of Indian liberals, especially Rammohan Roy and Ram Raz, who were "among the first to elaborate a politicised historicism of the Indian past to argue for Indian rights in the present."[101] As Bayly has suggested, liberal historicism was a discourse that appealed to an imagined past, a past that, in one form or another, was possessed of institutions that were based upon civic freedoms and liberties rather than despotism and arbitrary government.[102] While the liberal historicism of Rammohan and Ram Raz may have differed only in degree rather than kind from the Enlightenment historicism of Orientalists such as Munro and Elphinstone, what was new was the active participation of Indian liberals in the debate. For both Rammohan and Ram Raz, in many ways like Munro and Elphinstone before them, the resurrection or revivification of the panchayat, imagined as a jury, was a key element in the building of an Indian civil society.

[98] Ibid., p. 20. [99] Ibid., p. 22. [100] Ibid., p. 24. [101] Bayly, *Recovering Liberties*, p. 69.
[102] C. A. Bayly, "Rammohan Roy and the Advent of Constitutional Liberalism in India," pp. 30–2

6

THE PANCHAYAT AND TRIAL BY JURY, II

Military and criminal justice

The failure of the East India Company's civil panchayat experiment in the Presidencies both pre-dated and presaged the decline of the civil jury trial in England. Courts of request in various jurisdictions throughout England had for long tried cases for small debts without the benefit of a jury, but the County Courts Act of 1846 extended the practice throughout the country by making the use of juries optional. As was the case in India, the summary justice of the English county courts proved to be significantly more popular than trial by jury. By 1860, only 0.23 percent of small debts cases before the county courts employed a jury, a percentage that fell to 0.17 by 1880.[1] A similar decline in the use of trial by jury occurred in criminal cases in nineteenth-century England as an ever-greater number of offences came under the purview of a magistrate's or judge's summary jurisdiction. This decline perhaps culminated in the passage of the Summary Jurisdiction Act of 1879, but further inroads into the criminal jury trial continued to be legislated thereafter.[2]

In British India, however, such was not precisely the same case. There, as we have seen, agitation among Indians, supported by some British radicals both in parliament and India, began in the 1820s and

[1] Michael Lobban, "The Strange Life of the English Civil Jury, 1837–1914," in John W. Cairns and Grant McLeod, eds., *The Dearest Birth Right of the People of England: The Jury in the History of the Common Law* (Oxford: Hart Publishing, 2002), p. 178, fn. 29; see also, Conor Hanly, "The Decline of Civil Jury Trial in Nineteenth-Century England," *Journal of Legal History*, Vol. 26, No. 3 (December 2005), pp. 253–78.

[2] R. M. Jackson, "The Incidence of Jury Trial during the Past Century, *Modern Law Review*, Vol. 1, No. 2 (September 1937), pp. 132–44.

1830s as judicial and political reforms were being adopted in England. However, only the most minimal reforms to the British judicial system were adopted in India in response to these demands for reform. In civil cases, litigants retained the right to have their cases heard before a panchayat, although very few did so, while judges gained the authority to appoint qualified Indians to aid and advise them in their decisions. These boards of advisors, in the form of panchayats, assessors, or juries, possessed no power to determine fact or apply the law, and judges could see fit whether to accept their recommendations or not.

In criminal cases, the Judicial Regulations in the Presidencies remained relatively unchanged. Indian juries, with significant restrictions, were not officially employed in criminal cases until the adoption of the Criminal Procedure Code in 1861. Even after that date, criminal jury trials were implemented in only a few places and, as one early twentieth-century commentator noted, trial with the aid of assessors remained the rule.[3] However, before 1857, this did not necessarily lessen the interest of some local officials and other Company administrators in either investigating the potential linkages between the English criminal jury and the traditional panchayat or proceeding to adapt the panchayat to the judgment of criminal cases in British-held territories not directly subject to the Presidency Regulations, such as the Deccan and the Ceded and Conquered Territories in the north-west.

One heretofore neglected source of British interest and experience with the panchayat is the way in which it was also adapted to and incorporated into the system of military justice. Often forgotten is the fact that many of the most vocal proponents of the panchayat in the several decades after 1815, such as Mountstuart Elphinstone and Thomas Munro, were first and foremost high-ranking military officers. In the Company's armies, panchayats were frequently used to resolve disputes between soldiers, officers, and local merchants. A form of the panchayat was also used in the courts martial of Indian soldiers, the sepoys. The extent to which these practices influenced Munro's or Elphinstone's interest in panchayats more generally is not known. However, their first experiences with the panchayat system undoubtedly occurred while they were stationed and fighting in India. Along with their intellectual predisposition in favor of the reinvigoration of

[3] A. G. P. Pullan, "Trial by Jury in India," *Journal of Comparative Legislation and International Law*, 3rd Series, Vol. 28, No. 3–4 (1946), p. 105.

the "customary" panchayat, it may very well have been these practical experiences that lent pragmatic support to their Orientalist theories.

MILITARY PANCHAYATS

Certainly the most common cases in which panchayat-like institutions were employed were those of the courts martial of sepoys, the Indian officers and soldiers employed by the East India Company. In 1776, General Orders were issued by the Company requiring that "the courts martial for the trial of sepoy officers and sepoys be composed of native officers only," although there is evidence that this was common practice before that date.[4] Throughout the first half of the nineteenth century, this order remained in effect and was repeated in subsequent codes of Military Regulations.[5]

Military law, as Douglas Peers has pointed out, was complicated and almost byzantine in its structure. Five different codes governed the disciplining of soldiers and officers, one each for the armies of the three Presidencies, another for European soldiers employed by the East India Company, and yet another for the armies of the Crown. Moreover, officers were given very little guidance as to its implementation and the infliction of punishments varied widely.[6] In the case of "native courts-martial," courts were comprised of Indian captains (*subadars*) and lieutenants (*jemadars*) supervised by a European officer. It is important to note here that in both the relevant parliamentary acts and the Presidency Regulations, in the military law of the early nineteenth century, courts martial were employed in criminal as well as civil cases and, in the case of these "native courts-martial," commanding officers were authorized to employ a panchayat, especially to resolve civil disputes.

The fact that panchayats were closely identified with "native courts martial" and that they often functioned in similar ways was certainly

[4] Edward Moor, A *Compilation of all the Government and General – Government – General – Brigade and Garrison Orders – Minutes of Council – Commands of the Hon. Company – or Regulations from whatever Authority Promulgated, from the Year 1750 to the 31st of July 1801* (Bombay, 1801), Sec. XXXII, No. 3, unpaginated.

[5] For example, see John William Aitchison, A *General Code of the Military Regulations in Force under the Presidency of Bombay* (Calcutta, 1824), p. 140.

[6] Douglas M. Peers, "Sepoys, Soldiers and the Lash: Race, Caste and Army Discipline in India, 1820–50," *Journal of Imperial and Commonwealth History*, Vol. 23, No. 2 (1995), pp. 222–3.

apparent to at least some British observers. During the British debate over the introduction of trial by jury to India in 1827, for example, Henry Graeme, the acting Governor of Madras after the death of Munro, declared:

> I conclude that the trial by jury, far from being considered an innovation, will be hailed by the natives as if it were the revival of a good old custom. Its principle is readily recognisable in the native courts-martial, which have existed throughout the Madras army for so long a period with such good effect, where the members are entirely natives, whose proceedings are in some degree regulated by an European officer officiating as a Judge-advocate.[7]

As Graeme suggests, British officials often asserted that the three institutions – the "good old custom" of the panchayat, the English-style jury, and the military courts martial – were analogous to one another. As early as 1812, W. E. Wright, Judge and Magistrate at Chittoor, explained:

> It has been supposed that the institution of trial by jury is not suited to the genius of the people of India; but if the objection be well examined, it probably will be found not to be true. That the institution would be very acceptable to all descriptions of people who have any opinions on the subject, there can be little doubt; and, so far from appearing novel in its nature, it bears an analogy to some of the customs of the inhabitants, particularly the Hindoos; and the trial by native courts-martial (a sort of jury) has been introduced with great success into the native army.[8]

In 1822, A. D. Campbell, Magistrate at Bellary, suggested the same identification. In reply to a question related to the introduction of trial by jury, he wrote, "it already exists in a modified shape in the army on native courts-martial ... it is also a mere extension of the punchayet system."[9]

Military courts martial of sepoy troops for such crimes as insubordination, desertion, drunkenness, and the like were relatively infrequent

[7] PP, *Return to an Order of the Honourable House of Commons, Dated 1 August 1833; – for, Copies of the Several Minutes of Council at the Presidency of Madras, by Sir Thomas Munro, Mr. Graeme, and Mr. Lushington and others, on the Subject of Extending Trial by Jury to the Natives in Criminal Cases* (1833), p. 11.

[8] "Extract of letter to the Secretary of Government in the Judicial Department," 1 July 1812, reprinted in PP, *Return to an Order of the Honourable House of Commons, Dated 1 August 1833*, p. 26.

[9] "Extract of letter from Mr. A. D. Campbell, Magistrate of Bellary," 2 December 1822, reprinted in PP, *Return to an Order of the Honourable House of Commons, Dated 1 August 1833*, p. 27.

events.[10] However, courts martial were frequently employed in military bazaars and cantonments to resolve what otherwise would have been considered civil disputes, especially debts, incurred by sepoy and European soldiers and officers to bazaar merchants, servants, petty traders, and other camp followers. As with military law generally, the relevant Regulations differed between the Presidencies, a subject that came under parliamentary scrutiny in 1842.[11] Yet the panchayat or forms of it were, by the early nineteenth century, commonly adapted to resolve these issues.

In Bengal, there appears to have remained an odd but determined resistance to employ the term "panchayat," an issue that will be discussed further in the following chapter, but it is clear nonetheless that, despite retaining the term "courts martial," dispute resolution in such cases occurred in de facto panchayats. Thus, Bengal Regulation XX of 1810 stipulated that for actions of debt "and all *personal* actions" for less than Rs. 200 against officers, soldiers, retainers, servants, and those attached to the military bazaar, cases would be tried before military courts. "Such courts," the Regulation specified, "shall be composed of *European* officers when *European* officers may be parties concerned, and, in all other cases, of *native* officers with an *European* officer to *superintend* and *record* all *proceedings*, and shall, in all practicable cases, consist of five members, and in no instance of *less* than three members, one of whom shall preside."[12] The choice of five presiding officers was unlikely to have been accidental. The panchayat, of course, was customarily comprised of five members, "panch" meaning "five."[13] A lithograph published in 1830 shows one such sepoy court martial before four sepoy officers and one presiding British officer (see Figure 6.1).

In the Bombay Army, on the other hand, panchayats had regularly been used to resolve disputes with merchants, small traders, servants, and others supplying goods and services to officers and soldiers. However, in 1824, the passage of a new Mutiny Act in parliament had specifically delegated this responsibility to the jurisdiction of local commanding officers operating through military courts of request.[14] As noted previously, civil courts of request had operated in various parts of

[10] Peers, "Sepoys, Soldiers and the Lash," pp. 214–17.
[11] PP, *Copies of the Special Reports of the Indian Law Commissioners: Military Courts of Request* (1842), pp. 131–91.
[12] William Hough and George Long, *The Practice of Courts-Martial*, 2nd edn. (London, 1825), pp. 595–6.
[13] The European officer seated to the left in the lithograph is recording the proceedings.
[14] 4 Geo. IV, cap. 81, sec. 57.

Figure 6.1 The Native Court Martial (Anne S. K. Brown Military Collection, Brown University Library)

England for several centuries, functioning as small claims courts meting out summary justice. They had also been established in the presidency towns as early as 1753.[15] The procedures of the new military courts of request, however, followed the procedures outlined in Bengal Regulation XX of 1810, which, as we have seen, were racially segregated and provided for separate European and "native" courts that largely imitated the form of the panchayat, albeit under European supervision. These reforms were then formally adopted for implementation throughout the Bombay Army in the revised Bombay Military Regulations of 1827.[16]

The commanding officers in the Bombay Presidency, however, did not universally welcome the introduction of military courts of requests. A great deal of confusion was caused by questions concerning the jurisdiction of the new courts of request, by questions over whether English or local laws and customs were to be applied, and by the lack of sufficient interpreters to operate the new courts.[17] Already in June 1828, Major-General Sir Lionel Smith, stationed at Pune, complained that the new

[15] William H. Morley, *The Administration of Justice in British India* (London, 1858), p. 25.

[16] PP, *Papers Relating to East India Affairs: viz. Regulations Passed by the Governments of Bengal, Fort St. George, and Bombay, in the Year 1827* (1829), Bombay Regulation XXII, 1827, pp. 283–95.

[17] MSA, EIC, Judicial Department, Civil Judicature, Vol. 8/155, 1828, Extract from Proceedings of Government in the Military Department. Dated 9th July 1828.

courts of request had more than 300 cases in arrears. Moreover, the commanding officers hated doing the extra work in addition to their military duties, were often harassed by the litigants, and at times even offered to pay the awards themselves to avoid the job. He concluded his letter to the Adjutant General J. W. Aitchison asserting, "when we were allowed to settle these disputes by Punchaits, the natives were well pleased, and we had then the satisfactory character of listening to their complaints, and rendering Justice with promptitude. But I am sorry to say we have lost this character by substituting Courts of requests, which give no certainty, except that of delay. I would entreat His Excellency therefore to submit to Government if it would not be advisable to abolish the Native Courts of requests, and allow us to revert to Punchaits which I am of opinion will better facilitate the ends of Justice."[18] General Smith's request was never fulfilled.

In the Madras Presidency, the story is somewhat different yet again. There, of course, the revival and adaptation of the panchayat to the *ryotwari* system had been an essential element of Thomas Munro's reforms. Perhaps it is not surprising, therefore, that Munro also sought to adapt the panchayat to the needs of the Madras Army and it was here that the panchayat remained inscribed in the Military Regulations until well after it had been abandoned elsewhere.

In all of the Presidencies, the authority to police military cantonments and bazaars had been delegated to the troops' commanding officer in 1809 and, in 1810, camp followers and retainers became subject to "native courts martial" for petty offenses and debts of less than Rs. 200.[19] In 1821, however, Munro significantly expanded the scope of those Regulations "for the better preserving of discipline in garrisons and cantonments, and over retainers and followers of the army." Commanding officers were thereby authorized to try offenses, including assaults, affrays, and petty thefts by courts martial. More importantly, however, commissariat officers as well as other officers in command of the military bazaars were delegated the authority, "according to former usage, to assemble punchayets for the settlement of disputes to any amount."[20]

[18] MSA, EIC, Judicial Department, Civil Judicature, Vol. 8/155, 1828, Extract from Proceedings of Government in the Military Department. Dated 9th July 1828.

[19] PP, *Report from the Select Committee on the Affairs of the East India Company*, Vol. IV, App. No. 6 (1831–1832), p. 739.

[20] PP, *Papers Relating to East India Affairs: viz. Regulations Passed by the Governments of Bengal, Fort St. George, and Bombay, in the Year 1821* (1822), Madras Regulation VI, 1821, pp. 30–6.

However, unlike Munro's civil panchayat system, whose function was more akin to a jury, these military panchayats were much more like Elphinstone's panchayats in the Bombay Presidency, where panchayats operated as tribunals of arbitration. The relevant language of the Madras Regulation emphasized that the panchayat's procedures were "according to former usage" and were accompanied by the "usual" documentation. However, it is also clear that the panchayats were to be conducted under British supervision, that procedures were created that mimicked a British sense of legality, and that enforcement was a matter conducted ultimately under British military authority.

Like British arbitration, military panchayats in Madras were wholly voluntary and the dispute resolution mechanism was initiated only with the consent of both parties. Each party to the dispute was instructed to nominate two members to the panchayat and the commissariat officer one member. The Regulations do not make it clear whether this fifth member appointed by the commissariat officer was authorized to act as the *sarpanch*, but surviving evidence elsewhere indicates that he did so. As in the Bombay Presidency, where a *razeenamah*, or bond to abide by the award, was required to be entered into by the litigants, a similar *muchilka* was required in the Madras military panchayats. The panchayat's award had to be signed by both parties and registered in the commissariat's office. Except in cases in which a litigant pleaded gross partiality, the award of the panchayat was final. Finally, the commanding officers of the cantonments or bazaars were authorized and responsible for enforcing the panchayat's awards.[21]

The correspondence relating to an individual case from 1827 to 1828 suggests the complicated position that commanding officers sometimes faced. Lieutenant Colonel J. D. Greenhill, Commander of the Light Field Division of the Hyderabad Subsidiary Force was presented with a case for debt between two camp followers in which the defendant refused to nominate his own *panchayatdars*. Given the fact that Munro's Regulations did not cover disputes between camp followers and that the amount in dispute exceeded Rs. 200, and thus could not be tried before a military court, Greenhill sought the advice of both his military and legal superiors who, he hoped, would help "define my authority." He explained that "disputes occasionally take place between Camp followers (Bazarmen [*sic*]) for debts of much greater

[21] PP, *Papers Relating to East India Affairs: viz. Regulations Passed by the Governments of Bengal, Fort St. George, and Bombay, in the Year 1821* (1822), Madras Regulation VI, 1821, § VIII–X.

amount [than Rs. 200], which I possess no means of settling except by Punchayet, and, to maintain regularity and conformity with the Bazar [*sic*] Regulations, it is necessary each of the parties should name two persons for the Punchayet, and enter into a Penalty Bond to abide by the decision given by them in conjunction with a fifth person nominated by the Officer in charge of the Bazar as Commanding Officer of the Camp."[22] Despite the fact that Greenhill imprisoned the defendant for a month, the latter continued to refuse to nominate *panchayatdars*. In the end, the Commander-in-Chief George Townsend Walker was only left to bemoan that this was indeed a significant loophole in the Regulations and that Greenhill could take no legal action against the defendant. The only remedy, he noted, was "that the sum of 200 Rs. over which Power is now given to the Military Courts to decide should be extended to any amount that may be brought under the jurisdiction provided the cause of action is not referrible [*sic*] to any other Court. [A]nd I recommend that a regulation to that effect may be established with as little delay as the circumstances may admit."

In general, cases brought before military panchayats appear to have involved significantly smaller claims than those brought before the commanding officer for a court martial. There are very few statistics with which to verify this claim, but at least one report from the cantonment at Secunderabad suggests that this may have been so.[23] There, in the five years between March 1833 and March 1838, of the 176 total cases recorded in panchayats and courts martial, 125, or 71 percent, were adjudicated by panchayats. The average amount of both the claims and the awards was significantly less in cases adjudicated by panchayat than those taken before a summary court martial. In the case of panchayats, the average claim was for Rs. 695 and the average award was Rs. 521. In cases in which litigants preferred the military court martial, the average claim was Rs. 4,020 while the average award was Rs. 1,692. Unfortunately, there is no further evidence that can help account for this notable discrepancy and

[22] IOR/F/4/1425/56238, Board's Collections, 1833–1834, *Enactment of Regulation 7 of 1832 for the Better Discipline of Military Bazars [sic] and Relative to the Establishments to be Entertained in Lieu of Troops at the Several Military Stations for the Execution of Civil Process*, 12 November 1833. The relevant letters included in this collection date are Lieut. Col. J. D. Greenhill to R. Clive, Secretary to Government, Military Department, Dated 29th – 1827 [no month provided]; Lieut. Col. J. D. Greenhill, Commanding Light Field Division, Hydrabad [sic] Subsidiary Force, to the Assistant Adjutant General, Hydrabad [sic] Subsidiary Force, Dated 29 March 1828; and, Minute of the Commander in Chief, Dated 17th April 1828.

[23] PP, *East India: Copies of the Special Reports of the Indian Law Commissioners*, No. III: Part I, Military Courts of Request (1842), p. 146.

these are both rather large amounts of money. Yet there seems little doubt but that litigants preferred the panchayat when their claims were moderately substantial ones and the summary courts martial when their claims were significantly larger. One must emphasize, however, that neither court operated as a small claims court, as one might expect, and the amounts of claims and awards in both cases were relatively significant.

Munro's military panchayat scheme of 1821 was also complicated by the passage of the 1824 Mutiny Act that amended the Articles of War and provided for the establishment of military courts of request for garrisons and cantonments beyond the jurisdiction of the courts already established in Calcutta, Bombay, and Madras.[24] To respond to the new Mutiny Act as well as to respond to a perceived increase in crime in the cantonments, bazaars, and garrisons, Madras introduced a new set of Regulations in 1832.[25] The new Regulations significantly expanded the authority of the commanding and commissariat officers and authorized them, among many other things, to apprehend and try persons charged with capital crimes, such as treason and murder, for misdemeanors such as abusive language or the use of false weights and measures, and, finally, to arrest "any vagrant or suspicious person, without ostensible means of honest livelihood, or person of notoriously bad character." Whether intentionally or not, the 1832 Madras Military Regulations failed to include provisions for the establishment of courts of request, a situation that later came under the scrutiny of the India Law Commission. Despite this omission, there is evidence that courts of request did actually operate in at least some of the Madras cantonments. As a result, potential litigants in at least some areas retained the option not only to voluntarily submit their disputes to a military panchayat but also alternatively submit their claims to courts martial or military courts of request.

The principal differences between the three institutions were complicated by considerations of race, authority, and jurisprudence. Military panchayats, as we have seen, were voluntary, their members selected by the litigants, and they were placed under the authority of a

[24] 4 Geo. IV, cap. 81, sec. 57; see William Hough, *The Practice of Courts-Martial and other Military Courts* (London, 1834), pp. 173–86.

[25] PP, *Papers Relating to East India affairs: viz. Regulations Passed by the Governments of Bengal, Fort St. George, and Bombay, in the Year 1832* (1833), Madras Regulation VII, 1832, pp. 18–31. On bazaar and cantonment society in the Madras Presidency, see Chandra Mallampalli, "Cosmopolitanism in the Hinterland?: Bellary District through Fresh Lenses, 1800–1840," *Indian Economic and Social History Review*, Vol. 46, No. 2 (2009), pp. 183–210.

European officer. Their rulings were bound neither by precedent nor law. Courts martial, on the other hand, were comprised of European or sepoy officers whose decisions were bound by the Articles of War and other Military Regulations peculiar to each Presidency. Finally, military courts of request were convened under the authority of a field officer and staffed by captains and subalterns. Like panchayats, they were bound neither by precedent nor the Articles of War and their decisions were to be based solely upon "equity and conscience."[26]

Where the courts of request operated, it appears that they were much more popular than either the military courts martial or the military panchayats, a circumstance that might explain General Smith's backlog of cases in Pune. Once again, the evidence is very slight indeed. At the major cantonment of Kamptee (Kamthi), near Nagpur in western Maharashtra, of the 1,150 cases tried between 1833 and 1838, 1,088, or 94.6 percent, of the cases were adjudicated before military courts of request. Thirty-eight further cases were tried before military courts martial and only twenty-four before military panchayats.[27]

Upon further analysis, it is clear that, at least in this situation, military courts of request were exceptionally popular institutions, popular, that is, in the sense that they responded to the needs of recovering much smaller debts. The average claim before the courts of request was Rs. 85 and the average award was Rs. 61. At the same time, the average of claims before the courts martial was Rs. 1,414 and the average award was Rs. 906. Before the military panchayats, once again both the claims and awards were significant, albeit not as large as those before the courts martial. Military panchayat claims averaged Rs. 851 and their awards averaged Rs. 450. Under the circumstances, one might logically infer, at least provisionally, that the expansion of the system of courts of request beyond the Presidency towns created a much more accessible venue in which the claims of small traders, merchants, servants, and other camp followers and employees might be adjudicated.

Still, considering the confusion caused by these various codes and regulations, it is not surprising to find officers complaining not only about their responsibilities in this area, which they apparently resented, but also about the complicated, convoluted, and burdensome procedures they were supposed to follow. In 1837, the Indian Law Commission

[26] On the juridical principles underlying military courts of request, see PP, *Special Reports of the Indian Law Commissioners*, No. III: Pt. 1 (1842), pp. 156–8.

[27] PP, *Special Reports of the Indian Law Commissioners*, No. III: Part I (1842), pp. 146–7.

sought to bring some order to this confusion, resulting in the *Act for Consolidating and Amending the Regulations Concerning Military Courts of Request for Native Officers and Soldiers in the Service of the East India Company* passed by the Council of India in 1841.[28] The Act sought not only to regularize proceedings in the courts but also to limit claims to Rs. 200.

Interestingly, the military panchayat system of the Madras Army was specifically excluded from the provisions of the Act.[29] Indeed, neither concern nor controversy over the role and function of the panchayat appears to have been expressed in the communications that had taken place prior to the passage of the Act. The only substantive contribution was that of the Judge-Advocate General of the Madras Army R. Alexander, who was less than supportive of any attempt to retain the panchayat. He admitted that although "acceptable as is the theory of punchayet jurisdiction, there are practical evils in the system."[30] His complaints reiterated many of those that the opponents of civil panchayats had previously enumerated: that members of panchayats often acted less like judges and more like interested advocates, that there were few men respectable enough to serve on panchayats, those who were willing to serve were overburdened by the responsibility, and that higher castes would not sit with lower castes. His suspicion of the panchayat even extended to the suggestion that there was an element of coercion in their decisions "when it is apparent to their imaginations that they have to decide in opposition to interests with which it is difficult for them not to identify the ruling authority."[31]

By 1850, therefore, the military panchayats in the Company's armies had virtually disappeared. Voluntary use of them survived only in the military code of the Madras Army, although even here they were barely functioning, if at all. One veteran of nearly forty years in the Madras Army, Colonel J. David Greenhill, suggested that the decline of the panchayat was an important indication of a more general decline in military discipline among the sepoys. Testifying before parliament in 1832, Colonel Greenhill attributed this decline to the greater bureaucratization of the Company's armies whereby the almost dictatorial power of the British officers of sepoy units in the field had been

[28] Act No. XI, 1841. See, George S. Fagan, *Unrepealed and Unexpired Acts of the Legislative Council of India*, Vol. I (Calcutta, 1862), pp. 299–306.
[29] Act No. XI, 1841, § I.
[30] PP, *East India: Copies of the Special Reports of the Indian Law Commissioners* (1842), p. 148.
[31] Ibid.

gradually undermined by the increasing authority of company and corps commanders in the cantonments.[32] Before then, he asserted, "all their disputes among themselves were settled by punchayet or arbitration. A great change has taken place. Punchayet has been forbid lately; and now when the corps comes to a large station, the soubahdar finds his commanding officer of no consequence; frequently hears him rudely spoken to on parade, and not able to prevent the issuing of orders which are sometimes obnoxious to the feelings of the sepoy."[33]

One need not wholly accept the accuracy of Colonel Greenhill's analysis to appreciate the significance he attached to the panchayat. Yet, as in the case of civil panchayats, Indian litigants do not appear to have felt the same way as he did. Military panchayats appear to have been the locus of dispute resolution when cases concerned relatively significant amounts of money. Why this may have been so is still not absolutely clear. But military panchayats do not seem to have catered to the concerns of the small merchants, petty traders, or servants whose cases involved much smaller amounts of money. In these cases, it seems, the military courts of request offered a much more amenable site for the collection of debts or wages or to resolve other more commonplace problems. At least in the military sphere, the panchayat may very well have been undermined both by the antipathy of British officials and its rejection by Indian litigants.

CRIMINAL PANCHAYATS

Before 1861, the British did not permit Indians to sit on juries in criminal cases. If a judge or magistrate so desired, he could make use of "native" assessors, panchayats, or advisory "juries," although, as in civil cases, the judge or magistrate was not bound by their decisions.[34] Thus the term "jury," in the normative sense, was a misnomer. Nor were Indian judges at the local level permitted to preside over criminal cases with the notable exception of the Madras Presidency, where, as early as 1827, the "native judge," or *munsif*, was given

[32] PP, *Minutes of Evidence taken before the Select Committee of the House of Commons on the Affairs of the East India Company*, Vol. V: Military (1833), p. 147.
[33] Ibid., p. 154.
[34] PP, *Reports from Commissioners: Judicial Establishments, &c., India*, Vol. 25, Appendix B: No. 8 (1856), pp. 226–7.

cognizance of crimes and misdemeanors, except those committed by Europeans and Americans.[35]

However, this did not deter many Company officials and officers from repeatedly re-visiting the issue during the first half of the nineteenth century. As in the case of civil trials, the apparent success of criminal trials by jury in Ceylon was often referred to in these discussions. Similarly, the perceived analogy between the jury trial and the panchayat was an important reference point. Many British officials assumed that the panchayat was only an institution used to resolve civil disputes, such as those for land, inheritance, or personal debts. Yet evidence collected by local Collectors often revealed that this was not the case. Not only did British Collectors and military officials in non-regulation territories employ the panchayat to resolve criminal cases, but they also often based their practices on models observed in the princely states. Thus the question of the criminal jury trial often became a critical axis upon which turned British desires to adhere to the customs of the country but at the same time to counter the perceived racial and cultural inferiority of India.

In the Bombay Presidency, Mountstuart Elphinstone initiated inquiries into the use of criminal panchayats as a form of trial by jury in 1822. In July of that year, he executed a minute requesting information from the Company government on the use of criminal juries in Ceylon and formal letters of inquiry were dispatched to judges, collectors, and residents in August. At the same time, he requested further information from Captain John Briggs, the Resident at Khandesh, and Captain James Grant, the Resident at Sátára, on criminal panchayats there. Elphinstone noted that he was particularly interested "as to the manner in which the Jury is selected and whether any means are taken to obviate the partialities arising from the division of the people into casts [*sic*]." However, he also was careful to note that "I do not mean to propose the sudden introduction of trial by Jury but as we are about to make permanent Regns. for our new possessions and are reconsidering those in our old, the subject deserves to be examined."[36]

Elphinstone had been aware of and interested in criminal panchayats for some time by then. He had first become aware of their existence in western India in the months after Khandesh had been ceded to the

[35] PP, *Papers Relating to East India Affairs: viz. Regulations Passed by the Governments of Bengal, Fort St. George, and Bombay, in the Year 1827* (1829), Madras Regulation VIII, pp. 50–1.

[36] IOR/P/399/14, Bombay Judicial Consultations, Minute by the Governor, 8 July 1822.

British in December 1817. However, it was his belief that criminal panchayats were uncommon occurrences. In his original report submitted in 1819 and later published as *Report on the Territories Conquered from the Paishwa*, he noted that criminal justice under the Peshwas had been administered summarily by local *patels*, *mamledars*, and *subhedars*.[37] He concluded, therefore, that, despite the fact that he had a report of them from Sátára, "I doubt whether Punchayets were ever generally employed in criminal trials."[38]

Yet sometime in December 1818 he had also received a lengthy report on criminal panchayats in Khandesh, the content of which revealed that the British had immediately begun to reinvent the institution. Briggs, the Resident in Khandesh, later admitted that he had misunderstood his orders to try only civil cases by panchayat and, upon his assumption of authority in Khandesh, had begun to convene panchayats to try criminal cases.[39] Nevertheless, the criminal panchayat under Briggs conducted its procedures much more like an English special jury or a court martial, than either an English criminal jury or an arbitration tribunal. Thus, it is more accurate to define the panchayat, as imagined by Briggs, as a panel of specially appointed assessors rather than judges of fact or arbitrators.

In criminal trials by panchayat, it appears that Briggs functioned not only as both prosecutor and judge but also selected the members of the panchayat "usually from among the Zemindars of the pergunnah in which the criminal case was tried, and from persons of respectability, commonly Brahmins, who accompany the cutcherry on business of their own." This may appear to be an abuse of power according to modern notions of justice, but Briggs' faith in the jury and panchayat

[37] "Report of the Honourable Mountstuart Elphinstone to the Governor General," 25 October 1819, in *Selection of Papers from the Records at the East-India House*, IV, p. 178. On criminal justice under the Peshwa, see Sumit Guha, "An Indian Penal Régime: Maharashtra in the Eighteenth Century," *Past & Present*, No. 147 (May 1995), pp. 101–26.

[38] "Report of the Honourable Mountstuart Elphinstone," *Selection of Papers from the Records at the East-India House*, IV, pp. 177–8.

[39] In 1822, Briggs had written: "the instructions we originally received on this head seemed to direct the authority to refer all causes of litigation to be decided by a Court of Punchayut, the decision by which was to be considered as final unless proof of gross corruption or palpable dereliction of justice was established. It was understood also that no new rules nor innovations of any sort were to be introduced lest they might altogether subvert what it was intended to improve. The object no doubt being to give a practical trial to the system which prescribed under the late Government as a substitute for our own Courts, untill [sic] it was deemed advisable to introduce them." See MSA, EIC, Judicial Department, Civil and Criminal Judicature, Vol. 9A/9A, 1823, J. Briggs to William Chaplin, 3 May 1822; see also Briggs to Chaplin, n.d., *Selection of Papers from the Records at the East-India House*, IV, p. 906.

system did not rest on the notion of being tried by one's peers. Instead, trial by jury and, by extension, the panchayat, was a fundamental liberty because it provided security against oppression. Thus, he did not see any objection to introducing the jury system into any country or any government "where there is a disposition to do impartial justice, and to protect its subjects from local oppression."[40]

Once selected, the panchayat – "never less than five, and sometimes seven or nine" – was asked to select a *mookh*, or foreman. In a letter written to William Chaplin, the Commissioner of the Deccan, in 1822, Briggs recalled in detail a seemingly methodical judicial process.[41] After the selection of the panchayat and the collection of witnesses,

> the prisoner, being brought to the bar, was told these persons were about to bear evidence for and against him, and to decide on his guilt, but that if he objected to any of them to do so. The evidence on the prosecution was then gone into, and subsequently the defence. At the close of the examination of each witness, the punchayet was applied to by me to know if any thing occurred to them to ask more of the witness, and the prisoner was likewise asked if he wished to put any questions. It was in this stage of the proceedings I frequently derived assistance from an intelligent juryman, when, from the mode in which the evidence was given, a further examination by him has led more clearly to elucidate an obscure fact.
>
> After the prisoner's defence, the punchayet or jury was then required to give its opinion as to the prisoner's guilt; upon which the Shastree was called on to pronounce the law on the case, which was promulgated, and sentence passed accordingly.

However, Briggs' initial report to Elphinstone, undated but probably dating from early December 1818, also describes a much less meticulous adherence to these procedures.[42] Shastris, for example, were not regularly called upon to declare the law. Indeed, it is not altogether clear whose "law" was being applied here. Thus, in the case of Hoosein Bin Shiekh Chaud and Bapoo Chimnajee Durimdully, charged and convicted of highway robbery on 10 December 1818, Briggs, as judge, declared: "The ordinary Sentence for high-way Robbery would be death. I am in hopes however by passing a more lenient Judgement on you that you may at a future period return to be useful Members of

40 Briggs to Chaplin, n.d., *Selection of Papers from the Records at the East-India House*, IV, pp. 906–7.
41 Ibid., pp. 906–9.
42 IOR/P/121/36, Bengal Political Consultations, No. 60. Briggs to Elphinstone,19 January 1819.

the community at large and that the example will deter others of your description from engaging in Similar practices. You are therefore sentenced to hard labor in Irons for the period of seven Years and I hope you will during that time repent of you crime and return to some honest occupation for the rest of your lives."

Similarly, prisoners do not seem to have been granted the opportunity to object either to members of the panchayat or prospective witnesses. In the case of Hoosein and Bapoo Chimnajee, Briggs recorded only that "the Prisoners being called into Court and the charge read over to them are called on to plead guilty or not guilty. The Prisoners plead guilty to the charge." In another highway robbery case heard the same day, Briggs also noted only "the Prisoner being called into Court pleads guilty to the Charge."

Finally, Briggs was certainly aware that a panchayat's usual function in civil cases was also to issue an award. In criminal cases, one might expect that such a civil award might be analogous to a criminal sentence. Instead, apparently aware of this possibility, he arrogated to himself the responsibility of sentencing the convicts. He explained to Elphinstone that sentencing might impose too great a burden upon the panchayat. "You will perceive," he wrote, "I have not left the award to the Punchayut. I found considerable inconvenience from imposing on a Punchayut this duty lately and I have therefore kept the quota of punishment to be awarded by the Sitting Magistrate."

Elphinstone was not pleased with Briggs' innovation. Believing that panchayats were institutions of civil arbitration and not criminal justice, in October 1819, he prohibited the use of panchayats to try criminal cases. "The system of Punchait in Candeish as applies to Criminal offences being neither consistent with former usage, nor attended with any manifest advantage," Elphsinstone ordered, "should be discontinued and the mode of trial adopted in other Districts should be substituted."[43]

Briggs' adaptation of the panchayat to criminal offenses was not, however, solely a matter of his misunderstanding of his original orders, as he later explained to his superiors. There is little doubt but that his familiarity with military "native courts martial" provided Briggs not only with the experience to adapt the panchayat to criminal cases but

[43] IOR/P/398/71, Bombay Judicial Consultations, 22 March 1820, "Circular of the Honble the Commissioner to the Collectors in the newly acquired Territories from the late Paishwa." Dated 25 October 1819, p. 1519.

also led him to later argue that trial by jury should be generally adopted throughout the Presidency. About his Khandesh experiment, he later wrote that "I commenced my criminal trials by assembling a punchayet, and from having been many years in the habit of superintending similar courts in the army, it did not occur to me there was any thing strange or novel in the proceedings."[44] More generally, Briggs believed that his experience with military courts martial had proven that the introduction of trial by jury would be productive of more good than evil, as he circumspectly put it. "We have had a long experience of military juries," he wrote, "the objections to them have not been such as to suggest the idea of abolishing them." Rather awkwardly, Briggs went on to suggest that just as courts martial were essential for military efficiency, so trial by jury was essential for the protection of civil society from arbitrary government. To those who objected to the introduction of trial by jury on the grounds that Indians were not suitable to act as jurors, Briggs again drew upon his military experiences to argue that British tutelage had succeeded there. "We have had experience," he insisted,

> that persons coming from the lower classes of society, as the privates of all armies must be, have been rendered by a long acquaintance with our habits and manners, fit to determine on the guilt or otherwise of persons tried for crimes, alike amenable to the civil as well as military law; and it is therefore likely, among the upper and middling classes of the society in general, we shall not be at a loss to select jurors equally respectable, intelligent, and free from prejudice, as among the native officers of the Indian army.[45]

Despite his prohibition against criminal panchayats in 1819, Elphinstone maintained a "considerable interest" in criminal trials employing Indian jurors.[46] As we have seen, the issue was raised once again in 1822. At this time, a Committee for the Revision of the Regulations requested that James Henderson, the Secretary to Government, circulate a list of thirteen questions related to "the introduction of the trial by jury among natives" to the Government of Ceylon as well as various judges, collectors, political agents, and political residents

[44] Briggs to Chaplin, n.d., *Selection of Papers from the Records at the East-India House*, IV, p. 906.
[45] Ibid., p. 915.
[46] "Letter from the Committee for the Revision of the Regulations to the Secretary to Government," 2 August 1822, in *Selection of Papers from the Records at the East-India House*, IV, p. 870.

throughout the Bombay Presidency.[47] Of the fourteen responses later recorded and published by East India House, eight judges and officials offered their often qualified support of the proposal while six rejected it.[48] It was common among those who supported the proposal to emphasize its tutelary aspects; certainly, there were no rights-based arguments, as there surely would have been in England. Moreover, there was a general sense that the introduction of trial by jury would inevitably teach Indians the alleged benefits of being ruled by their foreign conquerors. Thus James Sutherland, a *sadr adalat* judge at Surat, declared "the introduction of trial by jury will tend to disseminate more widely a knowledge of the constitution that governs the country ... Jurors will carry with them a complete knowledge of the trials in which they may be engaged, and by discussing them with others, will give the public an interest in these matters that no other measure is likely to excite with such advantages."[49] Similarly, H. D. Robertson, the Collector at Pune, explained that trial by jury would tend "to excite an interest in the people on subjects which they at present view with considerable apathy and indifference, and also (I should suppose), when the nature of the duty was fully understood, to impress the people with a high opinion of the humane principles of our justice."[50]

The opponents of the measure adopted a mixture of racial, cultural, and historical arguments. Several respondents, most notably William Chaplin, the Commissioner of the Deccan, argued that there was no historical precedent for criminal trials by panchayat and thus the introduction of trial by jury would be "an innovation not sanctioned by former practice."[51] In a related manner, several others asserted their opposition to trial by jury "as being unsuited to the genius, habits, and feelings of the people," as Judge Edward Ironside put it.[52] Finally, there were those who expressed their outright racial hostility, such as G. A. Anderson, the criminal judge at Broach, who complained of "the total want of ability, judgment, and integrity in natives."[53]

The Regulation Committee submitted their report to Elphinstone in November 1823 advising against the introduction of trial by jury in the Presidency. Their report combined elements of nationalistic hubris and seventeenth- and eighteenth-century British Commonwealth

[47] Letter from the Committee for the Revision of the Regulations to the Secretary to Government, 2 August 1822, in *Selection of Papers from the Records at the East-India House*, IV, p. 870.
[48] Ibid., pp. 870–922. [49] Ibid., p. 887. [50] Ibid., p. 898. [51] Ibid., p. 897. [52] Ibid., p. 892.
[53] Ibid., p. 874.

philosophy. The Committee accepted the argument that trial by jury generally was an essential bulwark of liberty against the impositions of an arbitrary government. Yet they went on to assert that the jury was a uniquely Anglo-American institution that had been born out of a unique set of historical struggles between the government and the people. "An institution of this kind," they wrote, "appears not only to afford the most efficient security for freedom, but to be necessary to its existence; for in free countries there will almost always be a struggle, more or less important and extensive, between the Government on the one hand, and the people on the other."[54] However, the Committee went on, this was not the situation in India where the British government was allegedly benign and protective, absolute but not arbitrary. In this sense, therefore, Indian liberties did not require protection from arbitrary government. "There is here," the Committee wrote,

> no freedom to require the protection of so powerful a safeguard, no struggle between contending parties to call for the employment of an umpire, constituted with such ease to resist the influence of power. The Government of India can never suppose itself to have an interest in augmenting its power over its subjects, and if it were to entertain such an opinion, it would never, in order to put it in practice, have recourse to influencing judicial proceedings, when it has at its disposal means so much more prompt and efficacious.

Given the alleged absence of conflict between the interests of the Indian people and their British governors, as well as the absolute dominance of the British military forces, there was no need for the introduction of the jury system. In this situation, government-appointed judges were free to issue their rulings without bias, especially since power–political questions between the governed and the governors had been removed from the administration of justice. Therefore, the Committee reasoned, "we see no reason why [a judge's] decision should not be as likely to be just as that of a jury."[55]

[54] Ibid., p. 922.

[55] Ibid., p. 923. Other observers of the judicial system in India often repeated this historical argument. Thus, George Campbell of the Bengal Civil Service and author of *Modern India: A Sketch of the System of Civil Government* (London, 1852) noted the following with regard to trial by jury: "In England, a free country, formerly menaced by tyranny in the judicial form, and where criminals are sufficiently opposed by public opinion and public effort, the object of all these rules has been solely to protect the innocent against Government, and English rules have been imitated in India, where the state of things is quite different, where the Government is avowedly absolute, and at the same time cannot be suspected of any designed injustice or wish to make judicial tribunals the instruments of political oppression." See p. 520.

Thereafter, the question of criminal jury trials and criminal panchayats lay in abeyance until the question of juries in India was briefly revived once again upon the introduction of Peel's Jury Bill in 1825. As we have seen, the Juries in India Bill was eventually introduced to the House of Commons in March 1826 and quickly passed into law a month later. The Act to Regulate the Appointment of Juries in the East-Indies, or the India Juries Act, was merely permissive in nature, allowing each Presidency to promulgate its own rules and regulations for service on juries. Only Joseph Hume, the radical MP, complained that the bill did not specify whether or not Indians and "half-castes" were to be allowed to serve as jurors.[56] The following year, 1827, witnessed Munro's introduction of a regulation in the Madras Presidency allowing qualified Indians to sit on criminal juries. However, that regulation was quickly rescinded by his successor, Stephen Lushington.

In 1831, the issue was raised yet again and this appears to have been the last time that Indians serving on criminal juries were seriously considered by the Company before they lost control of their possessions to the Raj. The petition submitted to parliament by the residents of Bombay in that year was broadly conceived to include service on grand and criminal juries as well as serving as justices of the peace.[57] The subsequent bill, submitted by Charles Grant in May 1832, however, lacked any provisions for the introduction of criminal trials to India. Moreover, the bill, it will be recalled, was introduced in the midst of the Reform Bill crisis, a fact that led at least some, including Sir John Malcolm, the prominent Company military officer and former Governor of Bombay, to question the timing of the measure.[58]

However, Hume, who was active in the debates once again, continued to raise the issue and requested copies of the correspondence that had been conducted between Company officials in 1827 and 1828 concerning Munro's regulation introducing criminal juries into the Madras Presidency.[59] The regulation, he discovered, had been proposed by two provincial court judges and immediately received Munro's

[56] *Hansard*, Commons Debates, Vol. 15, 20 March 1826, cc. 1–2 and Vol. 15, 7 April 1826, cc. 107–8.
[57] *Hansard*, Commons Debates, 3rd Ser., Vol. 6, 1 September 1831, c. 956. [58] Ibid., cc. 967–8.
[59] PP, *Juries in India. Return to an Order of the Honourable House of Commons, Dated 1 August 1833; – for, Copies of the Several Minutes of Council at the Presidency of Madras, by Sir Thomas Munro, Mr. Graeme, and Mr. Lushington and Others, on the Subject of Extending Trial by Jury to the Natives in Criminal Cases* (1833).

support. At that time, Munro had emphasized the tutelary aspects of such a measure, claiming "a public spirit may be created in all nations, varying of course in degree according to the freedom of their institutions. In order to excite such a spirit in India, we must make the people eligible to all offices. In proportion as we do this, we may be sure that they will qualify themselves for them; that they will endeavour to outstrip their rivals; and that they will seek distinction, not only in offices of profit and honour, but also by serving their countrymen in those of utility, such as members of punchayets or juries, from which they derive no reward."[60] Munro himself had "long been satisfied that criminal cases among the people of the provinces under this Presidency, ought to be tried by native punchayets or juries" and had become convinced that as long as the courts were administered by both European judges and the Muslim law officers who advised them, justice would be "entirely in the hands of strangers."[61]

Munro's regulation was very short-lived although the debate over it continued after Lushington had suspended it. The extent of the opposition to the regulation among the Madras judiciary was only revealed in a subsequent exchange of letters between Lushington and his immediate predecessor, the former acting Governor, Henry Graeme. After Lushington had suspended the Regulation, he proceeded to circulate a list of questions on the matter among the circuit and *sadr adalat* judges in the Presidency. The responses he received were overwhelmingly negative, save for that of one circuit judge.[62] The racial animosity and cultural hubris expressed by the Madras judge mirrored that of their colleagues in Bengal when they had resisted the earlier attempt to introduce civil panchayats there.[63] The themes of mendaciousness, corruption, and prejudice were repeated once again. Justice Oliver of the *sadr adalat* complained of "the almost total want of veracity and integrity among the natives" which made them "as little fitted as can well be imagined to receive an institution which requires truth and honesty."[64] A circuit court judge predicted that thieves and robbers would rejoice at the opportunity to bribe and corrupt jurors.[65] Several judges argued that caste prejudices would inevitably defeat the "ends of justice."[66]

A second common theme expressed by the Madras judges argued that the failure of civil panchayats in the Madras and Bombay Presidencies

[60] "Minute of the President," n.d., *Juries in India*, p. 3. [61] Ibid.
[62] "Lushington Minute," 19 April 1828, *Juries in India*, p. 50. [63] See below, Chapter 7.
[64] "Lushington Minute," 19 April 1828, *Juries in India*, p. 37. [65] Ibid., pp. 43–4.
[66] Ibid., pp. 39; 42–3; 49.

indicated that Indians no longer valued the institution and therefore would not value the jury system. Justice Oliver noted, "if any judgment can be formed from the reluctance shown by natives either to submit to the decision of a punchayet or abide by the award of arbitrators, I should say that most unquestionably the trial by jury would not be agreeable to them."[67] Justices Bird and Woodcock similarly explained, "the natives of the Southern countries at least, have no confidence in punchayets in civil matters, and therefore we cannot imagine that the introduction of similar institutions in those of a criminal nature would be at all popular."[68]

Despite Hume's intervention, Grant's reform bill omitted any mention of Indian criminal juries and focused almost exclusively upon the appointment of justices of the peace in India. Like the earlier 1826 Act, Grant's bill and act, passed in August 1832, were merely permissive in nature, allowing the governors-in-general of all the Presidency towns to appoint any properly qualified person to the office.[69] There was, however, a small measure of jury reform included in the Act, which repealed the requirements that only Christians could serve on grand juries as well as the requirement that only Christians could serve on juries in which Christians were on trial. Nevertheless, criminal justice in much of India remained largely summary in nature and unencumbered by a jury.

This is not to say, however, that criminal juries and panchayats did not exist, although they do not appear to have been very common. As in the case of Captain Briggs in Khandesh, what happened in the non-Regulation Provinces was sometimes much different than what happened in the other Indian territories occupied and controlled by the British. G. R. Clark, the Lieutenant Governor of the North-western Provinces, explained before the Commons Select Committee on Indian Territories in 1852, "the criminal cases referred to the punchayets would be comparatively few; certainly I have been in the habit of referring cases of assault and land disputes, and even cases of homicide, to the punchayets,

[67] Ibid., p. 38. [68] Ibid., p. 47.

[69] 2 & 3 W. IV, c. 117, An Act to amend the Law relating to the Appointment of Justices of the Peace, and of Juries, in the East Indies (1832). Grant's bill engendered the determined resistance of the East India Company to permit Indians to serve as justices of the peace. The Company felt strongly enough, in fact, to petition the House of Lords to reject it. See *Hansard*, House of Lords, 3rd ser., Vol. 14, 15 August 1832, c. 1361 and the correspondence between Grant and the Company in PP, *Juries, India. Copy of Correspondence between the Directors of the East India Company and the Commissioners for the Affairs of the East Indies, on the India Jury Bill* (1831–1832).

but it is not ordinarily done; it has, however, worked satisfactorily."[70] Indeed, Clark was determined to defend the panchayat in the face of rather hostile questioning from R. D. Mangles, the Liberal MP from Guildford and a director of the East India Company:

MANGLES: You speak very highly of the system of punchayet; are you aware that many very able men have spoken of it as a rude system of arbitration, which has been superseded in the opinions and feelings of the natives, wherever ordinary good courts of justice have been established?

CLARK: I have heard that said, and testing it myself, I have not found it to be the case. I have generally found them very glad to resort to the punchayet, and willing to abide by its decision.

MANGLES: Are you aware, that in Madras, under Sir Thomas Monro's [*sic*] system, great facility was given to the punchayet by making resort to it cheaper than to the courts of justice; and yet, when courts of justice were established, the courts of justice had business as 100 to 1 above the business referred to the punchayets?

CLARK: I think in certain parts we have damaged the punchayets by our interfering with them so much, making it compulsory, and leaving the litigants less choice in the selection of arbitrators.

MANGLES: Have you not heard in some parts of India, about Agra, that such punchayets have very often ended in pitched battles; in the case of boundary disputes, for instance?

CLARK: Yes, but I have often terminated pitched battles by means of punchayets.[71]

Certainly, in at least some of the princely states criminal panchayats functioned as well. In Mysore, for example, the long-time Commissioner there, Mark Cubbon, reported in 1855 "that no criminal investigation is permitted to be carried on without a Punchayet."[72] In most criminal cases, *killadars*, or police officers, investigated the crime and reported their findings to a panchayat, which pronounced a judgment on the evidence. Panchayat decisions were then referred to the local magistrate (*amildar*) for execution.[73] In suspected murder cases, the panchayat functioned less as a trial jury and much more as a grand jury. When a death occurred, the local police "at once assembles a Punchayet, when a careful examination of the body is made, and if the

[70] PP, *First Report from the Select Committee on Indian Territories* (1852–1853), p. 190.
[71] Ibid., p. 191.
[72] "Memorandum showing the System of Judicature in Mysore," n.d., *Selections from the Records of the Government of India (Foreign Department)*, No. XI (Calcutta, 1856), p. 80.
[73] Ibid., p. 77.

Punchayet give it as their opinion that it is only a case of accidental, or sudden death, unattended with suspicious circumstances," then a report was made to the magistrate and the body released. In suspicious circumstances,

> the Punchayet examine the body, they note any apparent marks of violence, and the probable means by which life was destroyed. They next inquire into all circumstances which may throw any light upon the matter, such as the habits, connections, circumstances, associates, mode of life, &c., of the deceased, and should suspicion attach upon any individual, the proper researches are made to fix the guilt upon him, or to clear him of the crime. This preliminary investigation, which is made with all practicable speed, hardly ever fails in eliciting the true facts of the crime.[74]

However, in robbery cases, the panchayat in Mysore functioned as a jury. In these cases, either the local police or the magistrate investigated the crime and reported his findings to a panchayat, which issued a preliminary decision. The reports of both the local panchayat and the police or magistrate were then forwarded either to the European Superintendent or the regional judge (*munsif*). Either supervising official then convened another panchayat, which, after considering the evidence, drew up its own decision (*mahazur*). The Superintendent or, in more serious cases, the Commissioner, finally reviewed the case and, if necessary, sentenced the individual.[75]

Still, despite occasional calls for the creation of criminal trials by panchayat, the widespread British aversion to employing both the panchayat and the jury in Indian criminal trials and the arrogation unto themselves of summary criminal justice predominated throughout the first half of the nineteenth century.[76] Even in instances in which panchayats, assessors, or juries could be called upon to assist British judges after 1832, they were rarely used.[77] In the Bengal Presidency's Lower Provinces, for example, in 1849 and 1850, no Sessions judges ever convened a panchayat while deciding more than 2,300 criminal cases (see Table 6.1). Indian assessors were called upon in only 217 cases and the so-called jury 327 times.

[74] Ibid., pp. 78–9. [75] Ibid., pp. 79–80.

[76] One notable exception was that of Henry Lushington, a Sessions Judge at Fatehpur, who advocated the introduction of criminal trials by panchayat in 1846. See, Henry Lushington, "Notes on Trial by Jury" in *Selections from the Records of Government, North Western Provinces*, 2nd edn. (Agra, 1855), pp. 18–36.

[77] Bengal Regulation VI, 1832.

TABLE 6.1 Employment of panchayats, assessors, and juries in criminal cases, Lower Bengal Provinces, 1849 and 1850

	Panchayats (% of total cases)	Assessors (% of total cases)	Juries (% of total cases)	Total cases decided by Sessions Judges
1849	–	125 (9.9)	189 (15.0)	1,258
1850	–	92 (8.1)	138 (12.2)	1,131
Total	–	217 (9.1)	327 (13.7)	2,389

Source: PP, *Returns and Papers relative to the Affairs of the East India Company: Abstract Statements Relative to the Administration of Criminal Justice in the Lower Provinces for 1850* (1853), Abstract Statement No. 8, pp. 434–5.

TABLE 6.2 Employment of panchayats, assessors, and juries in criminal cases, North-Western Provinces, 1848 and 1849

	Panchayats (% of total cases)	Assessors (% of total cases)	Juries (% of total cases)	Total cases decided by Sessions Judges
1848	–	280 (6.7)	840 (20.0)	4,192
1849	–	560 (10.7)	819 (15.6)	5,254
Total	–	840 (8.9)	1,659 (17.6)	9,446

Source: PP, *Returns and Papers Relative to the Affairs of the East India Company: Report of the Sudder Dewanny Adawlut, North-western Provinces, on the Administration of Criminal Justice for the Year 1849* (1853), Abstract Statement No. 2, p. 304; Abstract Statement No. 8, p. 308.

The aggregate reports from the North-western Provinces reveal relatively similar accounts (see Table 6.2). There in 1848 and 1849, of the almost 9,500 cases heard before Sessions Judges, only 840 employed Indian assessors. In the case of the employment of jury-advisors, the numbers were slightly better; over 1,650 juries were employed over those two years. However, once again, no panchayats were convened.

Perhaps most surprising of all is the fact that these types of so-called native assistance in criminal matters appear nowhere in the similar accounts of criminal judicature from either the Madras or Bombay Presidencies. These had been, after all, the areas in which British experiments with panchayats were first implemented. In the Madras Presidency, village and district civil panchayats first created under Munro still existed, although virtually moribund, and would continue to do so throughout the remainder of the century. However, in the Bombay Presidency, all formal connections, both civil and criminal, between British governance and the panchayat had disappeared by mid-century.

When the Indian Law Commission issued its reports on the judicial establishments of India in 1856, the panchayat appeared only as an afterthought. The great bulk of the evidence they collected on the institution related to its military role and the jurisdictions of courts martial, the military panchayat, and courts of request.[78] Otherwise, panchayats were mentioned only in the report on the Madras Presidency. Here, the Commissioners' attitude might best be described as benign neglect. There is some irony to the fact that, unlike Munro, who believed the panchayat was analogous to the English common-law jury, the Commissioners understood the panchayat only as an arbitration tribunal.[79] As such, they concluded that the village and district panchayats in the Presidency, although hardly ever resorted to, probably did do some good. They admitted to having no proof of this, but urged that they be retained until or unless some other investigatory body may recommend their dissolution.[80]

Regarding the criminal jury trial, the Commissioners issued only slightly more vigorous recommendations. Given the fact that panchayats were no longer being convened to advise judges anywhere in the Presidencies, the subject did not merit being mentioned. Once again, the requirements for jury service were to be left to the discretion of the Governor-Generals in Council because, in their words, "in a country with such a diversified population as India comprehends, it would be extremely difficult to insert in a legislative measure any positive rule of national or local distinctions which would not be open to grave objections."[81] Nevertheless, they did recommend that judges be prohibited from overturning unanimous

[78] PP, *East India. (Indian Law Commission) Copies of the Special Reports of the Indian Law Commissioners* (1847), pp. 519–606.

[79] PP, *Fourth Report of Her Majesty's Commissioners Appointed to Consider the Reform of the Judicial Establishments, Judicial Procedure, and Laws of India, &c.* (1856), pp. 6–7.

[80] Ibid., p. 7.

[81] PP, *First Report of Her Majesty's Commissioners Appointed to Consider the Reform of the Judicial Establishments, Judicial Procedure, and Laws of India, &c.* (1856), p. 141.

jury verdicts, a recommendation later adopted in the 1861 Criminal Code of Procedure.[82]

The 1861 Criminal Code of Procedure is perhaps most notorious for codifying restrictions on the employment of Indians as jurors in criminal trials of Europeans, Britons, and Americans.[83] However, while the Code may have codified these restrictions, it certainly did not invent them. As we have seen in the case of civil trials, the East India Company and the Presidencies had acted to implement similar restrictions since the passage of Charles Williams Wynn's Juries in India Act of 1826. By the 1860s, the panchayat and the jury system had largely ceased to be linked together in the minds of British governors as well as in the practice of British governance in India.

During the remainder of British rule, the panchayat was gradually revived and reshaped into an institution of local and municipal governance largely, but not altogether, shedding its function as an adjudicatory institution.[84] After Independence, numerous attempts were undertaken to resurrect the panchayat's adjudicatory role, the *nyaya panchayats* being the most notable of them.[85] Yet as several prominent observers remarked in the early 1980s, that institution was marked by significant "ideological confusion," combining, as it did, the functions of both adjudication and local governance.[86] As of the writing of this book, that connection has been severed altogether by the Indian state although not necessarily by all Indian citizens. While Panchayati Raj Institutions (PRIs) now form the constitutional basis of local self-governance in India, the so-called *khap panchayats* administer their own forms of rough justice in some villages.

[82] Ibid., p. 142; Act XXV of 1861, Ch. XXIII, § 328.

[83] See Elizabeth Kolsky, "Codification and the Rule of Colonial Difference: Criminal Procedure in British India," *LHR*, Vol. 23, No. 3 (Fall 2005), pp. 631–83.

[84] Catherine S. Meschievitz and Marc Galanter, "In Search of Nyaya Panchayats: The Politics of a Moribund Institution," in Richard L. Abel, ed., *The Politics of Informal Justice, Volume 2: Comparative Studies* (New York: Academic Press, 1982), pp. 47–77.

[85] See, for example, the *114th Report on Gram Nyayalaya* (1986) prepared by the Indian Law Commission.

[86] Meschievitz and Galanter, "In Search of Nyaya Panchayats," pp. 55–6; Upendra Baxi and Marc Galanter, "Panchayat Justice: An Indian Experiment in Legal Access," in M. Cappelletti and B. Garth, eds., *Access to Justice: Vol. III: Emerging Issues and Perspectives* (Milan: Guiffre; Alphen aan den Rijn: Sijthoff and Noordhoff, 1979) pp. 341–86.

7

THE PANCHAYAT DEBATE IN THE BENGAL PRESIDENCY, 1814–1830

During the late eighteenth and early nineteenth centuries, the judicial establishments in the Indian Presidencies struggled to keep pace with a mounting backlog of cases. Acutely aware of this problem, the Board of Directors of the East India Company encouraged a variety of experiments that were intended to expedite the resolution of disputes, facilitate the reform of the judiciary, and improve access to justice. Certainly, one of the most unique experiments was the attempt to revive the "customary" panchayat and to adapt this tribunal to the needs of the Company's courts of justice. As we have seen, serious and determined attempts to revive and invigorate the panchayat as a tribunal to resolve civil disputes were undertaken both in southern India in the Madras Presidency under Thomas Munro and in western India in the Bombay Presidency under Mountstuart Elphinstone.[1] However, there were no similar efforts to resurrect panchayats in Bengal. Indeed, there appears to have been no figure in Bengal with the authority, stature, and Orientalist perspective on "native" justice similar to that either of Munro or Elphinstone.

The fact that there was little interest or will to attempt this panchayat experiment in the Bengal Presidency has received very little attention.

[1] Catherine S. Meschievitz, "Civil Litigation and Judicial Policy in the Madras Presidency, 1800–1834" (Ph.D. thesis, University of Wisconsin-Madison, 1986); Burton Stein, *Thomas Munro: The Origins of the Colonial State and his Vision of Empire* (New Delhi: Oxford University Press, 1989); Kenneth Ballhatchet, *Social Policy and Social Change in Western India, 1817–1830* (Oxford: Oxford University Press, 1957); and Meera Singh, *British Revenue and Judicial Policies in India: A Case Study of Deccan (1818–1826)* (New Delhi: Har-Anand Publications, 1994).

This is despite the fact that the Company's Board of Directors repeatedly ordered the Bengal government to implement it as a necessary reform to reduce the overwhelming caseloads of the judicial officers, to improve the efficiency of the courts, and to minimize the expenses of the judicial establishment. Indeed, the attempt to implement the panchayat system in Bengal engendered a notable conflict between Company authorities in both London and Calcutta. Conducted over the course of a decade and a half and across thousands of miles, the Company's efforts to enforce the adoption of the panchayat system in Bengal were continually thwarted by administrative officials and judicial officers in that Presidency. Eventually, the failure to resurrect the panchayat system in Bengal during this era of Orientalist reform was not a function of the failure of either leadership or vision. Instead, the failure of panchayat reforms in the Bengal Presidency was the result of bureaucratic in-fighting, administrative foot-dragging, and a notable contest of political wills between the Board of Directors of the Company in London and their political and judicial officers operating in India.

During the late eighteenth century, the judicial administration of the Bengal Presidency had been subject to a series of significant reforms. Throughout the period between the 1770s and 1790s, judicial procedures had been altered and re-altered, judicial offices established and abolished, judicial authority delegated and re-delegated, and judicial principles formed and re-formed.[2] Even *Hobson-Jobson*, a standard Anglo-Indian dictionary, refers to these attempts at reform as a "constant succession of revolutions in the judicial system" in its definition of the *adalat*, or court. Eventually, on the civil side, Cornwallis' reforms of 1793, separating the judicial from the revenue functions of the Company, thereafter established the system of district *zillah* courts, provincial Courts of Appeal, and the *sadr diwani adalat* at the Bengal Presidency.

If there had been any hope that these reforms would expedite the legal process, those hopes were quickly dashed. Writing in 1814, the Company had hoped that "the great objects which Lord Cornwallis had in view, in forming the Judicial Code of Bengal, consisted, not only in the desire of providing for an upright distribution of justice, but also in

[2] See PP, *Copy of the Fifth Report from the Select Committee of the House of Commons on the Affairs of the East India Company, 28th July 1812* (1812), pp. 4–28.

that of securing a promptitude and facility of obtaining it."[3] But by January 1807, the backlog in the Presidency's courts had surpassed 120,000 cases, and six years later, by January 1813, the "cases in arrears," as they were called, had grown to well over 140,000.[4]

The causes of this massive backlog of cases were much in dispute and the blame for it was spread quite widely. Naturally, some argued that Indian litigiousness was partly to blame, although one judicial officer, John Shakespear, the Superintendent of Police of the Western Provinces, tried to place this in as favorable a light as possible. "The litigiousness and perseverance of the natives are noticed in the Regulations of 1772," he wrote in 1816, "and it is not that our laws have given birth to, and fostered this evil – the spirit of variance always prevailed, the only difference is, that, under the native Government, the inhabitants were accustomed to decide their contentions by the sword, whilst, at present, they are compelled to seek redress for their grievances, real and supposed, in our Courts, and turbulence and dissension find vent by a less objectionable channel than formerly."[5] Other judicial officers, such as those in the Judicial Department of the Bengal Presidency, alternatively attacked litigants for their mendaciousness. "It is needless to remark," they wrote to the Court of Directors in London, "how much the Proceedings of all our tribunals are delayed and embarrassed by the notorious disregard for truth so generally displayed by Natives in giving Evidence and from their want of moral principle."[6]

In London, however, the Court of Directors viewed things quite differently. They believed that one cause lay in the provisions for dispute resolution originally adopted by Cornwallis in 1793. According to those Regulations, local *zillah* Judges were accorded summary jurisdiction to decide disputes over crops and rights to land. But by bringing these cases before the courts, the effect had been not only to unnecessarily delay decisions on these matters but also to

[3] PP, *East India Affairs: Papers Relating to the Police, and Civil and Criminal Justice under the Respective Governments of Bengal, Fort St. George, and Bombay from 1810 to the Present Time* (1819), p. 33; see also IOR/E/4/682, "Draft of a Dispatch Proposed to be Sent to Bengal, on Judicature and Police," 20 September 1814, ff. 307–11.

[4] Ibid., pp. 33–4; IOR/E/4/682, "Draft of a Dispatch Proposed to be Sent to Bengal, on Judicature and Police," 20 September 1814, ff. 307–11; see also *Copy of the Fifth Report*, pp. 165–73.

[5] IOR/V/27/140/12, *Papers Regarding Judicial System, Bengal Presidency 1814–1818*, J. Shakespear to W. B. Bailey, 16 December 1816, p. 8.

[6] IOR/L/PJ/3/252, Letter to the Honorable Court of Directors from Judicial Department (Lower and Western Provinces), 22 February 1827, ff. 439–441.

unwittingly encourage the use of violence to settle disputes more immediately. "The consequence [of this Regulation]," the Directors wrote, "has been that the affrays and all their attendant evils and outrage, which the Regulation was meant to prevent, have become more prevalent than ever."[7]

In addition, the Court blamed the revised Regulations of 1799 for delegating authority to local *zamindars* to distrain the property of *ryots* in default of revenue payments. Only after a *zamindar* had distrained a *ryot's* property was the latter allowed access to the courts, a process that necessarily led to disputes and to the increase of the courts' case-loads. The Regulations, the Directors argued, offered "very feeble protection . . . against the injustice and extortions of Zemindars."[8]

However, the most striking explanation without doubt came from the Presidency's own Judicial Department. The Department admitted the "justness" of the Directors' remarks but placed the blame squarely on the Permanent Settlement itself that had failed to establish a system of property rights before being implemented. In reply to the Directors' dispatch, they wrote:

> [W]e are led to ascribe the alleged inadequacy of our civil tribunals in the Lower Provinces to meet the demands upon them, to the precipitation with which the permanent Settlement was carried into effect, without previously defining the relative rights and interests of the zemindars and other Landholders; and the various classes of the cultivating population[,] or without providing such means as would have enabled the Courts of Justice to ascertain those rights and interests by recourse to recorded Documents, in those controversies which form directly or indirectly not only the most numerous but often the most embarrassing of all the questions which are brought forward for judicial adjudication.[9]

Recourse to the courts to settle these matters had certainly been entertained by Cornwallis when drafting the Permanent Settlement. Indeed, Cornwallis considered it futile to even attempt to record and classify those "rights and interests" because no reliable records existed with which to do so. Instead, he believed it was better left to the courts

[7] PP, *East India Affairs: Papers Relating to the Police, and Civil and Criminal Justice*, p. 36; IOR/E/4/682, "Draft of a Dispatch Proposed to be Sent to Bengal, on Judicature and Police," 20 September 1814, ff. 346–8.

[8] Ibid., ff. 339–40.

[9] IOR/L/PJ/3/252, Letter to the Honorable Court of Directors from Judicial Department (Lower and Western Provinces), 22 February 1827, ff. 439–441.

to decide disputes both between individuals and between individuals and the government.[10] But the result, the Bengal Judicial Department argued, had been costly. "The real pressure upon our tribunals arises from the Mass of litigation connected with the rights, tenures, and interests of the proprietors and occupiers of land," they wrote.

> It is now too late to apply an effectual remedy to an evil which might have been guarded against when the permanent Settlement was formed but it is and will be our anxious wish to adopt such measures, both in the Revenue and Judicial Departments as may be feasible, with a view to define the rights and interests of the cultivators, and to secure those rights.[11]

Needless to say, this did not go very far toward answering the Directors' concern regarding the Presidency's mounting caseloads. In a lengthy dispatch of 9 November 1814, they therefore ordered a number of reforms to be implemented throughout the Bengal judiciary. Perhaps the most logical reform, that of increasing the number of judicial officers on the grounds of relieving the courts of their backlogs, was immediately dismissed as not only being too expensive but also unlikely to solve the problem. "The actual & growing inadequacy of the existing administration of Civil Justice," they wrote, "is neither remedied in the one case nor prevented in the other, by any augmentation of the European part of the Establishment, even if the embarrassed condition of our Finances enabled us to incur an additional expenditure on that account. Double the number of Zillah judges, we are persuaded, would do little more than palliate, and that most feebly, the evil; and by no means reach the seat of the disease."[12]

The solution to the problem therefore was not to employ more British Judges and Magistrates but instead to extend "as far as may be necessary to meet the wants & necessities of the people, the instrumentality of the natives in conducting this branch of internal regulation."[13] Toward that end, the Directors ordered Bengal to adopt the same system recently adopted in the Madras Presidency and later to be adopted in the Bombay

[10] H. R. C. Wright, "Some Aspects of the Permanent Settlement in Bengal," *Economic History Review*, New Series, Vol. 7, No. 2 (1954), p. 213.

[11] IOR/L/PJ/3/252, Letter to the Honorable Court of Directors from Judicial Department (Lower and Western Provinces), 22 February 1827, ff. 441–3.

[12] PP, *East India Affairs: Papers Relating to the Police, and Civil and Criminal Justice*, p. 40; see also, IOR/E/4/682, "Draft of a Dispatch Proposed to be Sent to Bengal, on Judicature and Police," 20 September 1814, ff. 395–7.

[13] Ibid.

Presidency; that is, to shift the burden of resolving civil disputes out of the courts and onto the backs of both the local heads of villages, the *patels*, and the local village panchayats.

The Court's decision was obviously influenced by Orientalist thought, and while the imprint of Thomas Munro's thinking is quite prominent, he was not the only source upon which they had drawn. Upon the renewal of its Charter in 1813, the Company had instituted an inquiry into the administration of justice in India.[14] In part, as a result of the queries sent out in that year, the Directors claimed that if financial necessity made it imperative that "natives" be employed in the judicial branch, the question then arose as to how they could be employed most effectively. Their answer was that "no arrangement for this purpose can proceed on a right principle nor operate satisfactorily in the fulfilment [*sic*] of its aim, which has not a reference to the ancient & long established customs & institutions of the Country, & which does not accommodate itself to the habits, the feelings & the understanding of those for whose benefit it is designed."[15]

Interestingly, the Court was aware that much of the information regarding the "customary" activity of *patels* and panchayats had been derived from reports from Southern India, especially those of Mark Wilks and Thomas Munro, who had reported at length on panchayats in Mysore and the Ceded Districts of Madras.[16] Nevertheless, the Directors were convinced that the same principles could be equally applied to Bengal. "That the same authorities exist within the Territory under your charge," they wrote, "we have very clear evidence, though they may be found in a more mutilated and deformed condition than in other parts of our possessions."[17] In Bengal, the *patels* may be referred to as "Munduls, Moccudims, or Gomashtahs," but they and the panchayats traditionally "settled and adjusted ... the litigations occurring

[14] For the replies from officers who had served in Bengal, see *Selection of Papers from the Records at the East-India House, Relating to the Revenue, Police, and Civil and Criminal Justice under the Company's Governments in India*, Vol. II (London, 1820), pp. 1–93.

[15] PP, *East India Affairs: Papers Relating to the Police, and Civil and Criminal Justice*, p. 40; IOR/E/4/682, "Draft of a Dispatch Proposed to be Sent to Bengal, on Judicature and Police," 20 September 1814, ff. 395–7.

[16] Mark Wilks, *Historical Sketches of the South of India* (London, 1820), but Munro's influence in London was essential. See his 1807 Minute "Trial by Panchayat" reprinted in Alexander J. Arbuthnot, *Major-General Sir Thomas Munro, Bart., K.C.B., Governor of Madras: Selections from His Minutes and other Official Writings*, Vol. II (London, 1881), pp. 3–6; Meschievitz, "Civil Litigation and Judicial Policy," pp. 145–61; Stein, *Thomas Munro*, Chapter 4.

[17] PP, *East India Affairs: Papers Relating to the Police, and Civil and Criminal Justice*, p. 40.

among their neighbours."[18] Crucial to the Directors' decision to employ panchayats for the resolution of civil disputes was their understanding and perception of how customary panchayats functioned. For this, they relied not only on the reports of functionaries operating in the field but, more importantly, on the analogy that they believed to exist between Indian panchayats and English civil arbitration.

As we have seen, by the first decades of the nineteenth century, arbitration had come to be viewed as a potentially efficient and effective remedy to the delays and expenses of civil litigation in England. In the arbitration process, individuals voluntarily agreed to abide by the decision of one or more mutually acceptable arbitrators in order to resolve their differences. Sometimes the arbitrators themselves were encouraged to nominate a third person as an umpire or referee who was given the authority to decide the issue at hand in the event that the arbitrators could not reach an agreement. Litigants were also often encouraged to enter into bonds to secure the performance of an arbitrator's award, although this was neither required nor necessary. The bond merely provided an alternative means of enforcement of an award. If the litigant failed to abide by the arbitrator's award, they could then be sued in court for non-performance of the bond, a potentially simpler option from enjoining the case *ab ovo*.

Furthermore, in arbitration, litigants were rarely represented by legal counsel, hearings were entirely informal, and the whole process was free of rules of pleadings, evidence, and procedure. The arbitrators themselves need not have had any legal training or experience. Instead, they were expected to be men of good reputation, honest, trustworthy, and with practical experience in the matter. They received little or no recompense and were bound to decide matters solely in "equity and good conscience," avoiding arcane language or obscure legal precedents.[19]

Finally, purview of arbitration was extraordinarily broad. According to Stewart Kyd's late-eighteenth-century standard treatise on

[18] PP, *East India Affairs: Papers Relating to the Police, and Civil and Criminal Justice*, p. 40.

[19] Francis Russell, *A Treatise on the Power and Duty of an Arbitrator*, 5th edn. (London: Stevens and Sons, 1878), Chapter II and Stewart Kyd, *A Treatise on the Law of Awards*, 2nd edn. (1799; Philadelphia, PA: Farrand & Co., 1808), Chapter II. Further research may well indicate that this is the source of the "puzzling formula" by which British policy was guided in several important areas of civil law. See Marc Galanter, "The Displacement of Traditional Law in Modern India," *Journal of Social Issues*, Vol. 24, No. 4 (1968), p. 68 and, more generally, J. Duncan M. Derrett, "Justice, Equity and Good Conscience," in J. N. D. Anderson, ed., *Changing Law in Developing Countries* (New York: Frederick A. Praeger, 1963), pp. 114–53.

arbitration, nearly any dispute could be resolved through arbitration, excepting those involving titles to real property and high crimes against the state or the Established Church.[20] This might therefore include the arbitration of commercial and personal debts, which was especially championed by Lord Mansfield during the eighteenth century, but also trespass, misdemeanor assault, rights-of-way, contracts, fraud, embezzlement, and bankruptcy. Indeed by 1800, arbitration had become viewed as something of a panacea for some of the ills of the English courts and thus increasingly found its way into legislation. Arbitration provisions can be found in the Cotton Arbitration Acts of 1800 and 1804, the revised Combination Act of 1800, the Savings Bank Act of 1817, and the numerous Railway Acts passed by parliament after the 1820s.

Therefore, those persons choosing to resolve disputes through arbitration could enter into a relatively autonomous sphere of informal justice and private lawmaking that, unlike the courts, was flexible, efficient, and cheap. Blackstone was only one of a number of important jurists who heaped praise upon the "infinite importance of these peaceable and domestic tribunals" of arbitration that avoided "the inevitable delay and expence of public litigation."[21] Lord Mansfield was undoubtedly the most vigorous proponent of arbitration as he refashioned English commercial law during the late eighteenth century.[22]

As was the case for Elphinstone in Bombay, for many Company officials in London the correspondence between English arbitration and the "ancient" panchayat appeared to be obvious. Both systems, as we have seen, were based upon the voluntary compliance of the litigants. Litigants voluntarily chose to submit their dispute to a panchayat rather than go to the law and selected their own representatives to serve as members, or *panchayatdars*, on that tribunal. Like an English referee, a *sarpanch* was sometimes appointed to supervise the proceedings and to cast a deciding vote, if necessary. Finally, the *sarounsh*, *razeenamah*, and *yad* all had their equivalents in contemporary arbitration practices in England. It is important, in this regard, to emphasize the fact that both the Company officials in India and the Directors in

[20] Kyd, *Treatise on the Law of Awards*, pp. 10–11; 52–3; 63–64; 68–9; Russell, *Treatise on the Power and Duty of an Arbitrator*, pp. 3–13.

[21] William Blackstone, *Commentaries on the Laws of England*, Vol. III, 13th edn. (London, 1800), pp. 15–17.

[22] Henry Horwitz and James Oldham, "John Locke, Lord Mansfield, and Arbitration during the Eighteenth Century," *Historical Journal*, Vol. 36, No. 1 (1993), pp. 137–59.

London assumed that, as in the case of English arbitration, panchayats were institutions of dispute resolution that applied to broad areas of civil justice and not solely to caste discipline. They had come to rely on the notion, as Thomas Munro had put it, that the panchayat was an essential part of India's common law and that their jurisdiction included disputes over adoption, inheritance, wills, marriage, maintenance, village boundaries, trespass, commercial contracts, and personal debts.[23]

Before 1814, Company officers in London had frequently been informed that panchayats were simply "courts of arbitration." And in their orders of 9 November of that year to implement the panchayat system, the Directors repeatedly invoked and quoted the reports from local judges and other Company officials equating the panchayat to arbitration. For example, the Directors quoted Captain (later Colonel) Alexander Read's 1794 letter from the Madras Presidency who had written of the employment of panchayats in the following terms: "It is directed that when any differences arise relating to Municipal management or Cultivation a Punchayet or Native Court of Arbitration may be assembled to adjust them."[24] In 1801, John Melville, the judge-magistrate at Dacca, had reported that "authority and great encouragement should be given to procure an adjustment of petty disputes and quarrels thro' the means of Punchayets. This mode of arbitration, for in the present instance it is nothing more, was formally [*sic*] almost universally practised and it has not only the sanction of established usage in its favour but the members of such tribunals being as it were pointed out for the office by their established characters and by the acknowledged sentiment of the whole of their society the decision is at once acquiesced in and becomes happily unquestioned."[25] Sir John Malcolm's *Sketch of the Sikhs*, published in 1812, was quoted in the letter to Bengal in the same vein. "It is usual to assemble a Punchayet or a Court of Arbitration in every part of India under Native Government," Malcolm had written, "and as they are always chosen from Men of the best reputation in the place where they meet, this Court had a high Character for Justice."[26]

It is quite clear, however, that while these reforms were being implemented in both the Madras and later the Bombay Presidencies,

[23] See, for example, the breakdown of disputes recorded in MSA, EIC, Judicial Department, Annual and Periodical Reports, Vol. 1/102, 1826.

[24] IOR/E/4/912, Madras Dispatches 29 April 1814, ff. 579–82; Stein, *Thomas Munro*, pp. 180–2.

[25] IOR/E/4/912, Madras Dispatches 29 April 1814, ff. 589–93. [26] Ibid., ff. 586–7.

they evoked a great deal of resistance in Bengal. Initially, the Governor-General, Lord Moira, (later Marquess of Hastings) seemed to be quite sympathetic. In a minute written in 1815, he extolled the virtues of the panchayat, claiming that he had received reports that

> they reach the truth and unravel the cases which come before them better than we do, owing to their superior knowledge of the habits and customs of the people which are too minute or domestic for our view; that they consider the parentage, the cast [*sic*], the connections, and the circumstances in life of the witnesses when appretiating [*sic*] the credit due to their testimony, whether they are single or married, have children or other near relations whose welfare is superstitiously considered as identified with their own. All which are points of real importance in this country.[27]

Moreover, in an appendix to Lord Moira's minute, the reports of several local judges and magistrate had also praised the efficacy of panchayat justice. The Magistrate from Furruckhabad certainly wrote the most glowing report, noting:

> Above all things, the greatest encouragement should be given to the settlement of claims by Punchait or arbitration. To this ancient mode of terminating their differences of all descriptions, the natives are extremely partial. They are certain of obtaining hereby a just and equitable decision, without delay, expence, trouble, vexation, or fear of partiality. Therefore the decisions of Punches, when just and equitable, should in every practicable instance be confirmed by our Civil and Criminal tribunals and persons refusing, without just cause, to abide by them should be amerced. The more this custom prevails, the less will be the labours of our Judicial officers, the Government will be saved the great expence of new Officers and additional assistants to share the over-whelming labours of Judges and Magistrates; Property will be more secure; The people will be more happy; some lives and many limbs will be saved.[28]

However, by the following year, 1816, responses received from local judges, magistrates, and, especially, the *sadr diwani adalat* were noticeably more hostile to the proposed reforms. The *sadr* court's first

[27] IOR/V/27/140/12, *Papers Regarding Judicial System, Bengal Presidency 1814–1818*, "Minute by the Right Honorable Governor General on the Judicial Administration of the Presidency of Fort William, Dated 2nd October 1815," p. 38.

[28] IOR/H/Misc/776, Appendix to Lord Moira's Minute on the Judicial Administration of the Presidency of Fort William, 2nd October 1815. Reports of Judicial Officers of various Districts, n.p.

complaint focused on the enormous expansion of their supervisory functions that this reform would entail. They argued that given the extent of the territory and the number of village panchayats that would have to be established and supervised, the obstacles presented would be quite "formidable" and that "it would be impossible to exercise a proper and necessary control over such a number of petty courts." By their count, the *sadr* court estimated that each *zillah* judge would be responsible for the supervision of approximately 8,000 "village courts."[29]

Moreover, the *sadr* judges objected to the new elements of compulsion that the Directors proposed to adopt in order to promote the resolution of disputes through panchayats. Since the British perception of the "ancient and customary" panchayat was that it functioned in a way nearly identical to the modes of arbitration in England, litigants and arbitrators were wholly free to enter into or exit from arbitration in order to resolve their disputes, but they could not be compelled to do so. Indeed, until the twentieth century, the English courts consistently refused to sanction any form of "compulsory" or "mandatory" arbitration.[30] However, the Directors' plan to promote dispute resolution by panchayat included the institution of fines for those individuals who refused to serve on panchayats. In response, the *sadr* Judges argued that "some dissatisfaction, and consequent discouragement to Punchayets, might arise from the compulsory rule."[31]

In addition, the Judges questioned the appeals process suggested by the Directors. In the hope of limiting appeals from panchayat decisions, the Directors' plan allowed for appeals to the *zillah* courts, but only in cases of "gross error or partiality." This limitation, it was argued, may have had the unintended effect of driving potential litigants away from the panchayat rather than toward them. The *sadr* judges pointedly asked the Directors to consider "whether any attempt to alter the usual mode of convening Punchayets, to regulate their proceedings, and to bring their awards, or the personal conduct of the arbitrators, under the control of the regular Courts of Judicature, may not tend to defeat the object intended by discouraging, rather than promoting, the extension of this mode of arbitration to Civil disputes of a general nature, distinct from those of caste and discipline."[32]

[29] IOR/V/27/140/12, *Papers Regarding Judicial System, Bengal Presidency 1814–1818*, p. 18.
[30] William Holdsworth, *A History of English Law*, Vol. XIV (London: Methuen & Co., 1964), pp. 189–90.
[31] IOR/V/27/140/12, *Papers Regarding Judicial System, Bengal Presidency 1814–1818*, p. 21.
[32] Ibid.

The *sadr diwani adalat*, therefore, was unwilling to admit the panchayat into the formal judicial structure of the Presidency. While this may have been based at least in part on a suspicion of "native" judges, this was neither the language nor the justification used. Instead, the Court relied upon English legal doctrines and practices of arbitration to justify their opposition. Arbitration's very success and survival, as Blackstone had taught and Mansfield had implemented, was based on its informality, that is, the extra-judicial realm in which it operated, as well as the wholly voluntary participation of those who agreed to resolve their disputes in this forum. To bring the panchayat into the formal system of judicial administration was, in the Court's eyes, to vitiate and perhaps annul the sources of its effectiveness and success as a means by which to resolve disputes. They quoted at great length a report from a *zillah* judge in Rajshahi, East Bengal, who argued:

> It appears to me that any attempt to assimilate the proceedings of the Punchayet to those of our inferior Courts, would destroy that simplicity and locality of action, which is its best recommendation, and the main spring of its formation. As an established Court . . . numerous obstacles would occur in the nomination of its members; the enactment of rules for the guidance of so many thousand Courts, and in the enforcement of their decisions. That the satisfactory adjustment of disputes, without the vexation and uncertainty of a law suit, is highly expedient, every one must allow; but all kinds of adjustments, short of going to law, must be made with the free consent of the parties concerned, and by persons appointed by them.

In short, the judge concluded, "I am of opinion that the Punchayet can never be established so as to form an integral part of our judicial system."[33]

The court therefore recommended against the implementation of the "panchayat system," requesting instead "to defer giving a final opinion upon the expediency of enacting at this presidency, rules for assembling Village Punchayets, corresponding in substance with those now in force at Fort Saint George, until the result of their operation at that Presidency shall have been ascertained."[34]

For the next decade, the subject appears to have been either ignored or held in abeyance. Apparently, it was not until December 1824 that the Court of Directors brought up the issue again and then without any

[33] IOR/V/27/140/12, *Papers Regarding Judicial System, Bengal Presidency 1814–1818*, pp. 22–3.
[34] Ibid., p. 24.

direct reference to their order to institute panchayats. At that time, the Directors wrote to Bengal that they had "abstained from addressing you upon the many matters connected with your judicial system and the state of the courts . . . in the hope of receiving your detailed answer to our letter of 9th November 1814." The Directors reiterated their complaints about the unnecessary backlog of cases in the civil judiciary and, in a sign of exasperation, explained that "we think it useful to communicate the results of this examination of the state of your civil judicature, without referring to the various important matters contained in our letter of 9th November 1814, which will be more conveniently recurred [*sic*] to when we receive your long expected reply to our orders."[35]

When the Judicial Department eventually did reply in 1827, the tone and content of their response was aggressive and argumentative. As we already have seen, the Company's judicial officers in Bengal blamed the backlog of cases on a number of things, but most particularly on the manner in which the Permanent Settlement had been implemented. In addition, they argued that if the Directors had hoped to transfer the legal authority to settle disputes to the local heads of villages and panchayats, then they would be adopting a solution that would be the "very opposite from those benevolent objects to which your Honorable Court's instructions were directed."[36] In Bengal, the Presidency's dispatch insisted, the heads of village as well as other village officials were "either the proprietor of the Village, or the Gomashta or Agent paid and employed by the zemindar, or [a] farmer to manage and collect his rents." These people were obviously unfit to resolve disputes between local villagers or between the villagers and the *zamindar*. Regarding heads of villages, therefore, the Judicial Department concluded, it is

> our firm conviction that no modifications of the system adopted at Madras for the Regulation of the Office of Village Moonsiff which would not be subversive of the principle on which that Regulation is founded, could under the class of Officers indicated, be[?] generally useful in the regular administration of civil Justice in this part of India; but that on the contrary the attempt to introduce a similar system in Bengal would be attended with nearly insurmountable difficulties; and that if it

[35] *Selection of Papers from the Records at the East-India House, Related to the Revenue, Police, and Civil and Criminal Justice, under the Company's Government*, Vol. IV (London, 1826), pp. 32–3.

[36] IOR/L/PJ/3/252, Letter to the Honorable Court of Directors from Judicial Department (Lower and Western Provinces), 22 February 1827, ff. 454–5.

> were introduced it would be productive of results in the highest degree injurious to the interests of those very classes for whose benefit it is more particularly designed.[37]

In particular reference to panchayats, the Judicial Department was even more dismissive. Not only did the Bengal officials deny that the panchayat had ever been active in the territory, but they also dismissed the panchayat as a corrupt and ineffective tribunal. They admitted that the panchayat was ideally a "mode of adjusting civil controversies by arbitration" and that, in this, the panchayat did not differ "in principle from the systems general[ly] adopted in other countries." However, they insisted that Indian litigants did not trust panchayats and that "it is a subject of regret to ourselves and to our Judicial Officers that the Natives cannot be prevailed upon to have more frequent recourse to it."[38]

There were several reasons marshaled to explain the failure or demise of panchayats in Bengal. First, the Bengal officials claimed that it was extremely difficult to convene panchayats because too few people were willing to serve on them. *Panchayatdars*, in their estimation, both feared making enemies in the village and were quite aware of the likelihood that their decisions would be appealed. Potential *panchayatdars*, they wrote, "are not willing to sacrifice their time without remuneration for the benefit of their neighbours or for the public good. They know that their award will in all human probability make one of the parties their Enemy and they are too well aware of the Character of their Countrymen to doubt that the first mark of such enmity would generally be an accusation, that they had given such award under the influence of partiality or corruption."[39]

Second, the Judicial Department argued that panchayats, even when they could be convened, were both inefficient and time-consuming. The Department quoted at length a report from Richard Jenkins, the Resident at Nagpur, whose seven years' experience had "fully established the inefficiency of Punchaets when chosen by the parties themselves, as instruments for dispensing Justice with either impartiality or celerity." In Jenkins' opinion, the procedures by which representatives on the panchayat were selected by the litigants themselves only led to the inability of the tribunal to reach a decision. "It was found," Jenkins reported, "that the Members of the Punchaets usually considered

[37] Ibid., f. 463. [38] Ibid., ff. 463–5. [39] Ibid., ff. 465–6.

themselves and acted as partizans of the party by whom they were chosen, [and] in numerous cases it was found impossible to get them to come to any decision at all, the adherents on one side positively refusing to concur in a decision adverse to the interests of the person by whom they were elected."[40]

Third, the Judicial Department warned that panchayats, especially when they dealt with village boundary disputes, often led to violent clashes and affrays between villagers. Again, they quoted at length from a report, this time from John Wauchope, Judge and Magistrate of Bundelkhand. Bundelkhand, the Judicial Department carefully noted, "is one in which the Hindoo usages had been less affected by foreign rules than most other parts of Hindostan." There, he wrote, his knowledge of the operation of panchayats before British rule had led him to believe that "we shall find little to regret from the disuse of the system." "Under the former Government of this District," he continued, "the Superintendence or management of Punchaets was never from the earliest times that I have been able to trace confined to any particular Individual or body of Men whatever, and the consequence was, that they were very often either futile in their results, or terminated in a murderous conflict between the parties and their adherents." Boundary disputes, he went on to note, were indeed settled by a panchayat, but they also were attended by "a large assemblage of Men from all the surrounding Villages [who] were often invited by the parties to Witness the Settlement. This almost invariably led to violent affrays and the loss of many lives, and which again branched out into innumerable feuds, laying the foundations of continued future disorder and bloodshed."[41]

Fourth, the Judicial Department claimed that Indian litigants in fact preferred to bring their disputes before a British court rather than submit them to the decision of a panchayat. The Commissioner of Delhi reported to the Judicial Department in 1825 that panchayats were infrequently used there because they suffered not only from the lack of confidence that litigating parties reposed in the judgment of their opponent's *panchayatdars* but also "partly because they generally place greater reliance in the *Justice of the European Officers*."[42] In this regard, the Judicial dispatch also quoted approvingly from a letter to the Court of Directors from the Bombay Presidency in which the rise of litigation and the decline of the panchayat was attributed to the speedier and

[40] Ibid., ff. 476–7. [41] Ibid., ff. 469–73. [42] Ibid., ff. 474–5.

more accessible nature of the Company's courts. Indeed, the Judicial Department sought to explain the backlog of cases in Bengal by adverting not only to the problems created by the Permanent Settlement, as we have seen, but also to the rise in population, the growth of trade, the expansion of cultivation, and "the growing confidence of the people in the general proceedings of our tribunals."

Furthermore, the Judicial Department's dispatch emphasized the weaknesses and failures of panchayats in the Ceded and Conquered Districts east of Bengal. In areas such as the Saugor (Sagar) and Nerbudda (Narbada) Territories,[43] where the Regulations had not yet been introduced, the dispatch claimed that "it has been our object to maintain in vigor such of the Native Institutions as could be rendered available for the objects of good Government and more especially to encourage a resort to Punchaets in all practicable cases." But here, they noted, the panchayats had serious shortcomings. From Saugor, it was reported "that petty affrays and disputes regarding boundaries are constantly referred to Punchaets, but that the intrigues of both parties frequently protract the decision and at the commencement of each Season an affray may be anticipated unless some preventive measure is adopted."[44] Captain Hardy, Assistant in the Hutta Division, advised that "I think . . . that the employment of Punchaets should not be resorted to in ordinary cases, which can be decided equally well or better by the Assistant . . . because from their constitution they are necessarily slow – a frequent call on them for the performance of a voluntary and unpaid duty would be found inconvenient to the Members, and making it too common would render the character of these Courts less respected and would produce degrees [of] carelessness and inefficiency."[45]

Despite these numerous shortcomings, the Judicial Department was willing to concede that the panchayat could be used effectively in a very few categories of cases. In particular, several reports concluded that panchayats were best restricted to cases involving caste disputes and mercantile accounts. Captain Lowe, the Assistant in charge of the Baitool (Betul) district of the Saugor and Nerbudda Territories, reported that "The questions which I am chiefly in the habit of referring to the Punchaets are those in which there are disputed Village, and

[43] Saugor (Sagar) and Nerbudda (Narbada) Territories would later be incorporated into the Central Provinces (and even later into contemporary Madhya Pradesh).

[44] IOR/L/PJ/3/252, Letter to the Honorable Court of Directors from Judicial Department (Lower and Western Provinces), 22 February 1827, f. 480.

[45] Ibid., f. 485.

other accounts, in which it is exceedingly difficult to determine the degree of credit due to those produced by each party; and also claims of debt long standing in which the payment of the whole with interest, being impossible, there is a hope that some compromise may be effected."[46] But even in this regard there was notable resistance. The Judge and Magistrate of Agra, C. MacSween, reported that previous to the British administration of justice "Many questions of marriage, inheritance, cast [*sic*], claims to land &c. &c. were referred to Punchaets which here as elsewhere were corrupt and prejudiced. Questions were referred to them because each party hoped by some corrupt means to gain the cause not from any confidence in the honesty of the Punchaet or in the justice of cause."[47]

Nevertheless, the Judicial Department was willing to accept the fact that panchayats could be useful in these few areas, but not because they performed any specific judicial function. Instead, panchayats could be successful only when they functioned as an ad hoc mode of "simple arbitration," that is, as a voluntary and extra-judicial forum of dispute resolution.[48] The Judicial Department therefore concluded that "As an Institution for regulating questions of Caste, and of religious discipline of alleged breaches of the conventional rules or Bye Laws (if they may be so termed) of trades, professions, Societies, or Classes of people united for civil or religious purposes, We consider the Punchaet to be highly useful. Such Punchaets, aided by the heads of professions &c exercise a species of Jurisdiction for which our tribunals are peculiarly ill qualified, and it is highly important that the jurisdiction should remain as long as possible in those hands in which it is placed by the voluntary acquiescence of the parties most deeply interested."[49]

However, the Judicial Department's conclusions concerning the general role of panchayats in the administration of civil justice were much less sanguine. They correctly noted that the attempts to integrate the panchayat into the judicial system of the Madras Presidency had been largely a failure. There, the panchayat system "appears to have rendered no essential aid in the administration of Justice, the number of controversies settled by the Village and District Punchaets in those Territories bearing a very small proportion to the whole number decided by the Judicial tribunals."[50] Therefore, considering the Madras experience, the obvious defects of panchayats, and the reports from judges and magistrates throughout Bengal and the surrounding

[46] Ibid., ff. 486–7. [47] Ibid., ff. 468–9. [48] Ibid., f. 487. [49] Ibid., ff. 491–2. [50] Ibid., ff. 496–7.

territories, the Judicial Department concluded that, other than in cases in which the litigants themselves sought out or agreed to arbitration, the panchayat would not be adopted as a means to reduce the judicial backlog of cases. "We are," the Department announced, "decidedly averse to the introduction as a formal and legalized part of our Judicial system for the administration of Civil justice at this Presidency, of the Village and District Punchaet Institutions established in the Provinces under Fort St. George." Moreover, they added that "the Sudder Dewanny Adawlut, the Board of Commissioners in the Western Provinces, and almost without exception all the public Officers who have been consulted on the subject, have expressed a similar opinion."[51]

In retrospect, there is perhaps a great deal of justice in the Judicial Department's response. The panchayat system as adopted in both the Madras and Bombay Presidencies was an obvious failure. By the time of the Judicial Department's 1827 dispatch, the panchayats in the Madras Presidency were recording results in only forty-eight of the more than 65,000 cases brought before all of the Presidency courts. During the entire period 1820–1826, the panchayats had only settled an average of eighty-eight cases per year out of an annual average of 63,969 cases brought before the courts.[52] In the Bombay Presidency, as we have seen, the panchayat system was marginally more successful, although not nearly as successful as its proponents had hoped. There, between 1819 and 1827, panchayats decided 3,524 cases out of a total of just over 212,000, or about 4.5 per cent.[53] Therefore, the Bengal Judicial Department's evaluation of the panchayat system and the likelihood of its success there was more than justified by the experiences of the Madras and Bombay Presidencies.

However, Bengal's opposition to implementing the panchayat system was apparent long before the experiments in Bombay and Madras had yielded any results. As noted earlier, resistance within the Bengal establishment, with the notable exception of Lord Moira, who departed India in 1823, was apparent nearly upon receipt of the first instructions to adopt the panchayat scheme. Indeed, the Bengal Presidency's opposition to panchayats was based less upon observation and analysis and much more upon entrenched ideologies and bureaucracies.

[51] Ibid., ff. 497–8. [52] Meschievitz, "Civil Litigation and Judicial Policy," Table 5.3, p. 185.
[53] MSA, EIC, Annual and Periodical Reports, Civil Judicature, 1819–1827.

The judges of the *sadr diwani adalat* had opposed the panchayat reforms almost immediately upon receiving orders from London. In bureaucratic terms, the Court's initial resistance was based upon the perception that the plan would involve monitoring up to 8,000 villages, their civil law procedures, and their awards in each district. More importantly, however, was the question of whether the integration of the panchayat into the judicial structure of the Bengal system of courts would also inevitably involve greater judicial oversight, the enactment of rules, the enforcement of awards, and other aspects of a formal judicial body. If it did so, then that would, in their opinion, defeat the intention of the plan as well as destroy the customary practices of the panchayat.

By the time of the Judicial Department's second letter on panchayats in 1827, their resistance to the Directors' orders had noticeably stiffened. Their reasoning, as we have seen, was based in part on field reports the Department had collected from local judges, magistrates, agents, and police superintendents. However, a thorough analysis of the majority of reports received in Calcutta reveals that local officer-officials were much less hostile to the employment of panchayats than the Judicial Department's dispatch would suggest. In fact, there were several reports from across Bengal and the Ceded and Conquered Provinces that gave outright support to the panchayat plan. However, the Judicial Department ignored, understated, or kept entirely hidden these reports in their dispatches to London and, by doing so, willingly misled the Court of Directors as to the actual sentiment of many of the Bengal judicial officers in the localities.

Henry Middleton, the Agent and Superintendent at Ajmer in Rajasthan, for example, reported that panchayats there afforded justice both "cheaply and promptly." He concluded that "Seven out of ten of the summary causes would if unattended to, on their being first instituted grow into regular Suits, enrich Vakeels, and impoverish clients: by Punchait investigation the parties have a far fairer chance of justice than in our own Courts, and by it also both Plaintiff and Defendant are for the most part satisfied." Equally important to him was the fact that "the same man who might consider a regular decree of the Court as waste paper, would make it a point of honor to respect the verdict of a Punchait."[54]

[54] IOR/F/4/1316/52133, Henry Middleton, Agent and Superintendent at Ajmere to Sir Edward Colebrooke, Resident at Delhi, 5 October 1827, ff. 36–9.

Thomas Maddock, the Political Agent at Bhopal and eastern Malwa, similarly reported great success by delegating the resolution of disputes to panchayats. "Civil Suits," he wrote, "are decided by us on their merits without any fixed rules but general conformity to the usages of the Country[.] [W]e make use of Punchayets as often as possible and in this part of the Country they are capable of affording very efficient aid to Government. Since we have declined the cognizance of suits between parties neither of whom are our own Subjects, this branch of business has considerably diminished."[55]

Indeed, the reports from local agents in the field throughout Malwa often praised the economy and efficacy of panchayat justice. Nathaniel Alves, for example, reported that "Natives can more easily than Europeans get at all the intricacies of a dispute, and by making them dispense justice to themselves, we manifest the most sincere desire for its rigid and impartial administration, while we evince a practical regard for their institutions and customs, and keep greatly out of sight, and thereby render as little odious as possible that direct interference which circumstances will occasionally even in these minor cases impose upon political Officers in Malwa."[56]

In 1826, Sir David Ochterlony transmitted to the Bengal Secretary a copy of the instructions he had previously issued to Henry Hall upon the latter's appointment as Superintendent shortly after the British acquisition of Merwara. In that memo, he had explained that in civil disputes "When the accounts agree or truth is proved by evidence, but the case is not clear or involves any peculiar custom (as is frequently the case) the opinions of some respectable old Men not connected with either party or a Panchyte are had recourse to and a decision past [*sic*] accordingly – Always in support of a Panchyte when fairly submitted to by both parties." Unfortunately, he added, although the panchayat was "alway[s] very equitable, much encouraged, and decidedly supported since," it had lost much of its previous standing in the community.[57]

At Indore, Gerald Wellesley, the Resident, reported that panchayats were frequently used by creditors in cases of debts and, of course, in

[55] IOR/F/4/1024/28121, T. H. Maddock to Mr. Secretary Swinton, "Nature of the Duties Attaching to the Office of Agent in Bhopal, &c.," 1 December 1824, ff. 35–6.

[56] IOR/F/4/1038/28648, N. Alves, Local Agent, to G. Wellesley, 31 May 1825, ff. 92–4. Certainly, the Bengal Judicial Department could not have been pleased by the appearance in 1823 of Sir John Malcolm's *A Memoir of Central India, Including Malwa*, which also extolled the virtues of panchayat justice.

[57] IOR/F/4/994/27737, "Memorandum of Sir D. Ochterlony as to the Principles on Which the Superintendent Should Be Guided in the Management of Merwara," 31 May 1826, ff. 28–9.

matters relating to caste. His Political Agent at Bhopawar, Captain Robert Spears, concluded that the panchayat, "however defective it may be in some points, possesses the advantages of simplicity and economy, and is perhaps upon the whole better adapted to the conditions of the inhabitants" than the Company courts.[58]

The suppression of such information from the Bengal dispatch to the Court of Directors was matched by the manipulation of evidence of the failures and weaknesses of panchayats. As already noted, almost the entirety of the evidence presented by the Judicial Department was collected from reports from the Ceded and Conquered Provinces. The ostensible reason given for this was that it was here rather than in Bengal that the panchayat would most likely be functioning in its customary and traditional manner. However, with the exception of the report from Delhi, the Judicial Department studiously avoided the more positive evidence from places such as Merwara, Ajmer, and Malwa. Instead, they focused on reports from Hutta, Saugor, and Baitool, all of which were in the Saugor and Nerbudda Territories.

These territories in particular had long been bereft of any sort of British judicial administration since they had been acquired in 1818. According to A. A. Roberts, a civil judge at Saugor writing in the 1850s, the expulsion of the Maratha *mamledars* from their posts that occurred upon the British occupation and the devastation that resulted from the battles with the Pindaris had left the territories without any substantial body of local judicial or police officials, and this void was not filled until the 1840s.[59] "For years," Roberts wrote, "no machinery was organized for dispensing justice in civil matters, and that this department was almost wholly neglected."[60] After the British conquest, the entire administration of the territories, according to Roberts, was placed into the hands of only a few British officials, a situation that persisted for over two decades thereafter. "All the establishments," he wrote, "appear from the first to have been on a very limited and parsimonious scale, and were of course unequal to the work."[61] The two senior officers in the territories, Herbert Maddock and Charles

[58] IOR/E/4/735, Bengal Judicial Department, "Answer to Letter Dated 9th March 1830. Administration of Justice in the Provinces Not Subject to the Judicial Regulations, 28 November 1832," ff. 1365–7.

[59] A. A. Roberts, "Saugor Code of Civil Judicature," *Selections from the Records of Government: North Western Provinces*, Vol. IV (Agra: Secundra Orphan Press, 1856), pp. 285–92.

[60] Ibid., p. 286. [61] Ibid., p. 288.

Malony, were responsible for "maintaining Political relations; of collecting and securing the Land Revenue, Custom, and other duties, of superintending the Police, and of administering Criminal and Civil Justice in a new country, nearly the size of England, and with a population as large as that of Scotland," all with the aid of only two or three assistants.[62]

Apparently suffering under these administrative burdens, Maddock decided "to refer almost every Civil complaint to private arbitration," that is, to panchayats. Several years later, in 1826, four local "sudder amins" were appointed to help relieve the strain upon the administration of civil justice and all civil cases were required to be first entered before the local Assistants' courts. However, this seems to have had little effect. Roberts noted that as late as 1830–1, "extensive references of suits were still made to Punchayuts."[63]

Whether or not the abuses to the panchayat system described in the Judicial Department's 1827 dispatch were systemic throughout the Saugor and Nerbudda Territories will probably never be known. However, the Department's decision to emphasize them and, at the same time, to minimize the panchayat's potential as a source of civil justice appears to have been motivated far more by the Bengal judiciary's desire to protect and expand their prerogatives and authority and far less upon their desire to promote either judicial efficiency or access to justice.

About fifteen months prior to the Judicial Department's 1827 dispatch, the Bengal government had written to the Madras Presidency in May 1826 asking for a report on the progress and effects of the introduction of the 1814 Regulations regarding *patels* and panchayats, They received their reply from the Madras *sadr adalat* only in April 1829 and, based upon this report, dispatched another letter to London in June 1830.

The Madras report was almost wholly negative. With regard to village panchayats, the report recorded only 937 cases that had been settled by panchayats in the decade between 1817 and 1827. District panchayats, which had also been established by orders from London, reported only 505 cases having been settled during the same period. Even more distressing for the advocates of the panchayat system was the evident decline in their use by litigants. As the Madras *sadr* court noted,

[62] Ibid., p. 287. [63] Ibid., p. 290.

in the first five years after the promulgation of the Regulations, the village panchayats had disposed of 738 cases. But in the following six years that number had fallen to only 199. The district panchayats were less affected by this trend, but a decline was evident nonetheless. In the first five years of the Regulation, those courts disposed of 290 cases, while during the succeeding six years this number had fallen to 215.[64]

Not surprisingly, the Madras *sadr* court's conclusion was unequivocal: the panchayat experiment in that Presidency had been a failure. "The result of the experiment," they wrote, "seems to warrant the conclusion, that with the great mass of the people, this mode of settling lawsuits is held in little estimation; and it can now hardly be doubted that its prevalence in former times was a matter of necessity, from the want of other tribunals, rather than the effect of a prepossession in favour of an ancient institution." Moreover, they suggested that if British courts of justice were made more available and accessible, it was likely that the panchayat "would fall into disuse altogether."[65]

Therefore, the Bengal Judicial Department showed little hesitation in rejecting the idea entirely. In their 1830 letter to London, they lauded the success of the extension of British justice through the expansion of the number of village *munsifs* while dismissing the panchayat system in merely one sentence. The Governor-in-Council, they wrote, concurred in the assessment of the Madras *sadr* court. If litigants wanted to settle their disputes out of court, then they always had access to English-style arbitration. The fact that they did not do so was irrelevant. The Judicial Department simply concluded that "it does not appear why parties should not resort to it [arbitration] rather than go to law in this more than in any other country."[66]

The failure of the panchayat experiment in India can be ascribed to many causes. As the experience of the Madras and Bombay Presidencies revealed, the attempt to integrate this "ancient institution" into the structure of the British judicial establishment was fraught with difficulties. The panchayat's deliberative process was slow and often tedious, but probably no more so than British justice. It was difficult to get potential *panchayatdars* to volunteer their time and effort

[64] PP, *Appendix to the Report from the Select Committee of the House of Commons on the Affairs of the East-India Company*, Vol. IV (Judicial): Appendix No. 2 (1831–1832), "Extract from the Proceedings of the Court of Sudder Adawlut, under Date the 23rd April 1829," pp. 141–2.

[65] PP, *Appendix to the Report from the Select Committee*, App. No. 2, p. 142.

[66] PP, *Appendix to the Report from the Select Committee*, "Extract from the Minutes of Consultation, under Date 9th February 1830," p. 213.

to serve on these tribunals, especially if it meant doing so repeatedly. Some panchayats were undoubtedly subject to corruption, whether by emoluments paid to *panchayatdars* or by those who sought to use panchayats to delay justice and harass their neighbors. Moreover, panchayat justice was just as likely to arouse ill-feelings, enmities, and distrust between villagers as it was to resolve disputes and promote neighborliness among them. Finally, the panchayat was fundamentally weakened by the fact that it lacked any power other than its moral authority to enforce its decisions and awards and thus often encouraged disgruntled litigants to seek further recourse to the British courts.

Whether the British understanding and perception of the panchayat could ever have successfully served the function of delivering justice to every man's door, as Mountstuart Elphinstone had once written, is doubtful. As the post-Independence attempts to do so have proven, the vision of resurrecting the judicial panchayat has proven to be an attractive albeit elusive vision.[67] However, in the case of the Bengal Presidency of the early nineteenth century, the panchayat experiment was never seriously entertained. Unlike the examples of the Madras and Bombay Presidencies, entrenched bureaucratic interests, especially among the Company's judicial establishment, continually thwarted such efforts. Given the relative autonomy in which that Presidency could operate, without the support of the bureaucracy on the ground, it could hardly have been otherwise.

[67] See, for example, Upendra Baxi and Marc Galanter, "Panchayat Justice: an Indian Experiment in Legal Access," in M. Cappellett and B. Barth, eds., *Access to Justice Volume III: Emerging Issues and Perspectives* (Milan: Sijthoff and Noordhoff-Alphenaandenrijn, 1979), pp. 341–86; Catherine Meschievitz and Marc Galanter, "In Search of Nyaya Panchayats: The Politics of a Moribund Institution," in Richard L. Abel, ed.,*The Politics of Informal Justice, Vol. 2: Comparative Studies* (New York: Academic Press, 1982), pp. 47–77; and, Marc Galanter, "The Aborted Restoration of 'Indigenous' Law in India," *Comparative Studies in Society and History*, Vol. 14, No. 1 (January 1972), pp. 53–70.

PART II

LINEAGES AND LEGACIES

8

THE PANCHAYAT FROM VILLAGE REPUBLIC TO MUNICIPALITY

In 1806, Thomas Munro, later Governor of Madras, first described the Indian village as a "little republic" and India as "a mass of such republics."[1] This description of rural India was later repeated many times and became a standard trope among both Indian nationalists and their British governors. The classical, commonwealth, and European connotations of "republic" should not be lost upon either the modern historian or others interested in the history of the British in India. Well into the twentieth century, the term connoted village autonomy, autarchy, and immunity to change. To late eighteenth- and early nineteenth-century Britons, however, the term "republic" conjured up a very different set of images, analogies, and political and social references. The significance of these symbols, it must be added, was not confined to Britain's elite, who may or may not have learned

[1] Thomas Munro, "Report from the Ceded Districts," 15 May 1806 quoted in IOR/E/4/912, Madras Dispatches, 29 April 1814, p. 567. The actual source of this rather famous quote remains somewhat of a mystery. Later in the nineteenth century, it was almost always erroneously attributed to Charles Metcalfe's Minute of 1830 reproduced in "Minute on the Settlement of the Western Provinces" reprinted in PP, *Report from the Select Committee on the Affairs of the East India Company* (1831–1832), III: Revenue, App. No. 84, p. 331. Clive Dewey rightly notes that it first publicly appears in Wilks' *Historical Sketches* where it is cited as coming from Munro's "Report from Anantpoor" of 15 May 1806. See Clive Dewey, "Images of the Village Community: A Study in Anglo-Indian Ideology," MAS, Vol. 6, No. 3 (1972), p. 297, ff. 4 and Mark Wilks, *Historical Sketches of the South of India in an Attempt to Trace the History of Mysoor*, Vol. I (London, 1810), p. 121; see also Louis Dumont, "The 'Village Community' from Munro to Maine," *Contributions to Indian Sociology*, Vol. 9 (December 1966), pp. 67–89. However, there is no evidence of a report with this title nor does it appear either in T. H. Beaglehole's *Thomas Munro and the Development of Administrative Policy in Madras, 1792–1818* (Cambridge: Cambridge University Press, 1966) or other standard nineteenth-century biographies of Munro.

much in the public schools and universities. Indeed, by the early nineteenth century, a reference to a 'republic' would likely have meant equally as much to working-class radicals or to anyone else who had witnessed the creation of the American Republic, the First French Republic in 1792, or the Sister Republics of the French Directory.

Among historians of Britain, there has been much debate about the significance and meanings attached to the ideas of a republic and republicanism during the late eighteenth and early nineteenth centuries. However, we might begin by comparing its assemblage of meanings to Munro and one of his noted contemporaries, Mark Wilks. Munro (1761–1827) rose from a relatively modest commercial Scots background to become one of the leading officer-officials in the East India Company's army and was principally responsible for the construction of the British system of settlement and governance in India's Madras Presidency. Wilks (c. 1760–1831) came from a similarly modest background on the Isle of Man, made the Company's army a career as well, and eventually published the *Historical Sketches of the South of India*, one of the most notable books of the first generation of so-called Orientalists.[2] Both men received a classical education, Munro at Glasgow University and Wilks probably by private tutor. However, their perceptions of republicanism differed significantly from one another, revealing just two of the ways, although two of the most important, in which the term 'republic' conveyed different meanings to different people. It must not be forgotten that in the case of India these different meanings ultimately issued forth in policies that altered the daily lives of millions.

Munro's republicanism reflected many of the attributes of the commonwealth radicalism of seventeenth- and eighteenth-century Britain, albeit in a much diluted and attenuated form. This is not to suggest that Munro ever conceived of creating a radical republic in India: far from it. It is meant to say, however, that Munro's understanding of these ideals drew upon the well of ideas that had been born

[2] See the relevant entries in the *ODNB*: Martha McLaren, "Munro, Sir Thomas, First Baronet (1761–1827)," *ODNB* (Oxford University Press, 2004), online edn., May 2008, www.oxforddnb.com/view/article/19549, accessed 25 May 2011 and E. I. Carlyle, "Wilks, Mark (c. 1760–1831)," rev. Roger T. Stearn, *ODNB* (Oxford University Press, 2004), online edn., May 2008, www.oxforddnb.com.wam.leeds.ac.uk/view/article/29434, accessed 19 December 2012.

of a specific republican tradition.[3] Moreover, it would be quite fair to say that Munro applied the language of republicanism only when and where he saw fit, neglecting those aspects of the tradition that he did not endorse, and thereby adopting a new synthesis more suitable to commercial and colonial endeavors.[4] One should not expect a thorough treatise on the subject from him. Despite his university education, he was, after all, a military man by choice and training and not a political philosopher.

Yet, in many aspects of his thought and policies in India, there is ample evidence that he had absorbed some of the aspects of the commonwealth republican tradition and often expressed himself in the language, or discourse, if you will, that was part of the republican package of ideas. Like many other republicans, his attitude toward monarchy was notably ambivalent. Nowhere in Munro's writing does he ever evince a rejection of the monarchical form of government *in toto*, but he did heartily reject despotism.[5] He repeatedly contrasted India's arbitrary governments under the Mughals and Marathas to its prior "ancient constitution"; he emphasized the great importance of providing for the civic participation of Indians in the governing of the country; and he stressed the overriding significance of securing property rights in the land. He was not, however, immune to the contemporary notions of India that, as a backward nation, would require an experienced hand and careful management in order to restore republican virtues. Thus, in 1813, Munro wrote, "We are not to consider English maxims as always applicable to India, but to follow those rules which are most applicable to that country, as it now is. India has no political freedom, no voice in framing laws or imposing taxes; and many regulations

[3] For an admirably succinct survey, see Knud Haakonssen, "Republicanism," in Robert E. Goodin and Philip Petit, eds., *A Companion to Contemporary Political Philosophy* (Oxford: Blackwell Publishers: 1993), pp. 568–74.

[4] I have drawn heavily upon Steve Pincus, "Neither Machiavellian Moment nor Possessive Individualism: Commercial Society and the Defenders of the English Commonwealth," *American Historical Review*, Vol. 103, No. 3 (June 1998), pp. 705–36. The literature on this is very extensive. The *locus classicus* is J. G. A. Pocock, *The Machiavellian Moment: Florentine Political Thought and the Atlantic Republican Tradition*, rev. edn. (Princeton: Princeton University Press, 2003) and there have been many scholarly reviews of the literature, but see, in particular, Blair Worden, "English Republicanism," in J. H. Burns, ed., *The Cambridge History of Political Thought, 1450–1700* (Cambridge: Cambridge University Press, 1991), pp. 443–75.

[5] That this was common among republican theorists, see Worden, "English Republicanism," pp. 446–8. Pincus notes the same ambivalence in Milton, "Neither Machiavellian Moment nor Possessive Individualism," p. 710 while Britain's mixed constitution is an outstanding example of this ambivalence in practice, as noted by Haakonssen, "Republicanism," p. 568.

are now proper there, which might be otherwise under a state of greater freedom."[6]

When speaking of India's "village republics," he repeatedly emphasized their historical autonomy from arbitrary rulers, an autonomy that was based upon an ancient constitution that provided for order and justice. Unlike some other officers and officials in the Company's service, Munro did not believe that India's eighteenth- and early nineteenth-century institutions of government bore any relation to the feudal institutions of medieval Europe. Instead, he thought, "the nature of Indian governments, in general, is that of pure despotism, although mildly administered."[7] Under this "mild" despotism, Munro argued, the villages of India had been able to maintain their own structures of governance and systems of justice, which had remained largely unchanged and unaffected by the character and policies of their rulers until, that is, the British came. "The affairs of every Village are managed by two headmen – one is called the Potail and is usually a husbandman," he wrote. "The other is called the Curnam or Putwarre and is generally a Bramin. The Potail is the chief of the Village – he acts in it as Judge, Magistrate, and Collector, the inhabitants when dissatisfied with his decisions being at liberty to apply to the Amildar [district revenue collector]. The Curnam is the register of the Village and assists the Potail in all his transactions. The offices of both are hereditary, and in a Country where the Revolutions of Government are so frequent, they are regarded by the Inhabitants as their only natural and permanent superiors – for whoever rules the Province, they rule the Village."[8]

Upon the British occupation of portions of India, however, these vestiges of the "ancient constitution" were overthrown as British Judges and British courts replaced the villages' "natural and permanent superiors." "Too little attention seems to have been paid to this important point in the formation of the judicial system," he complained, "which is gradually undermining the whole fabric of the village constitutions, so admirably adapted for the preservation

[6] "Answers to Court's Queries, by Colonel T. Munro," 22 November 1813, in *Selection of Papers from the Records at the East-India House, Relating to Revenue, Police, and Civil and Criminal Justice, under the Company's Government in India*, Vol. II (London, 1820), p. 112.

[7] PP, *Minutes of Evidence Taken before the Committee of the Whole House, and the Select Committee on the Affairs of the East India Company* (1812–1813), p. 143.

[8] IOR/H/686, Papers concerning revenue, administrative and judicial matters in India, "Colonel Munro's Observations on Judicial System," n.d., pp. 760–2.

of internal peace and security."[9] The result of British intervention, therefore, was that the traditional social order based upon subordination and respect was giving way to "confusion and contempt for authority."[10]

Prior to the British arrival in India, the ancient constitution of the village republics provided for justice to be dispensed by the panchayat, which, according to Munro, was nothing less than a jury administering the common law of India. In one of Munro's most-often quoted passages dating from 1807, he argued, "the [British] Judicial Code in Civil Cases authorizes trial by referees, arbitrators & Munsiffs but says nothing of trial by Punchayet. It seems strange that the Code has been framed expressly for the benefit of the Natives should omit entirely the only mode of trial which is general & popular among them & regarded as fair & legal, for there can be no doubt that the trial by Punchayet is as much the common law of India in civil matters, as that by Jury is of England."[11] Not only was the panchayat part of India's "ancient constitution," but, like the village headman, it had continued to function largely independently under both strong and weak kings and princes. Under strong kings and princes, panchayat procedures were regular and orderly. However, "when the Government was weak and rapacious," Munro wrote,

> corruption descended from the head, through every gradation, to the lowest officer of the state, and justice was bought and sold; still, however, the evil was greatly diminished, by the universal practice of resorting to arbitration and punchayet, and by public opinion; for every interference of a public officer with their proceedings was extremely unpopular, and where undue influence had been exerted the successful party was always liable to lose what he had unjustly gained, by a new trial, on the first change of the administration of the province. The strong attachment of the natives to trial by punchayet has no doubt, in some degree, arisen from the dread of the venality of their rulers; but it has probably been increased and confirmed, by the conviction resulting from experience, that no Judge, however upright or active, was so competent as such a body to dispense justice correctly and expeditiously.[12]

[9] Colonel Munro, "Memorandum on the Revision of the Judicial System," n.d., *Selection of Papers from the Records at the East-India House*, II, p. 106.

[10] Munro, "Memorandum," *Selection of Papers from the Records at the East-India House*, II, p. 107.

[11] IOR/H/686, Papers concerning revenue, administrative and judicial matters in India, "Report of the Collector of the Ceded Districts 15th Aug. 1807, on the Advantages and Disadvantages of the Zemindarry Permanent Settlements and of the Ryotwar Settlements."

[12] Munro, "Answers to Court's Queries, by Colonel T. Munro," *Selection of Papers from the Records at the East-India House*, II, p. 116.

Along with his opposition to arbitrary rule and his adherence to notions of justice according to an ancient constitution, Munro also emphasized the moral imperative of civic participation in the quest for virtue, an essential commonwealth republican theme. In this tradition, the ownership of private property was the ultimate foundation of active citizenship. In this sense, Munro's *ryotwari* system in Madras, which devolved ownership of property upon the cultivators of the soil, was, in contrast to the *zamindari* system of Bengal, where the cultivators were made tenants of large landlords, as much a political and moral statement as it was a revenue policy.[13] Therefore, the employment of Indians in the civil service was not only a practical necessity but also an essential aspect of both character and civic virtue. In brief, Munro wrote in 1824, "in proportion as we exclude them from the higher offices, and a share in the management of public affairs, we lessen their interest in the concerns of the community, and degrade their character."[14] In a much more acerbic evaluation of British policy in India, he further pursued the connection between civic participation and civic virtue. It is worth quoting at length:

> If we make a summary comparison of the advantages and disadvantages which have accrued to the natives from our Government, the result I fear will hardly be so much in its favour as it ought to be. They are more secure from the calamities both of foreign war and internal commotions, their persons and property are more secure from violence, they cannot be wantonly punished or their property seized by persons in power, and their taxation is on the whole lighter. But on the other hand, they have no share in making laws for themselves, little in administering them, except in very subordinate offices; they can rise to no higher station civil or military; they are every where regarded as an inferior race, and often rather as vassals or servants than as the ancient owners and masters of the country.
>
> It is not enough that we confer on the natives the benefits of just laws and of moderate taxation, unless we endeavour to raise their character; but under a foreign Government there are so many causes which tend to depress it, that it is not easy to prevent it from sinking. It is an old observation that 'he who loses his liberty loses half his virtue.' This is true of nations as well as of individuals. To have no property scarcely degrades more in one case than in the other to have property at the

[13] On Munro's criticisms of the *zamindari* system, see PP, *Fort St. George. Copy of a Minute by the late Sir Thomas Munro, on the State of the Country, and Condition of the People under the Presidency of Fort St. George. Dated 31st December 1824* (1830).

[14] Munro, "Minute on the State of the Country," p. 18.

> disposal of a foreign Government in which we have no share. The enslaved nation loses the privileges of a nation as the slave does those of a freeman; it loses the privilege of taxing itself, of making its own laws, of having any share in their administration or in the general government of the country. British India has none of these privileges; it has not even that of being ruled by a despot of its own; for to a nation which has lost its liberty, it is still a privilege to have its countryman and not a foreigner as a ruler. Nations always take a part with their Government, whether free or despotic, against foreigners; against an invasion of foreigners the national character is always engaged, and in such a cause the people often contend as strenuously in the defence of a despotic as of a free Government. It is not the arbitrary power of a national Sovereign, but subjugation to a foreign one, that destroys national character and extinguishes national spirit. When the people cease to have a national character to maintain they lose the main-spring of whatever is laudable both in public and private life, and the private sinks with the public character.[15]

Despite this eloquent statement as well as his belief that India was possessed of a great civilization, Munro was as convinced as other Europeans that Indians needed to be tutored and trained to take their place in the modern world. He concluded that only by giving Indians a greater share of the administration of government could their moral collapse be averted. "Are we to be satisfied with merely securing our power and protecting the inhabitants, leaving them to sink gradually in character lower than at present," he rhetorically asked, "or are we to endeavour to raise their character, and to render them worthy of filling higher situations in the management of their country, and devising plans for its improvement [.]It ought undoubtedly to be our aim to raise the minds of the natives, and to take care that whenever our connection with India might cease, it did not appear that the only fruit of our dominion there had been to leave the people more abject and less able to govern themselves than when we found them."[16]

Munro's understanding of the "village republic" therefore rested largely upon commonwealth republican notions of freedom from absolutism, a property-owning citizenry, and the attainment of virtue through civic participation. Interestingly enough, during the first decade of the nineteenth century, the Company's Board of Revenue adopted many of Munro's recommendations although they substituted

[15] Ibid., p. 27. [16] Ibid., p. 28.

the term "petty commonwealth" to refer to the Indian village, rather than Munro's "little republics," when issuing directives for the revenue settlement of Madras in 1808.[17] However, this was not the only meaning that the terms "village republic" or "commonwealth" might convey. In the work of Munro's contemporary, Mark Wilks, the republic is shorn of many of its commonwealth and Machiavellian attributes and instead is expressed merely as a self-governing political unit based upon private property. As such, and much more so than in the case of Munro, Wilks' depiction of the Indian village as a republic appears more as a stage in the Lockeian state of nature rather than as a classical or commonwealth republic.

Wilks adopted the descriptor "republic" from Munro's 1806 Report from the Ceded Districts in modern Andhra Pradesh and, like Munro, believed that the village and its institutions had remained largely autonomous and unchanged despite a succession of many different princely rulers. Thus he noted, "conquests, usurpations, or revolutions, considered as such, have absolutely no influence on its [the village's] condition. The conqueror, or usurper, directly or through his agents, addresses himself as sovereign or representative of the sovereign to the head of the township; its officers, its boundaries, and the whole frame of its interior management remain unalterably the same; and it is of importance to remember that every state in India is a congeries of these little republics."[18]

For Wilks, however, the definition of the village as a republic had very little to do either with the rule of law through the headman and panchayat or the consequent importance of civic participation in village or national governance. Instead, the existence of widespread private property and the autonomous nature of governance marked the village as an ancient republic. "Every Indian village," he wrote, "is, and appears always to have been, in fact, a separate community or republic; and exhibits a living picture of that state of things which theorists have imagined in the earlier stages of civilization, when men have assembled in communities for the purpose of reciprocally administering to each other's wants."[19]

Indeed, Wilks was intent upon proving that Indian villages were historically based upon the private property of the cultivator and that

[17] Dumont, "The 'Village Community' from Munro to Maine," p. 71. Extracts from the original dispatch are reproduced in Romesh Chunder Dutt, *The Economic History of India under British Rule*, 2nd edn. (London, 1906), pp. 141–2.

[18] Wilks, *Historical Sketches of the South of India*, I, pp. 120–1. [19] Ibid., pp. 117–18.

only later changes, including those introduced by the British, were tending to weaken and destroy that institution. After analyzing the Code of Manu, for instance, he concluded, "it is manifest that this origin of landed property, so consonant to the dictates of reason, and to the general opinion of mankind, must have been familiarly known and acknowledged as a practical rule of society at the period when the code of Menu was compiled (for it professes to be a compilation), viz. about 880 years before the Christian æra, and 553 before the expedition of Alexander."[20] He warned, however, that the Bengal *zamindari* system threatened private property, but, at the same time, also hoped that "the British government may still restore property and its concomitant blessings to the great mass of its subjects." Referring to southern India, he went on to add:

> In this portion of India its ancient constitution may yet be revived. A company of merchants may confer a more solid benefit than was announced in the splendid proclamation of the Roman consul to the cities of Greece: freedom, in its most rational, safe, and acceptable form, may be proclaimed to the little republics of India, by declaring the fixed and moderate revenue that each shall pay, and leaving the interior distribution to themselves, interfering only on appeal from their own little magistrate, either in matters of revenue, or of landed, or of personal property. Under such a system, varying only from their ancient constitution in substituting for the tax on industry, involved in the exaction of a proportion of the crop, a fixed money payment, which is also of great antiquity in India; the waste would quickly be covered with luxuriant crops, because every extension of culture would be a clear profit to the proprietor; and without running into the wild fancies of a golden age, the mass of the people would be interested in the permanency of a government which had essentially improved their condition, and, with the religion and laws of their fathers, had revived their long forgotten proprietary rights.[21]

In Wilks' imagined village republic, therefore, the panchayat did not figure as a necessary adjunct either to the rule of law or as a bulwark against despotism. Their revivification would indeed be significant, he argued, but only because the British courts were "considered with terror as the instruments of a foreign rule."[22] Moreover, if Company policy was intended to rule in accordance with Indian laws and customs, as Company officials often claimed, then that policy had been violated. "If

[20] Ibid., p. 122. [21] Ibid., pp. 196–7. [22] Ibid., p. 500.

we profess to govern the Hindoos by their own laws," he wrote, "let us not falsify that profession by tearing them up by the roots on the pretence [*sic*] of pruning and amending them. They are no longer Hindoo if they are subject to innovation."[23] And yet, if the revival of the panchayat was considered to be important, it was largely because of its practicality in administering justice and not for its constitutional significance. "If Anglo-Indian legislators would throw off a little of that which they somewhat too largely ascribe to the natives of India, namely, the prejudice of education," he wrote, "they would find the rules of proceeding prescribed by the Hindoo code (with all its numerous imperfections on its head), combined with the local customs, or common law of India, not ill adapted to the state of society to which it is intended to apply; and in the *Panchaiet* or *Indian jury*, which is (or rather was) universally established in the south as the common law of the land, an admirable instrument of practical decision."[24]

One can certainly see in Wilks' description of the panchayat the rhetorical influence of Munro.[25] The identification of the panchayat as both an Indian jury and as part of India's common law was a trope that Munro introduced into the discussion of the Indian village. In Wilks' hands, however, a notable shift had taken place in which the village as commonwealth was replaced with the village as an ancient self-governing entity based upon private property; that is, the village as *polis*. For him, "the immemorial despotism of the East" was the "inevitable consequence" of the fact that both Hindu and Islamic theology were inextricably interwoven with their statecraft, a fact that he believed was also responsible for the result "that in the whole scheme of polity, whether of the victors or the vanquished, the very idea of *civil liberty* had absolutely never entered into their contemplation."[26] Therefore, there was little rhetorical space for the commonwealth form of republicanism. However, there was much more space for comparisons with ancient republics that, he believed, bore some similarity to India, including Sparta, Athens, and Rome. In those ancient states, too, Wilks simply argued, private property had formed the basis of self-governing communities.[27] Without the theological component of Hinduism and Islam, however, their historical trajectory had been much different.

[23] Ibid., p. 499. [24] Ibid., p. 501. Emphasis in original. [25] See Chapter 5.
[26] Wilks, *Historical Sketches of the South of India*, I, p. 22 and, more generally, pp. 21–30. Emphasis in original.
[27] Wilks, *Historical Sketches of the South of India*, I, pp. 137–49.

From a British perspective, the introduction and subsequent failure of the Company's panchayat experiments in the Madras and Bombay Presidencies did much to discredit the idea that the panchayat was either a part of India's common law or an essential instrument of civic virtue. As we have seen, the panchayat, which had played a central role in the Company's judicial policy in India after 1814, was largely abandoned after 1827. H. H. Wilson's addition to James Mill's *History of British India*, published in 1846, merely described the debate that had then taken place within the Company over the use of panchayats for the administration of justice. He was, however, dismissive of that attempt, declaring "the Panchayats, it appeared, had been highly prized, only as long as there was nothing better to be had."[28]

While legislators, collectors, and other judicial officials irregularly evinced an interest in panchayats after 1827, there was very little sustained discussion of the institution. Even Mountstuart Elphinstone, who had adopted the panchayat system in the Bombay Presidency and was certainly among the most well-qualified and experienced persons in this matter in either the Lords or Commons, appears to have given up on the panchayat and came to believe that they were resorted to "only in the absence of regular Courts."[29] During the second and third quarters of the nineteenth century, the integral connection thought to exist between the panchayat and the judicial administration of the Indian village community appears to have survived only in the Madras Presidency, and there in a very desiccated state. But it is during this period as well that we first encounter a radical rhetorical transformation of the village community from republic to municipality; that is, from republicanism to liberalism. Both the independence movement and the republic would subsequently inherit the consequences of this transformation.

The rhetorical and substantive transition began to take place within the terms of a discussion of the effect of changes in the administration of police in both the Madras and Bengal Presidencies.[30] In Madras, for

[28] Horace Hayman Wilson, *The History of British India. From 1805 to 1835*, Vol. II (London, 1846), p. 521.

[29] PP, *First Report from the Select Committee of the House of Lords Appointed to Inquire into the Operation of the Act 3 & 4 Will. 4, c. 85, for the Better Government of Her Majesty's Indian Territories* (1852–1853), p. 284. It is certainly striking that in Elphinstone's *History of India* the panchayat is specifically mentioned only once and then described merely as "bodies of arbitrators, called Panchayets, who sometimes act under the authority of the government, and sometimes settle disputes by the mere consent of the parties." See Mountstuart Elphinstone, *The History of India: The Hindu and Mahometan Periods*, 5th edn. (London, 1866), p. 91.

[30] On similar liberal reforms in the Bengal Presidency, see Chapter 9.

example, beginning in 1859, plans were implemented to remove the administration of police from the government's Revenue Department and to establish a separate police inspectorate. Such a change necessitated a "revision" of the Revenue Department: the introduction of significant cost-cutting measures to take into account the department's reduced resources. The Department decided that one way to do this was to resurrect the village headman's responsibility to collect taxes, thereby reducing the burden on the offices of the district sub-divisions (*taluks*). The plan, therefore, involved nothing less than to "restore these village establishments to their original and proper use of collecting the revenue."[31]

In order to carry this plan into effect, the Revenue Department recognized that the reform of the revenue administration also required a review of how the village headman and his subordinate officials were going to be paid for their new responsibilities. And this necessitated a reappraisal of the hereditary rent-free land (*inam*) previously granted to them for their services. As David Washbrook has shown, *inam* rights in southern India had been the subject of British concern for a very long time and played an important role in the "traditionalization" of south Indian society.[32] However, the British nineteenth-century "revenue offensive," as Washbrook describes it, had previously stopped at the boundaries of the village and the "allocation of the demand between rural families remained very much an intra-village affair, brokered by village officers and notables."[33] But now it threatened to breach those boundaries and this initiated a lengthy discussion among government officials concerning the possible effects that the reforms might have on the village community and its institutions.

The plan met with the vigorous opposition of C. V. Rangacharlu, later Diwan of Mysore, who was then serving as Special Assistant to the Inam Commission. Rangacharlu argued that the revenue proposal would further weaken the position of the village headman, making him much less of a "natural" head of the village and much more of a mere functionary of the state. He urged the Revenue Department "to pause and consider . . . whether these officers shall be restored to their

[31] *Correspondence Relating to the Revision Proposed in the Village Revenue Establishments of the Madras Presidency* (Madras, 1867), Pt. I, p. ii.

[32] David Washbrook, "Economic Depression and the Making of 'Traditional' Society in Colonial India, 1820–1855," *Transactions of the Royal Historical Society*, Sixth Ser., Vol. 3 (1993), pp. 237–63.

[33] Ibid., p. 253.

former and natural position of village heads and representatives, or shall remain, as at present, the last link in the chain of Government servants, the tool in the hands of Government officials for all purposes of corruption and torture, and the scape-goat for all their offences, and, in a word, whether they shall be wholly dependent on Government, and entirely independent of public opinion in the village."[34] Moreover, to fully restore the customary position of the headman, the judicial administration of village needed to be restored as well. Before the Muslim conquests, Rangacharlu contended, the headmen "were the natural heads of the village, elevated by the common consent of the village community and entrusted with all its best interests, deputed to act on their behalf in all matters with Government, and the arbiter and referee in all disputes in the village."[35]

Rangacharlu's imagining of the pre-conquest village headman certainly bears evidence of liberal, or perhaps even republican, notions of governance by consent and the institutionalization of systems of representation. However, it also reveals the impenetrability of the village to outside observers as well as the commonplace nature of abstract reasoning applied from an imagined past. Both Rangacharlu and the Revenue Department were arguing from historical precedent. However, their "pasts" were altogether different. For the Revenue Department, the headman had historically been an agent of government; for Rangacharlu, he had been a representative of the people.

Yet the debate over the headman's historical position also opened to question the role of the panchayat and the administration of justice in the village. Rangacharlu, who insisted upon the importance of raising the "respectability" of the headman, proposed that the headman be relieved of almost all of his revenue duties and that he serve almost exclusively as village judge or magistrate.[36] However, he also saw this reform as a means to revive the customary village panchayat as a civil court to replace the "impracticable Punchayet regulations" of Thomas Munro.[37] T. L. Strange, Puisne Judge of the Madras *sadr adalat*, similarly submitted a lengthy proposal to this effect, including plans for the establishment of revenue-based qualifications for service on the

[34] "Extract of a Letter from C. Runga Charlu, Special Assistant to the Inâm Commissioner, to G. N. Taylor, Esq., Inâm Commissioner, dated 15th November 1859," in *Correspondence Relating to the Revision*, Pt. I, p. 54.

[35] Ibid., p. 53. [36] Ibid., p. 55.

[37] C. Runga Charlu, "Memorandum Explanatory of a Scheme for the Revival of the Village Municipal Institutions," 15 February 1860, in *Correspondence Relating to the Revision*, Pt. I, p. 103.

panchayat and the creation of rotation lists. The panchayat thus created would then serve a double function. On the one hand, it would be responsible for electing the headman of the village. On the other, it would serve as a court of small causes in cases involving Rs. 20 or less.[38]

Despite these judicial proposals, the panchayat was simultaneously being re-imagined in this discussion as a municipal organization rather than as a judicial body. Thus, W. Robinson, the Inspector General of the Madras Police, suggested that a panchayat of three or four members might be created and given the authority to appoint village watchmen and fix their salaries. The panchayat might also be given the authority to levy a tax on the villagers to meet these expenses.[39] Hatley Frere, another Puisne Judge, suggested that a panchayat, composed of members selected from among village householders, might be given the authority to select the village headman.[40]

In both of these latter schemes, the dominant analogies of the early nineteenth century had obviously begun to change. Whereas the panchayat was once almost solely analogized to either an English jury or an arbitration tribunal, by the second half of the century analogies of the panchayat to town councils, parish vestries, or other ratepayers' institutions began to make a notable appearance. Indeed, by the end of the century, the municipal analogy came to dominate the imaginations of British governors and nationalists alike. As we shall see, this may have been one of liberalism's most significant legacies.[41]

The transition of the panchayat from judicial body to municipal corporation was both furthered and consolidated by a new generation of scholars, government officials, and others who began to seek out the origins and nature of the "village community." Most important in this regard was the publication of Henry Sumner Maine's *Village-Communities in the East and West* in 1871. Karuna Mantena has wisely pointed out Maine's key role in shaping post-1857 approaches to the British perception of Indian society and its practices of governance. As Mantena has succinctly put it, "Maine's social-theoretical model conceptualized native society as an apolitical, functional whole, held

[38] T. L. Strange to C. Pelly, 24 January 1860 in *Correspondence Relating to the Revision*, Pt. I, pp. 59–60.

[39] W. Robinson, Esq., Inspector General of the Madras Police, to J. D. Sim, Esq., Secretary to Government, Revenue Department, 20 April 1864, in *Correspondence Relating to the Revision*, Pt. I, p. 292.

[40] Hatley Frere to C. Pelly, 18 January 1860, in *Correspondence Relating to the Revision*, Pt. I, pp. 58–9.

[41] See Chapter 10.

together by stable bonds of custom and structures of kinship."[42] This was not wholly new, of course. We have seen many if not most of the elements of this approach already inscribed in the concept of the village republic and, to a somewhat lesser extent, in the Scottish Orientalist stadial theory of historical development. While Maine's contribution therefore may not have been "seminal," it was of overriding importance in the post-Rebellion era and it did revive interest in the purpose and function of the panchayat.

As was the case of those earlier generations who had argued that the panchayat was an Indian form of the Western jury, Maine also reasoned by analogy rather than direct observation. In *Village-Communities*, Maine uses the terms "council of village elders" and "village council" to refer to the panchayat, although he does make clear that this council "always bears a name which recalls its ancient constitution of Five persons," that is, a panchayat.[43] For him, the analogical source of his understanding of the panchayat was the Teutonic Aryan village assembly of free adult males. "India," he wrote, "has nothing answering to the assembly of adult males which is so remarkable a feature of the ancient Teutonic groups, except the Council of Village Elders."[44] Maine believed that the principal difference between the two, however, was that whereas the Teutonic village assembly was a democratic body, the panchayat was a representative institution. "The evidence of cultivators as to custom does not point, I am told, to any uniform mode of representation," he wrote, "but there appears to be a general admission that the members of the council should be elderly men."[45] In this sense, the Indian village was truly a "little republic," as Munro had first described it.

The difference between the democratic Teutonic village assembly and the republican panchayat arose largely from the historical contingencies of warfare and military organization. In the Teutonic village, Maine suggested, every adult male was armed for local defense and thus gained the right to participate in village governance. In India, on the other hand, despotic governments overwhelmed the village and young men were drawn off to serve in their armies. "Village communities," he wrote, "have always submitted without resistance to oppression by monarchs surrounded by mercenary armies. The causes, therefore,

[42] Karuna Mantena, *Alibis of Empire: Henry Maine and the Ends of Liberal Imperialism* (Princeton: Princeton University Press, 2010), p. 3.
[43] Henry Sumner Maine, *Village-Communities in the East and West* (London, 1871), p. 123.
[44] Ibid., p. 122. [45] Ibid., p. 124; see also p. 155.

which in primitive societies give importance to young men in the village assembly were wanting. [In India] the soldiers of the community had gone abroad for mercenary service, and nothing was required of the council but experience and civil wisdom."[46] Nevertheless, as the advocates of the Indian village republic had argued many years before, Maine also believed that the Indian village community was an autonomous and autarchic entity largely immune from "external interference."[47] The Indian village, he noted, contained within it "a nearly complete establishment of occupations and trades for enabling them to continue their collective life without assistance from any person or body to them."[48]

In Maine's account, however, the panchayat appears as an administrative body at only a certain stage of historical development. Like Wilks before him, Maine believed in an "original" state, in which property in the Indian village was equally divided; "an unmodified original equality," he called it.[49] In this state, he reasoned, the panchayat was the most appropriate form of village administration. However, as time passed and various conquerors intervened in village administration for the purpose of raising revenue, property amassed into the hands of one or several families and these larger landowners, now acting as village headmen, exercised the authority that earlier had been the responsibility of the panchayat. Maine sketchily described the process as follows:

> Villages frequently occur in which the affairs of the community are managed, its customs interpreted, and the disputes of its members decided by a single Headman, whose office is sometimes admittedly hereditary but is sometimes described as elective; the choice being generally, however, in the last case confined in practice to the members of one particular family, with a strong preference for the eldest male of the kindred, if he be not specially disqualified. But I have good authority for saying that, in those parts of India in which the village community is most perfect and in which there are the clearest signs of an original proprietary equality between all the families composing the group, the authority exercised elsewhere by the Headman is lodged with the Village Council.[50]

Therefore, the conquerors of the villages created rights to property in order to more easily collect revenue, which in turn allowed for the

[46] Ibid., pp. 124–5. [47] Ibid., pp. 113–14. [48] Ibid., p. 125. [49] Ibid., p. 155.
[50] Ibid., pp. 122–3. The process is described more fully at pp. 149–57.

growth of inequality and the rise of the village headman.[51] The original function of the panchayat was not fundamentally judicial, however. Instead, it acted as a communal body of village administration overseeing local customs and usages. In this sense, Maine argued, the panchayat was not a Benthamite or Austinian law-giver by command but a "moral" institution. "It would be altogether inappropriate to speak of a political superior commanding a particular course of action to the villagers," he wrote. "The council of village elders does not command anything, it merely declares what has always been. Nor does it generally declare that which it believes some higher power to have commanded; those most entitled to speak on the subject deny that the natives of India necessarily require divine or political authority as the basis of their usages; their antiquity is by itself assumed to be a sufficient reason for obeying them."[52] Therefore, the panchayat's principal function was not to administer justice but to declare the "unwritten usages" of the village.[53] As such, the panchayat was sometimes necessarily required to intervene in civil disputes.[54] However, his emphasis was undoubtedly upon the panchayat as a "moral" administrator of custom rather than as a "legal" institution to resolve civil disputes.[55]

The distinction Maine drew between the later, albeit more "primitive," village-headman system and the village-council system of community organization was an increasingly common one among British observers of India during the last third of the nineteenth century. Perhaps of greatest significance was the fact that this view was a reflection of changing attitudes toward the governing of India. Mantena has argued that Maine and his "intellectual successor", Alfred C. Lyall, had laid the foundations for indirect rule by privileging the retention of native institutions in order to maintain social continuity.[56] In this respect, it might be said that Maine was also laying the foundation for the re-appearance of the ancient panchayat within the structures of British colonial governance. However, when the panchayat did re-appear, it was re-imagined not as a court of small causes but in the new guise as an analog of the British municipal and village administrative council.[57]

[51] Ibid., pp. 170–1. [52] Ibid., p. 68. [53] Ibid., pp. 69. [54] Ibid., p. 71.

[55] Admittedly, Maine himself sometimes obscures this distinction. At one point, for example, he describes the panchayat's function as "half-judicial, half-legislative" even though he had previously argued that the panchayat did not legislate. See *Village-Communities*, p. 72.

[56] Mantena, *Alibis of Empire*, pp. 165–71. [57] See Chapter 9.

One notable exception to this general transformation of the imagining of the panchayat appeared in B. H. Baden-Powell's *The Origin and Growth of Village Communities in India* (1899), which was written largely in response to Maine's work. His reference to the panchayat was quite brief and, in his determined attempt to undermine Maine's work, he argued that the panchayat was merely an ad hoc body assembled only occasionally to resolve minor disputes within or between villages. In this work, Baden-Powell noted that Maine's theories of the Indian village were "in full possession of the field" and "beyond the reach of question."[58] However, Baden-Powell especially sought to discredit Maine's idea that there had been at one time in India's past an ideal type of village in which the land had been originally held in common.[59] Instead, he posited the existence of two different types of villages that had been founded upon different forms of property ownership. In the first type, the "severalty village," all property was owned and worked individually. In the second type, the "joint village," property was held by "a dominant class" that let all or a portion of their land to tenant-farmers.[60] In the latter case, Baden-Powell argued, earlier officials and observers had seriously mistaken "joint-ownership" for "communal property."[61] Joint-ownership might very well lead to joint responsibility for the governance in the form of a village council; however, the property itself had been divided according to the custom of joint inheritance.[62]

As Clive Dewey has pointed out, the intent of Baden-Powell's argument was to eradicate the notion that the Indian village was based upon some form of "indigenous communism," as Marx had called it.[63] However, it also had a significant effect upon Baden-Powell's understanding of the role and function of the panchayat. The logical corollary of the belief that property in the village was ultimately private was that the panchayat, as envisioned by Maine, had little or no role in protecting the customs and usages of the village.[64] "No one ever heard of a separate landholder being controlled or directed in his cultivation

[58] B. H. Baden-Powell, *The Origin and Growth of Village Communities in India* (London, 1899), pp. 2–3.

[59] Dewey, "Images of the Village Community," pp. 320–2.

[60] Baden-Powell, *Origin and Growth of Village Communities*, pp. 15–20. [61] Ibid., p. 115.

[62] Ibid., pp. 112–13.

[63] Dewey, "Images of the Village Community," p. 321; Karl Marx to Frederick Engels, 2 April 1858, in *Collected Works of Karl Marx and Frederick Engels*, Vol. 40: Marx and Engels, 1856–1859 (London: Lawrence & Wishart, 1983), p. 296.

[64] Baden-Powell admitted that villages might present a "union" to distribute taxation or create a "government by a committee of heads of families." However, he insisted that this was not a panchayat. His more general point was that whatever form of local governance that there may

by the *panchayat* or anyone else," Baden-Powell wrote.[65] Therefore, it is not surprising that Baden-Powell sought to portray the panchayat shorn of any civic responsibilities and functioning only as an ad hoc tribunal for the arbitration of petty disputes. Indeed, the lengthiest discussion of the panchayat in *The Origin and Growth of Village Communities* appears only in a footnote in which Baden-Powell attempted to distinguish the difference between the "constitutional" village council of a joint village and the panchayat:

> A *panchâyat* or committee of elders for settling disputes is assembled in every form and condition of village, whether in the north or south, and quite independently of what the village constitution is. It was, and still is, to some extent, the universal Indian mode of settling caste, social and land cases, and especially boundary disputes. But the body (consisting only of members of the proprietary families) which once governed the joint-village is a standing committee for reference in all affairs of common interest. It is not a mere occasional assembly of elders, called together when there is a dispute, but the continuing and ordinary governing body as opposed to a single "headman," or the oligarchy of a few chiefs and officers.[66]

Clive Dewey has also rightly remarked that the "village community" debate was largely a British and German one and, in Britain, closely connected to the broader political and economic issues of the era. And yet, while the debate over the form, structure, and political significance of the village community became increasingly "ideologically sterile," on the European continent, as Dewey asserts, this was not true for South Asia.[67] There, both the reality and the symbolic significance of the village community and its institutions, especially the panchayat, continued to survive among Indian nationalists and, of course, still does so today. Moreover, among Westerners, the importance of the village community and the panchayat continued to be maintained both by British administrators in India and by a few ideologically committed reformers.

The transformation of the panchayat into an agency of municipal administration will be discussed in further detail in the following chapter. However, the continued interest in the panchayat by British

be, it was in no way based upon the communal ownership of property. Baden-Powell, *Origin and Growth of Village Communities*, pp. 25; 59–60; 113.

[65] Baden-Powell, *Origin and Growth of Village Communities*, p. 122. [66] Ibid., fn. 2, pp. 12–13.

[67] Dewey, "Images of the Village Community," p. 295. This is not to dismiss the important German contributions, but solely to highlight their British permutations.

intellectuals, particularly the Fabians and Annie Besant, in the current context deserves more immediate attention. Sidney and Beatrice Webb's attention to the issue had been caught during their trip to India in 1911–1912. When they visited India, the indefatigable couple were in the midst of researching and publishing their massive, multi-volume history of English local government, the first volume of which had appeared in 1906. Thus it is not surprising that they should have taken an interest in the question of Indian village governance.

On Sidney Webb's part at least, his imagination was sparked by the panchayat, an institution that held multiple meanings for him. His remarks, albeit brief, appeared as the Preface to John Matthai's *Village Government in British India* (1915) and revealed many of the features that characterized socialist and collectivist idealization of the village as an authentic communal institution. More particularly, however, they also strikingly illustrated several of the themes that the Webbs had earlier elaborated in their studies of the history of English local government, especially the concept of "extra-legal democracy" that had appeared in the first volume of *English Local Government from the Revolution to the Municipal Corporations Act* (1906).[68]

By the term "extra-legal democracy," the Webbs had attempted to characterize "the democratic and efficient extra-legal constitution spontaneously worked out" in certain parish vestries before the nineteenth century. These constitutions, both written and customary, had no statutory basis, but they not only provided for the delivery of certain services, such as the hiring and payment of constables or the maintenance of poorhouses, schools, and highways, but also denoted such things as voter qualifications, electoral processes, and the structure of local administration. The Webbs valued this type of parish vestry because to them it was nothing less than a "far-reaching experiment in Local Democracy" that was later strangled by the centralization that was enacted by various acts of parliament during the first half of the nineteenth century.[69]

With regard to the panchayat, Sidney Webb argued by analogy the logic that had been common among British observers for over a century. To him, the panchayat was "a shadowy, local organization" that was

[68] Sidney and Beatrice Webb, *English Local Government from the Revolution to the Municipal Corporations Act* (London: Longman, Green & Co., 1906), p. 143.
[69] Webbs, *English Local Government*, p. 148.

> in fact, now and then giving decisions on matters of communal concern, adjudicating civil disputes, and even condemning offenders to reparation and fine. Such a Local Government organization is, of course, "extra-legal," and has no statutory warrant, and, in the eyes of the British tribunals, possesses no authority whatever. But it has gone on silently existing, possibly for longer than the British Empire itself, and is still effectively functioning, merely by common consent and with the very real sanction of the local public opinion.[70]

Therefore, like the parish vestries of seventeenth- and eighteenth-century England, despite strictures imposed "from above," the Indian village was largely governed by its own people through its panchayat.

Webb was also impressed by what he supposed was the civic culture that sprang out of these circumstances, the most important of which was the priority of civic obligations over individual rights. As the Webbs had written with regard to the governance of the English parish:

> The truth is, that the seventeenth-century parish, as an administrative unit, was regarded by no one as an organ of autonomous self-government. It was, if we may coin a new phrase, an organ of local obligation – a many-sided instrument by which the National Government and the Established Church sought to arrange for the due performance of such collective regulations and common services as were deemed necessary to the welfare of the State. And they did this, be it noted, not by the creation of a salaried hierarchy of government officials, working under the control of the King, but by the allocation of unpaid offices and burdensome duties among the ordinary citizens serving more or less in turn.[71]

The Webbs, therefore, regarded the English parish as the social manifestation of a "unit of obligation" rather than as a unit of mere local administration.

Sidney Webb understood the panchayat in much the same way. He decried the "Austinian pedantry of a century ago, which taught them [i.e., lawyers] that obligations are but the obverse of rights, and that nothing is a right which is not enforceable by judicial proceedings." Instead, he extolled the virtues of ancient village communities in both East and West in which individuals maintained obligations to the public. "The Indian Village, like the Early English Manor, emphasizes

[70] Sidney Webb, "Preface," John Matthai, *Village Government in British India* (London: T. Fisher Unwin, 1915), p. ix.

[71] Sidney and Beatrice Webb, *English Local Government*, pp. 40–1.

obligations rather than rights," he wrote, "and far from confining itself to rights on which some particular person could take action for his own benefit, devotes itself largely to the enforcement of obligations to the public."[72] As such, the panchayat epitomized "an organ of local obligation."

Based upon the brevity of this discussion, it would be difficult to say whether Webb had a specific theory of the historical development of the Indian village and the panchayat. His remarks suggest that he certainly adopted a broadly evolutionary approach, in which "the law of the geographical neighbourhood" replaced the "family law" of the tribe.[73] But even Locke might have been satisfied with this rather anodyne formulation. Rather than legal evolution, the Webbs tended to emphasize organizational evolution, such as in *Industrial Democracy* (1897), where the more evolved forms of worker representation, professional administration, and permanent organization of the trade union replaced the "naïve" and "primitive" forms of direct democracy in trade clubs.[74] Similarly, they admired the development of these same characteristics in the "organized democracy" of some English local governments as they began to appear in the form of established parish committees and the creation of salaried parish officials.[75] However, there were limits to the Webbs' admiration of bureaucratic invention at this time. Both in the case of the centralizing tendencies of government in Britain and the Raj in India, they disapproved of reforms "organized merely 'from above.'"[76] Of course, later they both became admirers of the Soviet experiment, as many collectivists and socialists did. However, at this time, they idealistically sought a new form of local governance based upon "the spontaneous groupings of the people themselves" and, in this sense, the panchayat appeared to them to be both the past and the future.[77]

Interestingly, Matthai's book itself was intended to rectify the portrait of the Indian village previously described by both Maine and Baden-Powell by providing an account of its daily internal governance, much of which was administered through various government-appointed officials.[78] Matthai's approach generally mirrored the findings of the 1907 Royal Commission on Decentralization in India and,

[72] Webb, "Preface," pp. xii–xiii. [73] Webb, "Preface," p. xi.

[74] Sidney and Beatrice Webb, *Industrial Democracy*, new edn. (London: Longmans, Green and Co., 1902), Chapter I.

[75] Sidney and Beatrice Webb, *English Local Government*, Chapter III.

[76] Webb, "Preface," p. xii. [77] Ibid. [78] Matthai, *Village Government*, pp. 1–4.

like that Commission, promoted the revival of panchayats as a form of local government administration.[79] For him, they potentially had an important role to play in areas as diverse as education, sanitation, poor relief, and policing.

However, like many other British observers, Matthai's advocacy of the panchayat was not based upon direct observation, but rather on a review of East India Company documents contained in the parliamentary papers and reports from the 1820s and 1830s, as well as the legal and historical foundations of the panchayat in the Hindu law codes. He noted that these types of traditional panchayats had only rarely been found to exist in India during the last quarter of the nineteenth century.[80] Although the British government had adopted the name panchayat and had attempted to apply it to several of its attempts to form local administrative bodies, Matthai rightly described them as "artificial administrative committees" often appointed and supervised by British officials.[81] In one sense, therefore, these Fabian Socialists stood in a long line of British observers who saw in the panchayat an ancient institution of voluntary and communal importance. In another sense, however, they had significantly diminished its role as a judicial institution. Instead, they had begun to re-imagine the panchayat as an Indian analog to the forms of "municipal socialism" that had gained currency in Europe before World War I. The Fabians, however, never relinquished their faith in the tutelary role of British colonial governance, arguing that the revival of the panchayat was not only a socialist objective but also a civilizing agent. Matthai's conclusion was that "when the load of indebtedness has been lifted off his shoulders and his mind awakened to the meaning of the things around him, we may well hope that the Indian villager may develop a new desire to make his personality, however feeble and broken, enter in some positive way into the government of his little world. Even amid the sound of war and the birth-throes of a new world, there is no higher call in India to the men of our generation than to see this process go forward."[82]

Matthai's work was well received not only among the Fabian Socialists, but it also was welcomed by the theosophist Annie Besant. Mark Bevir has provided us with an intricate account of the ways in which Besant's Western spiritualism contributed to her embrace of the

[79] On the Royal Commission, see Chapter 9. [80] Matthai, *Village Government*, p. 181.
[81] Ibid., p. 201. [82] Ibid., p. 38.

nationalist movement.[83] Works such as Besant's well-known *India: Bond or Free?* (1926) rely heavily upon Maine's theorization of the Aryan village community but are also firmly grounded in Matthai's research. As Bevir remarks, Besant's theosophy projected India as "an organic community bound together so as to pursue spiritual enlightenment through a recognition of personal duty" and the Indian village community administered through the panchayat was the embodiment of this pursuit.[84]

Little of what Besant had to say about the panchayat and the Indian village community was particularly new, although both her spiritualism and her emphasis upon the Aryan origins of the village community certainly set her apart from the Fabians. In *India: Bond or Free?* she described the Indian village system as an Aryan importation that had its own elected officials and "is always an organized community, organized for independent self-existence, containing the necessary elements for a full and satisfactory social life, educated and cultured."[85] Still, her dedication to the revival of the panchayat was clearly important. In her Presidential Address before the Indian National Congress in 1917, Besant declared, the "economic and moral deterioration [of India] can only be checked by the re-establishment of a healthy and interesting village life, and this depends upon the re-establishment of the Panchayat as the unit of Government."[86]

Thus, like Sidney Webb and Matthai before her, Besant imagined the revived panchayat principally as a body of municipal administration. The Commonwealth of India Bill, drafted by Besant and presented in 1925, therefore defined the purview of the prospective panchayats to include administration of local taxation, policing, education, recreational space, sanitation, civil registration, roads and bridges, tanks and wells, and many other civic responsibilities.[87] These new panchayats were also to have "civil and criminal jurisdiction in simple cases exercised by a court of summary jurisdiction," so their judicial functions had not been entirely dismissed or forgotten altogether. However, they were surely subsumed beneath the mass of municipal responsibilities proposed to be delegated to them.[88]

[83] Mark Bevir, "In Opposition to the Raj: Annie Besant and the Dialectic of Empire" (1989) UC Berkeley. Retrieved from: http://escholarship.org/uc/item/6mk025cf, 5 April 2013.
[84] Bevir, "In Opposition to the Raj," pp. 14–17.
[85] Annie Besant, *India: Bond or Free?* (Madras, 1926), p. 53.
[86] Annie Besant, *The Case for India* (London: n.d.), p. 48.
[87] Besant, *India: Bond or Free?*, p. 96. [88] See Chapter 10.

Thus, throughout the long nineteenth century, British observers had imagined and re-imagined the panchayat in terms of Western political and social theories. That they most often reasoned by analogy and historical inference should not be surprising given how little they actually knew of the panchayat's role in village life. In the case of the British renderings of the panchayat, its genealogy appears to have followed a unique trajectory. Heavily influenced by commonwealth republican discourse at the beginning of the nineteenth century, there seemed little place for it as a judicial institution during the liberal moment after mid-century. By the end of the century, the panchayat had been revived in theory and grafted onto Western models of local governance. It was as such that the nationalist movement embraced it.

9

THE PANCHAYAT AND THE BUILDING OF CIVIL SOCIETY

In 1947, when Gandhi explained to a group of women workers that "the panchayat should look after the public activities and act as the executive and legislature for the village," he was giving voice to an ideological construct that had been an element of colonial governance for over a century.[1] As C. A. Bayly has recently written, the panchayat "may never have been a unit of 'village democracy' in any meaningful sense ... [b]ut it was an iconic idea which could be constantly reinvented for political debate in the modern era."[2] Throughout the nineteenth and early twentieth centuries, British administrators played an important role in the attempts to reinvent the panchayat and to harness it to their modes of governance and administration. However, they were rarely successful and rarely had a precise idea of either the panchayat's form or its function. For some, the panchayat was an institution analogous to a board of arbitration; for others, it was a jury; for still others, it was an ancient system of local self-government. These iterations of the imagined panchayat were sometimes the result of extensive research into its historical role and its historical functions. More often, however, the British attempts to

[1] Mahatma Gandhi, *CWMG*, Vol. 94, p. 280. The importance of the panchayat in liberal, socialist, and nationalist thought cannot be stressed too much. As one prominent historian of India has noted, the panchayat "was one of the first all-India symbols of cultural autonomy and later entered the nationalist canon." See, C. A. Bayly, "Rammohan Roy and the Advent of Constitutional Liberalism in India, 1800–1830," *Modern Intellectual History*, Vol. 4, No. 1 (April 2007), p. 36. The panchayat as a form of local self-government is inscribed in Article 40 of the Indian Constitution.

[2] C. A. Bayly, *Recovering Liberties: Indian Thought in the Age of Liberalism and Empire* (Cambridge: Cambridge University Press, 2012), p. 347.

institute panchayat governance were reflections of contemporary European political and social ideologies.

Especially important in this regard were the attempts to promote the growth of civil society in India. The notion of a "civil society," of course, has been the subject of much research as well as the subject of much debate. In what follows, however, the focus is less upon the discourse of civil society than upon its adaptation to and implementation in colonial governance. If the generations of British administrators during the nineteenth century were not necessarily cognizant of the multiple meanings or discursive history of "civil society," they were nevertheless steeped in both a governing ideology and a colonial project that was obviously not only economic but social and political as well. In the most general terms, colonial governance was motivated, if only spasmodically, by attempts to create a civil society based upon the security of private property, the rule of law, and some form of limited participatory citizenship. Very few, if any, colonial officials ever thought that either democracy or independence were necessary corollaries of these reforms.

One recurring element in this colonial reform project was the desire to create a set of civil institutions that could aid in the administration of British conquests on the subcontinent. Both before and after the 1857 Rebellion, the panchayat was often seen as a key instrument of this policy and the implementation of a "panchayat system" an elementary step toward the creation of a modern civil society. As we have seen, the context and hence the meanings of "panchayat" varied considerably, however, changing in form, function, and purpose as political ideologies changed and evolved in the West. Thus the panchayat meant different things and was adapted to different purposes by Orientalist governors at the beginning of the nineteenth century and by Liberal governors at the end. Nevertheless, these colonial administrators were connected by an ideological thread that sought to devolve governance through the revival of an imagined panchayat while, at the same time, maintaining sovereignty.

In the most general terms, there are, of course, two competing notions of "civil society." The first, most commonly associated with the names of Habermas, Putnam, Shils, Walzer, and many others, arose largely in the aftermath of the 1989 Revolutions in Eastern Europe. Roughly put, this theory posits a distinction between the institutions of the state and its bureaucracy and the autonomous institutions and "public space" created by individuals and individual groups. There is, however, the much older notion of "civil society" that circulated principally among European elites during the second half of the eighteenth and much of the nineteenth centuries. A wide variety of philosophers, historians, and others contributed to this second stream of thought, among the most notable, perhaps, being Montesquieu, Rousseau, de Tocqueville, and Hegel.[3] However, of much greater significance for our purposes are the contributions of those individuals associated with the late eighteenth-century Scottish Enlightenment and, in particular, those who contributed to what has come to be called 'Scottish Orientalism.'

Like the republican notions discussed previously, this particular tradition grew out of the writings of David Hume, Adam Smith, and Adam Ferguson, but it was passed on and amended to a generation of "Orientalist" scholars principally through both Dugald Stewart, who had studied under Ferguson at the University of Edinburgh, and James Millar at Glasgow University.[4] As we have seen, among the most important figures in the history of colonial India who were educated in this tradition were Thomas Munro, later Governor-General of Madras, educated at Glasgow, and Mountstuart Elphinstone, later Governor-General of Bombay, and James Mill, who were both trained at Edinburgh.[5]

The tradition into which they were educated depended in part upon Smith's "conjectural theory" of history that posited a "ladder of civilization running from 'rudeness' to 'refinement.'"[6] For Smith, famously, the histories of societies progressed through four distinct stages of economic development, from hunting to pastoral to agricultural and, finally, to commercial society. However, Smith's was not the only, or even

[3] For a survey of the concept of "civil society" in British political thought, see José Harris, "From Richard Hooker to Harold Laski: Changing Perceptions of Civil Society in British Political Thought, Late Sixteenth to Early Twentieth Centuries," in José Harris, ed., *Civil Society in British History: Ideas, Identities, Institutions* (Oxford: Oxford University Press, 2003), pp. 13–37.

[4] Jane Rendall, "Scottish Orientalism: From Robertson to James Mill," *The Historical Journal*, Vol. 25, No. 1 (March 1982), pp. 43–69.

[5] C. A. Bayly, "Elphinstone, Mountstuart (1779–1859)," *ODNB* (Oxford University Press, 2004), online edn., January 2008, www.oxforddnb.com/view/article/8752, accessed 25 May 2011; Martha McLaren, "Munro, Sir Thomas, First Baronet (1761–1827)," *ODNB* (Oxford University Press, 2004), online edn., May 2008, www.oxforddnb.com/view/article/19549, accessed 25 May 2011.

[6] Rendall, "Scottish Orientalism," p. 43. On James Mill's departure from the premises of Scottish conjectural history, see Jennifer Pitts, *A Turn to Empire: The Rise of Imperial Liberalism in Britain and France* (Princeton: Princeton University Press, 2005), pp. 127–33. A different story of the impact of political economy in Bengal is told in Ranajit Guha, *A Rule of Property for Bengal: An Essay on the Idea of Permanent Settlement* (1981; Durham, NC: Duke University Press, 1996).

necessarily the dominant, "conjectural history" of this period. Much more important, for our purposes, was the theory proposed by Adam Ferguson in *An Essay on the History of Civil Society*, first published in 1767 and revised and corrected in many subsequent editions.[7]

Ferguson's influential and popular *Essay* presented a similar "ladder of civilization" developing, however, not in four stages but in three: from the "savage" to the "barbarous" to the "polished and commercial" stages of society.[8] Each stage was characterized by a unique combination of social and political institutions culminating in a "polished and commercial" civil society based upon private property, the rule of law, and a mixed government of monarchical, aristocratic, and representative institutions. Within a "polished" society, the arts, literature, and the sciences all flourished. As one commentator has noted, the fact that Ferguson's description of a "polished" society clearly described that of mid-eighteenth-century England certainly was one element in the *Essay*'s popularity.[9]

Ferguson's influence upon a generation of Scottish Orientalists need not have been immediate and direct, however. Instead, his influence appears to have been transferred most prominently through the work of William Robertson, a Scottish cleric and prominent historian. Born in 1721, Robertson had matriculated at the University of Edinburgh with Ferguson during the second half of the 1730s. In 1754, he was one of the first members of the Select Society, an Edinburgh debating society whose members were among the leaders of the Scottish Enlightenment, including Adam Smith, David Hume, and Lord Kames.[10] A close friend of Hume, Robertson's histories of Scotland, America, and Charles V were extraordinarily influential, so much so that Dugald Stewart, Elphinstone's and Mill's tutor at the University of Edinburgh, undertook to write a biography of him.[11]

[7] On the different strands of Scottish Enlightenment theory, see Fania Oz-Salzberger, "Civil Society in the Scottish Enlightenment," in Sudipta Kaviraj and Sunil Khilani, eds., *Civil Society: History and Possibilities* (Cambridge: Cambridge University Press, 2001), pp. 58–83. Of course, a very great deal has been written on Ferguson. A helpful starting point is provided by the Introduction and Bibliography in Adam Ferguson, *An Essay on the History of Civil Society*, Fania Oz-Salzberger, ed. (Cambridge: Cambridge University Press, 1995).

[8] Lisa Hill, "Adam Ferguson and the Paradox of Progress and Decline," *History of Political Thought*, Vol. 18, No. 4 (Winter 1997), pp. 678–9.

[9] Fania Oz-Salzberger, "Ferguson, Adam (1723–1816)," *ODNB* (Oxford University Press, 2004), online edn., October 2009, www.oxforddnb.com/view/article/9315, accessed 12 November 2012.

[10] Jeffrey R. Smitten, "Robertson, William (1721–1793)," *ODNB* (Oxford University Press, 2004), online edn., January 2008, www.oxforddnb.com/view/article/23817, accessed 12 November 2012.

[11] Dugald Stewart, *Account of the Life and Writings of William Robertson, D. D.* (1796).

For the Scottish Orientalists in India, Robertson's most influential work may well have been *An Historical Disquisition Concerning the Knowledge Which the Ancients Had of India*, published in 1791, a work that has received relatively little scholarly attention.[12] As the title indicates, the bulk of this treatise is comprised of a collection and explanation of observations on India drawn principally from ancient Greek and Roman sources. However, perhaps more important for the generation of Munro, Elphinstone, and James Mill was the book's appendix. This contained a unique account of the history and development of India, an account that Dugald Stewart later described as containing "all the most important information concerning" the character, manners, and institutions of India, "which was then accessible to the philosophers of Europe."[13]

The description of India contained in the *Appendix* to Robertson's *Disquisition* appears to be based almost exclusively upon Ferguson's criteria of a "polished and commercial" civil society. Indeed, in many ways it appears that Robertson was consciously ticking the boxes that Ferguson had created. If civil society required the presence of private property, for example, then Robertson went to great lengths to prove that Indian *ryots* possessed a type of leasehold tenure that "may be considered as perpetual, and at a rate fixed by ancient surveys and valuations."[14] If civil society also required a mixed government, then India possessed one, albeit one of a unique sort. In India, according to Robertson, "the sovereigns were far from possessing uncontrouled or despotic power." Unlike England, where despotic powers were limited by the institutions of both the aristocracy and commoners, India had developed different principles. But these principles had the same effect. Castes, he wrote, possessed privileges that were "inviolable" and "the sacred rights of the Brahmins opposed a barrier against the encroachments of regal power."[15] Moreover, if civil society required the rule of

[12] The work is briefly discussed in Karen O'Brien, *Narratives of Enlightenment: Cosmopolitan History from Voltaire to Gibbon* (Cambridge: Cambridge University Press, 1997), pp. 163–6 and placed in its contemporary intellectual milieu by Geoffrey Carnal, "Robertson and Contemporary Images of India," in Stewart J. Brown, ed., *William Robertson and the Expansion of Empire* (Cambridge: Cambridge University Press, 1997), pp. 210–30.

[13] Dugald Stewart, *Account of the Life and Writings of William Robertson, D. D.* in *The Collected Works of Dugald Stewart*, William Hamilton, ed., Vol. X, (Edinburgh, 1858), p. 166.

[14] William Robertson, *An Historical Disquisition Concerning the Knowledge which the Ancients had of India* (London, 1791), p. 267.

[15] Robertson, *An Historical Disquisition*, pp. 264–5. A similar narrative of India's constitutional history was later expressed by the influential Indian liberal Rammohan Roy; see, C. A. Bayly, "Rammohan Roy and the Advent of Constitutional Liberalism in India," pp. 29–30.

law, then the Hindus of India "have in their possession treatises concerning the laws and jurisprudence of their country, of more remote antiquity than are to be found in any other country." The Hindu Code, he wrote, was arranged in a "natural and luminous order"; it was comprehensive, acute, and subtle; and it was "founded upon the great and immutable principles of justice." "Whoever examines the whole work," he concluded, "cannot entertain a doubt of its containing the jurisprudence of an enlightened and commercial people."[16] Finally, if Ferguson had claimed that the achievements of civil society were reflected in the flourishing of the arts and sciences, then Robertson was intent upon providing proof that India's achievements placed that society upon a standing equal to that of the most civilized nations in the West. In the lengthiest portion of the *Appendix*, Robertson cited the architecture, manufacture, poetry, drama, philosophy, ethics, astronomy, and mathematics of India as conclusive evidence of its "early and high civilization."[17]

The importance of this intellectual inheritance was perhaps first made manifest in India after the second and third Anglo-Maratha Wars, the first of which ended in 1805 and the second in 1817–1818. In particular, Thomas Munro and Mountstuart Elphinstone appear to have relied to a very great extent both upon Robertson's vision of India and upon Ferguson's account of the stadial history of civil society. Unlike Smith, whose "conjectural history" was more decidedly linear, Ferguson had taken into account the fact that civil societies could fall as well as rise.[18] In his *Essay on the History of Civil Society*, Ferguson had charted the possibility that civil societies might descend into despotism when morality collapses, civil government becomes corrupted, or the desire for luxury and ostentatious wealth overwhelms the pursuit of virtue.[19]

For Munro, Elphinstone, and other Scottish Orientalists, this is the historical stage upon which they had entered and conquered large swathes of India. For them, the civil society of ancient India had already descended into despotism, although they sometimes disagreed as to the origins of this descent. For some, India's decline could be traced to the Mughal conquests, while to others it lay in the corruption and

16 Robertson, *An Historical Disquisition*, pp. 274–5. 17 Ibid., p. 311.
18 Oz-Salzberger, "Introduction," *Essay on the History of Civil Society*, pp. xx–xxi.
19 Adam Ferguson, *An Essay on the History of Civil Society*, 3rd edn., Part VI: "Of Corruption and Political Slavery" (London and Edinburgh, 1768).

despotism of the later Marathas.[20] In either case, the role of the British conqueror in India was, at least in part, to resurrect Indian civil society; that is, to secure landed property, to foster the growth of a landed class, and to promote the rule of law.

In order to accomplish the task of promoting the rule of law, the Orientalists and their subordinates in the field sought to revive what appeared to them to be one of India's most ancient institutions of civil society: the panchayat. As one local Political Agent reported in 1822:

> The conquests of the Mahomedans had only extended partially over the southern parts of the Peninsula of India, and accordingly in many of the Provinces under the Madras presidency we found several of the Hindoo institutions in existence, and as our information has extended we have gradually become more open to convictions of the advantages to be derived by the employment of the upper Classes of the people in directing, and of the masses of the people in carrying thru duties of Civil Justice, almost without the intervention of European authority; the antient [*sic*] Hindoo system of Punchayut has been distorted and trampled on, not only by the Mahomedans but by successive ignorant and oppressive Princes of their own Nation. Its name and some of the forms have still survived the rude shocks it has experienced and it is still venerated, however in practice it may [have] been misapplied. Like all other institutions under the iron grasp of tyranny it has assumed the form of the hand which wielded it. We I conceive are yet ignorant of the true shape of this machine, but it is quite necessary to comprehend its structure and restore it to its original functions, before we can hope to render it subservient to the purpose for which it is intended.[21]

Munro himself believed that the panchayat was one of the last vestiges of a civil order that had since become corrupt and venal. In his *Minute on the Administration of Justice*, written in 1813, he noted:

> When the government was weak and rapacious, corruption descended from the head, through every gradation, to the lowest officer of the State, and justice was bought and sold. Still, however, the evil was greatly diminished by the universal practice of resorting to arbitration and panchayat, and by public opinion; for every interference with their proceedings was extremely unpopular ... The strong attachment of the

[20] A related contemporary debate on the significance of Mughal rule is described in Bayly, *Recovering Liberties*, pp. 86–9.

[21] MSA, EIC Judicial Department, Civil and Criminal Judicature, Vol. 9A/9A, 1823, J. Briggs, Political Agent in Candeish, to William Chaplin, 3 May 1822.

> natives to trial by panchayat has, no doubt, arisen from the dread of the venality of their rulers.[22]

In a similar manner, Elphinstone, in his *Report on the Territories Conquered from the Paishwa*, planned to "purify and invigorate the Native System, so as to convert it from a mere engine of oppression into an instrument for a more extensive dispensation of justice."[23] Even under earlier despots, he wrote, "the right to demand a Punchayet was a bar to arbitrary decrees."[24]

Largely under the influence of Munro, who was in London between 1807 and 1814 and working closely with both the East India Company and the parliamentary Select Committee on the Affairs of the East India Company, the Company Directors and Board of Control were convinced to adopt the panchayat as the main instrument with which to provide civil justice in India.[25] It is perhaps likely that many at the Company did not share Munro's political ideology, but instead they saw the institution of the panchayat as a pragmatic means by which not only to reduce the expenditures in the judicial departments of India but also to clear the enormous backlog of cases that had accumulated in the British courts. Nevertheless, the orders that went out to India in 1814 to the Madras and Bengal Presidencies, and later the Bombay Presidency, bear the indelible imprint of Scottish Orientalism.

The Company's Board of Directors in London had become convinced, in their words, that "as the punchayets or native juries appear also to have uniformly prevailed under every native government of India, it is necessary that they should make a part of any consideration involving in it a return to the ancient form of judicial administration."[26] The jurisdiction of these reinvigorated civil panchayats was to be quite wide-ranging. As we have noted above, while caste panchayats and merchant and artisanal panchayats would retain their autonomy, civil panchayats were to be re-created, incorporated into the British judicial administrative system, and given jurisdiction over inter-personal matters

[22] Alexander J. Arbuthnot, ed., *Major-General Sir Thomas Munro, Bart., K.C.B., Governor of Madras: Selections from His Minutes and other Official Writings*, Vol. II (London, 1881), p. 16.

[23] Mountstuart Elphinstone, *Report on the Territories Conquered from the Paishwa* (Calcutta, 1821), p. 104.

[24] Ibid., p. 92.

[25] Burton Stein, *Thomas Munro: The Origins of the Colonial State and his Vision of Empire* (Delhi: Oxford University Press, 1989), pp. 149–67.

[26] PP, *East India Affairs: Papers Relating to the Police, and Civil and Criminal Justice under the Respective Governments of Bengal, Fort St. George, and Bombay; from 1810 to the Present Time*, Judicial Letter to Fort St. George, 29 April 1814 (London, 1819), p. 298.

such as small debts, contracts, property disputes (including partition, trespass and maintenance), personal injury, marriage, and adoption.[27]

However, the resurrection, or perhaps more appropriately, the re-invention of the panchayat was also intended to revive and re-invigorate Indian civil society by restoring the authority of the middle landed class as well as restoring Indian law to the Indian people. In the Company's 1814 orders to establish panchayats, John Melville, the Judge and Magistrate at Dacca, was quoted as reporting in 1801 that the attempt to introduce a British system of justice had the unintended effect of adversely affecting "the influence of paternal authority, and of castes," which previously had been "salutary checks" on the morals of Indians. The panchayat, on the other hand, not only served to resolve petty disputes but also promoted the prominence of those people who were "pointed out for the office by their established character, and by the acknowledged sentiment of the whole of their society."[28] In the Court's letter to Bengal in the same year, they quoted from Sir John Malcolm's *Sketch of the Sikhs*, which had been published in 1812. "It is usual to assemble a Punchayet or a Court of Arbitration in every part of India under Native Government," Malcolm had written, "and as they are always chosen from Men of the best reputation in the place where they meet, this Court had a high Character for Justice."[29] The panchayat reforms envisioned by the Company's Board of Directors would do nothing less than promote "some of the natives who are highest in rank and most worthy of trust."[30]

Indeed, as we have seen, the village headmen (*patels*) and panchayats were considered at this time to be the foundation of a civil society. They were, in the Company Directors' words, "regarded by the inhabitants as their natural and permanent superiors" whose influence was "founded as much in personal respect, as in the authority of their office." They were nothing less than "the native gentry of the country" and "the natural and only foundation on which to raise the superstructure of civil government."[31]

[27] See, for example, the list of disputes adjudicated in the Khandesh province of the Bombay Presidency in MSA, EIC, Judicial Department, Annual and Periodical Reports, Vol. 1/102, 1826. On caste panchayats during this era, see Amrita Shodhan, "Caste in the Judicial Courts of Gujarat, 1800–1860," in Edward Simpson and Aparna Kapadia, eds., *The Idea of Gujarat: History, Ethnography and Text* (New Delhi: Orient Blackswan, 2010), pp. 32–49.

[28] PP, *East India Affairs*, p. 299. [29] IOR/E/4/912, Madras Dispatches 29 April 1814, ff. 589–93.

[30] PP, *East India Affairs*, p. 301.

[31] PP, *East India Affairs*, p. 296. Similar ideas, of course, circulated among the British concerning the *zamindars* as well.

If the restoration of the panchayat was intended to promote the restoration of the "native gentry of the country," it was also intended to promote the rule of law. For most British officials, the two, of course, were inextricably connected. In eighteenth- and early nineteenth-century England, the rule of law was most often dispensed through the medium of the local justice of the peace who himself was typically a member of the landed gentry. Thus, the restoration of the social and judicial position of India's "native gentry" would inevitably restore the rule of law that had been undermined by the Maratha and Mughal despots.

Previous chapters have already noted that by 1814, at the latest, the Company had become convinced that the attempt to impose the English courts upon India, which had been a key element of Lord Cornwallis' 1793 Permanent Settlement, had failed to deliver justice to the people. The Company had noted that "the great objects which Lord Cornwallis had in view, in forming the Judicial Code of Bengal, consisted, not only in the desire of providing for an upright distribution of justice, but also in that of securing a promptitude and facility of obtaining it."[32] But by January 1813, the backlog had grown to well over 140,000 cases.[33] The Company became convinced that the solution lay not in the further expansion of the British judicial establishment but in the restoration of the ancient Indian constitution and its modes of dispensing civil justice.

In this regard, Munro's influence and experience were likely to have been critical. Certainly, his notions that village headmen were the "natural" leaders of the village and that the panchayat was analogous to the common-law jury trial were often repeated in Company dispatches.[34] And it was as such to promote a civil society based upon a middle landed class and the rule of law that the Company's Board of Directors declared that "we conceive the fittest and most proper agency we can primarily make use of in the distribution of civil justice, consists of those who form the permanent and natural authorities in the interior of the provinces."[35]

We have also seen that while British observers of the panchayat heralded their "rediscovery" of this ancient and landed institution, they nevertheless were unsure of what it exactly was. Thomas Fortescue, the

[32] PP, *East India Affairs*, p. 33.
[33] PP, *East India Affairs*, pp. 33–4; see also PP, *Copy of the Fifth Report from the Select Committee of the House of Commons on the Affairs of the East India Company, 28th July 1812* (1812), pp. 165–73.
[34] IOR/E/4/912, Madras Dispatches 29 April 1814, ff. 582–5. [35] PP, *East India Affairs*, p. 40.

Commissioner of Delhi, for example, obviously had great difficulty explaining the panchayat to a parliamentary committee in 1830. "I do not know whether I can call it a court," he said. "It is a self-constituted court among the people; it is an assembly rather, elected by the people, who decide whatever they choose to bring before it: it is not a thing they are called to; nor can we direct them to assemble a court."[36] Regardless of how the panchayat was understood by British officials, it was nonetheless understood that, as in England, this institution was sanctioned by the common law of India and thus was essential for the revival of Indian civil society and protection of their subjects' rights. As one anonymous observer wrote, the panchayat was "a precious relic of popular rights."[37] Thomas Maddock, the Political Agent at Bhopal and eastern Malwa, reported in 1829 that panchayats "are particularly useful . . . for deciding all points of dispute which hinge on local customs and the rights and usages of particular classes."[38] Most importantly, perhaps, the Board of Directors had as early as 1812 indicated in a revenue letter to Madras that "distributive justice appears . . . to have been chiefly conducted through the medium of potails and punchaets" and that through them "the protection of the people in their most important rights, were obtained."[39]

Therefore, beginning in 1814, the Company's Directors ordered the Presidencies to incorporate panchayats into the administration of civil justice. However, as described in previous chapters, within a decade, it had become clear that the Scottish Orientalist plan to revive Indian civil society through the panchayat had failed to meet even the most modest expectations. In the Bengal Presidency, the resistance of the high court judges there had prevented its implementation entirely and the panchayat survived only as an autonomous form of private mediation and arbitration. In the Madras and Bombay Presidencies, by 1827, panchayats were recording results in only a very small percentage of cases. As in the case of the failure of Cornwallis' Permanent Settlement, the obvious failure of the panchayat experiment was attributed to a variety of causes. Many of the British prejudices

[36] PP, *Report from the Select Committee of the House of Lords Appointed to Inquire into the Present State of the Affairs of the East India Company, and the Trade between Great Britain, the East Indies and China* (1830), pp. 35–6.

[37] "System of Punchayet, or Indian Trial by Jury," p. 457.

[38] IOR/E/4/735, 28 November 1832, Bengal Judicial Department, Answer to Letter Dated 9th March 1830. "Administration of Justice in the Provinces not subject to the Judicial Regulations," ff. 1337–40.

[39] PP, *East India Affairs*, p. 289.

concerning Indians and the courts were revived once again: the pervasiveness of perjury, alleged litigiousness, corruption, and even the climate were submitted as explanations for the failure of panchayats. However, the failure of civic virtue, and thus the project of building civil society, was also a recurring theme. As early as 1824, the Register at Pune, R. K. Arbuthnot, observed:

> I consider that the principal cause of the failure in the System, has originated in the false conclusion, that respectable men would easily be obtained to sit on Punchaets. At first it was probable that the people might think it necessary to obey an order of Government, whether to sit on Punchait or any other [*sic*], while the impression of the tyranny of their former superiors was still strong in their memory, but it was not to be expected they would long continue subservient to orders, to the disobedience of which, no penalty was attached, and which they themselves could not but feel irksome; Experience has proved that this is the case, and it is found that persons will not give up their own employment to attend to the business of others, and to subject themselves to the continual importunities of the parties, and most probably to the odium of both, but most certainly of one, without having some more greater interest in the duty than they derive from a mere reputation either with Government or their fellow Citizens. Respectable people may be induced to try the cause of a particular friend as a personal favor, if he has no other mode of redress, but I do not think that even a pecuniary remuneration, would induce them, to be continually called upon to arbitrate the causes of indifferent persons.[40]

In a similar vein, H. D. Robertson, in his half-yearly report on civil justice in portions of the Bombay Presidency, bemoaned the fact that panchayats were failing because the people "are seldom excited to activity but by personal and constantly recurring causes – they have not the slightest fellow feeling towards each other, as Citizens – they have no sentiment of public duty or of reciprocal obligation as members of one Community."[41]

After 1827, the panchayats had lost their position as "the main engine of civil justice," as Elphinstone frequently referred to them. For the next thirty years they existed only on the margins of British judicial administration, functioning as adjuncts to the British courts. In

[40] MSA, EIC, Judicial Department, Annual and Periodical Reports, Vol. 3/83, 1825, R. K. Arbuthnot to Captain H. D. Robertson, 14 August 1824.

[41] MSA, EIC, Judicial Department, Annual and Periodical Reports, Vol. 3/83, 1825, H. D. Robertson to William Chaplin, 19 November 1824.

this new, more restricted role, panchayats could function within the British legal system both as panels of advisors to British judges and as voluntary boards of arbitration.[42] The first iteration, as panels of advisors, may have been their most common function, but, in accordance with the English law of arbitration, litigants in all of the Presidencies always retained the option of submitting their disputes to an arbitral panchayat if both the plaintiff and defendant agreed to do so. By the late 1820s, the Board of Directors had become convinced that panchayats were voluntary boards of arbitration and, as such, should be protected and even encouraged. However, in their estimation, the previous failure of the panchayat as a system of judicature had been caused principally by the fact that it had been incorporated into the formal judiciary and thus had become compulsory.[43]

Nevertheless, the employment of panchayats as voluntary boards of arbitration was quite infrequent and this did not vary considerably between the Presidencies. In Bengal, for example, where Company resistance to panchayats had always been strongest, they virtually disappeared from the judicial records. As early as 1827, only fifty-seven cases were reported in the village and district panchayats there.[44] By the 1840s, there were none being reported.[45] In the Madras Presidency, the comparable figure between 1847 and 1850 was 130 cases, while in the Bombay Presidency it was 253.[46]

One must be careful to note, however, that these figures are derived from reports from only the so-called Regulation Provinces, that is, those areas in which the Presidency's Regulations were directly applied. Those dicta, however, did not apply in full to the other Ceded and Conquered territories that had yet to be fully incorporated into the Company's judicial system.[47] There is, as we have noted, some

[42] PP, *Reports from Commissioners: Judicial Establishments, &c., India* (1856), Appendix B: No. 3, "Outline of the Constitution and Procedure of the East India Company's Courts of Civil Judicature in the Presidency of Bombay," p. 200. Emphasis in original.

[43] See Chapter 1.

[44] PP, *Appendix to the Report from the Select Committee of the House of Commons on the Affairs of the East-India Company*, Vol. IV: Judicial (1833), Appendix No. 2, pp. 170–171.

[45] Colonel Sykes, "Administration of Civil Justice in British India, for a Period of Four Years, Chiefly from 1845 to 1848, Both Inclusive," *Journal of the Statistical Society of London*, Vol. 16, No. 2 (June 1853), pp. 103–8.

[46] Colonel Sykes, "Administration of Civil Justice," pp. 116; 123.

[47] In addition, of course, they do not take into account panchayats that may have been active in the Princely States or the autonomous panchayats of castes, merchants, or artisans. For some evidence regarding caste panchayats during this era, see Amrita Shodhan, "Caste in the Judicial Courts of Gujarat, 1800–1860," in Edward Simpson and Aparna Kapadia, eds., *The Idea of Gujarat: History, Ethnography and Text* (New Delhi: Orient Blackswan, 2010), pp. 32–49.

anecdotal evidence that panchayats were being employed more actively in these areas than in the Regulation Provinces. For example, in the early 1830s, according to one later observer, "extensive references of suits were still made to Punchayuts" in the Saugor and Nerbudda Territories of northern India.[48] Nevertheless, it would not be unfair to conclude that by the 1840s the panchayat had virtually ceased to be a functioning element of the British judicial administration of India.[49]

The panchayat as an institution of British administration nonetheless re-emerged later in the nineteenth century. In its new guise, however, it was no longer an appendage of the British judiciary, but was re-imagined as the cornerstone of municipal and village self-government. The translation of the panchayat from judicial to municipal institution in the British imagination in one sense marks the movement of the panchayat from an object for resurrection among Scottish Orientalists to the subject of reform among British Liberals. However, there were notable continuities. Late nineteenth-century British Liberalism bore many of the legacies of the Scottish Enlightenment tradition, especially that of the molding of civic virtues and fostering civil society.

In this context, there is some measure of irony to the fact that, in England, it is John Stuart Mill, whose father, James Mill, had wholeheartedly rejected the Scottish Orientalist tradition, who has been credited with merging local government reform into the mainstream of British Liberalism.[50] For the younger Mill, local governments, or "sub-Parliaments," as he called them, were "one of the fundamental institutions of a free government."[51] Local decentralized municipal governments, he wrote, could function, of course, as modes of local administration. More important, however, was the fact that they also functioned as "the chief instrument" of "the public education of the citizen."[52] In the words of one of Mill's followers,

[48] A. A. Roberts, "Saugor Code of Civil Judicature," *Selections from the Records of Government: North Western Provinces*, Vol. IV (Agra: Secundra Orphan Press, 1856), p. 290.

[49] Hugh Tinker, *The Foundations of Local Self-Government in India, Pakistan, and Burma* (New York: Frederick A. Praeger, 1968), pp. 32–3.

[50] Jan Palmowski, "Liberalism and Local Government in Late Nineteenth-Century Germany and England," *The Historical Journal*, Vol. 45, No. 2 (2002), p. 389. José Harris notes, however, that while Mill was obviously familiar with the "civil society" debates of the eighteenth century, he did not use the term very often. See Harris, "From Richard Hooker to Harold Laski," pp. 26–8.

[51] John Stuart Mill, *Considerations on Representative Government*, 2nd edn. (London, 1861), p. 274.

[52] Mill, *Considerations on Representative Government*, p. 275.

local self-government was nothing less than a "national school of civil liberty."[53] G. K. Gokhale, the liberal nationalist leader, was certainly one among many who adopted this perspective, paraphrasing Mill before the Bombay Legislative Council in 1901 to the effect that "the object of Municipal institutions is not merely to get local work efficiently done, but also to develop civic-spirit and raise the level of general intelligence among the people."[54]

Despite Mill's obvious antipathy to Indian self-government, the adoption of the term "panchayat" by British administrators to designate a variety of municipal bodies was coeval with this stream of British Liberalism.[55] We have seen earlier that in Madras during the late 1850s the re-imagining of the role of the panchayat had become inextricably connected to taxation reform.[56] A similar process occurred in Bengal as well. There, the 1856 Chaukidari Act authorized local magistrates to appoint a panchayat of between three and five persons to apportion taxes for the provision of *chaukidars*, or police.[57] Later amendments to this Act, such as the Bengal and Madras Village Chaukidari Acts of the 1870s, retained this terminology. However, the form and function of the "chaukidari panchayats" obviously bore little relationship either to earlier preconceptions of the panchayat or to previous British usages.[58] Instead, the panchayat had now become identified as a village or municipal committee appointed by British governors to help manage local government. Indeed, such a distinction between the "customary" village panchayat and the new municipal panchayat was implied in the annual report to parliament of Clements Markham prepared in 1873: "Municipal institutions, in India," he wrote, "were, in their present form, the creation of our Government, and are quite distinct from the old village communities."[59] He further explained that the municipal panchayat was intended to function as an elemental step on the path to self-government and representative institutions. "Where there is no election," Markham concluded, "there is local government through

[53] G. C. Brodrick quoted in Palmowski, "Liberalism and Local Government," p. 389.

[54] G. K. Gokhale, "Mofussil Municipalities Bill," in *Speeches of the Honourable* Mr. G. K. *Gokhale*, C. *I*. *E*. (Madras, n.d.), p. 461.

[55] On J. S. Mill's view of India, see Lynn Zastoupil, *John Stuart Mill and India* (Stanford: Stanford University Press, 1994) and Pitts, *A Turn to Empire*, pp. 133–50.

[56] See Chapter 8.

[57] PP, *East India (Progress and Condition). Statement Exhibiting the Moral and Material Progress and Condition of India, during the Year 1871–72* (1873), pp. 5–6.

[58] Tinker, *Foundations of Local Self-Government*, pp. 39–40; see also PP, *Minutes of Evidence Taken before the Royal Commission upon Decentralization in Bengal*, Vol. IV (1908), p. 9.

[59] PP, *East India (Progress and Condition)*, 1873, p. 5.

puncháyats, or boards composed of the inhabitants, so that throughout India the habit of self-government engendered by municipal institutions may be expected in course of time to have a marked effect on the inhabitants of towns, and through them on the mass of the people."[60]

Within a half decade, this imagining of the panchayat as a municipal institution was also incorporated into the 1860 Income and Property Tax Act.[61] Whereas under the Chaukidari Act panchayats were limited to apportioning taxes, the Income Tax Act extended that responsibility to include tax assessments as well. However, these panchayats were still appointed bodies and, if the Collector disagreed with the assessment, he reserved the authority to impose his own assessment without their consent.[62] Not surprisingly, neither incarnation of the panchayat was especially popular. As one historian of municipal government in India has noted, these panchayats were "regarded not as the representatives of the village folk, but as servants of the 'sarkar', the government."[63] Moreover, British officials eventually came to doubt their efficacy and complained that their payments were irregular and their books in disarray.[64]

The reforms pertaining to local self-government associated with Lord Ripon's Viceroyalty (1880–1884) were equally insignificant in this regard, but the continuities expressed in their ideological content should not be overlooked. The District Municipalities Acts for Madras, Bombay, and Bengal enacted between 1884 and 1888 provided not only for the creation of elected municipal councils in towns and cities but also for the creation of unions of villages administered by district "panchayats." These "union panchayats," or "village unions," were to be responsible for sanitation, roads, schools, and hospitals. Yet, as in the case of the "chaukidari panchayats," they failed to take hold in the countryside. By 1914, in Bengal, of the estimated 70,000 villages, only 60 union panchayats had been created. In Madras, the experiment was no more successful. There, among the 50,000 villages, only 382 panchayats had been created.[65] As one historian has noted, the failure to

60 Ibid., p. 7.
61 See PP, *East India (Property Tax). Copy of Act No. XXXII. of 1860, of the Government of India, Intituled "An Act for Imposing Duties on Profits Arising from Property, Professions, Trades, and Offices"* (1861).
62 PP, *East India (Property Tax)*, § CVI, p. 26.
63 Tinker, *Foundations of Local Self-Government*, p. 40.
64 PP, *East India (Progress and Condition). Statement Exhibiting the Moral and Material Progress and Condition of India during the Year 1884–85* (1886), p. 11.
65 Tinker, *Foundations of Local Self-Government*, pp. 55–6 notes 390 union panchayats in Madras. Testimony before the 1908 Royal Commission on Decentralization, however, noted 382. See

create these new-style panchayats was as much a failure of imagination as it was a failure of administration. In Hugh Tinker's estimation:

> This widespread failure betokens a fundamentally wrong approach. Village wants and obligations were visualised in artificial terms as money, as an extension of modern local government, instead of the traditional terms of personal effort in corporate society. The attempt was made to create village leadership by administrative fiat in the provincial secretariat, rather than by consultation with the village elders in the village street.[66]

At least one witness before the 1907–08 Royal Commission upon Decentralization agreed with this evaluation. Mahusudan Das, a local political leader, landowner, and merchant in Orissa, testified that there was still a "communal life, out of which could be developed a panchayat system." However, he went on to explain that "by panchayat I do not mean one person who is called a panchayat, but I mean what the word literally means – five people forming a body with certain powers."[67] Mohamed Aziz-Ud-Din, the Collector in the Anantapur District of the Madras Presidency, testified to the same effect. "These union panchayats are not held in any favour by the people, because they involve taxation," he noted. But "if by these panchayats is meant the old panchayats that we read of in history, it is a different matter; I think that some such system could be introduced, but not on the old arbitrary lines."[68]

The Village Chaukidari Acts and the District Municipalities Acts were nothing less than "a democratic façade to an autocratic structure."[69] Nevertheless, the drive to decentralize British administration and to promote local self-government bore witness to the way in which the impetus to create a civil society in India had been absorbed into the Liberal political project from the civic ideals of the Scottish Orientalists. This is made no clearer than in Lord Ripon's famous Resolution on Local Self-Government of 1882. In that Resolution, Ripon laid claim to John Stuart Mill's legacy of the educative function of local self-government, a claim that itself had been derived from Scottish Orientalism.

PP, *Minutes of Evidence Taken before the Royal Commission upon Decentralization in Madras*, Vol. II (1908), p. 230.

66 Tinker, *Foundations of Local Self-Government*, p. 56.

67 PP, *Minutes of Evidence taken before the Royal Commission upon Decentralization in Bengal*, Vol. IV (1908), p. 50.

68 Ibid., p. 218. 69 Tinker, *Foundations of Local Self-Government*, p. 70.

In the oft-quoted sections five and six of the Resolution, Ripon explained that the fundamental purpose of the reforms was not only to reduce the British establishment in India but equally important was the need "to foster sedulously the small beginnings of the independent political life" of India. He noted that "as education advances, there is rapidly growing up all over the country an intelligent class of public spirited men whom it is not only bad policy, but sheer waste of power, to fail to utilise." Therefore, it was necessary "to develop, or create if need be, a capacity for self-help in respect of all matters."

Needless to say, the intent of the Ripon reforms amounted to nothing less than a "system of tutelage."[70] However, such an approach was inherent in the liberal project both in India and in Britain. John Stuart Mill's *Considerations on Representative Government* asserted the same commitment vis-à-vis the British working class.[71] In Britain, he wrote, local self-government could be made to serve as a "school of political capacity and general intelligence." But, for Mill, local self-government did not mean democratic self-government. Instead, local self-government would serve as a school for civil society precisely because it would bring the lower orders into contact with the higher. The privileged classes could then serve to teach, train, and supervise the lower class. With regard to the educative function of local self-government, Mill doggedly pursued the analogy:

> A school supposes teachers as well as scholars: the utility of the instruction greatly depends on it bringing inferior minds into contact with superior, a contact which in the ordinary course of life is altogether exceptional, and the want of which contributes more than anything else to keep the generality of mankind on one level of contented ignorance. The school, moreover, is worthless, and a school of evil instead of good, if through the want of due surveillance, and of the presence within itself of a higher order of characters, the action of the body is allowed, as it so often is, to degenerate into an equally unscrupulous and stupid pursuit of the self-interest of its members.[72]

[70] Ibid., p. 60. See also Anil Seal, *The Emergence of Indian Nationalism: Competition and Collaboration in the Later Nineteenth Century* (Cambridge: Cambridge University Press, 1968), pp. 155–70.

[71] Generally, see Dale E. Miller, "John Stuart Mill's Civic Liberalism," *History of Political Thought*, Vol. XXI, No. 1 (Spring 2000), pp. 88–113; see also, Alan Kahan, *Aristocratic Liberalism: The Social and Political Thought of Jacob Burckhardt, John Stuart Mill, and Alexis de Tocqueville* (New Brunswick: Transactions Publishers, 2001).

[72] Mill, *Considerations on Representative Government*, pp. 281–2.

Nevertheless, the failure of the Ripon reforms did not extinguish attempts to revive the panchayat, although its re-creation continued to be an effort of historical imagination. Indeed, as had been the case for at least a century, the identification of the precise function, form, and authority of the village panchayat continued to bedevil its adherents and thus had become a screen onto which to project political, social, and ideological aspirations. The 1907–08 Royal Commission upon Decentralization bears ample evidence of both the continuing ideological importance of the panchayat and its fundamental mystery.

The Royal Commission was intent upon exploring the possibility of reviving the panchayat as an instrument of local self-governance. Members of the Commission repeatedly questioned witnesses on this point throughout its sessions and across the three Presidencies of Bengal, Madras, and Bombay. However, the Commission was confounded by the fact that both British and Indian witnesses imagined the panchayat in a myriad of ways. There were notable conflicts in the testimony over the nature of the panchayat's function, its jurisdiction, its composition, its supervision, and its possible role in the oppression of lower castes. All of these conflicts bear witness to the fact that the resurrection of the panchayat was as much an act of faith and imagination as it was a pragmatic solution to the problem of decentralization and local self-governance.

There was, for example, no clear answer to the question of what the panchayat could or should actually do. The acting Chief Secretary to the Madras Government H. Bradley, for example, was opposed to the delegation of administrative authority to village panchayats, but he thought that they should be allowed to dispose of petty civil and criminal cases.[73] A. M. T. Jackson, an Under-Secretary of the Bombay Government, on the other hand, believed that panchayats could be revived to administer village concerns such as water-tanks and schools but that they should not be given any formal judicial responsibilities, although they might be allowed to act as informal boards of arbitration.[74] Indian witnesses tended to express a more expansive interpretation of the possible role and functions of the panchayat. Both the radical Bal Gahandhar Tilak and the liberal Gopal Krishna Gokhale testified that, in Gokhale's words, "village panchayats must be

[73] PP, *Minutes of Evidence taken before the Royal Commission upon Decentralization in Madras*, Vol. II (1908), p. 47.

[74] Ibid., p. 46.

created" and given extensive judicial and administrative powers.[75] Tilak argued that "the village must be made a unit of self-government, and village communities or councils invested with definite powers to deal with all or most of the village questions concerning education, justice, forest, *abkari*, famine relief, police, medical relief, and sanitation."[76]

However, their position was not necessarily universal among Indian witnesses, the majority of whom were government employees. Mathradas Ramchand, a pleader from Hyderabad, believed that panchayats would be fundamentally undermined by communal conflicts.[77] Muhammad Habibullah, a former Chairman of the Vellore municipal board, thought that panchayats could be established, but only in villages "where persons of sufficient intelligence and public spirit may be forthcoming." Even in these villages, he suggested, their authority should be restricted to administering sanitation, water supply, schools, and public nuisances.[78] At the same time, P. Rajaratna Mudeliar, who served in many high offices, including Secretary to the Board of Revenue and Inspector-General of Registration in Madras, thought that village panchayats might be given authority to hear petty civil cases and to manage the water supply and sanitation but should not be granted authority over education and schooling.[79] In Orissa, the Collector and Magistrate, Khulna A. Ahmad, testified that "the village panchayat should have the power to impose chaukidari tax, drainage and sanitary taxes, and water and school taxes." However, judicial administration of petty cases was to be left to a separate court composed of government-appointed servants.[80]

These various imaginings of the authority of the panchayat were matched by a similarly creative construction of its possible composition. In the tradition of European Liberalism, neither British nor Indian witnesses expressed support for village democracy. Many witnesses expressed enthusiasm for the electoral principle in general, but with a franchise based upon gender and property qualifications.[81] Gokhale, for instance, argued that membership in the panchayat should be restricted

[75] Ibid., p. 59. [76] Ibid., p. 84. [77] Ibid., p. 180.

[78] PP, *Minutes of Evidence taken before the Royal Commission upon Decentralization in Madras*, Vol. II (1908), p. 272.

[79] Ibid., p. 110.

[80] PP, *Minutes of Evidence taken before the Royal Commission upon Decentralization in Bengal*, Vol. IV (1908), p. 131.

[81] Certainly, there was no support for female panchayat suffrage, which Gandhi would later advocate.

to the village headman, the *munsif*, the police headman, and "two or three other persons chosen by such of the villagers as pay a minimum land revenue of, say, rupees ten."[82] Veerasami Iyengar, a landowner in Tanjore, supported the creation of village panchayats, but he thought that the "selection of members ought to be made among those who belong to the middle class and who would be prepared to go out, and learn matters and give good and useful counsels."[83] Khandubhai Desai, a government civil engineer from Surat, testified that "if constituted, these Boards should have two-thirds elected members and one-third nominated members and the Chairman to be elected, the *patel* and village accountant being among the nominated members. Every payer of land tax, or other direct tax, and every man who can read and write, should be entitled to a vote and eligible to be a member, but a person convicted of any serious crime should be disqualified."[84]

As Khandubhai Desai's testimony indicates, many witnesses were suspicious of even a restricted franchise and advocated the government's nomination of at least a portion of the *panchayatdars*. Thus, Sundara Aiyar Avargal, a Madras *vakil*, recommended that the members of panchayats should be appointed by the Collector or Divisional Officer. Only later might the electoral principle be introduced.[85] In a similar manner, R. C. Artal, the Deputy Collector for Belgaum, agreed that "at the beginning it would be necessary for the Collector to nominate members and after some experience to allow the people the right of electing members by common consent."[86] M. Adinarayana Aiyar, who held various positions in the Madras Revenue Department, suggested that the villagers should "nominate" three members of the panchayat and the government appoint two.[87] Gokhale, as we have seen, preferred three appointed members and "two or three" elected ones.[88]

[82] PP, *Minutes of Evidence taken before the Royal Commission upon Decentralization in Bombay*, Vol. VIII (1908), pp. 59, 63.

[83] PP, *Minutes of Evidence taken before the Royal Commission upon Decentralization in Madras*, Vol. II (1908), p. 267.

[84] PP, *Minutes of Evidence taken before the Royal Commission upon Decentralization in Bombay*, Vol. VIII (1908), p 75.

[85] PP, *Minutes of Evidence taken before the Royal Commission upon Decentralization in Madras*, Vol. II (1908), p. 320.

[86] PP, *Minutes of Evidence taken before the Royal Commission upon Decentralization in Bombay*, Vol. VIII (1908), p. 28.

[87] PP, *Minutes of Evidence taken before the Royal Commission upon Decentralization in Madras*, Vol. II (1908), p. 91.

[88] PP, *Minutes of Evidence taken before the Royal Commission upon Decentralization in Bombay*, Vol. VIII (1908), p. 63. C. A. Bayly has recently described Ghokale's position on panchayats as part of the "tutelary instincts" of Indian liberals. See Bayly, *Recovering Liberties*, p. 274.

Despite these significant differences over both form and function, there was a striking continuity in the way in which the panchayat was imagined as a school for civil society.[89] Kesava Pillai, a member of the *taluk*, or sub-district, board in Gooty (in contemporary Andhra Pradesh), was unequivocal as to the panchayat's educative function. Panchayats, he said,

> will infuse new life into the villagers and make them alive to their duty and responsibility for the detection and suppression of crime, for sanitation, for the preservation of trees and *topes* near the villages ... for protecting people from starvation in famine times, and in short for hearty co-operation with the Government in their aims and administration. Panchayats may not come up to expectations for some time, but panchayats, if sympathetically encouraged, will just like in any other country evolve, through struggles and experiences, into self-respecting, useful and loyal institutions.[90]

He concluded that with the revival of panchayats, "the people will then begin to be a people."[91]

The Sessions Judge at Ahmedabad, Dayaram Gidumal, placed equal emphasis upon the educative importance of panchayats for the growth of civil society, testifying that the formation of panchayats had to depend "upon the public spirit shown" in each village.[92] Even more specifically, Rev. A. Andrew, a missionary from the United Free Church of Scotland, was convinced that "what you want in India is the development of local self-government, and this goes to the very root of the matter. The development of the education of the people so far as self-government is concerned ought to begin at the village panchayat."[93] B. G. Tilak was certainly the most eloquent advocate of the panchayat as the school for civil society. Arguing that the village panchayat must be made the basis of self-government, he warned the Commissioners not to be afraid either of the possible inefficiencies or the ultimate result of handing power over to village panchayats. "It should be the aim of the British Administration," he said, "to educate the people in the management of their own affairs, even at the cost of some efficiency and without entertaining any misgivings regarding the ultimate growth and result of such a

89 On the rise of "civic virtue" among Indian liberals, see Bayly, *Recovering Liberties*, pp. 142–4.
90 PP, *Minutes of Evidence taken before the Royal Commission upon Decentralization in Madras*, Vol. II (1908), p. 166.
91 Ibid., p. 167. 92 Ibid., pp. 37; 38. 93 Ibid., p. 215.

policy."[94] He concluded his statement before the Commissioners with another thinly veiled warning couched in the same civic language: "The fluctuating wave of decentralization may infuse more or less life in the individual members of the bureaucracy, but it cannot remove the growing estrangement between the rulers and the ruled, unless and until the people are allowed more and more effective voice in the management of their own affairs in an ever expansive spirit of wise liberalism and wide sympathy, aiming at raising India to the level of the governing country."[95]

As several historians of British political thought have argued, there are complex connections that link republican notions of civil society and nineteenth-century liberalism.[96] Unlike the post-1989 vision of an autonomous civil society, however, the nineteenth-century Scottish Orientalists and Victorian Liberals drew upon a set of ideals derived both directly and indirectly from the civic republican tradition that emphasized the necessity of civic participation for the creation of a civil society. This line of thought can be traced at least from Adam Ferguson, through the reforms of Munro and Elphinstone, and then to the attempts to implement local self-government and decentralization during the late nineteenth and early twentieth centuries. Throughout this period, the panchayat was often seen as an essential institution through which to manage the transformation of India into a civil society. However, the result was never intended to be a democratic or independent nation-state. Indeed, Victorian Liberalism feared democratic despotism as much as it reviled Oriental despotism.[97] By reviving the panchayat in the form of judicial bodies or municipal boards, the invigoration of Indian civil

[94] PP, *Minutes of Evidence taken before the Royal Commission upon Decentralization in Bombay*, Vol. VIII (1908), p. 84.

[95] Ibid., p. 84.

[96] E. F. Biagini, "Neo-Roman Liberalism: 'Republican' Values and British Liberalism, ca. 1860–1875," *History of European Ideas*, Vol. 29 (2003), pp. 55–72; Mark Bevir, "Republicanism, Socialism, and Democracy in Britain: The Origins of the Radical Left," (2000) UC Berkeley. Retrieved from: http://escholarship.org/uc/item/51h4m12z. More generally, liberalism's roots in seventeenth-century civic republicanism are discussed in Steven Pincus, "Neither Machiavellian Moment nor Possessive Individualism: Commercial Society and the Defenders of the English Commonwealth," *American Historical Review*, Vol. 103, No. 3 (June 1998), pp. 705–36.

[97] On the liberal fear of democracy, see John Roach, "Liberalism and the Victorian Intelligentsia," *Cambridge Historical Journal*, Vol. 13, No. 1 (1957), pp. 58–81; Karuna Mantena, *Alibis of Empire: Henry Maine and the Ends of Liberal Imperialism* (Princeton: Princeton University Press, 2010), pp. 41–4; and, Pitts, *A Turn to Empire*, pp. 251–4.

society was intended to transfer the administration of India to its 'natural' leaders while, at the same time, retaining India within the Empire.[98] The panchayat, in the meantime, had taken on its own meanings for the generation of the nationalist independence movement.[99]

[98] For the debate among British progressives before World War I, see Nicholas Owen, "British Progressives and Civil Society in India, 1905–1914," in José Harris, ed., *Civil Society in British History: Ideas, Identities, Institutions* (Oxford: Oxford University Press, 2003), pp. 149–176.

[99] The "apotheosis" of the panchayat in twentieth-century thought is a theme taken up by C. A. Bayly, *Recovering Liberties*, pp. 279–90.

10

THE PANCHAYAT LEGACY AND THE INDEPENDENCE MOVEMENT

Throughout the second half of the nineteenth century, the panchayat continued to be re-imagined and redeployed by British administrators in a variety of ways. During the Bengal famine of 1896–7, for example, R. H. Renny, the Deputy Commissioner of Palamau, formed village panchayats whose appointed members were responsible for assessing the needs of villagers and distributing "gratuitous relief."[1] In the states of British Rajputana, Lt. Col. J. Sutherland, the Governor-General's Agent, established a series of panchayats before which litigants could "seek redress for any robbery or loss of property." These panchayats were comprised of local pleaders and adopted the impressive title of the International Courts of *Vakils*. "Besides the Punchayet at Ajmere entitled 'The International Court of Vukeels of Rajpootana,'" Sutherland wrote in 1848, "similar Punchayets have been formed at each of the Political Agencies composed of the Vukeels of States nearest the residence of the Political Agents."[2] Interestingly enough, these judicial panchayats continued to function throughout the second half of the nineteenth century.

Yet, as we have seen, the most common reinvention of the panchayat took the form of the introduction of village and town councils. As early as 1856, panchayats could be appointed by local magistrates throughout the Bengal Presidency to assess and allocate taxes to

[1] PP, *Appendix to the Report of the Indian Famine Commission, 1898, Being Minutes of Evidence, etc, Vol. I. – Bengal* (1899), p. 49.

[2] *Bombay Times and Journal of Commerce*, 15 April 1848.

support the provision of police, a practice that was later extended beyond the regulated Bengal Presidency under the terms of the 1870 Village Chaukidari Act.[3] By 1873, there were sixty-eight municipalities in Bengal and 315 in the North-western Provinces, the Punjab, and Oudh in which the distribution of tax assessments was allocated by British-appointed panchayats.[4] Yet, as early as 1875, the extent and efficacy of the panchayats' operation was already being questioned.[5] The annual report on the state of India for 1884–5 noted that "at present the Punchayets are responsible for the collection of the rates and for the payment of the Chaukidars, but the payments are often irregular, and the accounts are not strictly kept."[6] As late as 1905, British administrators were still expressing the hope that the necessary reforms "will lead to the selection of a better class of men to serve on panchayats, to a decided improvement in the village police organization, and to a more equitable incidence of the chaukidari tax."[7]

At the same time, in the Madras Presidency, British-appointed union, or local fund, panchayats were empowered to levy house taxes to maintain local roads, lighting, and improve sanitation. By the early 1890s, there were reportedly 270 of these union panchayats in the Presidency, a number that would rise to nearly 400 by the first decade of the twentieth century.[8] Moreover, the village panchayats, first instituted by Thomas Munro in 1816, continued to be available throughout the nineteenth century to resolve disputes of any amount upon the request of the litigants although they were, by all accounts, moribund.[9]

Surprisingly, it was in the Bombay Presidency where British administrators felt the least inclined to adopt the term "panchayat" for their own governing purposes. And yet, it was also here that the panchayat

[3] Act No. XX (1856) to make better provision for the appointment and maintenance of Police Chowkeydars in Cities, Towns, Stations, Suburbs, and Bazaars in the Presidency of Fort William in Bengal; see also, PP, *East India (Progress and Condition). Statement Exhibiting the Moral and Material Progress and Condition of India, during the Year 1872–73* (1874), pp. 23–4.

[4] *Statement Exhibiting the Moral and Material Progress 1872–73*, p. 5; PP, *East India (Progress and Condition). Statement Exhibiting the Moral and Material Progress and Condition of India during the Year 1882–83*, Vol. 19, No. 1 (1884–1885), p. 53.

[5] Anand A. Yang, *The Limited Raj: Agrarian Relations in Colonial India, Saran District, 1793–1920* (Delhi: Oxford University Press, 1989), pp. 106–111.

[6] PP, *East India (Progress and Condition). Statement Exhibiting the Moral and Material Progress and Condition of India during the Year 1884–85* (1886), p. 11.

[7] *Report on the Administration of Bengal, 1904–1905* (Calcutta, 1906), p. 20.

[8] S. Srinavasa Raghavaiyangar, *Memorandum on the Progress of the Madras Presidency during the Last Forty Years of British Administration* (Madras, 1893), p. 322; PP, *Report of the Royal Commission upon Decentralization in India*, Vol. I (1908), p. 238.

[9] *Report on the Administration of the Madras Presidency during the Year 1875–6* (Madras, 1877), Part II, p. 124.

ideal appears to have retained its greatest hold upon members of the first generation of political activists and nationalists. In part, this is understandable. Parsi panchayats, for example, continued to thrive in Bombay, Surat, and elsewhere in the region. To the south, in the neighboring princely state of Coorg, panchayats actively settled disputes involving small claims of between Rs. 50 and Rs. 200.[10] In the princely state of Mysore, during the 1880s, the British government even urged the *diwan* to adopt village judicial panchayats in order to facilitate access to justice, a suggestion that ultimately was rejected.[11] On the other hand, it is notable that many of the leading figures of the early nationalist movement in western India, including Mahadeo Govind Ranade, G. V. Joshi, Bal Gangadhar Tilak, and Gopal Krishna Gokhale, were all Chitpavan Brahmins from Pune, a caste that had no panchayat system to regulate domestic matters.[12]

Nevertheless, in the Bombay Presidency, the panchayat ideal appears to have emerged as an increasingly significant element of nationalist ideology as a result of the so-called Deccan riots that shook Ahmednagar, Pune, and neighboring areas in the mid-1870s. The drought and subsequent famine of 1875–6 exacerbated an already precarious position among peasant landholders. The so-called riots were a relatively non-violent affair during which indebted peasants sought out local moneylenders and burned or otherwise destroyed their bonds of indebtedness. E. W. Ravenscroft, the Secretary to the Government of Bombay, reported in 1877:

> The absence of serious crime is a very remarkable feature in the outbreak. In many cases where the money-lenders themselves, at the ryots' demands, tore up their bonds, no further harm was done, and ferocity was shown in only one case where an attempt was made to burn a money-lender alive. Even in that instance, too, certain of the rioters themselves saved the banker's life.[13]

[10] Lewis Rice, *Mysore and Coorg: A gazetteer compiled for the Government of India*, III: Coorg (Bangalore, 1878), pp. 353–7.

[11] *Report on the Administration of Mysore, 1881–82 to 1885–86* (Bangalore, 1887), pp. 10; 17; 36.

[12] Gordon Johnson, *Provincial Politics and Indian Nationalism: Bombay and the Indian National Congress, 1880 to 1915* (Cambridge: Cambridge University Press, 1973), p. 57.

[13] Letter from the Secretary to the Government of Bombay, Revenue Department, to the Secretary to the Government of India, Department of Revenue, Agriculture and Commerce, No. 2202, dated 6th April 1877, *Papers and Proceedings Connected with the Passing of the Deccan Agriculturists' Relief Act, XVII, of 1879, Selections from the Records of the Bombay Government*, No. CLVII, n.s. (Bombay, 1882), p. 2; Of the several studies of the Deccan Riots, see Neil Charlesworth, "The Myth of the Deccan Riots of 1875," *Modern Asian Studies*, Vol. 6, No. 4 (1972), pp. 401–21; *Peasants and Imperial Rule: Agriculture and Agrarian Society in the*

Nevertheless, the peasants' actions brought into sharp relief the scale of peasant indebtedness, the shortcomings of the British system of revenue settlement, and the failure of the civil courts to deal efficiently and fairly with peasants who had been sued by moneylenders. "Sufficient chance," Ravenscroft noted, "is not at present given to a defendant to say his say" because the courts were too far away from the peasants' homes, the legal process was too lengthy, and the Judges had neither the time nor expertise to examine fully each case.[14]

Among the several proposals suggested to remedy these disadvantages, certainly the most influential among the Indian elites of the region was that of Sir William Wedderburn to resurrect the panchayat and restore its judicial functions. Wedderburn, who would later become chairman of the British Committee of the Indian National Congress, had a substantial career in the Indian Civil Service (ICS), including service as a judge in both Sind and Pune.[15] Ideologically, he was also part of the politically diverse circle of disciples of Henry Maine that included such disparate elements as the imperialist Sir Bartle Frere, who had served both in the ICS at Pune and then as governor of Bombay, and the free-trader Sir James Caird, a member of the Indian Famine Commission.

These men shared not only a significant measure of experience in western India but also the perspective derived from Maine's "historicist revision" that entailed "protecting the customary practices of the village-community."[16] Wedderburn himself also was obviously influenced by the success of the Pune Arbitration, or *Lawád*, Court. Established in 1876 and vigorously promoted by G. V. Joshi, a prominent local *vakil* and leading member of the Pune Sarvajanik Sabha, the Arbitration Court was a voluntary association of "most classes of the people" who agreed to serve as arbitrators in any dispute voluntarily brought before them.

Bombay Presidency, 1850–1935 (Cambridge: Cambridge University Press, 1985), especially, Ch. 4; Ravinder Kumar, *Western India in the Nineteenth Century: A Study in the Social History of Maharashtra* (London: Routledge & Kegan Paul, 1968), Ch. V; Parimala V. Rao, "New Insights into the Debates on Rural Indebtedness in 19th Century Deccan," *Economic & Political Weekly*, 24 January 2009.

14 Letter from the Secretary to the Government of Bombay, *Papers and Proceedings*, p. 14.

15 Edward C. Moulton, "Wedderburn, Sir William, Fourth Baronet (1838–1918)", *ODNB* (Oxford University Press, 2004), online edn., January 2012, www.oxforddnb.com/view/article/41165, accessed 1 February 2014; On Wedderburn's tenure as chairman of the British Committee, see Nicholas Owen, *The British Left and India: Metropolitan Anti-Imperialism, 1885–1947* (Oxford: Oxford University Press, 2007), pp. 36–59.

16 Karuna Mantena, *Alibis of Empire: Henry Maine and the Ends of Liberal Imperialism* (Princeton: Princeton University Press, 2010), pp. 145–6, *et seq.*

Within two years, branch Arbitration Courts had been established in more than ten towns throughout the Bombay Presidency and, by 1878, the courts claimed to have settled nearly 3,000 cases, most of which dealt with "agricultural matters."[17] Wedderburn's desire to resurrect the panchayat was also based in part upon his belief that the Raj had over-centralized the administration of India, thereby subverting the ancient customs of its village communities. His plan to revive the ancient panchayat system, he believed, would "have the support of all those who wish to see our measures founded on the sure basis of popular usages and popular approval."[18]

Wedderburn was steeped in the eclectic liberalism that had rather easily merged together the intellectual inheritances of Munro, Elphinstone, and Maine. He openly acknowledged that his imagining of the panchayat owed much to the legacy of Munro and Elphinstone, but, unlike them, he viewed the panchayat less as an element of an ancient Indian constitution displaced by Maratha and Mughal despots and much more as a primeval institution in need of protection and nurturing. "In order therefore that these Village Councils may be preserved and developed," he wrote, "it is necessary that Government should extend to them a hearty and watchful support."[19] In this, he shared the approach of many post-Mutiny commentators who had adopted Maine's historicist perspective and "were animated by a concern to halt the impending collapse of native societies."[20]

Exactly when Wedderburn became convinced of the efficacy of restoring the panchayat is unclear, but he obviously worked closely with Joshi in promoting its resuscitation. In March 1878, Wedderburn addressed the East India Association in London and there appears to have first publicly advocated his proposal. Wedderburn's paper was interesting, first of all, for the way in which he framed his argument, positing his "economic" theory of judicial reform against the government's "paternal" intervention between peasants and moneylenders. For Wedderburn, post-riot attempts by British revenue officers to make the peasant independent of the moneylender constituted a violation of political economy. Instead, he likened the relationship between the peasant and the moneylender to that of the capitalist and laborer in

[17] *Gazetteer of the Bombay Presidency: Poona*, Vol. XVIII: Pt. III (Bombay, 1885), pp. 29–30; W. Wedderburn, "The Pancháyat: Conciliation as a Remedy for Agrarian Disorders in India," *Journal of the East India Association*, Vol. XI (London, 1878), pp. 129–30.

[18] Wedderburn, "The Pancháyat," pp. 126–7. [19] Ibid., p. 127.

[20] Mantena, *Alibis of Empire*, p. 151.

Europe. There the "text-books of political economy" showed that while there may be struggles over the distribution of profits, the interests of both capital and labor to produce any profit were essentially identical. In this sense, the peasant cultivator and the moneylender were like "Siamese twins, who could quarrel and inflict blows on each other, but whose comfort lay in harmony, and to whom separation meant death."[21] Wedderburn's solution, therefore, was to revive the panchayat specifically "as a means not only of putting an end to the internecine warfare now going on between the classes, but also as the most efficient agent for procuring harmonious and profitable co-operation for the future." As such, Wedderburn's imagined panchayat would serve as both a Board of Conciliation to settle disputes between "classes" and as a Court of Arbitration to settle suits between individuals.[22]

Wedderburn's proposal not only obviously projected European notions of class, class struggle, and political economy onto the Indian situation, but it was also of a piece with European, and more specifically British, developments in the law and practice of industrial relations. Perhaps most significantly, boards of arbitration and conciliation had become an increasingly popular remedy to industrial strife in Britain among both industrialists and lawmakers. In particular, the 1867–9 Royal Commission on Trade Unions had brought significant attention to the arbitration and conciliation systems that had been established autonomously in several industrial sectors, and in both 1867 and 1872 parliament had provided enabling acts to provide for their creation and administration.[23]

Yet Wedderburn undoubtedly was unique among British administrators in presenting the causes of the Deccan riots as basically an industrial relations problem. Several months later, in February 1879, however, Joshi testified before the Indian Famine Commission and, in much more specific terms, promoted the re-creation of panchayats as a means to solve the problem of peasant indebtedness. The court fees and stamp duties imposed by the British courts, he argued, had helped to impoverish the peasantry who were forced to spend crores of rupees in

[21] Wedderburn, "The Pancháyat," pp. 117; 120; 123. [22] Ibid., p. 126.

[23] 30 & 31 Vict., c. 105, Councils of Conciliation Act, 1867, and 35 & 36 Vict., c. 46, Masters and Workmen (Arbitration) Act, 1872. Generally, see Lord Amulree, *Industrial Arbitration in Great Britain* (London: Oxford University Press, 1929), Chs. VIII–XI and Roger Davidson, "Government Administration," in C. J. Wrigley, ed., *A History of British Industrial Relations, 1875–1914* (Amherst, MA: University of Massachusetts Press, 1982), pp. 159–83.

the courts. "The only measure that can be taken to remedy these evils produced by litigation," he noted, "is to strongly encourage the *adjustment of suits by arbitration*, as this method has been found by experience to be highly beneficial."[24] The "experience" to which Joshi referred was both the Pune Arbitration Court and Elphinstone's pre-1827 panchayat experiment in the Bombay Presidency. According to Joshi, in Elphinstone's time, "justice was not taxed with stamp duties or such other duties" and complicated cases were subject to the arbitration of panchayats.[25] Therefore, as the Pune Arbitration Court had proven already, Joshi concluded, "litigation would not increase, reconciliation between the Sowcar and the debtor would be attained, and the parties would not be reduced to poverty."[26]

Upon their return to India in May 1879, Wedderburn and Joshi addressed a public meeting held in Pune to petition T. C. Hope, the Bombay Civil Service Officer deputed to draft the Agriculturists' Relief Act, "to consider what proposals regarding the establishment of Panchayats" should be added to the Bill.[27] The meeting was organized by the Pune Sarvajanik Sabha, the organization founded in 1870 as a "mediating body" between "the Government and the people," and was attended by British District and Assistant Judges from the areas immediately affected by the Bill as well as by Indian judicial and legal figures and other members of the Sarvajanik Sabha, including S. H. Chiplunkar, Editor and owner of *Dnyan Prakash*, B. S. Shesho, President of the Pune Arbitration Court, and the "moderate" nationalist leader G. K. Gokhale.[28]

Joshi opened the meeting extolling the virtues of the "time-honoured institution of the Panchayat" and submitted the draft of a Panchayat Bill that he and Wedderburn had prepared. When Wedderburn rose to speak, he emphasized the efficacy of arbitration

[24] PP, *East India (Report of the Famine Commission), Appendix II: Proceedings of the Commission, and Selected Evidence* (1882), p. 82. Emphasis in original.

[25] *East India (Report of the Famine Commission)*, p. 80. [26] Ibid., p. 83.

[27] "Proceedings of a Public Meeting of the Inhabitants of Poona," *The Quarterly Journal of the Poona Sarvajanik Sabha*, Vol. II, No. 1 (July 1879), p. 78.

[28] *The Constitution of the Poona Sarvajanik Sabha and Its Rules* quoted in Rosalind O'Hanlon, *Caste, Conflict and Ideology: Mahatma Jotirao Phule and Low Caste Protest in Nineteenth-century Western India* (Cambridge: Cambridge University Press, 1985), p. 190; see also Kumar, *Western India in the Nineteenth Century*, pp. 174–6, and S. R. Mehrotra, "The Poona Sarvajanik Sabha: The Early Phase (1870–1880)," *Indian Economic & Social History Review*, Vol. 6, No. 3 (September 1969), pp. 293–321, and, more generally, Gordon Johnson, *Provincial Politics and Indian Nationalism: Bombay and the Indian National Congress, 1880 to 1915* (Cambridge: Cambridge University Press, 1973), pp. 91–101. The list of attendees was published in "Proceedings," p. 78.

and conciliation and urged it to be adopted in rural India. "A system of conciliation," he said,

> would put an end to the internecine warfare between Sawkars and raiyats. And in carrying it into effect, in giving new life to the Panchayat, the ancient and honoured council of the village elders, Government would not only enjoy the sympathy of all educated Natives, but would secure the support of that mighty factor of Indian administration, "Mamul" or customary usages which for the inarticulate masses serves in the place of thought and opinion.[29]

As we have seen, such derogatory sentiments regarding the "inarticulate masses" were typical of Liberal sensibilities in both India and England. Nevertheless, Gokhale suggested that the proposals be submitted to a select committee for review and revision, if necessary. The committee, composed predominantly of acting and former sub-judges, including the influential judge and intellectual Mahadev Govind Ranade, submitted its report and a proposed bill on 23 May 1879.[30] The committee's draft drew heavily upon the much older Madras and Bombay Regulations from the era of Munro and Elphinstone, although it limited the jurisdiction of the panchayat to suits brought by money-lenders against peasants. The composition of the panchayat, however, bore little relation to any imagined "ancient and honoured council of the village elders." Its eligible members were to be selected jointly by the local subordinate judge and a representative of the Collector, although provision was also made for "personal consultation with the people." The resulting list of government-approved *panchayatdars* was to be published in the *Government Gazette*.

Procedures in the proposed panchayat, however, were to be much like those adopted in Elphinstone's time. The plaintiff was to be afforded the opportunity to bring the case before a panchayat and to select an initial list of *panchayatdars*. If the defendant agreed to have the case heard by the panchayat, he or she could accept the proposed list or they could move that both parties select an equal number of *panchayatdars*. In the latter event, both parties then would jointly appoint a *sarpanch* to serve as an umpire. If the defendant did not agree to have the case heard by the panchayat, then the case would be transferred to the subordinate judge for disposition or, in special cases, to the civil courts for trial. Finally, the panchayat itself was not to be bound by

[29] "Proceedings," p. 81. [30] Ibid., pp. 89–94.

formal rules of evidence and would be directed to "pronounce an award according to justice and right."

Unlike in Elphinstone's era, however, these panchayats were to be provided with some exceptional powers of enforcement. They could summon witnesses and fine those who failed to appear; they could administer oaths and subject those who gave false testimony to the penalties provided for by the Indian Penal Code; and they could subpoena documents considered to be necessary for the resolution of the case. Although the panchayat was intended to be free of any fees or stamp duties, its awards were nonetheless subject to a filing fee.

Thus the panchayat proposed by the committee was once again a hybrid institution that combined elements of imagined customary practices with British civil procedure. Moreover, drawing upon the Elphinstonian legacy, it reflected a certain imagining of the panchayat as an analog of British systems of arbitration rather than Munro's jury system and sought to obviate those earlier panchayats' most obvious limitation by providing significant although not absolute powers of enforcement. Nevertheless, *The Quarterly Journal of the Poona Sarvajanik Sabha* heralded the proposal not only as a laudable means by which conciliation might be promoted but, more importantly, as an essential step toward self-government. "It should be remembered," the *Journal* wrote,

> that the Village Panchayat is one of the oldest institutions known to this contending country, simple in its character, and least costly to the parties. These Panchayats have of late ceased to be useful to the community, owing to the establishment of regular courts of justice, and also to the discouragement they have received at the hands of the Government. But the institution has not died out altogether; for, under the form of Arbitration Courts, it has been, since the last few years, revived at Poona, Surat, and elsewhere. We think the time has come when its traditionary [*sic*] status may be restored and recognized with benefit to the people, by giving it a certain position in our judicial system. Nothing, in our opinion, will better popularize the principle of conciliation and amicable arbitration, or more effectively discourage useless and expensive litigation, or more successfully educate the people in self-government[31]

This discursive shift was another critical moment in the history of the panchayat for it first linked the panchayat's revival not only to the

[31] "The Deccan Agriculturists' Bill," *Quarterly Journal of the Poona Sarvajanik Sabha*, Vol. II, No. 2 (October 1879), p. 55.

goal of gaining greater access to justice but, more significantly, to the goal of self-government. The Famine Commission, however, viewed the proposal as little more than an unnecessary duplication of already existing British-styled arbitration law and dismissed the idea. They reasoned, "the existing law makes ample provision for recognising references to arbitration by the consent of the parties, and for giving to the awards of arbitrators so appointed the form of a decree. It has not, however, been found that this mode of settling disputes is generally popular."[32] Nevertheless, in the succeeding decades, the panchayat would increasingly come to be viewed, particularly among many nationalists, as an essential aspect of Indian self-governance.

The acceptance of the panchayat as an fundamental feature of self-governance, however, was neither an immediate one nor was there a common understanding of its composition or function. As we have seen, the 1880s and 1890s witnessed a significant rehabilitation of the vocabulary of the panchayat among British administrators, albeit in forms as disparate as the administration of local policing and limited municipal and village governance.[33] Yet, even British administrators were eventually forced to recognize the fact that these were "artificial administrative committees."[34] Moreover, the idea of the panchayat was continually being expanded to include new and unique objectives and purposes. In 1911, for example, G. K. Devadhar of Gokhale's Servants of India Society moved a resolution before the Allahabad Congress to promote the creation of panchayats to resolve differences between Hindus and Muslims as well as between castes. In his estimation, these panchayats would be the equivalent of "conciliation boards" where the people would be "trained in the habits of working in perfect harmony and unison for the common good."[35] Perhaps most significant, however, was the fact that even when the Indian National Congress formally adopted self-governance as a goal in 1916, neither panchayats nor *panchayati raj* were mentioned.[36] Thus the function of the panchayat as well as its role in a self-governing India continued to be debated, re-imagined, and contested throughout the early nationalist period.

[32] PP, *Report of the Indian Famine Commission. Part II. Measures of Protection and Prevention* (1880), pp. 132–3.

[33] See Chapter 9.

[34] *Indian Local Self-Government Policy, 1915: Being a Resolution Issued by the Governor General in Council on the 28th April 1915* (Calcutta, 1915), p. 36.

[35] *The Mahratta*, 5 February 1911, p. 71.

[36] *Report of the Thirty-First Indian National Congress held at Lucknow on the 26th, 28th, 29th and 30th December, 1916* (Allahabad, 1917), pp. 70–97.

Certainly, as noted in the previous chapter, one of the more prominent voices promoting the reinvigoration of the panchayat was that of Annie Besant. As President of the 1917 Calcutta Congress, she declared that "the economic and moral deterioration [of India] can only be checked by the re-establishment of a healthy *and interesting* village life, and this depends upon the re-establishment of the Panchayat as the unit of government."[37] Besant, who relied to a significant extent upon a 1916 bill presented to the Madras Legislative Council and drafted by Dewan Bahadur T. Rangachariar, imagined the panchayat largely stripped of its judicial function and instead functioning as a multi-tiered administrative organization. By the late 1920s, she had come to call these bodies village panchayats, *taluq* (sub-district) panchayats, and district panchayats.[38] At the village level, the panchayat would have "complete control" over roads, lighting, health, and, most importantly, primary education.[39] The higher levels of administration would possess authority over the inter-village and regional provision of these services. However, both the franchise and eligibility for political participation at each level would be selective. At the village level, universal suffrage would be appropriate, Besant argued, but at the *taluq* and district level "higher qualifications" would be required for "the higher responsibilities." Without apparent irony, Besant concluded:

> If you want a real democracy you will have to introduce some graduated system of this kind, in which the more difficult questions demand higher qualification for those who choose the people who are to act for them, those upon whom the welfare of the Empire depends.[40]

At nearly the same time, the British government in India began to make further efforts to re-deploy the term "panchayat." In 1918, the publication of the Montagu–Chelmsford Report raised the issue once again, although its recommendations were vague, unsubstantial, and equivocal. "It is recognized," the Report concluded,

> that the prospect of successfully developing panchayats must depend very largely on local conditions, and that the functions and powers to be allotted to them must vary accordingly; but where the system proves a success, it is contemplated that they might be endowed with civil and

[37] Annie Besant, *Speeches and Writings of Annie Besant*, 3rd edn. (Madras, 1921), p. 360. Emphasis in original.
[38] Annie Besant and A. Ranganatham, *The Indian Village System* (Madras, 1929?), p. 48.
[39] Besant, *Indian Village System*, p. 50. [40] Besant, *Indian Village System*, p. 55.

> criminal jurisdiction in petty cases; some administrative powers as regards sanitation and education, and permissive powers of imposing a local rate. It is hoped that wherever possible an effective beginning will be made.[41]

Nevertheless, several of the post-Report reformed provincial governments, especially those in Bengal, the United Provinces, Bombay, the Punjab, and Madras, quickly moved to devolve administrative and judicial powers upon the newly created councils and village panchayats.[42] The Oxford don, L. F. Rushbrook Williams, who prepared the 1924–5 survey of the progress and condition of India for the British government, was favorably impressed by the reformed provincial governments' willingness to experiment with new forms of local administration, "among the most interesting" of which, he wrote, was "the revival of the Village Panchayat."[43] There was, however, a great deal of variety in the authority, responsibilities, and longevity of these village panchayats. In Bombay city, for example, elections to panchayats were based upon a wide male suffrage and the panchayats themselves were given extensive authority over local governance. However, villages were required to apply for permission to create a panchayat and, once created, they possessed no judicial authority except for that of judging offenses against their own by-laws.[44] B. R. Ambedkar noted that as late as 1932, there were only 323 panchayats in the Presidency of 30,000 villages.[45] In Uttar Pradesh, on the other hand, village panchayats were authorized to try petty civil and criminal cases. According to Rushbrook Williams, there were 6,001 of these panchayats established throughout the province by 1923–1924.[46]

In the rush to create these new institutions of self-governance, many panchayats were created, but many were short-lived as well. In Madras, for example, the Village Panchayat Act of 1920 eventually led to the creation of thousands of panchayats, but between 1930 and 1947 the number of panchayats varied between approximately six and 8,000.[47]

41 PP, *East India (Constitutional Reforms). Report on Indian Constitutional Reforms* (1918), p. 161.

42 Hugh Tinker, *The Foundations of Local Self-Government in India, Pakistan and Burma* (New York: Praeger, 1968), pp. 116–19; N. Srinivasan, "Village Government in India," *The Far Eastern Quarterly*, Vol. 15, No. 2 (February 1956), p. 209.

43 PP, *East India (Progress and Condition). Statement Exhibiting the Moral and Material Progress and Condition of India during the Year 1924–25* (1924–1925), p. 73.

44 Tinker, *Foundations of Local Self-Government*, pp. 117–18.

45 Vasant Moon, ed., *Dr. Babasaheb Ambedkar Writings and Speeches*, Vol. 2 (Bombay: Government of Maharashtra, 1979), p. 105.

46 PP, *East India (Progress and Condition) 1924–5*, p. 73.

47 Srinivasan, "Village Governments in India," p. 209.

Moreover, not all of these panchayats chose to function in both an administrative and judicial capacity. There, in 1934, it was reported that just over 4,100 villages operated "panchayat courts."[48] Thus, perhaps one-third to one-half of the village panchayats opted not to exercise judicial authority.

In Bengal, the Self-Government Act of 1919 provided for the creation of "union boards" and "union courts" that replicated the administrative and judicial functions of the traditional panchayat. The jurisdiction of the union courts was quite limited and restricted to suits involving contracts and moveable property valued at less than Rs. 25, while the elected union boards were responsible for policing, sanitation, and public health. By 1924, nearly 1,500 union boards had been created and their judicial functions reportedly were especially popular. "The Union Courts and Union Benches work well," Rushbrook Williams wrote,

> many of them succeeding in amicably settling a large proportion of the cases brought before them. It is a remarkable testimony to the growing popularity of these humble tribunals that in order to secure the speedy settlement of cases, creditors have been known to reduce their demands so that these institutions might have jurisdiction.[49]

As late as 1940, as many as 2,166 "union benches" were enumerated by the British government.[50]

Yet the attachment of the panchayat to the goals of self-governance and later independence was to be of the most lasting significance, even though its form and function continued to be a matter of some debate and experimentation. Without doubt, the eventual intervention of M. K. Gandhi ultimately proved to be decisive. In retrospect, Gandhi's transformational role is somewhat surprising. His imagining of the panchayat was neither unique nor particularly distinctive and drew upon distinctly Western models and theories of ancient village democracy and governance. Moreover, Gandhi's advocacy of *panchayati raj*, at least in his public pronouncements, was sometimes cryptic and relatively infrequent. In his vast *oeuvre*, there are relatively few instances in which he laid out in any detail his vision of the panchayat's form and functions.

[48] PP, *East India (Statistical Abstract). Statistical Abstract for British India with, Where Available, Relating to Certain Indian States from 1926–27 to 1935–36* (1937–1938), pp. 212–13.

[49] PP, *East India (Progress and Condition) 1924–5*, p. 74.

[50] PP, *East India (Statistical Abstract). Statistical abstract for British India* (1942–1943), pp. 210–11.

Indeed, Gandhi's first pronouncement regarding the role of the panchayat was not made in India at all, but in South Africa. Within a year of arriving there in May 1893, Gandhi had become involved in the protest movement against the Franchise Law Amendment Bill, which threatened to further disenfranchise those Indians in Natal who met the already strict property qualifications. In June 1894, he drafted a petition to the Natal Legislative Assembly with the ostensible object of countering the argument presented by the Bill's backers that Indians had no experience with elective institutions and "have never exercised the franchise in the land they come from."[51] Intentionally drawing upon English authorities, Gandhi's petition sought to prove not only that "all the facts and history point the other way" but also that "the Indian nation has known, and has exercised, the power of election from times far prior to the time when the Anglo-Saxon races first became acquainted with the principles of representation."

Although it has not heretofore been noted, a good portion of this section of Gandhi's Natal Petition was copied directly from Sir Pherozeshah Mehta's inaugural address to the sixth Indian National Congress held in Calcutta in 1890.[52] Thus Gandhi copied verbatim from Mehta's address the claim that Henry Sumner Maine "has shown that the Teutonic Mark was hardly so well organized or so essentially representative as an Indian village community until the precise technical Roman form was engrafted onto it."[53] He also copied a rather lengthy quote from a paper delivered to the East India Association by Thomas Chisholm Anstey, a Bombay barrister who had died in 1873, to the effect that "Local Self-Government in the widest acceptation of the term is as old as the East itself."[54] Finally, he took from Mehta's speech the claim that the workings of caste assemblies in India are "exact prototypes of the Saxon Witans, from which the English parliamentary institutions have sprung."[55]

[51] CWMG, Vol. 1, 28 June 1894. Among the voluminous number of works that chronicle Gandhi's life, see Ramachandra Guha, *Gandhi before India* (London: Allen Lane, 2013), pp. 72–81 and Judith Brown, *Gandhi: Prisoner of Hope* (New Haven: Yale University Press, 1989), pp. 30–94. On the Natal Petition, see also Crispin Bates, "The Development of Panchayat Raj in India," in Crispin Bates and Subho Basu, eds., *Rethinking Indian Political Institutions* (London: Anthem Press, 2005), pp. 173–4.

[52] D. V. Gokhale, ed., *Inaugural Addresses by Presidents of the Indian National Congress with Mr. Charles Bradlaugh's Speech* (Bombay, 1895), pp. 79–104.

[53] *Inaugural Addresses*, p. 91. Gandhi's petition italicized the words "essentially representative."

[54] *Inaugural Addresses*, pp. 90–1.

[55] Ibid., p. 91. In this sentence, Gandhi's phrasing is slightly different from Mehta's original. Gandhi's Natal petition stated in full "Every caste in every village has its own rules or regulations,

Unlike Sir Pherozeshah, however, Gandhi elaborated upon this last observation by explaining, as he understood it, the role and function of the panchayat. "The word *Panchayat*," he wrote,

> is a household word throughout the length and breadth of India, and it means, as the Honourable Members may be well aware, a Council of Five elected by the class of the people to whom the five belong, for the purpose of managing and controlling the social affairs of the particular caste.[56]

Precisely from where Gandhi derived the idea that caste panchayats were elected is unclear. Shortly before his assassination, Gandhi indicated that he had never actually seen a "real panchayat" that functioned as it had "in former times."[57] At that time, Gandhi suggested that "real panchayats" undertook agricultural improvements, improved sanitation, and regulated morality, including the elimination of cinema-going, gambling, alcohol, *ganja*, and *bhang*. When this was accomplished, he concluded, "Then I shall feel that your Panchayat has done some good work."[58]

However, as we have seen, the notion that the Indian village was an autonomous republic was and remained common currency among Indian intellectuals throughout this period and thereafter. Further, in an interview published in 1946, Gandhi even suggested that "panchayat" and "republic" were synonymous: "Independence must begin at the bottom," he said. "Thus, every village will be a republic or *panchayat* having full powers. It follows, therefore, that every village has to be self-sustained and capable of managing its affairs even to the extent of defending itself against the whole world."[59]

Certainly, the clearest exposition of Gandhi's later imagining of the panchayat was published in *Young India* only in 1931. Here, as we shall see, he took direct issue with the view that panchayats were judicial institutions and instead re-asserted his contention that they were "an assembly of five elected by the villagers."[60] Gandhi's antipathy to the panchayat re-imagined as a judicial institution or village court undoubtedly stemmed from his experience in the Non-Cooperation Movement of 1920–1922. In July 1920, a month before the beginning

and elects representatives, and furnishes an exact prototype of the Saxon Witans, from which have sprung the present Parliamentary institutions.

[56] Emphasis in original. [57] CWMG, Vol. 98, 27 December 1947, p. 121. [58] Ibid., p. 122.

[59] M. K. Gandhi, *Hind Swaraj and Other Writings*, Anthony J. Parel, ed., (Cambridge: Cambridge University Press, 2009), p. 181. Italicization in original.

[60] CWMG, Vol. 52, 28 May 1931, pp. 191–3.

of the movement, Gandhi's plan had included the provision that "Lawyers will give up practice and help people to settle their civil disputes among themselves."[61] Of course, Gandhi's critique of the role of lawyers in supporting imperial dominance dated back at least to the publication of *Hind Swaraj* in 1909, but his attack upon the law and the courts in 1920 was especially compelling:

> The lawyers should, for the time being, give up practice and intending litigants or those who find themselves dragged into litigation should boycott the courts and get their disputes settled through *arbitration boards*. It is my confirmed belief that every Government masks its brute force and maintains its control over the people through civil and criminal courts, for it is cheaper, simpler and more honourable, for a ruler that instead of his controlling the people through naked force, they themselves, lured into slavery through courts, etc., submit to him of their own accord. If people settle their civil disputes among themselves and the lawyers, unmindful of self-interest, boycott the courts in the interest of the people, the latter can advance in no time. I have believed for many years that every State tries to perpetuate its power through lawyers.[62]

It is notable, however, that as late as this 4 July 1920 statement Gandhi still did not refer to these new judicial institutions as panchayats, but instead he called them "arbitration boards." The statement issued by the Non-Cooperation Committee three days later also requested the "suspension by lawyers of practice and settlement of civil disputes by private arbitration."[63] The September 1920 All-India Congress Committee similarly announced that "lawyers should help in inducing parties not only to refer future disputes to arbitration but also to withdraw cases now pending in the British Courts and submit them to the National Arbitration Courts."[64]

At a very early point during the Non-Cooperation Movement, both Gandhi and Congress ceased to refer to these new bodies as arbitration courts and instead adopted the term panchayat. It is unclear exactly

61 CWMG, Vol. 21, 4 July 1920, p. 5.

62 Ibid., p. 7. Emphasis added. In *Hind Swaraj*, Gandhi claimed not only that the law, as a profession, teaches immorality, but also that it was the means by which the English perpetuated their power. "If [Indian] pleaders were to abandon their profession and consider it just as degrading as prostitution," he wrote, "English rule would break up in a day." Gandhi, *Hind Swaraj*, pp. 56–59. Notably, however, he did not propose the resurrection of the panchayat as a remedy at this time.

63 CWMG, Vol. 21, 7 July 1920, p. 13.

64 *The Indian National Congress, 1920–1923* (Allahabad, 1924), p. 18. Interestingly, in the Index to this work, the entry for "panchayats" reads: "see arbitration courts."

when or why Gandhi became convinced that the ancient panchayats were intended to function as boards of arbitration and lawyers as arbitrators. As a lawyer, Gandhi was certainly more familiar with this function of the legal profession, having employed it himself in Dada Abdulla's case, the case that had first brought him to South Africa.[65] Shortly after arriving in South Africa, Gandhi had also taken on another case involving a longstanding dispute over the terms of the dissolution of a partnership. In this case, the terms of the settlement had been established by a "panchayat" that appears to have functioned as a board of commercial arbitration among Indian merchants in Durban. The panchayat had been chaired by Dawad Mahomed, a prominent Durban merchant and later President of the Natal Indian Congress.[66] These experiences may very well have led Gandhi to first declare in the Natal Petition that the Indian familiarity with representative institutions was exemplified through the existence of a panchayat among Indian merchants in Durban that can deliberate on "matters of pressing importance."

Nevertheless, as the Non-Cooperation Movement proceeded, where these "arbitration boards" did spring up they were almost universally referred to as panchayats, a description that Gandhi quickly embraced as well, and they functioned much less as an arbitration board and much more as non-state popular court. Certainly, during the immediate post-World War I period, some of the discussion concerning the role of panchayats had focused upon their revivification as judicial institutions. The 1918 Montagu–Chelmsford Report, as we have noted, while not specifically endorsing the immediate creation of panchayats, did recommend that an "effective beginning" be made to encourage them and endow them "with civil and criminal jurisdiction in petty cases" as well as permissive powers for assessing local taxes for the provision of sanitation and education. Nevertheless, by the end of 1920, Gandhi had come to fully endorse the panchayat as a judicial institution, and throughout the Non-Cooperation Movement he repeatedly referred to them as sites for "settling local disputes,"[67] to "decide your cases,"[68] and "to deal out justice."[69] As late as 1924, he was still extolling

[65] Goolam Vahed, "Passengers, Partnerships, and Promissory Notes: Gujarati Traders in Colonial Natal, 1870–1920," *International Journal of African Historical Studies*, Vol. 38, No. 3 (2005), pp. 459–60.

[66] Vahed, "Passengers, Partnerships, and Promissory Notes," p. 459; Guha, *Gandhi before India*, pp. 62–72.

[67] CWMG, Vol. 22, 15 December 1920, p. 97. [68] CWMG, Vol. 22, 16 February 1921, p. 354.

[69] CWMG, Vol. 25, 17 November 1921, p. 144.

the virtues of these "panchayat courts" that along with the creation of national schools, *swadeshi*, and the removal of untouchability would lay the foundation for *swaraj*.[70]

However, after the cessation of the Non-Cooperation Movement, Gandhi admitted that the panchayat courts had been a practical failure, a conclusion that was echoed by the Indian National Congress.[71] In particular, the implementation of panchayat courts across India had been noticeably uneven. They appear to have been most successful in areas such as Bihar, Oudh, Orissa, and the Punjab, areas that had been key to Gandhi's support.[72] In June 1921, nearly eighty panchayats were reported to be functioning in the Punjab.[73] In Oudh, the government reported in February 1921 that the Kisan Sabhas (Cultivators' Associations) had resolved "to decide all disputes by Panchayats" and that, as a result, "few cases [were] instituted in civil courts."[74] In Bihar, the government reported that "panchayats had been established in a large number of villages ... and were being established every day."[75] Elsewhere, however, the establishment of panchayat courts was a notable failure. In Delhi, for example, Congress reported that eleven panchayat courts had been established. In Tamil Nadu, there were ten; in Maharashtra, sixteen; in Kerala, six; in Madras, eighteen; and in Bombay, none.[76]

In addition, relatively few lawyers or *vakils* joined the movement and, in some places, *vakils* were reported to have attacked those who tried to participate in the panchayat courts.[77] In the Bombay Presidency, only six pleaders were reported to have joined the boycott and, as Judith Brown notes, four of them had never practiced before, while the remaining two were already on the verge of retirement.[78] The Congress Civil Disobedience Committee estimated that only between 1,200 and 1,500 lawyers throughout the country suspended practice in support of the Movement; the 1921 Census of India recorded over

70 CWMG, Vol. 27, 11 April 1924, p. 221; 17 April 1924, pp. 259–61; 1 May 1924, pp. 326–7; 8 May 1924, p. 369.

71 CWMG, Vol. 52, 28 May 1931, p. 191; *Report of the Civil Disobedience Committee Appointed by the All India Congress Committee* (Allahabad, 1922), pp. 48–51.

72 Judith Brown, *Gandhi's Rise to Power: Indian Politics, 1915–1922* (Cambridge: Cambridge University Press, 1972), pp. 258–60; 269–71.

73 CWMG, Vol. 23, 8 June 1921, p. 239. 74 NA, CAB 24/120/64, 21 February 1921.

75 Quoted in K. K. Datta, *History of the Freedom Movement in Bihar, Volume One: 1857–1928* (Patna, 1957), pp. 338–9.

76 *Report of the Civil Disobedience Committee*, Appendix V, pp. 1–3; Brown, *Gandhi's Rise to Power*, p. 279.

77 CWMG, Vol. 25, 22 December 1921, p. 324. 78 Brown, *Gandhi's Rise to Power*, p. 280.

36,500 lawyers in British India alone and nearly 53,000 in all of India.[79] Moreover, in some provinces, such as Assam and Bihar, the government had taken extraordinarily repressive measures to disrupt the panchayats.[80] Finally, there was general agreement that the relative failure of the panchayat courts was also due in part to the fact that they lacked any powers of enforcement. In several instances, the Civil Disobedience Committee reported that panchayats were "not popular, there being no power for enforcement behind their decrees."[81]

Despite these setbacks, Gandhi nevertheless suggested that the panchayat court experiment, although a practical failure, was an ideological success. The "halo" and "artificial prestige" surrounding the British law courts, he wrote in 1924, had disappeared and, after the Non-Cooperation Movement, "people believe, much more than they did before" in the "settlement of disputes by panchayats."[82] In December 1921, shortly before the suspension of the Movement, Gandhi had already come to the conclusion that although the boycott of the British courts had not been successful, "we have demolished their prestige" and they "neither worry nor dazzle us."[83]

Over the succeeding years, however, Gandhi ceased to visualize the panchayat as a forum for the settlement of disputes and re-imagined them principally as institutions of village administration. His 1931 article in *Young India* outlined a set of proposed rules for the establishment of elected village panchayats that were among the most detailed explications of his imagining of the panchayat.[84] The limits placed upon the judicial functions of panchayats were notable: they were to have no criminal jurisdiction, they might try civil suits but only upon the voluntary consent of both parties, no party could be compelled to go before a panchayat, and panchayats had no authority to impose fines with "the only sanction behind its civil decrees being its moral authority." In effect, Gandhi's vision of the judicial function of the panchayat was now nearly identical to that of Elphinstone's a century earlier:

[79] *Report of the Civil Disobedience Committee*, p. 48; *Census of India, 1921*, Vol. I: Pt. II – Tables (Calcutta, 1923), pp. 206–7.

[80] *Report of the Civil Disobedience Committee*, Appendix V, p. 3; CWMG, Vol. 22, 5 March 1922, p. 436.

[81] *Report of the Civil Disobedience Committee*, Appendix V. Rajendra Prasad, India's first president, was less pessimistic about the efficacy of panchayats although he admitted that there were practical problems, especially their lack of enforcement powers. See Rajendra Prasad, *Autobiography* (Bombay, 1957), pp. 134–5.

[82] CWMG, Vol. 27, 17 March 1924, p. 259.

[83] *Young India*, 8 December 1921, quoted in *Report of the Civil Disobedience Committee*, p. 50.

[84] CWMG, Vol. 52, 28 May 1931, pp. 191–3.

the imagining of the panchayat as a British-style voluntary board of arbitration.

Of greater importance for the future of the panchayat was what Gandhi listed as Clause 9 of his proposed set of rules, including his declaration of what "every Panchayat will be expected to attend to." Gandhi enumerated the following responsibilities:

(a) The education of boys and girls in its village
(b) Its sanitation
(c) Its medical needs
(d) The upkeep and cleanliness of village wells or ponds
(e) The uplift of and the daily wants of the so-called untouchables.[85]

Only attention to this "constructive work," Gandhi argued, could make the panchayat "really popular" and greatly enhance its "moral prestige."[86]

Not all nationalist leaders were willing to forego the notion of the panchayat as the revival of a customary judicial or arbitration tribunal. However, many had also been chastened by the experience of the Non-Cooperation Movement and the imagining of the panchayat as a unit of village or municipal administration became the dominant theme among them after 1922. This relatively narrow space within which the panchayat might be re-imagined is perhaps no better illustrated than in the case of C. R. Das, the Bengali barrister and ardent nationalist. Upon the founding of his Swaraj Party in 1923 to counter Gandhi's policy of non-cooperation, Das drafted an *Outline Scheme of Swaraj*. Like Gandhi, Das' plan provided for panchayats to function as boards of arbitration, but more importantly, their principal tasks were to exercise authority and jurisdiction over education, police, medical care, and wells, tanks, and canals. Unlike Gandhi, Das' political orientation also led him to imagine the panchayat as the governing authority of an agrarian commune. Thus, Das thought that the panchayat would also be responsible for overseeing co-operative stores and rural banks and for ensuring "that arable lands are properly tilled, and village commons, playing-grounds, pasture-lands, groves, orchards, etc., are properly

[85] Ibid., p. 193.
[86] Incidentally, the newly gained moral authority of the panchayat would serve to strengthen its enforcement powers. As Gandhi noted in full, "by the constructive work of the kind suggested in clause 9, it will find its judgments and authority respected by reason of its moral prestige. And that surely is the greatest sanction any one can possess and of which one cannot be deprived." Ibid.

maintained, and a sufficiency of necessaries, specially [*sic*] corn, cotton, and cattle, (or other forms of food, clothing, and accessories in specially circumstanced tracts), for the use of the Commune, is always available within their jurisdiction."[87]

After World War II, Gandhi's followers continued to pursue the Mahatma's vision. S. N. Agarwal's *Gandhian Constitution for Free India*, for example, published in 1946, received the qualified imprimatur of Gandhi himself. By this time, Agarwal's imagining of the panchayat had become quite commonplace. Metcalfe's 1830 Minute on the Indian village republic was reproduced once again as was Maine's work on the village community:[88] British law and governance had corrupted and destroyed this ancient institution,[89] and the ancient village republic was remarkable for its "genuine democracy and local self-government."[90] Agarwal did arrogate to the panchayat "wide legal powers, both criminal and civil" in order "to provide cheap and speedy justice to villagers."[91] More importantly, however, the restoration of *panchayati raj* promised to usher in a utopian post-modern society. The village economy would find a "golden and happy mean between Capitalism and Socialism."[92] "Hectic and noisy urban life" would be replaced by the "peaceful life of health-giving labour in the fields, cottage factories and workshops."[93] Consequently, national health and hygiene would improve and that would bring "renewed gaiety, enjoyment and recreation to the masses."[94] Inevitably, "India would stand like a shining Lighthouse always guiding other nations amid the darkness of exploitation and imperialism," leading the world to a new era of international harmony.[95]

Of course, it would be easy to scoff at such utopian fantasies. Yet they bear obvious witness to the iconic standing and ideological power that the panchayat had gained in Indian political and social thought by the mid-twentieth century. The fact that this standing was largely due to the panchayat's imaginative recreation by East India Company officials and the "nativist" interpretation of later British liberal intellectuals was not ignored. Ironically, instead they were provided as evidence of the legitimacy of an authentic Indian past.

[87] Chitta Ranjan Das, *Outline Scheme of Swaraj* (1923; Government of West Bengal, 1973), pp. 19–21. Das, like Besant, also expanded the received definition of panchayat to include any popularly elected consultative body. Thus, in the *Outline Scheme*, panchayats existed at every level of state administration and culminated in an "All-India Panchayat" at the national level.

[88] Shriman Narayan Agarwal, *Gandhian Constitution for Free India* (Allahabad: Kitabistan, 1946), pp. 47–8; 84; 97–8. Thanks to Marc Galanter for directing me to this work.

[89] Agarwal, *Gandhian Constitution*, pp. 47–8. [90] Ibid., pp. 49. [91] Ibid., pp. 84; 97–8.

[92] Ibid., p. 52. [93] Ibid., p. 59. [94] Ibid., p. 61. [95] Ibid., p. 67.

Although few voices in the nationalist movement were raised in open opposition to the goal of *panchayati raj* and there was no unanimity as to its priority within the nationalist movement, the most notable and powerful dissident was B. R. Ambedkar, the widely acknowledged leader of the "Untouchables." Ambedkar had first made known his opposition to the resuscitation of the panchayat during a 1932 debate in the Bombay Legislative Council. At that time, the Council was considering the amendment of the 1920 Bombay Village Panchayat Act, which, as noted above, provided for the voluntary delegation of extensive administrative authority to locally elected panchayats but possessed no judicial authority, save for the adjudication of violations of its own by-laws.[96] The principal amendment debated in 1932 entailed the extension of the panchayat's legal jurisdiction to include both civil and criminal cases, thereby creating what was, in effect, an elected local judiciary.

Ambedkar's opposition to the resurrection of the panchayat remained a remarkably consistent aspect of his thought and actions throughout his life, but it also forced him to tread a very narrow path between nationalism, democracy, and communalism. He was alone in rejecting the myth of the panchayat as an ancient republic, a myth, he astutely noticed, which was a legacy of colonial rule.[97] Moreover, he consistently rejected *panchayati raj* as a "very dangerous system" and the "bane of public life in India" because it "saturated" the people with "local particularism," prevented the development of a "larger civic spirit," and reproduced the inferior status of the "depressed classes," as they were called at the time. While he was not opposed to the principle of devolving administrative responsibilities upon local authorities, he was adamantly opposed to those who "eulogized the ancient system of village panchayats" and who wanted to revive them solely for their own sake.[98]

In 1932, Ambedkar's opposition to the Bombay Village Panchayat Bill was based upon two principles, the first of which was his long-standing opposition to majoritarian electoral politics.[99] In every village, he stated, Dalits were a minority and the election of members of the panchayats would only serve to confirm that status. "Adult

96 *Ambedkar Writings and Speeches*, II, pp. 105–20.

97 B. R. Ambedkar, "Outside the Fold," in Valerian Rodrigues, ed., *The Essential Writings of B. R. Ambedkar* (New Delhi: Oxford University Press, 2002) pp. 323–5; *Constituent Assembly of India Debates (Proceedings)*, Vol. VII, 4 November 1948.

98 *Ambedkar Writings and Speeches*, II, pp. 106–7.

99 For Ambedkar's early support of "communal representation," see Eleanor Zelliot, "Dr. Ambedkar and the Mahar Movement" (Ph.D. thesis, University of Pennsylvania, 1969), pp. 150–1.

suffrage cannot convert a minority into a majority," he declared; "Consequently, I am bound to insist that if these village panchayats come, there shall be special representation for the minorities [. . .] Now I agree that this is communalism. But I am also convinced that communalism must be my policy. I am not ashamed of it."[100] When a fellow councilor rose to ask whether communalism was compatible with nationalism, Ambedkar responded that "special representation" was needed in order to protect the rights of the "depressed classes." In this sense, he concluded, "without communalism there can be no self-government for India."[101]

Ambedkar's strongest words, however, were reserved for the proposal that the disposal of civil and criminal cases should devolve upon Judges chosen from among the elected members of the village panchayat. Such a judiciary, he noted, would not only promote men of little or no legal training to positions of authority, but it would also lead to American-style electoral and judicial corruption. However, it was the inevitability that an elected village judiciary would be dominated by Brahmins that evoked his greatest ire. In this case, he argued, "special representation" on village benches was absolutely necessary in order to prevent the creation of "a conspiracy to utilise the political and judicial power that they will get to put down the other classes."

Ambedkar never made his opposition to the revival of the panchayat a vital issue in his campaigns for Dalit representation. Indeed, he was dismissive of the idealization of the panchayat within the Independence movement generally. This is no more apparent than during his presentation of India's draft constitution to the Constituent Assembly in 1948. Responding to criticisms that the draft constitution had not incorporated the system *panchayati raj*, Ambedkar joked that "the love of the intellectual Indians for the village community is of course infinite if not pathetic." More seriously, he also rightly explained that this love for panchayats was derived from the "fulsome praise" heaped upon them by British administrators who lauded the village community's immunity from historical change.[102] Yet such longevity, he continued, was irrelevant; much more important were the values which the village transmitted and the principles upon which it functioned. "Surely," he explained, they continued to exist only "on a low, on a selfish level."

[100] *Ambedkar Writings and Speeches*, II, p. 107. [101] Ibid., p. 107.

[102] In particular, Ambedkar emphasized the influence of Charles Metcalfe to whom he attributed the notion that the Indian village was a "little republic." As we have noted above, this analogy was actually put forth first by Thomas Munro.

Famously, Ambedkar then derided the intellectual tradition of the village republic in the most critical terms:

> I hold that these village republics have been the ruination of India. I am therefore surprised that those who condemn provincialism and communalism should come forward as champions of the village. What is the village but a sink of localism, a den of ignorance, narrow-mindedness and communalism? I am glad that the Draft Constitution has discarded the village and adopted the individual as its unit.

Against the passionate opposition of several members of the Assembly, Ambedkar was not able to exclude the panchayat entirely from the Constitution. He did, however, exclude it from the Constitution's enumeration of Fundamental Rights and delegate it instead to its Directive Principles. In his speech presenting the draft constitution, Ambedkar objected to the general notion that the Directive Principles were mere "pious declarations" by arguing that even if the Principles were not enforceable at law, elected officials would "certainly have to answer for them before the electorate at election time." Nevertheless, Article 40 of the Constitution notably provided only for the potential delegation of municipal powers to panchayats, omitting entirely any claim to judicial authority.[103] In this sense, Ambedkar had achieved the goal he had first expressed before the Bombay Legislative Council in 1932.

Following the debates on the panchayat in the Constituent Assembly, Ambedkar wrote a short piece, unpublished until 1989, excoriating the Hindu idealization of the Indian village, its invention as a republic, and the means by which village customs and institutions kept Dalits in perpetual servitude and beggary.[104] He condemned the Hindu members of the Constituent Assembly not only for their ecstatic faith in the Indian village as a unique and ideal form of social organization but also for their fanatical support of the idea that the autonomous Indian village unit should form the basis of the Constitution. For

[103] *Constituent Assembly of India Debates (Proceedings)*, Vol. VII, 9 November 1948; 17 November 1948. Article 40 of the Constitution of India reads in full: "The State shall take steps to organise village panchayats and endow them with such powers and authority as may be necessary to enable them to function as units of self-government." Opposition to the Article came from a number of political perspectives. Many extolled the democratic virtues of the panchayat system while others viewed the panchayat as a vehicle for substantive economic reform. The latter group included, for example, K. T. Shah, who tried to amend the Article to require the introduction of co-operative panchayats, and N. G. Ranga, who opposed co-operatives.

[104] Ambedkar, "Outside the Fold," pp. 323–31. See also, Surinder S. Jodhka, "Nation and Village: Images of Rural India in Gandhi, Nehru and Ambedkar," *Economic & Political Weekly*, Vol. 37, No. 32 (10–16 August 2002), pp. 3350–52.

Untouchables, he wrote, "there could not have been a greater calamity. Thank God the Constituent Assembly did not adopt it."[105]

The panchayat ideal, Ambedkar wrote, was a legacy of colonial governance adopted by Hindus who felt "flattered" by the favorable attention given to them by their British governors. Ambedkar traced this legacy back to the British idealization of the Indian village republic and, in particular, to Charles Metcalfe's famous nineteenth-century description of their autonomy and longevity. Although Ambedkar was obviously not fully aware of the lineages of the concept of the Indian "village republic" in the British historical imagination and instead drew upon the account of Metcalfe provided by Baden-Powell's *Land Systems of British India*, he nonetheless maintained that "this belief of the Hindus is not ancestral belief, nor does it come from the ancient past." Instead,

> Having read this [Metcalfe's] description of an Indian village given by a high-placed member of the governing class, the Hindus felt flattered and adopted this view as a welcome compliment. In adopting this view of the Indian village, the Hindus have not done any justice to their intelligence or their understanding. They have merely exhibited the weakness common to all subject peoples.[106]

Ambedkar went on to list the numerous ways in which "the Touchables occupy the position of a ruling race" in the village "while the Untouchables occupy the position of a subject race of hereditary bondsmen," a situation that led him to question the entire meaning of the "village republic." Ambedkar's assessment of the "village republic" ideal for the Dalit is worth quoting at length:

> In this republic, there is no place for democracy. There is no room for equality. There is no room for liberty and there is no room for fraternity. The Indian village is the very negation of a republic. If it is a republic, it is a republic of the Touchables, by the Touchables, and for the Touchables. The republic is an Empire of the Hindus over the Untouchables. It is a kind of colonialism designed to exploit the Untouchables. The Untouchables have no rights. They are there only to wait, serve and submit. They are there to do or die. They have no rights because they are outside the so-called republic, they are outside the Hindu fold. This is a vicious circle. But this is a fact that cannot be gainsaid.[107]

[105] Ambedkar, "Outside the Fold," p. 323. [106] Ibid., p. 324. [107] Ibid., pp. 330–1.

Ambedkar's opposition notwithstanding, given the relative marginalization of the panchayat to the Constitution's Directive Principles, it is not surprising that the role of the panchayat continued to be debated among some nationalists during the first decade after Indian independence.[108] Both Gandhians and socialists were the principal heirs to the Mahatma's panchayat vision and several Congress leaders, especially H. D. Malaviya and S. N Agarwal, continued to actively promote the panchayat cause. These voices were relatively quiet during the years immediately after Independence. They appear to have willingly assented to the "central objective" of India's First Five-Year Plan (1951–1956), which concerned the "promotion of rapid and balanced economic development."[109] Reform of local government along the lines of the panchayat ideal had certainly not been entertained seriously at that time. However, as preparations began for the Second Five-Year Plan, these voices reasserted themselves.

In 1954, the Congress Working Committee appointed a separate subcommittee, the Village Panchayat Committee, to consider the place of the panchayat as both a judicial and administrative institution in independent India. Included among the six-member subcommittee were three of the leading proponents of *panchayati raj*: Agarwal, Malaviya, and K. N. Katju, the Congress General Secretary.[110] Not surprisingly, in the pages of the *A.I.C.C. Economic Review*, the journal published by Congress's Economic & Political Research Committee, the appointment of the subcommittee was hailed by Agarwal as "a big step in the direction of establishing such panchayats in accordance with the genius and traditions of India through the Ages" and by Malaviya as a "historic" event that promises to "restore the authority of the village community and achieve socialism."[111]

Nevertheless, the discussions that took place at the various committee meetings and often recorded within the pages of the *A.I.C.C. Economic Review* revealed just how difficult it was to recreate an imagined institution within the confines of a democratic society divided by class,

108 See Marc Galanter, "The Aborted Restoration of 'Indigenous' Law in India," *Comparative Studies in Society and History*, Vol. 14, No. 1 (January 1972), pp. 53–70.

109 Second Five-Year Plan, Chapter 1 available at http://planningcommission.nic.in/plans/planrel/fiveyr/index2.html.

110 On Katju, see Galanter, "Aborted Restoration," p. 56, fn. 20.

111 S. N. Agarwal, "Economics of Village Panchayats," *A.I.C.C. Economic Review*, Vol. VI, No. 2 (1 June 1954), p. 3; H. D. Malaviya, "Reflections on Village Panchayats," *A.I.C.C. Economic Review*, Vol. VI, No. 4 (15 June 1954), pp. 11; 14.

caste, and creed.[112] For example, all contributors to the debate accepted the premise that from ancient times the panchayat had been a democratic institution, but there was certainly no agreement as to exactly how democracy was to be implemented at the village level. Katju, for instance, proposed that rather than implement a system based upon the enfranchisement of the individual, each family (*ghar*) should be allowed to nominate a member to the panchayat.[113] Agarwal, on the other hand, assumed that panchayats would be elected, but insisted that these elections be made free from party politicking.[114] In Bihar, the state government had already instituted a "unanimity principle" for election to village panchayats and, according to its Local Self-Government Minister, this had proven to be "very satisfactory."[115] Further disagreements arose over the size of panchayats, whether panchayats should be organized based upon individual or several villages, whether voting should be by secret ballot or public acclamation, the representation of women, and reserved seats for Scheduled Castes and Tribes. Finally, by this time, most states had already passed separate acts establishing both civil and judicial panchayats, the latter being commonly known as *nyaya panchayats* (justice panchayats).[116] Thus the question arose as to how to incorporate these pre-existing institutions with their distinct constitutions into a uniform national system of *panchayati raj*. Even on this point, however, no agreement could be reached because determined proponents of decentralization resisted the idea of creating a national ministry or government department for panchayats.

Yet these differences should not overshadow the fact that among these Committee members there was unanimous agreement that the panchayat, whatever its future form or composition, historically had possessed both administrative and judicial authority and selection to the panchayat had been based upon democratic principles. Moreover, while excoriating the destructive effects of the British colonial state, the Village Panchayat Committee nevertheless drew upon the language and imagination of Munro, Elphinstone, and, especially,

112 The Village Panchayat Committee met six times between 25 May and 16 July 1954. In June 1954, Agarwal, Malaviya, and Katju were also invited to the Local Self-Government Ministers' Conference at Simla where further discussions took place.

113 K. N. Katju, "Economic, Non-economic and Judicial Aspects of Village Panchayats," A.I.C.C. *Economic Review*, Vol. VI, No. 5 (1 July 1954), pp. 5–6.

114 "Panchayats and Politics," A.I.C.C. *Economic Review*, Vol. VI, No. 5 (1 July 1954), pp. 11–12.

115 "Panchayats and Politics," p. 12.

116 On *nyaya panchayats*, see Catherine S. Meschievitz and Marc Galanter, "In Search of Nyaya Panchayats: The Politics of a Moribund Institution," in Richard L. Abel, ed., *The Politics of Informal Justice, Vol. 2: Comparative Studies* (New York: Academic Press, 1982), pp. 47–77.

Metcalfe to assert that the Indian village historically had been an autonomous and self-governing "village republic" that had been immune to the great changes of government above it. Thus, as Malaviya wrote, "our Village Republics continued to function during the Hindu, Muslim and Peshwa governments as remarkable experiments in genuine democracy and local self-government."[117]

Jawaharlal Nehru's Second Five-Year Plan ultimately rejected these plaints in favor of more rapid industrialization in which the function of the panchayat was to act principally as an administrative adjunct to economic development, a position confirmed by the 1957 Mehta Report, which advocated democratic decentralization through the establishment of a three-tiered system of panchayats.[118] Notably, however, the success or failure of these panchayats was to be "graded" solely "on the basis of their performance in the administrative and development field."[119]

The Mehta Report expressed significant doubts as to the efficacy of the panchayat's judicial function, particularly noting that their judicial powers could not be exercised freely "without inviting the wrath of the party which loses the civil suit or criminal case." More significantly, the Report took notice of the fact that democratic elections in the village often aggravated village feuds as well as caste differences, a critical problem for which they provided no solution. All that they could hope for was to find "a satisfactory democratic solution" that would not leave "a trail of bitterness, animosity and feuds."[120]

Officially, *panchayati raj* came into existence only with the passage of the Constitution (Seventy-third Amendment) Act of 1992. As of the writing of this book, India's Ministry of Panchayati Raj enumerated 237,452 village panchayats endowed "with such powers and authority as may be necessary to enable them to function as institutions of self-government."[121] Most importantly, this included the authority to levy taxes in order to administer a wide range of municipal functions,

[117] H. D. Malaviya, "Village Panchayats in India: A Peep in the Past," *A.I.C.C. Economic Review*, Vol. VI, Nos. 6–7 (24 July 1954), p. 13.

[118] Second Five-Year Plan, Chapter 7 available at http://planningcommission.nic.in/plans/planrel/fiveyr/index2.html; *Report of the Team for the Study of Community Projects and National Extension Service* (hereafter Mehta Report), Vol. I (New Delhi, 1957), § 2, pp. 5–23. Thanks to Marc Galanter for pointing out this latter source.

[119] Mehta Report, Summary Recommendations No. 17. [120] Mehta Report, I, pp. 18–19.

[121] Constitution (Seventy-third Amendment) Act, 1992, § 243G.

including education, health and sanitation, transportation and communication, family welfare, and agricultural improvement. Notably, however, the new panchayats were not accorded any judicial functions, thus finally severing the last link to their original functions as envisioned by Munro and Elphinstone.

Ironically, the judicial functions of the panchayat, once its most admirable attribute, have now become most closely associated with India's most conservative, repressive, and anti-modern impulses. Thus, the actions of the so-called *khap panchayats*, especially in Haryana, are regularly identified in the newspapers as "kangaroo courts" that issue "diktats" and are principally engaged in "honor killings." In one academic journal, *khap panchayats* are even more menacingly described as "killer machines."[122] This is by no means intended to minimize the legitimate horror and revulsion evoked by these honor killings, nor is it intended to dismiss the claims of those who see in the *khap panchayat* the persistence of caste and patriarchy in modern India. However, it is to take note once again of the contradictions, contested meanings, and imaginings of the panchayat ideal in India.

[122] Kavita Kachhwaha, "Khap Adjudication in India: Honouring the Culture with Crimes," *International Journal of Criminal Justice Sciences*, Vol. 6, Nos. 1 & 2 (January–June/July–December 2011), p. 299.

CONCLUSION

The profound mystery of the panchayat is perhaps no better illustrated than in Premchand's famous short story *Panch-Parmeshwar* (1916). The story's title was first translated into English as *The Holy Panchayat*, although the phrase is now more commonly translated as "God is in the five."[1] Nevertheless, the phrase was well known to the East India Company's officer-officials from at least the early nineteenth century. In his *Report on the Territories Conquered from the Paishwa*, Mountstuart Elphinstone noted, "the decision of a Punchayet was always respected, as the proverbial expression of Punch Prumaishur, (A Punchayet is God Almighty) fully testifies."[2]

In the story, two lifelong friends, Jumman, a Muslim, and Algu, a Hindu, have a falling-out over a case brought before the village panchayat. The case involved Jumman's aunt who had devised her property upon her nephew in return for her own care and maintenance. After the transfer of property, however, both Jumman and his wife treated her poorly, gave her little food, and constantly complained of the burden she had placed upon them. After three years of this kind of treatment, the aunt finally decided to bring her complaints before the village panchayat.

When the panchayat convened, the aunt nominated Algu to serve as its *sarpanch*. Jumman was overjoyed at this selection, believing that his

[1] This is the title as it appeared in the readings for the BA (Honours) course in English at the University of Delhi. See Department of English, University of Delhi, *Modern Indian Literature: Poems and Short Stories* (New Delhi: Oxford University Press, 1999), pp. 53–69.

[2] Mountstuart Elphinstone, *Report on the Territories Conquered from the Paishwa* (Calcutta, 1821), p. 82.

friend would undoubtedly act in his favor. Algu, however, questioned Jumman closely and skillfully. Algu's interrogation eventually led to the panchayat deciding in favor of the aunt and requiring Jumman to pay his aunt a monthly allowance. Jumman was stunned by the decision and, as a result, the two old friends parted ways, Jumman feeling betrayed and determined to take revenge upon Algu. Whenever the two met, "they greeted each other coldly as a sword greets a shield."

Jumman's opportunity for revenge arose when Algu became involved in a dispute over the sale of his ox to a local trader. The trader had acquired the ox from Algu, but never paid for it. When the ox subsequently died from overwork, the trader refused to pay altogether. A panchayat was assembled to hear the dispute and, to Algu's horror, Jumman was nominated as *sarpanch*. Algu reluctantly agreed to the nomination. However, as soon as he was appointed *sarpanch*, Jumman was infused with the spirit of the panchayat: "I am sitting on the highest throne of justice and *dharam* [righteousness]," he thought to himself. "Whatever comes from my lips will be treated with the same respect as the words of God. I must not stray even an inch from the truth." Jumman also understood now that Algu had behaved justly in his own earlier case. He told his old friend, "today I have learnt as a panch that I am neither anybody's friend nor anybody's foe. A panch cannot see anything but justice. Today I am convinced that God speaks through a panch's lips."

The mystical element of justice is certainly not unique to Indian society and culture. Perhaps, it is the very mystery of the panchayat that accounts for its ideological longevity in both East and West. While the mystique of the panchayat obviously sparked the imagination of both the British colonizers and the Indian leaders of independence throughout the nineteenth and twentieth centuries, the various forms and practices that characterized the attempts to implement *panchayati raj* could never hope to match such lofty hopes and expectations. It would be too simplistic, however, to claim that the ideal of the panchayat was and always would remain unattainable as long as it expressed such other-worldly aspirations. This is undeniable. Much more significant is the fact that such ideals inevitably clashed with and were refashioned to serve the powers of the state and of governance.

It is in this sense that the history of panchayat practices is as much the history of ideas as it is the history of ideologies. Moreover, both the ideas and ideologies need to be viewed in their transnational perspective as they circulated not only between London and India but also within India itself. The first section of this book was intended to illustrate not only the Western imagination of "customary" legal practices in India but also the ways in which the resurrection of the imagined panchayat under British control collided with the perceived necessities of colonial governance. Indeed, the British imagination of the panchayat was remarkably limited. Although it drew upon contemporary "high theory" as explicated in the works of such noted authors as William Robertson and Adam Ferguson, in practice the British imagination was limited to reasoning by analogy. Thus the panchayat as implemented in the Madras Presidency under Thomas Munro was understood as an equivalent to England's ancient common-law jury, while in the Bombay Presidency under Mountstuart Elphinstone it was perceived as an analog to English modes of arbitration. In both instances, moreover, the resurrection of the imagined panchayat was also intended to relieve the colonial state of its judicial costs while at the same time restoring only a measure of autonomy to India's "village republics."

Within a decade, the panchayat experiment in both Presidencies proved to be a failure. Litigants voted with their feet and they overwhelmingly sought to resolve their disputes before British and Indian judges and magistrates who themselves were armed with exceptional summary powers. Why this was so remains a mystery. Evidence from much later suggests that litigants understood that these British-style panchayats lacked the authority to enforce their decisions and awards. In the case of plaintiffs coming before the panchayats in the Bombay Presidency, there may have been a decided preference for a winner-take-all decision rather than a decision crafted to satisfy both parties. Of equal importance, however, was the continuing bureaucratic rationalization of panchayat procedures intended to meet the needs of efficiency and governance. Ultimately, such reforms to the panchayat fatally undermined any efforts, however modest and however illusory, to resuscitate village India and restore its ancient constitution.

By the second half of the nineteenth century, the Orientalist perspective that had provided a significant part of the foundation and rationale for the panchayat experiments in Bombay and Madras was absorbed into and reconfigured by the British liberal movement. Particular elements of the Orientalist project, especially the tutelary role of British-sponsored institutions in the making of Indian civil society as well as the idealization of village India, remained essential aspects of the ideology of liberal colonialism. However, the most notable change was the reimagining of the panchayat as an institution of local self-governance rather than as an institution for the administration of justice. Of course, the judicial role of the panchayat never disappeared altogether, but it became increasingly less significant, especially after the perceived failure of judicial panchayats during the Non-Cooperation Movement. Once again, the origins of this transformation can be traced to the transnational movement of ideologies of governance, particularly the influential responses of British ideologues to the democratic challenges to aristocratic and bourgeois political dominance in the metropole.

Obviously, the political and social context into which these ideas were introduced was an altogether different one from the post-war situation of the early part of the nineteenth century. The nascent nationalist movement once again absorbed and reconfigured the panchayat ideal. As the long nineteenth century came to a close, village India was still idealized and the creation of civil society in India was still an essential objective. However, the resuscitation of the panchayat was slowly transformed from it being an agent of colonial local governance to it becoming an authentic pre-colonial mode of Indian self-government. Given the fact that the revival of the panchayat was an act of political and historical imagination, it should not be surprising that there was no unanimity among its advocates as to the panchayat's function, organization, or membership. Nevertheless, the panchayat had now entered into the nationalist vocabulary and had begun to establish its iconic standing within the movement.

In retrospect, Gandhi's adoption of the panchayat ideal ultimately secured that status. As that ideal had evolved and accumulated new meanings over the course of the nineteenth century, the panchayat came to signify many of Gandhi's most closely held beliefs, especially local autonomy and self-sufficiency (*gram swaraj*). Gandhi's most critical contribution, however, was his reimagining of the panchayat as a democratic institution. Yet democracy in India was riven with what Marc Galanter has called "competing equalities," and no one revealed these fissures more clearly than B. R. Ambedkar. Ambedkar was eventually successful in relegating *panchayati raj* to a Directive Principle rather than a Fundamental Right when drafting independent India's Constitution. However, the ultimate responsibility for derailing the resurrection of the panchayat as a national institution at that time lay with the first government of Jawaharlal Nehru, which gave priority to economic development and industrialization.

On the national scene, therefore, the 1992 Constitutional Amendment was only the latest iteration of the panchayat ideal, an ideal that had long been embedded in colonial governance. The sources of this ideal lay in a particular Orientalist reading of Maratha history, its reconfiguration under the influence of nineteenth-century liberalism, and, finally, its incarnation as an institution of the modern state in accordance with international standards of rights and human development. Nevertheless, despite these various attempts to incorporate the panchayat into the structures of the modern state, it has always been an institution open to multiple interpretations of both its forms and functions. It is the very elasticity of the panchayat ideal that has been both its greatest strength and its greatest weakness.

GLOSSARY

Note: The transliteration of terms by the British was neither consistent nor uniform. Therefore, what follows also includes some, but not all, of the most common spellings that appear in the archival material of the period.

amildar	– revenue collector
amin	– Indian urban magistrate superior to a *munsif*
bandobast	– *jati* trading rules and customs
chaukidar	– village police or watchman
curnum	– village accountant or clerk
desmukh, deshmukh	– hereditary office exercising police and/or revenue authority
despande	– hereditary revenue accountant
diwan	– royal court; minister of state
gotra	– clan
gramsabha	– village court
gumashta	– personal agent
inam	– hereditary land grant
jati	– birth group
jumaut	– assembly
kachari, cutcherry	– court house
kamavisadars	– local revenue officers or local commissioners
karkun, carcoon	– clerk or auditor
kulkarni, coolcurnee	– village accountant
mamledar, mamlatdar, mamlutdar	– district officer under the Marathas; district commissioner or revenue officer under the British
muchilka	– bond or deed

munsif, moonsiff	– Indian civil magistrate
nyayadesh	– chief justice minister under the Peshwa governments
panchayat, punchaiet, punchayet	– village council, village tribunal (later, unit of local governance)
panchayatdar	– member of a panchayat
pargana, pergunna, pergunnah	– territorial or administrative unit comprising several villages; several *parganas* constitute a *zilla*
patel, potail, patail, patil	– village headman
peshwa	– prime minister of the Maratha state; after ca. 1750, the de facto head of government in the Maratha territories
razeenamah	– bond; written agreement to abide by decision of panchayat
ryot, raiyat, ryut	– peasant cultivator
sabha	– assembly
sadr, sudder, sudr	– chief or supreme; sadr station – headquarters of British collectors
sadr adalat	– chief court of justice
sadr diwani adalat	– Civil Court of Appeals
sarounsh, sarunsh	– written decision of a panchayat; award
sarpanch, sirpunch, sirpunj	– head or presiding member of a panchayat
sepoy	– Indian soldier under Company or British command
shastri	– Hindu law scholar
sheristadar	– record-keeper
sirkar, circar	– regional administrator under the Peshwas
subhedar, subadar	– provincial governors of the Marathas; Indian captain of a sepoy unit
sunnud, sanad	– grant or charter
taluk	– territorial division of a province
tukaza, takaza, tugaza	– forms of shaming often employed to encourage settlement of debts
vakil	– pleader
watan, wutun	– hereditary estate

yad	– memo, often attached to a panchayat award
zamindar, zemindar	– hereditary landholder
zilla, zillah	– territorial and administrative unit comprised of several parganas

MANUSCRIPT SOURCES

BRITISH LIBRARY, EUROPEAN MANUSCRIPTS (MSS. EUR)

Elphinstone Papers
Munro Collection

BRITISH LIBRARY, ASIA, PACIFIC, AND AFRICA COLLECTIONS, INDIA OFFICE RECORDS

Bengal Criminal and Judicial Consultations
Bengal Dispatches
Bengal Political Consultations
Bengal Proceedings
Bengal Secret Consultations
Board's Collections
Bombay Dispatches
Bombay Dispatches, Judicial Department
Bombay General Proceedings
Bombay Law Proceedings
Bombay Mayor's Court Proceedings
Bombay Judicial Consultations
Bombay Proceedings
Bombay Revenue Proceedings
East India Company Correspondence
Judicial Letters from Bombay
Judicial Letters from Bengal
Judicial Papers, mainly concerning Bombay
Law Cases and Opinions of Council, 1704–1826
Madras Dispatches
Miscellaneous
Papers on Judicial Matters

MAHARASHTRA STATE ARCHIVES, EAST INDIA COMPANY PAPERS

Deccan New Judicial Arrangement
Judicial Department, Annual and Periodical Reports
Judicial Department, Appeals
Judicial Department, Castes
Judicial Department, Civil Judicature
Judicial Department, Civil and Criminal Judicature
Judicial Department, Court of Requests
Judicial Department, Local Courts
Judicial Department, Magisterial and Police
Judicial Department, Native Officers of Court
Judicial Department, Deccan New Judicial Arrangement
Judicial Department, New Judicial Code Deccan
Judicial Department, Petitions
Judicial Department, Regulations

BIBLIOGRAPHY

(Place of publication is London unless otherwise noted.)

NEWSPAPERS AND JOURNALS

A.I.C.C. Economic Review
Asiatic Journal and Monthly Register
Bombay Times and Journal of Commerce
Calcutta Magazine
Gentleman's Magazine
Journal of the Royal Asiatic Society
The Mahratta
Oriental Herald
The Quarterly Journal of the Poona Sarvajanik Sabha

PRINTED PRIMARY SOURCES

Aitchison, John William, *A General Code of the Military Regulations in Force under the Presidency of Bombay*, Calcutta, 1824.

Aitchison, C. U., *A Collection of Treaties, Engagements, and Sunnuds Relating to India and Neighbouring Countries*, Vol. VI, 1864.

Ambedkar, B. R., *Dr. Babasaheb Ambedkar Writings and Speeches*, Vol. 2, Vasant Moon, ed., Bombay, 1979.

Anon., "Administration of Justice in India: Sir Alexander Johnston's Plan of Reform," *Law Magazine and Review: A Quarterly Journal of Jurisprudence*, Vol. 3, No. 2 (1830).

Arbuthnot, Alexander J., ed., *Major-General Thomas Munro, Bart., K. C. B., Governor of Madras: Selections from His Minutes and Other Official Writings*, 1881.

Bentham, Jeremy, *The Elements of the Art of Packing, as Applied to Special Juries, Particularly in Cases of Libel Law*, 1821.

Blackstone, William, *Commentaries on the Laws of England*, 13th edn., 1800.

Borradaile, Harry, *Reports of Civil Causes Adjudged by the Court of Sudur Udalut, for the Presidency of Bombay, between the years A.D. 1800 and A.D. 1824*, Bombay, 1825.

Briggs, John, *Letters Addressed to a Young Person in India*, 1828.

Chaplin, William, *A Report Exhibiting a View of the Fiscal and Judicial System of Administration Introduced in the Territory above the Ghauts*, Bombay, 1824.

Charters Relating to the East India Company from 1600 to 1761, John Shaw, ed., Madras, 1887.

Constituent Assembly of India Debates (Proceedings), Vol. VII, 4 November 1948.

Correspondence Relating to the Revision Proposed in the Village Revenue Establishments of the Madras Presidency, Madras, 1867.

Duff, J. C. Grant, *A History of the Mahrattas*, 1826.

Elphinstone, Mountstuart, *Report on the Territories Conquered from the Paishwa*, Calcutta, 1821.

Elphinstone, Mountstuart, *The History of India: The Hindu and Mahometan Periods*, 5th edn., 1866.

Fagan, George S., *The Unrepealed and Unexpired Acts of the Legislative Council of India*, Vol. I, Calcutta, 1862.

Ferguson, Adam, *An Essay on the History of Civil Society*, Fania Oz-Salzberger, ed., Cambridge, 1995.

Gokhale, G. K., *Speeches of the Honourable Mr. G. K. Gokhale, C. I. E.*, Madras, n.d.

Hamilton, Walter, *A Geographical, Statistical, and Historical Description of Hindoostan, and the Adjacent Countries*, 1820.

Hamilton, Walter, *The East-Indian Gazetteer; Containing Particular Descriptions of the Empires, Kingdoms, Principalities ...* 2nd edn., 1828.

Hansard, Commons Debates.

Hockley, William B., *Pandurang Hàrì: or, Memoirs of a Hindoo*, 1826.

Hough, William, *The Practice of Courts-Martial and Other Military Courts*, 1834.

Hough, William and George Long, *The Practice of Courts-Martial*, 2nd edn., 1825.

Inaugural Addresses by Presidents of the Indian National Congress with Mr. Charles Bradlaugh's Speech, D. V. Gokhale, ed., Bombay, 1895.

Indian Local Self-Government Policy, 1915: Being a Resolution Issued by the Governor General in Council on the 28th April 1915, Calcutta, 1915.

The Indian National Congress, 1920–1923, Allahabad, 1924.

Karaka, Dosabhai Framji, *History of the Parsis, Including Their Manners, Customs, Religion and Present Position*, 1884, repr. Whitefish, MT, 2004.

Kaye, John William, *The Life and Correspondence of Major-General Sir John Malcolm, G. C. B., Late Envoy to Persia, and Governor of Bombay, from Unpublished Letters and Journals*, 1856.

Kyd, Stewart, *A Treatise on the Law of Awards*, 2nd edn., 1799; Philadelphia, 1808.

Letters Patent Establishing New Courts of Judicature at Fort St. George and Bombay in the East-Indies, 1798.

Mackintosh, Sir James, *Memoirs of the Life of the Right Honourable Sir James Mackintosh*, R. J. Mackintosh, ed., Vol. II, 2nd edn., 1836.

Malcolm, John, *Sketch of the Political History of India*, 1811.

Malcolm, John, *Sketch of the Sikhs; A Singular Nation, Who Inhabit the Provinces of the Penjab*, 1812.

Malcolm, John, *Report on the Province of Malwa, and Adjoining Districts*, Calcutta, 1822.

Malcolm, John, *A Memoir of Central India, Including Malwa, and the Adjoining Provinces*, 2 vols., 1823.

Materials towards a Statistical Account of the Town and Island of Bombay, Vol. III: Administration, Bombay, 1894.

Montesquieu, Baron de, *The Spirit of the Laws*, Vol. II, 1st American edn., Worcester, 1802.

Moor, Edward, *A Compilation of All the Government and General – Government – General – Brigade and Garrison Orders – Minutes of Council – Commands of the Hon. Company – or Regulations from Whatever Authority Promulgated, from the Year 1750 to the 31st of July 1801*, Bombay, 1801.

Papers Respecting the Pindarry and Mahratta Wars; [and], Treaties and Engagements with Native Princes and States in India, Concluded for the Most Part in 1817 and 1818, 1824.

Papers and Proceedings Connected with the Passing of the Deccan Agriculturists' Relief Act, XVII, of 1879, Selections from the Records of the Bombay Government, No. CLVII, n.s., Bombay, 1882.

Parliamentary Papers.

Poona Residency Correspondence, Volume 13: Poona Affairs (Elphinstone's Embassy), Part II, 1816–1818, G. S. Sardesai, ed., Bombay, 1958.

Report on the Administration of the Madras Presidency during the Year 1875–6, Madras, 1877.

Report on the Administration of Mysore, 1881–82 to 1885–86, Bangalore, 1887.

Report on the Administration of Bengal, 1904–1905, Calcutta, 1906.

Report of the Thirty-First Indian National Congress held at Lucknow on the 26th, 28th, 29th and 30th December, 1916, Allahabad, 1917.

Report of the Civil Disobedience Committee Appointed by the All India Congress Committee, Allahabad, 1922.

Report of the Team for the Study of Community Projects and National Extension Service, New Delhi, 1957.

Robertson, William, *An Historical Disquisition Concerning the Knowledge Which the Ancients Had of India*, 1791.

Roy, Rajah Rammohun, *Exposition of the Practical Operation of the Judicial and Revenue Systems of India*, 1832.

Russell, Francis, *A Treatise on the Power and Duty of an Arbitrator*, 5th edn., 1878.

Selections from the Records of Fort St. George: Papers Regarding the Village Punchayet and other Judicial Systems of Administration, 1812–1816, Madras, 1916.

Selection of Papers from the Records at the East-India House Relating to the Revenue, Police, and Civil and Criminal Justice, under the Company's Governments in India, Vols. I–IV, 1820–1826.

Selections from the Records of the Bombay Government, Bombay, 1869.

Selections from the Records of the Government of India (Foreign Department), Calcutta, 1856.

Selections from the Records of Government, North Western Provinces, Agra, 1855–1856.

Stewart, Dugald, *Account of the Life and Writings of William Robertson, D.D.*, 1796.

Sykes, Colonel, "Administration of Civil Justice in British India, for a Period of Four Years, Chiefly from 1845 to 1848, Both Inclusive," *Journal of the Statistical Society of London*, Vol. 16, No. 2 (June 1853), pp. 103–36.

Wedderburn, W., "The Pancháyat: Conciliation as a Remedy for Agrarian Disorders in India," *Journal of the East India Association*, Vol. XI (1878), pp. 115–49.

Wilks, Mark, *Report on the Interior Administration, Resources, and Expenditure of the Government of Mysoor, under the System Prescribed by the Orders of the Governor General in Council, Dated 4th September 1799*, Fort William, 1805.

Wilks, Mark, *Historical Sketches of the South of India, in an Attempt to Trace the History of Mysoor; from the Origin of the Hindoo Government of that State, to the Extinction of the Mohammedan Dynasty in 1799*, London, 1810.

Wilson, Horace Hayman, *The History of British India. From 1805 to 1835*, 1846.

BOOKS

Agarwal, Shriman Narayan, *Gandhian Constitution for Free India*, Allahabad, 1946.

Ambedkar, B. R., *The Essential Writings of B. R. Ambedkar*, Valerian Rodrigues, ed., New Delhi, 2002.

Amulree, Lord, *Industrial Arbitration in Great Britain*, 1929.

Appadurai, Arjun, *Worship and Conflict under Colonial Rule: A South Indian Case*, Cambridge, 1981.

Baden-Powell, B. H., *The Origin and Growth of Village Communities in India*, 1899.

Ballhatchet, Kenneth, *Social Policy and Social Change in Western India, 1817–1830*, Oxford, 1957.

Bayly, C. A., *Recovering Liberties: Indian Thought in the Age of Liberalism and Empire*, Cambridge, 2012.

Bayly, Susan, *Caste, Society and Politics in India from the Eighteenth Century to the Modern Age*, Cambridge, 1999.

Beaglehole, T. H., *Thomas Munro and the Development of Administrative Policy in Madras, 1792–1818*, Cambridge, 1966.

Bear, Laura, *Lines of the Nation: Indian Railway Workers, Bureaucracy, and the Intimate Historical Self*, New York, 2007.
Besant, Annie, *Speeches and Writings of Annie Besant*, 3rd edn., Madras, 1921.
Besant, Annie, *India: Bond or Free?*, Madras, 1926.
Besant, Annie, *The Case for India*, n.d.
Besant, Annie and A. Ranganatham, *The Indian Village System*, Madras, n.d.
Brown, Judith, *Gandhi's Rise to Power: Indian Politics, 1915–1922*, Cambridge, 1972.
Brown, Judith, *Gandhi: Prisoner of Hope*, New Haven, 1989.
Charlesworth, Neil, *Peasants and Imperial Rule: Agriculture and Agrarian Society in the Bombay Presidency, 1850–1935*, Cambridge, 1985.
Chatterjee, Partha, *Nationalist Thought and the Colonial World: A Derivative Discourse*, 1986; repr. Minneapolis, 2011.
Choksey, R. D., *Twilight of the Maratha Raj, 1818*, Poona, 1976.
Das, Chitta Ranjan, *Outline Scheme of Swaraj*, 1923; repr. Government of West Bengal, 1973.
Datta, K. K., *History of the Freedom Movement in Bihar, Volume One: 1857–1928*, Patna, 1957.
Davis, Jr., Donald R., *The Spirit of Hindu Law*, Cambridge, 2010.
Davis, Natalie Zemon, *Fiction in the Archives: Pardon Tales and their Tellers in Sixteenth-Century France*, Stanford, 1987.
Dodwell, H. H., ed., *The Cambridge History of India, Volume VI: The India Empire, 1858–1918*, Delhi, 1958.
Dutt, Romesh Chunder, *The Economic History of India under British Rule*, 2nd edn., 1906.
Fisher, D. R., *The History of Parliament: the House of Commons 1820–1832*, Cambridge, 2009.
Franks, H. George, *Panchayets under the Peshwas*, Poona, 1930.
Gandhi, M. K., *Hind Swaraj and Other Writings*, Anthony J. Parel, ed., Cambridge, 2009.
Gatrell, V. A. C., *The Hanging Tree: Execution and the English People, 1770–1868*, Oxford, 1994.
Gazetteer of the Bombay Presidency, Volume XIX: Sátára, Bombay, 1885.
Gazetteer of the Bombay Presidency: Poona, Vol. XVIII: Pt. III, Bombay, 1885.
Gazetteer of the Bombay Presidency: Gujarat, Vol. II: Surat and Broach, Bombay, 1887.
Gazetteer of the Bombay Presidency, Vol. I, Pt. II: History of the Konkan, Dakhan, and Southern Maratha Country, Bombay, 1896.
Guha, Ramachandra, *Gandhi before India*, 2013.
Gune, V. T., *The Judicial System of the Marathas*, Poona, 1953.
Heerma van Voss, Lex, ed., *Petitions in Social History*, International Review of Social History Supplements, Cambridge, 2002.
Inden, Ronald, *Imagining India*, Bloomington, 1990.

Indian Law Commission, *114th Report on Gram Nyayalaya*, Delhi, 1986.
Jaffrelot, Christophe, *Dr. Ambedkar and Untouchability*, Delhi, 2005.
Jayal, Niraja Gopal, *Citizenship and Its Discontents: An Indian History*, Cambridge, MA, 2013.
Johnson, Gordon, *Provincial Politics and Indian Nationalism: Bombay and the Indian National Congress, 1880 to 1915*, Cambridge, 1973.
Kahan, Alan, *Aristocratic Liberalism: The Social and Political Thought of Jacob Burckhardt, John Stuart Mill, and Alexis de Tocqueville*, New Brunswick, 2001.
Kumar, Ravinder, *Western India in the Nineteenth Century: A Study in the Social History of Maharashtra*, 1968.
Maine, Henry Sumner, *Village-Communities in the East and West*, 1871.
Mantena, Karuna, *Alibis of Empire: Henry Maine and the Ends of Liberal Imperialism*, Princeton, 2010.
Matthai, John, *Village Government in British India*, 1915.
Mehta, Uday Singh, *Liberalism and Empire: A Study in Nineteenth-century Liberal Thought*, Chicago, 1999.
Metcalf, Thomas, *Ideologies of the Raj*, Cambridge, 1995.
Mill, John Stuart, *Considerations on Representative Government*, 2nd edn., 1861.
Miller, William Ian, *Bloodtaking and Peacemaking: Feud, Law, and Society in Saga Iceland*, Chicago, 1990.
Morley, William H., *The Administration of Justice in British India; Its Past History and Present State*, 1858.
O'Brien, Karen, *Narratives of Enlightenment: Cosmopolitan History from Voltaire to Gibbon*, Cambridge, 1997.
O'Hanlon, Rosalind, *Caste, Conflict and Ideology: Mahatma Jotirao Phule and Low Caste Protest in Nineteenth-century Western India*, Cambridge, 1985.
Orth, John V., *Combination and Conspiracy: A Legal History of Trade Unionism, 1721–1906*, Oxford, 1991.
Owen, Nicholas, *The British Left and India: Metropolitan Anti-Imperialism, 1885–1947*, Oxford, 2007.
Pitts, Jennifer, *A Turn to Empire: The Rise of Imperial Liberalism in Britain and France*, Princeton, 2005.
Pocock, J. G. A., *The Machiavellian Moment: Florentine Political Thought and the Atlantic Republican Tradition*, rev. edn., Princeton, 2003.
Prasad, Rajendra, *Autobiography*, Bombay, 1957.
Raghavaiyangar, S. Srinavasa, *Memorandum on the Progress of the Madras Presidency during the Last Forty Years of British Administration*, Madras, 1893.
Raman, Bhavani, *Document Raj: Writing and Scribes in Early Colonial South India*, Chicago, 2012.
Rice, Lewis, *Mysore and Coorg: A Gazetteer Compiled for the Government of India, III: Coorg*, Bangalore, 1878.
Robb, P. G., *Ancient Rights and Future Comfort: Bihar, the Bengal Tenancy Act of 1885, and British Rule in India*, Richmond, Surrey, 1997.

Roberts, Simon, *Order and Dispute: An Introduction to Legal Anthropology*, 2nd edn., New Orleans, 2013.

Seal, Anil, *The Emergence of Indian Nationalism: Competition and Collaboration in the Later Nineteenth Century*, Cambridge, 1968.

Sharafi, Mitra, *Law and Identity in Colonial South Asia: Parsi Legal Culture, 1772–1947*, Cambridge, 2014.

Siddiqi, Majid, *The British Historical Context and Petitioning in Colonial India*, Delhi, 2005.

Singh, Meera, *British Revenue and Judicial Policies in India: A Case Study of Deccan (1818–1826)*, New Delhi, 1994.

Stein, Burton, *Thomas Munro: The Origins of the Colonial State and His Vision of Empire*, Delhi, 1989.

Tinker, Hugh, *The Foundations of Local Self-Government in India, Pakistan, and Burma*, New York, 1968.

Travers, Robert, *Ideology and Empire in Eighteenth-Century India: The British in Bengal*, Cambridge, 2007.

Webb, Sidney and Beatrice Webb, *Industrial Democracy*, new edn., 1902.

Webb, Sidney and Beatrice Webb, *English Local Government from the Revolution to the Municipal Corporations Act*, 1906.

Wink, André, *Land and Sovereignty in India: Agrarian Society and Politics in Eighteenth-century Maratha Svarajya*, Cambridge, 1986.

Yang, Anand A., *The Limited Raj: Agrarian Relations in Colonial India, Saran District, 1793–1920*, Delhi, 1989.

Zastoupil, Lynn, *John Stuart Mill and India*, Stanford, 1994.

ARTICLES

Bates, Crispin, "The Development of Panchayat Raj in India," in Crispin Bates and Subho Basu, eds., *Rethinking Indian Political Institutions*, 2005, pp. 169–84.

Baxi, Upendra and Marc Galanter, "Panchayat Justice: An Indian Experiment in Legal Access," in M. Cappelletti and B. Garth, eds., *Access to Justice: Vol. III: Emerging Issues and Perspectives* (Milan: Guiffre; Alphen aan den Rijn: Sijthoff and Noordhoff, 1979) pp. 341–86.

Bayly, C. A., "Maine and Change in Nineteenth-century India," in Alan Diamond, ed., *The Victorian Achievement of Sir Henry Maine: A Centennial Reappraisal*, Cambridge, 1991, pp. 389–97.

Bayly, C. A., "Rammohan Roy and the Advent of Constitutional Liberalism in India, 1800–30," *Modern Intellectual History*, Vol. 4, No. 1 (April 2007), pp. 25–41.

Beuscher, J. H., "The Use of Experts by the Courts," *Harvard Law Review*, Vol. 54, No. 7 (May 1941), pp. 1105–27.

Bevir, Mark, "In Opposition to the Raj: Annie Besant and the Dialectic of Empire" (1989) UC Berkeley. Retrieved from http://escholarship.org/uc/item/6mk025cf.

Bevir, Mark, "Republicanism, Socialism, and Democracy in Britain: The Origins of the Radical Left" (2000) UC Berkeley. Retrieved from http://escholarship.org/uc/item/51h4m12z.

Biagini, E. F., "Neo-Roman Liberalism: 'Republican' Values and British Liberalism, ca. 1860–1875," *History of European Ideas*, Vol. 29, No. 1 (2003), pp. 55–72.

Charlesworth, Neil, "The Myth of the Deccan Riots of 1875," *Modern Asian Studies*, Vol. 6, No. 4 (1972), pp. 401–21.

Davidson, Roger, "Government Administration," in C. J. Wrigley, ed., *A History of British Industrial Relations, 1875–1914*, Amherst, 1982, pp. 159–83.

Derrett, J. Duncan M., "Justice, Equity and Good Conscience," in J. N. D. Anderson, ed., *Changing Law in Developing Countries*, New York, 1963, pp. 114–53.

Dewey, Clive, "Images of the Village Community: A Study in Anglo-Indian Ideology," *Modern Asian Studies*, Vol. 6, No. 3 (1972), pp. 291–328.

Dumont, Louis, "The 'Village Community' from Munro to Maine," *Contributions to Indian Sociology*, Vol. 9 (December 1966), pp. 67–89.

Dwyer, Déirdre M., "Expert Evidence in the English Civil Courts, 1550–1800," *Journal of Legal History*, Vol. 28, No. 1 (April 2007), pp. 93–118.

Galanter, Marc, "The Aborted Restoration of 'Indigenous' Law in India," *Comparative Studies in Society and History*, Vol. 14, No. 1 (January 1972), pp. 53–70.

Galanter, Marc, "The Displacement of Traditional Law in Modern India," *Journal of Social Issues*, Vol. 24, No. 4 (1968), pp. 65–90.

Galanter, Marc and Jayanth K. Krishnan, "'Bread for the Poor': Access to Justice and the Rights of the Needy in India," *Hastings Law Journal*, Vol. 55, No. 4 (March 2004), pp, 789–834.

Gluckman, Max, "The Peace in the Feud," *Past & Present*, No. 8 (November 1955), pp. 1–14.

Guha, Sumit, "An Indian Penal Régime: Maharashtra in the Eighteenth Century," *Past & Present*, No. 147 (May 1995), pp. 101–26.

Guha, Sumit, "The Politics of Identity and Enumeration in India, c. 1600–1990," *Comparative Studies in Society and History*, Vol. 45, No. 1 (January 2003), pp. 148–67.

Haakonssen, Knud, "Republicanism," in Robert E. Goodin and Philip Petit, eds., *A Companion to Contemporary Political Philosophy*, Oxford, 1993, pp. 568–74.

Hanly, Conor, "The Decline of Civil Jury Trial in Nineteenth-Century England," *Journal of Legal History*, Vol. 26, No. 3 (December 2005), pp. 253–78.

Harris, José, "From Richard Hooker to Harold Laski: Changing Perceptions of Civil Society in British Political Thought, Late Sixteenth to Early Twentieth Centuries," in José Harris, ed., *Civil Society in British History: Ideas, Identities, Institutions*, Oxford, 2003, pp. 13–37.

Hay, Douglas, "The Class Composition of the Palladium of Liberty: Trial Jurors in the Eighteenth Century," in J. S. Cockburn and Thomas A. Green, eds., *Twelve Good Men and True: The Criminal Trial Jury in England, 1200–1800*, Princeton, 1988, pp. 305–57.

Hill, Lisa, "Adam Ferguson and the Paradox of Progress and Decline," *History of Political Thought*, Vol. 18, No. 4 (Winter 1997), pp. 677–706.

Horwitz, Henry and James Oldham, "John Locke, Lord Mansfield, and Arbitration During the Eighteenth Century," *Historical Journal*, Vol. 36, No. 1 (March 1993), pp. 137–59.

Jackson, R. M., "The Incidence of Jury Trial during the Past Century," *Modern Law Review*, Vol. 1, No. 2 (September 1937), pp. 132–44.

Jodhka, Surinder S., "Nation and Village: Images of Rural India in Gandhi, Nehru and Ambedkar," *Economic & Political Weekly*, Vol. 37, No. 32 (10–16 August 2002), pp. 3350–52.

Kaviraj, Sudipta, "The Imaginary Institution of India," reprinted in *The Imaginary Institution of India: Politics and Ideas*, New York, 2010, pp. 167–209.

Kolsky, Elizabeth, "Codification and the Rule of Colonial Difference: Criminal Procedure in British India," *Law and History Review*, Vol, 23: No. 3 (Fall 2005), pp. 631–83.

Kotani, Hiroyuki, "The 'Caste Autonomy' Policy in the Nineteenth-century Bombay Presidency," in H. Kotani, *Western India in Historical Transition: Seventeenth to Early Twentieth Centuries*, New Delhi, 2002, pp. 86–111.

Lobban, Michael, "The Strange Life of the English Civil Jury, 1837–1914," in John W. Cairns and Grant McLeod, eds., *The Dearest Birth Right of the People of England: The Jury in the History of the Common Law*, Oxford, 2002, pp. 173–215.

Ludden, David, "Orientalist Empiricism: Transformations of Colonial Knowledge," in C. A. Breckenridge and P. van der Veer, *Orientalism and the Postcolonial Predicament: Perspectives on South Asia*, Philadelphia, 1993, pp. 250–78.

Mallampalli, Chandra, "Cosmopolitanism in the Hinterland?: Bellary District through Fresh Lenses, 1800–1840," *Indian Economic and Social History Review*, Vol. 46, No. 2 (2009), pp. 183–210.

Mehrotra, S. R., "The Poona Sarvajanik Sabha: The Early Phase (1870–1880)," *Indian Economic & Social History Review*, Vol. 6, No. 3 (September 1969), pp. 293–321.

Mendelsohn, Oliver, "The Pathology of the Indian Legal System," *Modern Asian Studies*, Vol. 15, No. 4 (1981), pp. 823–63.

Meschievitz, Catherine S. and Marc Galanter, "In Search of Nyaya Panchayats: The Politics of a Moribund Institution," in Richard L. Abel,

ed., *The Politics of Informal Justice, Volume 2: Comparative Studies*, New York, 1982, pp. 47–77.
Miller, Dale E., "John Stuart Mill's Civic Liberalism," *History of Political Thought*, Vol. 21, No. 1 (Spring 2000), pp. 88–113.
Moog, Robert, "Indian Litigiousness and the Litigation Explosion," *Asian Survey*, Vol. 33, No. 12 (December 1993), pp. 1136–50.
Moore, Erin P., "Gender, Power, and Legal Pluralism: Rajasthan, India," *American Ethnologist*, Vol. 20, No. 3 (August 1993), pp. 522–42.
Oldham, James, "Special Juries in England: Nineteenth Century Usage and Reform," *Journal of Legal History*, Vol. 8, No. 2 (1987), pp. 148–66.
Oldham, James, "Truth-Telling in the Eighteenth-Century English Courtroom," *Law and History Review*, Vol. 12, No. 1 (Spring 1994), pp. 95–121.
Owen, Nicholas, "British Progressives and Civil Society in India, 1905–1914," in José Harris, ed., *Civil Society in British History: Ideas, Identities, Institutions*, Oxford, 2003, pp. 149–76.
Oz-Salzberger, Fania, "Civil Society in the Scottish Enlightenment," in Sudipta Kaviraj and Sunil Khilani, eds., *Civil Society: History and Possibilities*, Cambridge, 2001, pp. 58–83.
Palmowski, Jan, "Liberalism and Local Government in Late Nineteenth-Century Germany and England," *The Historical Journal*, Vol. 45, No. 2 (2002), pp. 381–409.
Peabody, Norbert, "Tod's Rajast'han and the Boundaries of Imperial Rule in Nineteenth-Century India," *Modern Asian Studies*, Vol. 30, No. 1 (February 1996), pp. 185–220.
Peers, Douglas M., "Sepoys, Soldiers and the Lash: Race, Caste and Army Discipline in India, 1820–50," *Journal of Imperial and Commonwealth History*, Vol. 23, No. 2, pp. 211–47.
Pincus, Steve, "Neither Machiavellian Moment nor Possessive Individualism: Commercial Society and the Defenders of the English Commonwealth," *American Historical Review*, Vol. 103, No. 3 (June 1998), pp. 705–36.
Pullan, A. G. P., "Trial by Jury in India," *Journal of Comparative Legislation and International Law*, 3rd Series, Vol. 28, No. 3–4 (1946), pp. 104–9.
Rendall, Jane, "Scottish Orientalism: From Robertson to James Mill," *Historical Journal*, Vol. 25, No. 1 (March 1982), pp. 43–69.
Rao, Parimala V., "New Insights into the Debates on Rural Indebtedness in 19th Century Deccan," *Economic & Political Weekly*, 24 January 2009, pp. 55–61.
Roach, John, "Liberalism and the Victorian Intelligentsia," *Cambridge Historical Journal*, Vol. 13, No. 1 (1957), pp. 58–81.
Robb, Peter, "The Colonial State and the Construction of Indian Identity: An Example on the Northeast Frontier in the 1880s," *Modern Asian Studies*, Vol. 31, No. 2 (May 1997), pp. 245–83.

Rocher, Rosane, "British Orientalism in the Eighteenth Century: The Dialectics of Knowledge and Government," in Carol A. Breckenridge and Peter van der Veer, eds., *Orientalism and the Postcolonial Predicament: Perspectives on South Asia*, Philadelphia, 1993, pp. 215–49.

Sahai, Nandita Prasad, "Collaboration and Conflict: Artisanal Jati Panchayats and the Eighteenth Century Jodhpur State," *Medieval History Journal*, Vol. 5, No. 1 (2002), pp. 77–101.

Sahai, Nandita Prasad, "Artisans, the State, and the Politics of Wajabi in Eighteenth-century Jodhpur," *Indian Economic and Social History Review*, Vol. 42, No. 1 (2005), pp. 41–68.

Sharafi, Mitra, "The Marital Patchwork of Colonial South Asia: Forum Shopping from Britain to Baroda," *Law and History Review*, Vol. 28: No. 4 (November 2010), pp. 979–1009.

Shodhan, Amrita, "Caste in the Judicial Courts of Gujarat, 1800–1860," in E. Simpson and A. Kapadia, eds., *The Idea of Gujarat: History, Ethnography and Text*, Hyderabad, 2010, pp. 32–49.

Singha, Radhika, "Settle, Mobilize, Verify: Identification Practices in Colonial India," *Studies in History*, Vol. 16, No. 2 (August 2000), pp. 151–98.

Snyder, Francis G., "Anthropology, Dispute Processes and Law: A Critical Introduction," *British Journal of Law and Society*, Vol. 8, No. 2 (Winter 1981), pp. 141–80.

Srinivasan, N., "Village Government in India," *The Far Eastern Quarterly*, Vol. 15, No. 2 (February 1956), pp. 201–13.

Sundar, Nandini, "Caste as Census Category: Implications for Sociology," *Current Sociology*, Vol. 48, No. 3 (July, 2000), pp. 111–26.

Vahed, Goolam, "Passengers, Partnerships, and Promissory Notes: Gujarati Traders in Colonial Natal, 1870–1920," *International Journal of African Historical Studies*, Vol. 38, No. 3 (2005), pp. 449–79.

Washbrook, David, "Economic Depression and the Making of 'Traditional' Society in Colonial India, 1820–1855," *Transactions of the Royal Historical Society*, Sixth Ser., Vol. 3 (1993), pp. 237–63.

Worden, Blair, "English Republicanism," in J. H. Burns, ed., *The Cambridge History of Political Thought, 1450–1700*, Cambridge, 1991, pp. 443–75.

UNPUBLISHED DOCTORAL DISSERTATIONS

Meschievitz, Catherine S., "Civil Litigation and Judicial Policy in the Madras Presidency, 1800–1843," University of Wisconsin-Madison, 1986.

Zelliot, Eleanor, "Dr. Ambedkar and the Mahar Movement," University of Pennsylvania, 1969.

INDEX

Books in the Series

Diseases of the Will
Mariana Valverde

The Politics of Truth and Reconciliation in South Africa: Legitimizing the Post-Apartheid State
Richard A. Wilson

Modernism and the Grounds of Law
Peter Fitzpatrick

Unemployment and Government: Genealogies of the Social
William Walters

Autonomy and Ethnicity: Negotiating Competing Claims in Multi-Ethnic States
Yash Ghai

Constituting Democracy: Law, Globalism and South Africa's Political Reconstruction
Heinz Klug

The Ritual of Rights in Japan: Law, Society, and Health Policy
Eric A. Feldman

The Invention of the Passport: Surveillance, Citizenship and the State
John Torpey

Governing Morals: A Social History of Moral Regulation
Alan Hunt

The Colonies of Law: Colonialism, Zionism and Law in Early Mandate Palestine
Ronen Shamir

Law and Nature
David Delaney

Social Citizenship and Workfare in the United States and Western Europe: The Paradox of Inclusion
Joel F. Handler

Law, Anthropology and the Constitution of the Social: Making Persons and Things
Edited by Alain Pottage and Martha Mundy

Judicial Review and Bureaucratic Impact: International and Interdisciplinary Perspectives
Edited by Marc Hertogh and Simon Halliday

Immigrants at the Margins: Law, Race, and Exclusion in Southern Europe
Kitty Calavita

Lawyers and Regulation: The Politics of the Administrative Process
Patrick Schmidt

Law and Globalization from Below: Toward a Cosmopolitan Legality
Edited by Boaventura de Sousa Santos and Cesar A. Rodriguez-Garavito

Public Accountability: Designs, Dilemmas and Experiences
Edited by Michael W. Dowdle

Law, Violence and Sovereignty among West Bank Palestinians
Tobias Kelly

Legal Reform and Administrative Detention Powers in China
Sarah Biddulph

The Practice of Human Rights: Tracking Law Between the Global and the Local
Edited by Mark Goodale and Sally Engle Merry

Judges Beyond Politics in Democracy and Dictatorship: Lessons from Chile
Lisa Hilbink

Paths to International Justice: Social and Legal Perspectives
Edited by Marie-Bénédicte Dembour and Tobias Kelly

Law and Society in Vietnam: The Transition from Socialism in Comparative Perspective
Mark Sidel

Constitutionalizing Economic Globalization: Investment Rules and Democracy's Promise
David Schneiderman

The New World Trade Organization KnowledgeAgreements: 2nd Edition
Christopher Arup

Justice and Reconciliation in Post-Apartheid South Africa
Edited by François du Bois and Antje du Bois-Pedain

Militarization and Violence against Women in Conflict Zones in the Middle East: A Palestinian Case-Study
Nadera Shalhoub-Kevorkian

Child Pornography and Sexual Grooming: Legal and Societal Responses
Suzanne Ost

Darfur and the Crime of Genocide
John Hagan and Wenona Rymond-Richmond

Fictions of Justice: The International Criminal Court and the Challenge of Legal Pluralism in Sub-Saharan Africa
Kamari Maxine Clarke

Conducting Law and Society Research: Reflections on Methods and Practices
Simon Halliday and Patrick Schmidt

Planted Flags: Trees, Land, and Law in Israel/Palestine
Irus Braverman

Culture under Cross-Examination: International Justice and the Special Court for Sierra Leone
Tim Kelsall

Cultures of Legality: Judicialization and Political Activism in Latin America
Javier Couso, Alexandra Huneeus, and Rachel Sieder

Courting Democracy in Bosnia and Herzegovina: The Hague Tribunal's Impact in a Postwar State
Lara J. Nettelfield

The Gacaca Courts and Post-Genocide Justice and Reconciliation in Rwanda: Justice without Lawyers
Phil Clark

Law, Society, and History: Themes in the Legal Sociology and Legal History of Lawrence M. Friedman
Robert W. Gordon and Morton J. Horwitz

After Abu Ghraib: Exploring Human Rights in America and the Middle East
Shadi Mokhtari

Adjudication in Religious Family Laws: Cultural Accommodation: Legal Pluralism, and Gender Equality in India
Gopika Solanki

Water on Tap: Rights and Regulation in the Transnational Governance of Urban Water Services
Bronwen Morgan

Elements of Moral Cognition: Rawls' Linguistic Analogy and the Cognitive Science of Moral and Legal Judgment
John Mikhail

A Sociology of Constitutions: Constitutions and State Legitimacy in Historical-Sociological Perspective
Chris Thornhill

Mitigation and Aggravation at Sentencing
Edited by Julian Roberts

Institutional Inequality and the Mobilization of the Family and Medical Leave Act: Rights on Leave
Catherine R. Albiston

Authoritarian Rule of Law: Legislation, Discourse and Legitimacy in Singapore
Jothie Rajah

Law and Development and the Global Discourses of Legal Transfers
Edited by John Gillespie and Pip Nicholson

Law against the State: Ethnographic Forays into Law's Transformations
Edited by Julia Eckert, Brian Donahoe, Christian Strümpell and Zerrin Özlem Biner

Transnational Legal Process and State Change
Edited by Gregory C. Shaffer

Legal Mobilization under Authoritarianism: The Case of Post-Colonial Hong Kong
Edited by Waikeung Tam

Complementarity in the Line of Fire: The Catalysing Effect of the International Criminal Court in Uganda and Sudan
Sarah M. H. Nouwen

Political and Legal Transformations of an Indonesian Polity: The Nagari from Colonisation to Decentralisation
Franz von Benda-Beckmann and Keebet von Benda-Beckmann

Pakistan's Experience with Formal Law: An Alien Justice
Osama Siddique

Human Rights under State-Enforced Religious Family Laws in Israel, Egypt, and India
Yüksel Sezgin

Why Prison?
Edited by David Scott

Law's Fragile State: Colonial, Authoritarian, and Humanitarian Legacies in Sudan
Mark Fathi Massoud

Rights for Others: The Slow Home-Coming of Human Rights in the Netherlands
Barbara Oomen

European States and their Muslim Citizens: The Impact of Institutions on Perceptions and Boundaries
Edited by John R. Bowen, Christophe Bertossi, Jan Willem Duyvendak and Mona Lena Krook

Religion, Law and Society
Russell Sandberg

The Experiences of Face Veil Wearers in Europe and the Law
Edited by Eva Brems

The Contentious History of the International Bill of Human Rights
Christopher N. J. Roberts

Transnational Legal Orders
Edited by Terence C. Halliday and Gregory Shaffer

Lost in China?, Law, Culture and Society in Post-1997 Hong Kong
Carol A. G. Jones

Security Theology, Surveillance and the Politics of Fear
Nadera Shalhoub-Kevorkian

Opposing the Rule of Law: How Myanmar's Courts Make Law and Order
Nick Cheesman

The Ironies of Colonial Governance: Law, Custom, and Justice in Colonial India
James Jaffe

Lightning Source UK Ltd.
Milton Keynes UK
UKOW06n2008170316

270408UK00004B/65/P

9 781107 087927